JEW BOY

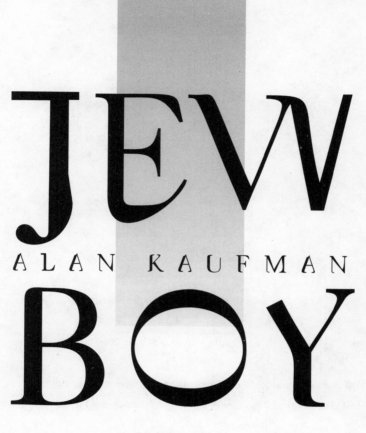

JEW

ALAN KAUFMAN

BOY

A Memoir

FROMM INTERNATIONAL
NEW YORK

For Diane

CONTENTS

CONTENTS

SCARS

BOARDING THE FREIGHT

AMONG POETS AND THIEVES

JEW BOY

TALES OF CHILDHOOD

THE AUDITION

IT WAS 11 P.M. My father had already left for his night shift post office job an hour ago. I had school tomorrow. I had gone to bed. But she woke me with her sobbing. I came out, rubbing a fist in my eye, asking, "Whatsamattah, Mommy? Why are you crying?"

I found her seated on the bed beside the open valise, face flushed a dark red, tears rolling down her cheeks, her hair all frazzled. "He was so young, so young, a young boy and they killed him." "Mommy, do you mean Mario?" "Yes, Mario. Of course I mean Mario. You don't understand anything. You don't even know how sick I am, you and your brother and your stupid father. Gosh!" "Please, Mommy," I said, picking with my fingers at my pajama leg. "Don't cry. I'll get us a beautiful mansion! You'll see! Like Eddie Fisher." I tried to put my arms around her but she shoved me away. "Oh, sure," she said. The skepticism in her voice stung me to the quick. She made me feel like such a fool for believing in her dream of making me a singing star.

In fact, to me it was no dream, was already reality, and only a little more time was needed before we could start building the pool. I didn't understand why the pool was so important, since she didn't like the beach and I couldn't swim. But it was going to be built. Soon I'd be in the movies like Shirley Temple, whom she idolized. In real life she and Shirley were about the same age during the war. Both had blonde hair and blue eyes. But while one tap-danced before cameras to the organ-grinder's music, the other hid in a chicken coop gripped by a nauseating fear as SS men hunting for Jews prowled the vicinity. Mario was an Italian partisan tenor murdered by the Germans. He would sing "Santa Lucia" to her in their hideout, his favorite song. The partisans operated in the mountains of the north, where they waged a running battle with Heinrich Himmler's Death's Head division and where she, an escaped French Jew, slept on cases of dynamite. Once she saw an informer shot through the mouth and later, in passing the spot, scraped at the grass with her toe, exposing his hair: he had been buried standing up. For although this unit was Communist, they were also Catholics. Denied a horizontal burial, his soul would not reach heaven. Mario was killed as the result of this informer's betrayal, first cruelly tortured, then paraded into the town square, covered in a red sheet to signify his Communism and publicly hung. My mother watched all this through a field telescope from the mountain hideout.

"Mario had such a beautiful voice! A future Eddie Fisher, so handsome!" "Did you love him?" I asked. "No! He was not a boyfriend!" she said indignantly. "No! Just a friend! Of course not!" But secretly I suspected that she did.

I sat on her bed, between us the open suitcase—the "valise" as she called it—filled with old, yellowing photographs. She plucked out the snapshot of the grinning young man with curly black hair, leaning casually against a tree. I had seen it a thousand times. "This is Mario," she said, eyes shining. Is Mario the reason, I wondered, pained, why I am practicing day and night to master "Santa Lucia"? I had never thought of this before. In a trembling voice I asked, almost dreading to know: "Did Mario used to sing that song good?" She answered, "You never heard anyone sing it like him. You should only sing it so good. But, you never will." Her unexpected scorn came like a surprising knife-thrust into my belly. My understanding of my life, her life, the whole point of life ran out of me unchecked, blood of my hope. How would I compensate for her robbed childhood? How would I fulfill my appointed destiny of redeemer? From the day of my birth I had been led to believe that I was the messianic promise, risen from the ashes of extermination. Hollywood was going to open the door to a new life for all of us. But now, in a moment, it slammed shut. I stood before it naked, ashamed, a little boy, fat, who was not talented enough to get an audition and so deserve his mother's love.

But perhaps even she now saw how untenable this was, even for herself. Neither of us could afford not to dream. Reality stood all around us, an unbearable prison. The Bronx darkness of screaming sirens, the bickering voices of neighbors, the barking of stray dogs, all hung in the air, threatening, oppressive. Her voice intruded, tremulous with disgust at her own lies while forcing herself to repeat them, for she had seen the brink of truth but drawn back. "You could . . . do it . . . if you worked hard. But . . . you don't want . . . to practice. You won't listen to me." "I'll listen, I'll listen," I gasped, ever so grateful. "I'll listen, Mommy, I swear on everything holy, I will, I will." I felt so thankful to regain my appointed purpose, though now a pang of doubt stained my confidence. But I pushed on through. My psyche knew no other route. I began to cry, to plead, "Please, believe in me, oh, please, Mommy." She gave me a look that I had never seen before, that I could not have known, was yet too young to identify as insanity. She said, in a voice full of betrayal, "He sang it so beautifully and they killed him. They murdered him. And you, you aggravate your poor mother who went through hell." She began to wail: "I had such hopes for you. But you turned out to be like your father. Look at him! What have we got? Nothing!" "No, Mommy, no, please. Don't say that! Don't! Oh, God, please no. . . ." My voice gagging, each word she uttered opening wider an abyss from which I somehow sensed there was no turning back. She raged: "You'll end up like him! Breaking your back! For nothing, in the post office. The *putz* office! You'll be a putz like your father! You'll see!" "No, Mom!" I screamed. Whereupon she slapped me once hard across the face, and then once more. And stunned I stopped, body stiff, shoulders hunched, fists clenched, wide-open eyes shocked in surprise, and moaned in anguish. And she, in turn, began to pace back and forth, back and forth, ranting to herself in an eerie, bitter voice: "This is what I get for marrying your father. This is what I get. I should have listened to my parents. They told me, 'Mashala, don't marry him. He's poor. You'll end up with nothing. He's coarse. A lowlife.' And so what do I have now? My own son talks back to me!" While I howled in protest how sorry, oh, Mommy, how sorry I was to deaf ears, she disappeared and I heard her rummaging in the closet and then move to the kitchen where a drawer scraped open and utensils rattled heavily. But I dared not move, decided it was safer to remain in the living room with eyes squeezed tight so that her search would go unseen by me, as if somehow blindness would protect me. I knew that I was in serious trouble. I knew that what was about to ensue would entail more than the usual slap. Instinct told me to go find a corner, quick, hide in it, face to the wall. As if refusal to open my eyes, to countenance this event, could somehow prevent its occurrence.

I ran to the wall, hid my eyes in my arm, cried, "No, no, please, no," with all the conviction inside me, softly, gently, an appeal to a kind universe. She grabbed my arm and pulled me to a chair that she had placed in the center of the room. Beside it on the floor lay a wire hanger and a rolling pin. My eyes jumped away from them. I dared not look. She sat in the chair, offered her hands to me: "Take them," she ordered, "and sing 'Santa Lucia.'" I noticed my brother, Howard, watching, terrified, from the bedroom. My eyes met his in mute appeal. But what could he do? His lips pressed tight with helplessness was the only support he could offer. I was alone. The utter aloneness of my predicament drove me to despair. I began to cry out of control. She picked up the rolling pin and brought it down on the arm that shot up reflexively from my side. The hard wood shivered through my elbow. I screamed and ran. She gave chase and managed to land another blow on my arm. She then dropped the rolling pin, ran to fetch the hanger. This she brought down whistling on me in a stinging rain of fire, again, again, again, again, again. The sound of my voice in my own ears surprised me, as though I heard its continuous, choked scream from a far distance. She dragged me by my hair to the chair, barked: "Sing!" and grabbed my hands. "Look into my eyes when you sing."

"San-ta," I began, barely able to mouth the word. She slapped me. "'Santa Lucia.' Sing it!" and she hummed the melody as though I didn't know it. As if I hadn't practiced singing it a thousand times. As if my whole life had not become predicated upon singing it as well as Eddie Fisher in order to build her a house with a big swimming pool. I had always thought that I could sing it well enough to conquer show business, but now I must sing it as well or better than Mario.

She struck me and I sang and each time she laced into me with blows it was to perfect my rendition of some phrase or stanza. I was literally being tuned like an instrument, but with pain, blows, lashes in order to sing as well as a ghost once had. And I don't know if I sang as well but at one point I was singing while she calmly listened. She no longer insisted that I meet her eyes. Perhaps the sight of my face killed the illusion of my performance, as though by no stretch of the imagination, singing or not, could I resemble Mario. But perhaps with my voice I could retrieve some sense of him, and I sang beautifully. I sang with understanding. I sang with unsuspected Italianesque empathy.

I sang better than Shirley Temple, better than Eddie Fisher, better even than Mario, I believe.

THE PURPLE JEW

IN SCHOOL HE was average, inconspicuous, his somewhat silly face obscured behind thick-lensed black horn-rimmed glasses through which his walleyed stare rushed at you like some bizarre, near-blind cave fish from the ocean depths. But when the eighth period bell shrilled, Bruce Weiss rushed from our world into the pages of an animated Marvel comic book surreality with the zeal of a Kali-worshipping thug. Ordered to slay in the name of his panel-strip paradigm, he would surely have done so. A fan of Spiderman before most had ever heard of the troubled superhero, he emulated the wall-climber in every detail, down to a perfect imitation of the webhead's neurotically obsessed alter ego, Peter Parker. But after a time Bruce Weiss came to know that there could be only one true Spiderman in the world, and so he invented a hero for himself to inhabit: Voodoo Kid. And in a brilliantly tailored superhero costume he skulked about the neighborhood, performing deeds of mayhem and mischief that my brother, Howard, in his role as Bruce's personal cameraman, captured on an 8-millimeter handheld Bell & Howell. The footage was to be used in a forthcoming Voodoo Kid flick.

In fact, Bruce displayed a keen knack for cross-promotion. There was also a hand-drawn and inked Voodoo Kid comic, self-published on mimeograph, as well as a Voodoo Kid plastic toy model made by Bruce's father, Bob Weiss, a professional illustrator who not only aided and abetted his son's fantasy world but encouraged Howie and I to become comic book collectors.

Father and son inhabited a dingy one-bedroom that had been converted into a workshop for their capricious pursuits and where they talked aloud of the Fantastic Four, the Incredible Hulk, and Doctor Strange as if they were blood relations. Supposedly there was a Mrs. Weiss somewhere, but one never saw her: Howie and I presumed her dead, murdered for her failure to indulge Bruce and Bob's obsession.

Atop every available inch of dusty furniture surface posed handcrafted plastic models of superheroes, ranging from Spiderman to Superman to Daredevil. At a kitchen table spread with inkpots, drawing pens, and large panel boards, Bob drew the strips he published in "underground zines" out of San Francisco, all containing a grotesque superabundance of dripping snot, drooling lips, and penises of exaggerated sizes with human faces. Along the walls his rare comic archive filled enough shoeboxes to pack a store; these jostled for space with unmailed stacks of his personal newsletter, *Bob's Comix World*, which posted tips on rare comic book editions alongside fees of up to two and three hundred bucks per "collector's item."

Bob, his massive girth settled in a creaking chair, wiped his clammy face with a soiled handkerchief and said: "As you see, there's a lot of bread to be made in this comic collecting business."

To get rich, he explained, one simply hunted in secondhand stores or in the closets of one's own friends and relations for first, second, and third edition issues, stole or bought them, and preserved the booty in individual plastic sleeves he had bought for a nickel apiece from the Bronx Hobby Shop on Jerome Avenue. The treasures were then stored at room temperature in shoeboxes or manila folders marked with the series title and the numbered sequence. For example: AVENGERS #1–9, or X-MEN #6–15. The most prized issues were either the first edition or else that issue containing the origin of the superhero's transformation from an ordinary mortal into costumed avenger.

I loved the grandiosity of the word origin; longed for a day when I would be so famous that young boys in obscure places would speak of my "origins" as something exotically remote, fabulous.

Sometimes, though, the origins of a particular superhero appeared only incidentally in a publication series of a different name. For instance, the first appearance of Spider-Man, containing the tale of his origins, debuted in *Amazing Fantasy* #15 in a trial run for only one issue before fan demand led to his very own series. Needless to say, possession of such an item was tantamount to ownership of the Lost Ark.

My personal hero was Captain America (origin in *Avengers* #4), whose red, white, and blue leotards symbolized an American essentialness I desperately craved as the son of a French-Jewish Holocaust survivor. Divorced from the realm of common American experience, not only by her accent but by her survival of an historical event of such extreme savagery and magnitude that it made the violence-prone Bronx seem rather innocent, I felt estranged from the country of my birth, ambivalent about my *own* origins. But Captain America, who had risen from a twenty-year frozen sleep after an earlier career in WW II as a fighter against the Nazis, understood quite well, it seemed to me, about gas chambers and mass graves. This brought him closer to my experience than other characters.

His boy sidekick, Bucky, had been blown up midair over London during the Blitz while trying to defuse a Nazi buzz bomber. In despair, Captain America dropped into the North Atlantic, where a glacier encased him. Two decades later a team of researchers thawed him out, still garbed in his red, white, and blue togs. As he came to, his old despair raged as fresh as a minute ago. Dazed, he found himself trapped between the present and the past, unsure, historically speaking, of what era it was or his place in it—my predicament exactly.

Bob held out as a reward for all this collecting that once our stock had grown fat, we could haul it off to a comic book convention to sell or swap. Not only could we make thousands of dollars, but through smart trading we could consolidate our holdings and multiply their value.

"Where are the conventions held?" I asked, amazed.

"All around the country," said Bob. "Boston, Miami . . . it depends on the collectors' associations. But don't worry. I'll be glad to rep you. I'm sure I can cut you some great deals."

That settled it. Bob next showed us how he constructed plastic model superheroes, this a full decade before their like would roll en masse from a factory conveyor belt. For Captain America's basic form he used an existing model of a Roman gladiator and with a soldering iron and the melted wire of a clothing hanger such as my mother used to hit me, slowly, patiently sculpted muscles and mask. I shivered to see my hero emerge from the same painful instrument used to punish me. Bob's power struck me as Godlike. With slow, patient applications, he painted Cap's costume. He then fashioned little mask wings and Cap's shield from loose bits of plastic, wire, and opaque enamel paints. He had brushes of such delicacy that you could paint an eyelash on the head of a tiny figurine. He showed us a brush with a single hair. "Look at that," he said, turning it before the light, a tightrope across which dreams and heroes walked against a backdrop of dirty Bronx kitchen walls perspiring with gleams from a naked ceiling fixture.

Bruce, dressed in mask and cape, led us on a Voodoo Kid film shoot. I was to play an FBI agent on Voodoo Kid's trail. For the role, Bruce lent me a jacket and Bob calmed my unruly hair with a smelly layer of Brillcream. I recoiled from the touch of his pudgy fingers but held still, for he was the key to my future comic book millions.

Out we slipped into the dingy, almost completely deserted streets. Our first stop: an alley where I took up the camera, while Howie and

Bruce leaned their heads close to privately confer. Bruce then sidled over, his silly grin showing through the mask's mouth hole. "OK," he told me. "Whatever happens, just make sure you film it all, and don't stop shooting till I say quits."

He showed me how to hold the camera, which buttons to press. He then poked his head from the alley, looked left and right, and said: "All's clear! Action!"

I raised the camera.

Now Howie appeared, a villanous Hindu mystic swathed in a turban fashioned from a beach towel that read: NATHAN'S ORIGINAL CONEY ISLAND HOT DOGS. Scowling, he swaggered to a row of big aluminum trashcans, pulled one out, hoisted it over his head, and hammed an angry face for the camera. He then turned and heaved the trashcan through a first-floor residential window. The glass exploded with a shattering crash. The camera shook in my hands.

"Why!?" I shouted.

"Keep shooting!" cried Bruce. He charged the lens, leaped onto Howie's back, and began to ride him around the alley as Howie hammed and growled. In the meantime, a shocked, angry old crone poked her head from the shattered glass and screamed: "What the fuck is going on out here?! Police!! Police!!"

"Keep shooting!" Bruce spit.

"No way!" I shouted, and ran.

Bruce and Howie caught up with me about six blocks later as police sirens wailed past.

"Oh, you blew it! You blew it!" Bruce ranted in despair. "Look at that! We could have filmed police cars and cops with guns drawn! You blew it!"

"Well, I'm sorry," I said, "but I don't want no trouble."

Howie shook his head with a sad smile. "You know how much money they'd pay for a scene like that in Hollywood? And we could have had the real thing for free."

"Well, all right," said Bruce. "Let's do the next shoot. We have to go to Townsend Avenue."

We zigzagged through the streets, hugging walls to avoid the patrol cars that were out there searching for us. On Townsend Avenue we slipped into a tall, swank building with an intercom system. Bruce rang every bell and a cacophony of voices called "Who is it?" and "Yes?" Finally, one stupid enough just buzzed and we got in.

We rode the elevator to the roof, stepped through the exit door. The sooty Bronx stretched in an ugly labyrinth before us. We could see Yankee Stadium and the nearby Bronx Courthouse. It all ended at the 149th Street Bridge in hazy smog from which the only escape seemed death's route, straight up into heaven.

"There it is," said Bruce. He approached a box that he unpacked and pulled out a dummy of sewn-together pillows dressed in a mock Voodoo Kid outfit. The dummy exactly matched Bruce in size.

"Howie! Take the camera and when I say to, shoot!"

Bruce lifted the dummy, placed its "hands" around his neck, and said, "Alan! Tie it up!" I tied the dummy's hands by attached strings that I knotted around Bruce's throat so it hung with its head on his chest.

Bruce shouted, *"Shoot!"*

"This," he said, speaking to the camera, "is my sinister double, sent here by my archenemy, Krockton, to slay me!" They wrestled back and forth furiously, director and doll, against the filthy backdrop of the city, Bruce and his mirror image rolling on the hot tar, slamming into air vents, Bruce's skull now inches from a ventilation fan's decapitating blades. At one point he hung so far over the roof's ledge that I grabbed his leg to save him.

"No," he gasped, "get out of the picture! Keep shooting!"

Finally, the deadly duel ended, though somewhat inconclusively.

"So, who won?" I asked.

"It's not over," he panted, unmasked. He frowned at my impatience. "Howie, take Alan with you. You know what to do."

"C'mon," said Howie with kindly tolerance. We charged down the fire exit stairs, ten flights at least, to avoid residents. Out in the street, we crossed the road to have the broadest possible view of the entire building. Howie hoisted the camera. "OK!" he shouted through a cupped hand. But nothing happened. Bruce couldn't hear. Technical problem. "Alan, yell with me."

"*Okaaayyyy!*" we howled in unison.

At that moment the heads of Voodoo Kid and his deadly double appeared locked in ferocious combat, and then the air was pierced by a savage scream as the puppet Voodoo Kid plummeted to earth, where it landed on the head of a boy walking a bicycle, who happened to be passing by and fell to the ground. Howie of course kept shooting with a steadfastness that I could but admire. I was already halfway across the street, shouting, "Are you OK?" as I dodged past slowing cars. I helped the dazed boy to his feet.

"What the fuck is this?" he hissed, pushing off the fake Voodoo Kid.

"We're filming a movie," I said. "I'm sorry."

"Oh, yeah? Well, what the fuck, man!? What the fuck!" He lifted his bike, spun the rear wheel, which ticked with undamaged gears, sighed with relief, looked at the doll on the ground and then up at me, and then at Howard across the street who, unbelievably, continued to shoot, and said: "Stupid shit, man! Stupid shit!" and continued on his way.

Bruce rushed from the building, arms outstretched, fingers splayed, voice issuing pointless, neurotic proclamations and directions: "Keep calm! Everyone just keep calm! Help is on the way! Let's get an ambulance for this man. I saw the whole thing!"

"Bruce," I said dryly, "the guy's already took off. Forget it."

Across the street, Howie doubled over with laughter, howled. "Did you see Bruce's hands? His fingers? Just like Peter Parker, like Spider-Man! Bruce, you're nuts! You *are* Spider-Man!"

The first thing I would need as a budding comic book collector was investment capital. So I got a job for two afternoons a week in the local stationery store. My mother fully approved of this, and even my father nodded and yawned at the supper table and said: "Oh, yeah? That's good. It's good to work."

But at work I found it difficult to understand instructions or to con-
centrate on tasks. The shop was narrow, crowded to the ceiling with
cheap toys, greeting cards, notebooks, etc., and there was nowhere to
sit. The owner was Mr. Shwab, a pudgy bald man with a very pink face
who wore the same short-sleeve shirt and bow tie, day in and day out—
the shop stank of his perspiration. He explained to me at great length
how to find things on the shelves and in the stockroom, and my head
even nodded with a kind of dim comprehension, but the instant he
stepped away I forgot everything. Consequently I stood frozen to my
spot, ears burning with shame and heart thumping as he called out with
weary impatience: "Alan? Are you going to bring me the Number Two
pencils I asked for? Our customer is right here waiting." This drove me
to make a desperate rush at the shelves, where I pulled out rolls of crepe
paper as boxes of rubber bands tumbled to the floor and the customer's
precious time was wasted to the loud drumroll of my heart, and finally
the stationer was at my elbow, whispering in a huff: "Here! The pencils
are here! Just follow the code the way I showed you." I groaned:
"Ohhhhhhhhh! That's where it is," flooded with the relief of sudden
insight; but moments later darkness again descended and I waited,
hands in pockets, dreading the next customer.

Once my mother came in, expecting, no doubt, to find her boy
genius perched on a high stool behind the cash register, ringing up sales
with a smile and exchanging pleasantries with the customers while
directing a battalion of clerks rushing about with No. 2 pencils behind
their ears and the owner seated in a chair behind the counter, beaming
with contentment. Instead she found me hiding timidly behind a
revolving display stand of Magic Markers in a side aisle.

"What are you doing back here?" she asked, disappointed. "Why
aren't you up front, helping Mr. Shwab?"

"This is where he wants me," I lied.

"Go," she said crossly, "introduce me to your boss."

He had no time for small talk, was busy with a customer, but my
mother's voice droned on as Shwab nodded stiffly. I heard her say the
words "He's brilliant" and "a little Einstein." Shwab's face looked uncon-

vinced, but he offered a tight-lipped smile. She cooed effusive thanks. He apologized for being so busy. A week later I was fired.

Collecting my fifteen bucks, I went up the street to work for the other stationer, who hired me at half my former salary. However, I fared better in this establishment. The owner, Mr. Caspetti, a slender man in his late thirties who wore casual Italian sportswear like my father, wasn't interested in the quality of service so much as the quantity of turnover.

The stockroom was an insane, disorganized mess: there were rubber bands mixed in with pencil sharpeners, rulers entangled in kite string, loose-leaf binders so long in their place that weak lightbulbs had burned their silhouettes into the cheap paper lining the shelves. I joined one of a small army of incompetent elves working "off the books."

The other boys on my shift were Tony and Buzzy. Tony was a slight Italian boy who showed up for work in a paint-spattered black T-shirt bearing the faded words TRIUMPH MOTORCYCLES. I would have given my life to own such a garment. Buzzy was a freckled, chubby Irish boy with a flattop crew cut and a lower lip that protruded stupidly. Naturally, Tony was our leader.

Our jobs were to watch admiringly as he worked and say, "Gosh, Tony," and, "Boy, you got that figured out all right." Our worshipful incompetence fueled his performance. He responded with kind reassurance to our effusive and constant apologies.

"Aw, that's OK. Look, this is how you find it . . ." and we would listen, nodding our heads intently, but as soon as the lecture ended, our minds again went peacefully blank. Why bother to learn? Tony would do it.

Mr. Caspetti seemed glad for the arrangement. He never once came to the back of the store to check on our performance. When things were needed from the stockroom, Tony found it and we brought it.

"Howzitgoin back dere?" Mr. Caspetti'd ask with a brief, indifferent sidelong glance as I handed him the requested pen or box of paper clips.

"Great!" was all I said, and to the back I dutifully returned. I made fifteen dollars a week, no questions asked, as Tony hunted through the stationery jungle and I gasped with amazement when he found what I had been searching for.

Thus, armed with cash, in no time I discovered with Howie a local network of secondhand book stores in which to shop for collector's items. These stores presented to me a new and revelatory world all their own. Their old, dated bookwares wore an air of decrepit abandonment. Those displayed up front were considered valuable not for their heroic rarity but for their lurid ambiance, such as *Collected Works of the Marquis de Sade* and *Mass Murderers in America*. I would open the de Sade book a crack, quickly skim a page or two of whipped white skin, shackled hands, pert breasts, pleas for mercy, gasps of pleasure—snap it shut and, ashamed, make a quick red-faced tour through the world of mass murderers, gaping at black-and-white photos of naked corpse torsos bound tight with fat-digging rope and electrical tape, and crisscrossed by slash wounds with gaping, black abrasions. Blood always appeared black in such photos. Sometimes the victim's face was shown, eyes closed, dark-ridged, a kind of simple smile on lifeless lips. The faces of the mass murderers were horrible in their averageness. I could have been perusing a photo album of postal workers or stationers. And they were all, as a rule, male.

The back shelves of such stores belonged to stag magazines and comic books. No archaeologist excavating ruins experienced more intoxication than I flipping through these low-priced stacks. If I found a coveted first issue, my hand trembled and my eyes lowered furtively as I handed over to the unwitting proprietor—usually a pimply or unshaven overweight man with a listless masturbatory gaze—the ten or twenty-five cents it cost. Then my brother and I ran down the street shrieking with ecstatic disbelief that we had actually acquired an *Amazing Fantasy* #15 or an *Avengers* #4 such as we had first seen at the Weiss's.

At home we slipped the precious find into a plastic sleeve and stored it away in an appropriately marked manila envelope. We even had a card index, each issue marked with an identifying number and chronicling the comic's name, issue number, date, author, illustrator and fettle: *Fantastic Four*, issue #7, written by Stan Lee and illustrated by Jack Kirby, mint condition.

Also at this time I began to draw a comic strip of my own: *The Purple Jew*.

One morning I took out some paper and colored pencils and drew the origins of my own hero, with balloon boxes for him to speak in. He was a poor Bronx boy, went the narrative, walking up the Grand Concourse, minding his own damned business when suddenly for no reason a gang of teenagers beat him to a pulp. They left him dying on the sidewalk. No one came to his aid, though traffic flowed by and pedestrians stepped around him. By nightfall, he still lay there, about to die when, suddenly, the voice of God broke the silence. "Jim! Jim! Stand up!" said the voice of God. Jim stood up, miraculously all right. "I have saved you for a special mission," said God. "You will fight evil! You will be my champion, a modern Jewish knight, with the strength of a lion and the prowess of a cat, and you will wear purple fighting togs bearing the Jewish star on the front. You will be: The Purple Jew!"

I drew all through the morning while my mother slaved over pots steaming with boiled potatoes, corn, broccoli, and a meatloaf baked in the oven. Despite the intense heat, I drew on, oblivious.

"What is this, Abie? A cartoon? You should only do your math homework with the same kind of patience. Four hours you've been sitting there. Enough already. Go outside. Play! There's not so many days left in the summer. Then school starts and, believe me, you won't have time for your cartoons!"

"I'm OK, Mom," I said abstractedly, "thanks." My disposition grew kindly. I felt well disposed toward everyone. A pleasant sense that I had been blissfully emptied spread through my body. My smile was genuine.

"What's this?" asked my father when he shuffled in for lunch, dressed in white T-shirt and boxer shorts, his house slippers slapping on the floor. His thick fingers isolated a page of panels and his brow wrinkled. A slow, condescending smile spread over his face as he read. "The

Purple Jew?" he chuckled in disbelief. "Do I read correctly? The Pur-ple Jew?" enunciating each separate syllable slowly to better savor the pre-posterous whole.

"Whatzamattah wit it?" I asked sullenly, my vision deflated. "It's a comic book. I'm gonna try to publish it."

"Publish? Tee hee hee! The Pur-ple Jew! Hee hee hee hee! Sure, you'll publish! Sure. Tee hee hee! Sure. Tee hee! The Pur-ple Jew!" but I received this stiffly, said: "That's right. The Purple Jew."

That he read comic books, was something of an early aficionado himself, familiar with Superman, Captain Marvel, and Batman, lent his devastating weight to his sarcastic critique: here was yet another world, like that of sports or of the streets, the nature of which I just didn't "get" according to him, but which, of course, he did.

Still, I had gone about my collecting in deadly earnest, inspired by Bob Weiss's confidence in its lucrative benefits, worked hard to save, and felt myself to stand on more solid ground than I had ever before, so I said to this man who had never, according to my mother, succeed-ed at anything: "You can laugh, but I'm gonna make a lot of money from the comics. You'll see!" And this sent my father into paroxysms of laughter, as though it was all too much for him and he couldn't bear a single minute more. "You'll see!" I repeated, voice rising angrily. I stood up, gathered my papers together, tears springing from my eyes. "I'm gonna collect comics, become a millionaire, and draw my own comic books! That's right! The Purple Jew will make me rich!"

When I left him, he was close to choking.

And that's how summer went. Absorbed in collecting, drawing the Purple Jew, shooting films, and tolerating my father's constant gibes. Ridicule lurked in other quarters, too. When filming we avoided the schoolyard, the potentially painful contact with other kids our age who wouldn't understand. They were beginning to trickle back from summer vacations in greater numbers as fall drew near.

My life became an adventure imagined by the writers and artists of Marvel Comics. Each week's newly purchased issue explained me to myself. Lying in bed on my side, with flies buzzing in the blast-furnace heat of the room, I stared at . . . no, *fell into* each panel on the page, where I experienced life in the character's ink-sketched skin and lived more intensely than I could ever hope to as myself. Reading Captain America, I felt like him: knew myself as stiff around others, unable to relax, haunted by a painful, private sense of special destiny. Like him, I fought against the phantoms of the Nazi past, and like him, the battle took place entirely in my own mind. We each mistook the present for the past and the past for the present. Like him, I had lost a dear loved one when I was just a child—his loss was his young sidekick, Bucky; mine, my own mother, who even before I was born watched her own childhood and faith in humanity murdered when *she* was still only a child.

September brought the excitement of a new school year, and children and parents crowded the local stores to shop for school supplies. Unfortunately, I had to quit my job, and once again was broke.

I was enrolled in the class for intellectually gifted children, as a student of Mrs. Shwartz, the toughest and most dedicated teacher in the school. Though mere children, we, her students, were already deemed to be Harvard-bound. If we played our cards right, excelled in our studies, saved up our pennies, and accepted her rule as law, we would certainly go to the Ivy League. So we were told. We were told that the Ivy League was the scholastic equivalent of professional baseball, a place where they paid you to study in a program that combined travel with exciting adventures, and of course after four years of Ivy League they found you a job in your chosen field. As a writer, which I professed to my teachers to want to be, I could expect to earn about one hundred thousand dollars per book advance. I would live in a mansion in Westchester until I could afford something better. By the time I had won the coveted Nobel Prize for Literature, certainly I would inhabit a castle and bring in annually upwards of a million dollars.

However, all of this rested on Mrs. Shwartz's assessment of one's chances, and to win her approval was very hard. She was already disposed, I knew, to certain students. All during fifth grade she had appeared in our homeroom to chat with Mrs. Adler, who nodded at students in the room who had a look of combined wonder and confident satisfaction; Mrs. Shwartz took careful note of these with her fierce, green-blue eyes. In particular, she seemed enamored of Mark Steinberg, whom she knew intimately. Steinberg's parents were personal friends of Mrs. Shwartz's. I envied Steinberg his gold-rimmed spectacles, which lent him a distinctive, worldly air; imagined the glasses to be a kind of totem that somehow magically invoked the self-discipline necessary for the single-minded pursuit of academic goals. Probably also, I thought, they made studying more fun, a masquerade as intelligent! To see the world through magnifying lenses—there was the key! To seem as dignified as a doctor or a teacher by virtue of something so portable that it could fold away in one's pocket was an easy way of gaining Mrs. Shwartz's elusive approval.

I decided that there was something wrong with my eyes. So much reading of comic books weakened them. From so much drawing of comics I was going blind! I imagined my appearance in Mrs. Shwartz's class on the first day, wire-frames perched on the ledge of my nose, a long cane in my hand, and the astonished look on her face as she rose to help me to my seat, where I would settle myself with great dignity, fold my cane, and give my glasses a slight adjusting tap that would put Mark Steinberg's scholarly affectations to shame. It was clear what I must do.

I announced to my mother that my eyes were bad.

She laughed. "The school tested you. You have twenty-twenty vision."

"But Mom . . . !" I groaned.

"Don't be stupid! You have eyes like me! Perfect! Your poor brother has to wear glasses, that's bad enough. You should be grateful you don't have this problem. Look how ugly they are. You want people to call you four-eyes? You have a handsome face! Why do you want to cover it with glasses? Instead, you should worry about that posture of yours! Look at how your shoulders stoop! I saw an ad in a magazine for a brace. I'm thinking of getting you one."

"Noooooooooo!" I moaned, clenching my fist. She always managed to divert discussion of my concerns to the dark preoccupations of her own twisted mind. "I don't need no brace. Nobody in school wears back braces!"

"Of course they do. My own brother wore one when he was a little boy."

"But that was long ago, in the past. That's not today! This is America! Not France! Sixth-grade students don't wear no back braces!"

"What a liar! Don't tell me! I saw the ad in *National Enquirer!* An American magazine!"

"That's the newspaper for stupid people," I screamed. "Mark Steinberg's parents read the *New York Times!* They know when he needs glasses! They buy him H.I.S. shirts and corduroy pants and penny loafers. And his parents are teachers, both of them!"

"Hey!" shouted my father from the bedroom where he slept all day, resting up from his night shift post office job. "Cut out all that yelling in there! I'm trying to sleep!"

"Your son is making me crazy," she shouted back. "He's criticizing us that we're not teachers like this stupid Mark Steinberg or Steinway. Gosh, my English is so bad. Still. And my memory is shot from so many pills." These last comments were aimed at me. "You should be ashamed," she said. "I'm taking pills for blood pressure. And your poor father works so hard to feed and clothe you when all he has is a fourth-grade education. But you criticize him because of this Mark Steinway! So, who cares if his parents are teachers? Did they have Nazis chase them for five years, trying to put them in ovens when they were only your age? You should be ashamed! What's wrong with the clothes you wear? I clean and iron them every day. Every day you have fresh underwear. Everyone says to me: 'Look how beautiful you take care of your two boys. Look how you comb their hair. Their teeth are white like pearls.' Twice to the dentist you've been already in the last two years. And Siegal's visits to give injections for your asthma—you know what that costs? You think money grows on trees?!"

She didn't understand. I wanted to try yet again, but my throat wouldn't speak. I stood there swaying dizzily, eyes welling with tears, lips trembling.

"Why do you stand there looking at me with that stupid expression? George! You should see your son! Gosh, what a crybaby he is!"

I struck my head with my fists. Then I did it again. I growled: "*Arghhhhhhgh!*" A kind of gurgling noise.

"What are you doing?" she said uneasily. "You're behaving like those retard boys they put in football helmets to stop from hurting themselves. Are you a retard boy? Should we put a football helmet on your head? To stop from hurting yourself? A brace is what I should put on you! Stoopie!" And then, she called again: "Stoopeeeeeeeee!" with such determined derision that my tears stopped and, struck mute, I walked into my room and fell on the bed.

I was not going to win the war of spectacles, this I knew. All pleas to have my eyes checked were ignored; forced to read and write great novels, and to do homework, without glasses, one day I awoke in bed, my sight gone. At first my parents did not believe me and tried to force me to dress unassisted. However, when I stumbled against the corner of a table, fell, and cut a deep gash into my head, they quickly saw the error of their ways. As I lay bleeding, head supported in my mother's lap, I heard her say: "You better call school to tell them he's not going in. And summon Dr. Siegal to have a look at him."

After a silent, extensive examination, Siegal removed his glasses, rubbed his eyes wearily, rolled down his shirtsleeves, and said: "There's no doubt about it. He is completely and permanently blind!" I was made comfortable. Mrs. Shwartz and the class were informed. As a joint volunteer effort, students agreed to visit my bedside with school books and assignments, and helped me complete my studies. Mark Steinberg was assigned to take dictation for my composition exercises. "Unbelievable!" he gasped as he wrote down the words pouring from my lips. "Astonishing!" Several times he blew his nose in a handkerchief, moved to tears. Mrs. Shwartz personally returned the papers to me, graded with a bold blue A+. "We misjudged you," she said as she sat my latest piece down on the radiator steam cover, which served as my private night table. "It is you who should be teaching us." I smiled weakly and held out my hand, which she pressed to her lips. "But what about the Steinbergs?" I gently teased. "Please," she blushed. "Don't, don't!"

Reaching under my bed, I pulled out the shoebox containing my most prized comics and flipped through them, gently pressing my fingertips to their plastic sleeves, assessing their "mint condition," weighing the possibility of their sale in exchange for funds sufficient to buy gold-rimmed spectacles. I would need at least one hundred dollars. But when I raised with Bruce the possibility of his father effecting a quick sale, he hedged; adjusted his horn-rims and his cave-fish eyes rushed out at me, then retreated back into the bottle-glass lenses, where they hung motionless as in a fishbowl. His father, he said, would not attend a comic book convention for a few more months at least! Even then, he couldn't say if his father would agree to rep my collector's items on this particular trip. It would depend on the state of their own finances, etc., etc. In other words, forget it, I was screwed.

This last fact was reinforced by a shopping expedition that Saturday. All summer I had alluded, for my mother's edification, with alternating force and gentleness, to certain currently fashionable clothing trends that I deemed essential to my success in Mrs. Shwartz's class: Levi's, H.I.S. shirts, Thom McAn penny loafers. But when zero hour came, she took us to Modell Davega Army and Navy Surplus on Fordham Road because, as she put it: "You eat twice as much as those other students. You're husky boys! You need clothes that last. Besides, your father doesn't make enough. He's not a teacher. He works in the *putz* office. One day you'll go to college and make a lot of money. Then you'll buy yourself H.I.S. Gosh, you should be grateful to have any-thing to wear. Do you know how I shivered from the cold in the mountains when I hid from the Nazis? My teeth chattered. I would have given my right arm for a coat." So it made sense to dress us in Army/Navy gear, uniformed to serve in a war that had never ended.

In the store, under harsh fluorescent lights, sandwiched between bins heaped with military apparel, like a recruit receiving his gear before basic training, I went along in a daze, the corner of my mouth turned up in chagrin as she filled our arms with the usual work shirts, polyester slacks, and $4.99 black dress Navy oxford shoes with rippled soles.

She then took us to John's Bargain Stores for loose-leafs and pencil cases bearing the images of Bugs Bunny and Elmer Fudd. As for the rest of what was needed—compasses, rulers (calibrated not only in inches but in millimeters), special laboratory notebooks containing graph paper, colored plastic tab dividers, etc., etc.—there was no point in even raising these with her. Still, I tried. I was met with: "Oh, gosh. You're dragging me someplace else now? I don't feel well. I'm not a well person. Abie, tell your teacher we can't afford all these things she wants you to get! Such nerve! Tell her to raise twins on a putz office salary! Who ever heard of such a thing?!"

On the first day of class I showed up squeaking in stiff black clunkers, rustling in polyester, my pale blue long-sleeved shirt already malodorous with perspiration and an excremental musk rising from the seat of my old-fashioned black trousers. I, who had worked in two stationers over the summer, now bore garish Looney Toons–illustrated vinyl school supplies. Dragging my feet, all hopes shattered, I waddled to secure a seat in the back, where I could hide from view all year.

Mrs. Shwartz lifted her face only to squint as we filed in through the door, point her pencil at a student, and attempt to guess the name.

"You're . . . Kaufman."

"Yes," I said sadly, "I'm Kaufman," which seemed to irritate her.

Clearly she had formed an opinion of me based on previous discussions with Mrs. Adler. But she held her peace, checked a box on the document laid before her on the desk, and said: "Just find yourself a seat. Keep in mind that you're tall and that the person behind you might have trouble seeing the blackboard."

Her eyes followed me with such approval to the last seat of the last row in the classroom that in a sudden blush of pride I doubled back, waded in among the desks in the middle row, chose the most centrally located one I could find, and plopped myself down in it. Her face grew hard at this, and I could tell by the sudden opacity of her eyes that she was making a mental note for herself.

Minutes later, three girls in a row entered, the prettiest in the class—Michelle Hyman, Vickie Cantor, Laura Winkler—and took up in a cluster of nearby seats. My body odors now seemed to roll off me in spreading waves. I couldn't be sure, but I thought that Laura Winkler stared hard at Vickie Cantor, shot a look my way, then back at Vickie, and wrinkling her nose made a face. She then put a hand quickly to her mouth to smother a laugh, and Vickie Cantor did the same.

Naturally, Mark Steinberg took up his throne in the front row, right under Mrs. Shwartz's nose. He had the added advantage of being not only weak-sighted but short. Mrs. Shwartz, of course, welcomed his arrival with a smile that still contained the warmth of her recent dinner in his parents' home. She did not want to seem biased, though, so she quickly composed herself, but by that very effort magnified her preference. As for him, he wore a secret little smile too: there was so little wrong that he could do and he knew it.

When the full class was present, accounted for, and all the rules spelled out, she launched into the first lesson. Covered the blackboard with chalk strokes that seemed to spring from a demonic core of cold rage. She put up an incomprehensible equation with such fury that I felt my heart rate increase. I looked around at the bowed heads of my fellow students. Their pencils moved furiously to keep up. A raging symphony was in progress: she the conductor, they the orchestra. I sat there like a janitor stumbled somehow into the pit during a performance and waved into a chair. I should pretend to play, I decided. Slowly I opened my loose-leaf binder, began to take notes. But as I wrote I could not shake the feeling that others around me were gagging secretly from the smells of my body and clothes, and I felt a painful urge to leave the room. My hand shot up.

Mrs. Shwartz glared. "What is it?"

"I need to go to the bathroom, please," I said.

"Not now!" she snapped.

"I gotta go bad," I whined. Giggles down the rows. Only Mark Steinberg's pen scratched ahead uninterrupted, his cheek resting on fist, brow furrowed with concentration, a model picture of intellectual effort and in his H.I.S. shirt with button-down collar points, corduroy Levi slacks, thick tartan plaid wool socks and buff-polished loafers with a bright new penny wedged into the bowstrap of each shoe, as at ease as in his own living room. Of course it was his gold wire-framed spectacles that—more than scholastic achievement, his structured and enlightened home environment, or inculcation with the finest middle-class virtues—guaranteed his future attendance at Harvard University, a college about which I knew nothing more than that my acceptance there would heal my mother of cancer if she should ever contract it, and also would probably end world hunger for once and all.

"All right! Go!" said Mrs. Shwartz. "But be warned! This is difficult material. I am not going to repeat myself! If you miss out, then it's your responsibility to find another student to explain it to you, but only after school! And there will be a graded quiz today . . ."

"Awwwwwwww!" the class groaned in unison.

"That's what I said. It will be a graded quiz. Every week we will have one. The grade will be part of your cumulative report card grade. And if you fail you must bring the quiz back to me signed by a parent."

The room now had grown perfectly still. We were like the soldiers of a new unit formed from high-spirited recruits who have just learned that some of us would probably not return home alive from the war. Everyone looked at each other as though trying to guess who wouldn't make it. The decisive pity evident in the eyes of those peering my way was virtually unanimous. Like an innocent man condemned in the field by a kangaroo court of officers responsible for a failed offensive, I stood to my feet, a half-smile of unconvincing gallantry on my face, shuffled self-consciously past desks, odors emanating from my tush, brushed Laura Winkler's knees, smiled a doltish grin of apology and, clutching the lavatory key ring in my unwashed hand, my body apologized its way out of the room. When the door slammed, faintly rattling the glass window in its insecure frame, the chalk resumed its flogging of the board.

I returned home after school on that first day, tears welling up in my eyes alternating with gasps of disbelief and exclamations of "Darn it! Oh, darn it!" At Walton Avenue I hurriedly departed from my usual route, trying to avoid as far as possible the spreading pool of students spilling from the school, my brother Howard somewhere back there among them.

I moved up toward Mount Eden Avenue at a huffing trot, stopped, pulled the quiz from my pocket, again gaped at it walleyed, and shook my head. I walked up to a building, the quiz dangling from one hand and my fingertips gently grazing the dirty ochre-colored walls, leaned my forehead against cold stone and uttered a moan so deep that it seemed to rise from within the belly of another, second person hidden within me whom I failed to fully recognize yet knew, with a kind of peaceful acceptance, was me.

Perhaps victims of criminal abduction, realizing their imminent execution by torture in undiscoverable waste places, groan this way, with the same surprised discovery of their innermost being poised on the verge of annihilation. It was not only an emotion; the dread I felt of what I faced at my mother's hands found no consolation in anything around me, and questioned everything with a kind of mournful reproach. From where would help come? From the owner of that green-and-white Bel Air convertible parked on the curb? Was the owner a family person? How would he or she feel to know of the torments that lay ahead for me? Would such intervene for a complete stranger? Would anyone take my mother aside and say: "Mrs. Kaufman, your Alan is a wonderful, gifted boy. He is not a Nazi. He is not the enemy. He is only a child who likes comics and is having problems with math." But there was no one in the world who would help me.

"George! Sheshi! Come in to eat! The imbecile is home!" she shouted as I plodded through the door, head bowed, hands hanging at my
sides, incontinent with the utter futility of it all, shoulders sloped so
badly that they practically begged to be saddled by a humiliating pos-
ture-corrective brace from some mail-order house in Georgia. I was
hoping to communicate, by an ashen, worried expression, that my
scholastic condition resulted not from a defective character but from a
genetic deficiency of some sort, one that warped my back and slowed
my mind, made me cretinous.

She wiped her hands angrily in her apron, flushed face drenched in
perspiration, shiny blue eyes dimmed to an inhuman opalescence like
eggs from some nearly extinct species of predatory bird that were at
any moment about to hatch their full-blown menacing brood.

"Where were you? Do you know we were worried about you? Did
they keep you at school? What happened?"

"No" is all I said.

She stared at me, her eyes dancing with the movements of mine,
which waltzed to avoid her direct gaze. "So, what is the matter? Did
you get into trouble already with that big mouth of yours? George, look
at your son. He's standing there. Something is wrong but he won't say
what it is. Did they beat you up, those stupid kids? Gosh, they raise
them like animals in this country. People have no brains. So? Say something!"

"I failed a quiz."

I was careful not to say "test," to assert the distinction in the way I
drew out the word "quiz" in an incredulous tone of voice, as though to
say, Can you believe it? I went to the post office to buy a stamp. I handed them my money; they handed me back a tomato.

"So, he failed a quiz. So what?" said my father as he shuffled past us
through the almost kinetic field of her sudden anxiety and swiftly
mounting anger. Already sensing her changed mood, he tried to defuse
it, not for concern for me but because he had to work tonight and wanted to catch a few hours more of undisturbed sleep after supper.

"Go, wash up," he said to me with a meaningful look. "Your face is all dirty."

I touched my fingers to my forehead where I had leaned against the building. "Go, fer cryin' out loud," he said, sitting. "What, you been cryin' over a stupid quiz?"

"What are you telling?!" my mother exploded. "What do you know, with your fourth-grade education! You want him to end up like you in the putz office working all night on a cold deck, like your father did?!"

Under the dinette table his white, oak-solid legs underweared in boxer shorts and his callused feet shod in house slippers shifted uneasily.

"I told you," he said, his voice sounding younger, pleading almost, "don't talk to me like that in front of the kids or I'll rap you in the mouth!"

"Oh, yes? You will hit your sick wife? Like that crazy brother of yours, Arnold, the *meshugener*, hits his wife, Ray?"

"Hey!" he barked reflexively. "Leave my brother out of it!"

She turned suddenly to me like an actor in a sitcom confiding low-voiced to the studio audience: "Look at the trouble you're making between your father and me. You won't be happy till you see us divorced!"

The thought that my math performance could be responsible for the destruction of my parents' marriage filled me with despair. "Nooooooo!" I urged. "Please don't say that! It's not true!"

Just then, Howie brushed past. "What happened? You failed a test?"

And she: "You told me it is a quiz, not a test! Did you fail a test?!"

"No, look!" I unfolded the sheet of mimeographed paper. It bore only a few questions and answers, but the words "Very Poor" and the grade 45% were written boldly in bright red ink, as well as Mrs. Shwartz's angry red-ink cross-outs, made it seem important.

"Oh, Gosh!" my mother moaned softly, all her college dreams for me shattered by the proof of failure in her trembling hands. Then her face grew hard and she looked at me without pity. "So. What do you want me to do with this?" She held it out for me to take. "Here. You don't have as much of my family in you as I thought. You're more like your father's side. You should have seen how brilliant my brothers were in school. Sure. Because they studied. They didn't spend their time with stupid comic books! You know what the comic books will get you? Like your father and his father you'll end up, broke, illiterate! You watch! In ten years you'll tell me: 'Momma, you were right!' But by then it will be too late! Wait. You'll see. Here, take back this. Your life will be wasted. Go. Your father is right. Wash your stupid face. It's all dirty. Take it! Go. What were you doing, hugging the wall? Get away from there! Did you get the new clothes we bought you dirty too? Go. Take this away. Your father is hungry. He has to go to work tonight. Ten hours on his feet in the freezing cold. That's what you get with a fourth-grade education! Go read comic books like he did instead of studying. Hitler I survived, five years I was hungry, afraid, running, hiding, so that you could read comic books. Go, stupid! What do you know? All day I cooked."

I didn't accept the quiz back, swallowed hard. "I need you to sign the quiz. Mrs. Shwartz wants proof that I showed it to you."

"Forget it!" She laughed bitterly. "George, look at this stupid son of yours. You watch. He's gonna get me in trouble with the Department of Immigration! He wants me to sign the test. Watch. It'll end up in the wrong hands! They'll send me back to France. Won't that be nice?"

"Your mother's here illegally, she don't sign no nothin'," growled my father. "Mash-a-la. Bring me some of that soup. I'm starvin' here, fer krissakes!"

He glared while Howie observed me, shaking his head from side to side with a sad smile. "What's wrong wit you?" my father said. "Why do you always gotta make trouble? You got a test, so pass the test! You failed the test, so study more. But don't bring here no tests from no teacher to sign. You tell that teacher that she should sign! She's the teacher, not your mutha! Is your mutha teachin' you or is the teacher teachin' you? Well, which is it?"

"The teacher is teaching me," I said, trying hard not to smile with relief that no physical punishment seemed in the offing.

"OK. So, is it me and Momma's fault that you failed the test?"

"Quiz," interrupted my mother. "Quiz. It's not a test." Again she turned to me as to an audience to confide: "He doesn't know the difference. He's only got a fourth-grade education. He never made it to the sixth grade . . ."

My father had already heard this once too often and said, "What do you know about what I know or don't know? You know, you got a bigger mouth than that stupid kid of yours, you know that? Bring me the food already! I'm sick and tired of the both of ya!"

And that should have been that. She turned to the stove. He picked up the *Daily News*. Howie's face dropped to read the comic book hidden on his lap under the table. Suppertime's well-oiled machine was set into motion. The atmosphere resettled into a mist of steamed and charred food smells floating on a pond of stove heat. But it all came to an abrupt halt when I said again: "I need to get the paper signed."

My father's face grew crimson. "You know, now you're beginning to get on my nerves! I told you, no one's signin'! Your mother's here illegally. Now get out of here! Beat it! Discussion's over! You wanna go witout supper, you can go wit-out supper! But stop makin' trouble, ya hear, or I'll make you trouble like you'll never forget!"

"But it's gotta be signed!" I cried out. "Mrs. Shwartz said so! She's the teacher! I'll get left back! She'll think I didn't show it to you! Please! It's not my fault! I didn't know there was a quiz. I'm not good in math anyway! But this really screws me up! Please, oh, please, you gotta, you gotta." I removed a pen from my pocket, held it out, struck such a pathetic picture standing there, I thought.

And then my mother snapped. My father shoved his chair away from the table, the torn-out center of a slice of Wonder Bread swelling his cheek. I heard her mutter very low: "No more talk. Now I'll take care of this the way I know how," as she brushed past him with a glassy look in her eyes, as though I were a perfect stranger in no way connected to her plan. But I understood very well my place in it.

"Pop," I begged, talking very fast—there was so little time. "Pop. She's going to get the hanger. Please! Pop! Don't let her!"

"Too late, mister," he said, moving his chair back to the table. "You asked for it. And you know what? I hope she gives it to you but good!"

"Pop!" I pleaded. He was my last hope. "Pop, please. I beg you, Pop!"

"You beg me? Don't go begging me, I ain't got nothing to do with it."

I imagine that while she laid into me with the wire hanger, he and Howard helped themselves to warm food from the stove; supped with heads bowed low, not from shame but concentration, with my screams and pleas for help seasoning their mouthfuls.

What finally caught their attention was my appearance with a welt across my forehead to announce, in a drained voice of numb disbelief, that they had better go look, because she's throwing out our comic book collection.

They rushed past me even before all the words had left my lips.

"Put that down, put that down!" shouted my father, as Howie stood beside him chanting: "She's lost it, Dad, look. She's nuts." Howie had convinced my father that some day, say five years from now, we'd all cash in on our *Captain Americas* and *Spider-Mans*, convinced him that the future lay in comic book investments, and he had looked forward to their eventual auction to the tune of tens of thousands of dollars. Having them was like owning stock in a commodities exchange, a gentlemanly form of speculation perfectly suited to a poor sort raised on Captain Marvel comics and Buck Rogers matinees and who had never gotten past fourth grade. Besides, he enjoyed reading them as much as we did. So, he said again in a voice of wavering conviction: "You're not throwing out nothin' until I say so. Put 'em down!"

Eyes crazed, hair wild, she had an armful of first editions hugged tightly to her breast, among which I recognized the cover of *Avengers* #4 announcing Captain America's star-spangled resurrection from the black sleep of war. She hunched her shoulders and neck when she spoke, like some deranged kidnapper backed into the corner on a rooftop and threatening to jump with the abducted babe in his arms.

"Out they go!" she shrieked. "I'm not going to have our kids' education ruined by putz office comic books! And if you make me trouble, I divorce you! I leave! You make your own food! And raise these sons of yours! Don't you try to stop me! . . ."

"She's crazy, Dad," Howard muttered. "Get them out of her hands. They're worth money. Do something. In five years we'll be rich!"

He looked at her, then back at us, torn between future prosperity and the current state of peace, and said to my brother: "Five years? Who knows if we'll even be alive in five years? Let this be a lesson to the two of you. Your momma works hard. All day she's been slavin' in that kitchen to make you food. We don't need no trouble. Your teachers got papers to sign, let them sign them. Your mother wants to throw out the *fa-cac-tah* comics, so throw 'em out. It's time you two grew up already. When I was your age I worked for a living."

And that was it. Howie followed her out the door wailing indignantly as she marched to the incinerator chute in the corridor. I stumbled after, while my father returned to the kitchen mumbling to himself: "I'm telling ya, they're a bunch of goddamned nuts, the whole lot of 'em, and they're driving me crazy."

The incinerator for garbage disposal was located in the corridor by a dim window, just before the dark stairwell. It was only large enough to squeeze an arm into and stuff trash down the cast-iron chute. It opened like an oven mouth by a wooden handle to reveal a brick throat glowing below with fire, and sparks shot past like tracer bullets. It reminded me of the pictures of the crematoria that I had seen in the book about death camps, in the Grand Concourse public library. Whenever I threw out the trash I'd stand for a moment staring into the fiery darkness, trying to feel what it meant to be shoved dead—or worse even, alive, as some of the prisoners had—into such a space. But I could never quite grasp it. Here she now stood, Howard behind her, pleading, while I watched coldly from a distance as she stuffed down comic after comic, all first editions still in their plastic sleeves, and at one point I glimpsed the tricolor costume of Captain America before he too was consigned to the flames, killed a second time by the war, first by its villains, now by its victims, and it seemed to me that none of us could escape from what had happened in WW II to Jews like my mother, everything was burning in the ovens of Time, my childhood too, and there was no escaping, no rescue possible, from the ultimate destruction awaiting us all.

THE ADVENTURES OF THE PURPLE JEW

Gun in hand, I kicked down a door behind which sat a table full of bald Nazis in suspenders and riding boots, playing poker and smoking ill-smelling cigarettes. "Take that, you Nazis," I shouted as I pumped them full of lead. Then, cloaking myself in an overcoat I found hanging on the wall, I slipped out of the building with my collar turned up. I strolled over to a guard stationed at the gate of the camp, put a cigarette to my lips, and asked in perfect German: "Gotta light?"

The guard responded, "Yes, mein Commandant," and with the automatic gesture of an obedient robot brought out a cigarette lighter and complied.

"Thank you," I said and blew a smoke ring in his face that hung on his big nose like a ghostly horseshoe and dissolved. "At ease," I said, and drawing my revolver I shot him too.

Now the sounds of sirens, barking dogs, shots, and the boots of alerted troops charging down steps clamored in the night and spotlights lit up the sky. I shrugged off the coat to reveal my purple fighting togs, adorned with the emblem of a Jewish star, and melted into the shadows of the woods.

I next showed up in Stockholm, Sweden, at the home of its most famous math professor, Dr. Olaf, an old man who lived in scholarly solitude with Brigitte, his voluptuous daughter.

When he saw me at the door, gaunt with fatigue, dirt-smudged and smelling of gunpowder, he gave a start and gasped: "Why, you're Abie Kaufman, alias The Purple Jew! Good heavens, what on earth has happened to you!" His beautiful daughter appeared at that moment at the head of the stairs, saw me, and came hurrying down, holding up the hem of her gown to keep from tripping.

"Good evening, Dr. Olaf," I said grimly, brushing past him. "Would you mind terribly if I sat down? I need a rest."

"Mind?!" exclaimed the doctor. "Why, I am honored! Brigitte! Brigitte! The Purple Jew in the flesh! Bring him something cool to drink. Sir, what is your pleasure?"

"A tall glass of milk mixed with some Bosco chocolate syrup will do just fine, thanks. And here, you can put this away somewhere. Don't worry: it's not loaded. I won't be needing it for the rest of the night."

The touch of cold gun metal sent a thrill through his pudgy soft white hands as he bore my gun to a cabinet and stored it in a drawer.

"I see you've been up to your usual business of killing Nazis," he said with admiration, returning.

I nodded grimly. "They're out there all over the place. I kill one and two more pop up." Then I chuckled and added, "Heh! Doesn't leave me as much time as I'd like for math. But, it's gotta be done."

"Oh, I wouldn't worry about that, Abie. Why, tomorrow you're to get the Nobel Prize!"

"Funny," I said, "I'm only twenty. They've never given the prize to a mathematician so young."

"How does it feel?" asked the good professor, "to be so brilliant and so early recognized?"

I shrugged.

Just then Brigitte returned with the milk. Also, she had slipped into something more comfortable, a Frederick's of Hollywood black silk babydoll pajama outfit.

Her father smiled his approval. "Ah, I see you've made yourself nice for our guest."

She leaned over me to hand me the glass, cried "Oooooh!" and the glass crashed to the floor, shattering and turning the costly beautiful rug dark-stained with chocolate milk.

"Your shoulder," she said tearfully, "it's bleeding," and with manicured dainty fingers turned back the torn fabric of my costume to expose a hole in my flesh. "You've been shot!"

"It's nothing," I said. "I caught a slug as I made my escape. Just a flesh wound." But in no time she had my togs off and was bandaging the hole as I sipped a fresh glass of chocolate milk prepared by the professor. "Look," I said to both of them when the dressing was done. "Whatever you do, don't let on about my injury to my mother. She's gonna be there tomorrow. I don't want her to worry."

Both nodded deferentially that they understood.

The next day the professor and his daughter helped me into my tuxedo and rode to the King's palace for the awards ceremony. In an auditorium very like the one in my old grade school, P.S. 64 in the Bronx, the world's greatest mathematicians sat assembled. In addition, my parents, my uncle Arnold and his family, my grandparents (all four risen from the dead and sitting as happy as Topper up in the balcony), plus just about everyone I had ever known and who had doubted the special nature of my destiny, including all my classmates, were there. Mrs. Adler was there and Mrs. Shwartz. When I entered they all rose to their feet and sang "God Bless America" as I sauntered nonchalantly to the stage. Then they burst into a din of thunderous applause and shouted, "Bravo! Bravo!"

The King, after a brief, dull speech, handed me the Prize: an enormous trophy and a check for a million dollars. "I trust," he said, "that this will make you comfortable for a long time to come. You were very brave not to follow your mother's silly suggestion to become a teacher and marry rich. Instead you became an avenger, went hungry, and, learning math on your own in dingy basement rooms, wrote your name in the stars. . . ."

"Don't talk bad against my mother or I'll knock your head in," I snarled, and the King bowed his head in shame.

"Of course," he said, "I never intended . . ."

"Right," I said, and he skulked off stage.

I now stood at the podium, the trophy in one hand, check in the other. A hush fell over the hall.

"Mom," I said, looking down into her eyes, which glowed with pride, "now you can rest. This one is for you. The Nazis put your childhood in a concentration camp, filled your heart with dead people and fear, and in turn you did the same to me, but that's over now. I'm gonna build you the house you shoulda had. And I'm gonna send you to the Sorbonne for that diploma you always wanted. And I'm gonna get you the best doctors money can buy to take care of your high blood pressure, kidney stones, and rectal polyps. Because what happened to you is not fair! And there's God and he gave me the talents to make it right! So don't you ever cry again, my little momma, and don't you worry no more about no Nazis either. I'm taking care of that!" I allowed my tux jacket to slip aside, revealing underneath the costume of the Purple Jew and the blue steel handle of my gun. I grinned handsomely.

"Oh, Abie! Be careful!" she shrilled. "Is it loaded? Oy! Don't hurt yourself!"

"Goodbye, Mom," I chuckled. "Goodbye Professor, goodbye Brigitte." I slipped behind the curtains, melting back into the shadows, underground, to calculate groundbreaking equations on the run as I made my vengeance raids on the enemies of innocence.

ASTHMA

THERE WAS NO chance to run. We were too small, too fat, too slow. Twenty-year-old, two-hundred-pound Butch Brunet would have caught us easily. As we passed Al and Lou's candy store, one of the owners, Fat Al, peered out at us and nodded in greeting. I nodded back, afraid to alert him. We turned into the entrance of the building. The door gave to Brunet's hand. We marched into the cool, dark lobby to an alcove under the stairs, lined with copper-plated mailboxes. He took Howie by the shoulders and stood him up against the mailboxes. Then, clasping my shoulders, he stood me next to Howie.

"Please," we both pleaded. "Don't kill us."

"Kill?" He giggled. "I'm not planning to kill you. I'm gonna hurt you, though. Both of you. It's for your own good. Gotta toughen you

Jewboys up. How are you gonna survive in the schoolyard if you don't get tough? You'll see, you'll thank me someday for this. You want kids to beat up on you like a couple of faggots? Huh? Is that what you are? Couple of faggots?"

"We're not faggots," I protested.

"Jew shit," he hissed. His fist landed squarely in my solar plexus, knocking the wind completely out. I had been dropped into silent space from an airplane, falling to earth too fast to draw breath. A great stillness enveloped my shock. And then I began to emit a low whine. Tried to speak. My lips moved but no words came. My hands waved helplessly. Now Brunet was pounding away with both fists at Howie, who crouched behind crossed arms, without much luck it seemed. I tried to mouth a protest, but still no words or breath came. My breathing had shut down. And then, suddenly, my first intake of air occurred with a miraculous, wheezing groan like an old accordion, and I leaned on hands and knees with head hung low, vanquished, a dog, grateful just for breath, and could hear Howie now gasping, "Enough! Enough!" as Brunet pummeled him.

I regained sufficient wind to find my feet but stood helplessly by, watching as Brunet worked my brother over. Nothing could be done but hope that it would soon end. Finally his arms dropped and, panting hard, he examined his handwork. He had closed Howie's left eye, raised the cheek on that side, bloodied his mouth. He had avoided collapsing him completely in order to better keep him on his feet for extended sport. Howie leaned against the mailboxes, yet despite his injuries seemed strangely collected, even unfazed, and showed no sign of emotion whatsoever.

Bitterly, I said to Brunet, "What do you want? We don't got nuthin. We're new in the neighborhood. We're poor. Please, leave us alone. We're not bothering nobody."

Whatever had driven him to this had spent itself, and he stood dully, the giggliness gone.

"I want money. How much money you two Jews got?"

"Money!" I exclaimed in exasperation and despair. "We don't got no money! We're pooooor! My father works in the post office. He's got loan sharks after him. We eat potatoes. We don't got no money! Please! Leave us alone!"

"Jews always have money."

"Don't beg him," snapped Howie. "You don't got to explain nothing to him." He spoke calmly with his hand cupped over his eye. The sight of him so badly hurt enraged me. I would have killed Brunet if I had been strong enough. But I understood that it was important to show some humility or he might start up again.

"You hurt us bad, mistuh," I said. "We're sorry, whatever we done. But we don't got no money to give. That's for sure. Look, why don't you let us go and forget about it? You beat us up good. Jeez. Look at my brother. And I could hardly breathe from that punch. You knocked out all my air. We got no money."

Brunet seemed pleased by my little speech.

"I wish I was strong like you," I said, pretending admiration. "But we're just a couple of fat Jewish kids. We got nothing, really. Let us go."

"Now and then, I'm gonna take you in here and kick the shit out of you, kike. That's just a fact. But go ahead. You paid your dues. See you around."

We rushed out, down the steps, and turned the corner of 170th Street, hurrying away in a zigzagging route, glancing back every so often to be sure that he wasn't following.

The sight of Howie's face was greeted at home by an outburst of hysterical rage. Since I bore no visible wounds, I was blamed for Howie's injuries. I was older, my mother shouted, I should have seen it coming, gotten us out of there before trouble started.

"Who is this boy?" she demanded to know.

He's no boy, I tried to explain, but a man twice our age and powerfully built. A real killer.

My father shuffled in. "Oh, yeah? What did he look like? I'll go down there and rip his head off!"

This angered my mother even more. What if my father were injured? His Blue Cross hadn't even begun yet! What if he were hurt too badly to work? Then we'd really starve. And how!

And so on. She concluded that it had been all my fault, that I was a troublemaker with a big mouth, and so from now on we were forbidden to return to the schoolyard. From here on in we should go play at P.S. 70, ten blocks north. It was more of a Jewish neighborhood over there, with the *shul* and the nearby Cohen Funeral Home.

My parents pressed ice cubes wrapped in a towel to Howie's eye. They then retired behind their bedroom door to confer in Yiddish-language whispers. When the door reopened, my father emerged fully dressed. My mother followed, wringing her hands. "George," she pleaded, "don't do anything stupid!"

"I told you," he retorted with mock irritation, "I'm only going to look for this punk. If I find him I'll give him a warning, to stay off my kids or else!"

The door slammed. I lay in my bed, excited, imagining my father hunting for Brunet. I knew in my heart that he wouldn't find him. Wondered if he really was searching.

My mother came into the room. "Your father is sick from what happened," she said. "You should have seen how he looked when he saw your brother's face. White as this sheet."

Howie laughed. "Oh yeah? Where'd he go? To the Greeks for a cheeseburger?"

"Stupeed! He went to find this bully. I hope he controls himself. That's all we need, he should go to jail for assault, God forbid!"

"They're not gonna send Pop to jail for sticking up for his kids," I jeered.

"Sure they will," she said plaintively. "What do you know? They can put him in jail for assault. Didn't you ever hear of assault? What do they teach you in that stupid school of yours anyway?"

Over an hour later he returned with his hands full of packages.

"So. What did you see? I've been worried sick!"

My father looked at her nonplused as he laid his load down on the new dinette table. "I didn't see no one in there. It was empty. I had myself a cheeseburger by the Greeks. And I stopped off in Florsheim's to get some shoe polish. Wait'll you taste the delicious peach pie from Friedhoffer's. They got 'em on sale. The clerk let me taste a *bistle*. D'licious! And here I got us a few mags."

She flipped through them: *Ring, True Men Adventures, Stag.*

We stood behind her to catch a glimpse of the spoils from his expedition. "Can we have a piece of pie? For being good?"

My father laughed uneasily. "A piece of pie for being good? I don't know anybody who's being good. What kind of reason is that?"

"Oh, George, don't be cruel. The poor kids took some beating. Look at your son's face!"

"All right! I'm just joking. You think I'd begrudge the kids a piece of pie, fer krissakes! Go on, Mashala, get out the plates. I'll div-vy it up!"

We came away with a small slice each and sat down to feast. He got the rest. Then we retired to the bedroom, where the four of us sprawled on the bed, flipping through magazines with the TV on.

"You know," he said, "I don't like the kids lookin' through my magazines. It's not exactly meant for dopes their age."

But I was far too absorbed in a lurid story in *Stag* about the human sacrifice of a young virgin by Satanists in nineteenth-century Paris to turn back now, and whined, "Oh, Daddy, please! We're grown up!"

"Sure," said my mother, "your sons have seen a lot already. Besides, you think they don't look at this junk on the outside? Of course they do. And how! Better this filth than the filth they read out there."

On the television, Tarzan, played by Johnny Weissmuller, was attempting to explain to Jane, played by Maureen O'Hara, why elephants are more trustworthy than human beings, while in the magazine story a naked buxom young woman clamped spread-eagle to a blood-spattered altar and ringed by grim-looking men garbed in hooded robes screamed and writhed orgasmically, as the high priest drew the blade of a gigantic knife in a slow skin-slicing incision across her waist and another held a golden goblet to catch the blood, which they drank, an act described in gruesome detail. Horrible tortures then followed, climaxing in the sawing open of the virgin's chest, and the tearing out of her beating heart. I developed an erection that I tried to hide between my squeezed thighs.

Every so often I lifted my face to find relief from the sadistic ritual in the boyishly primitive goodness of Tarzan's husbanding of Jane. He really was a miracle worker, summoning elephants to assist in the construction of their honeymoon abode, creating stampedes of gazelles to deter unwelcome curiosity seekers with cameras and guns, and jockeying Jane around the jungle by means of his ingenious cost-free public transportation system of treetops and vines. She seemed totally happy.

By contrast, my mother, who had moved to the recently acquired E-Z Boy reclining chair, was anxious, fretting, her brow beetled in worry. She flipped through a snuff magazine but seemed unable to focus. When she did find herself absorbed in an article, her face assumed a kind of dull expression, like that of a postoperative patient doped up on pills and nourished through intravenous infusion.

A fast reader, I was able to lap up two or three more of the magazine stories before my father put a stop to it, despite my mother's dismissal of his displeasure: a crew-cutted homicidal rapist with a scarred upper lip leaves the naked corpse of his coed victims in woods near a university campus, a Pentecostal star carved into their torsos and their heads removed; in a jungle torture camp run by Japanese soldiers in World War II, a group of Australian nuns are suspended naked upside down and immersed in huge vats of boiling oil; finally I came to an illustration of a grinning, shirtless, heavily muscled Nazi thug in riding boots poised to lash his whip against the crisscrossed naked back of a luscious-looking blonde whose expression is a strange mixture of absolute terror and sexual anticipation.

In other parts of the depicted SS dungeon, women are broken on massive-looking wheels or screaming under the application of white-hot brands. Again I developed an erection, but this time with a keener-than-usual interest marked by an intensely uncomfortable stirring of guilt.

As I read the account of rape and torture I flipped back again and again to the illustration, trying to better grasp the exquisite pleasures of taking one's sexual satisfaction and inflicting unbearable pain on a beautiful woman, though in these fantasies real woman did not suffer but only underwent the ritual of its infliction. The pain the women endured was to them desirable. The women were not real women but doll-women, a new kind of subgroup of females created expressly for the fulfillment of fantasy. In other words, they were inhuman or less than human. I then imagined my mother as a beautiful young doll-woman turned in the capable pain/pleasure–inflicting hands of big blond Nazi torture-masters. Of course, I myself now became the biggest and blondest Nazi torture-master of all, unsurpassed in my ability to inflict cruel suffering and overwhelming sexual fulfillment. At this point I dreaded nothing more than to glimpse the reality of my actual mother just a few feet away, her body crisscrossed with the scars of cesareans and of kidney stone operations—not whips—and smelling of chopped onions and pine-scented disinfectant, not of perfumed sweat and vaginal musk.

My concentration developed a kind of enervated rapturous focus in envisioning the dull slap of leather cat-o'-nine-tails against glistening skin, the sexual writhe of the shackled prisoner. In this world the victim could not respond with anything but a "plea" or a "moan." Her flesh contained nerve endings that did not connect with her mind but drained off their pain into an insensate gland that made it disappear. The victim's flesh was not actually cut, seared, or bruised. Instead, the lashes were a form of foreplay coaxing the woman to fulfill herself in orgasm, the white-hot brand a fierce surprise that would catch her self-possession off guard with an urge to explode in "juices" down her thighs. Orgasm was a kind of birth from which the Nazi torture-masters would be transformed into respectful knights with knees bent to their released victims, who would don silken garments and lounge on gorgeous settees, gratefully awaiting the pleasures of other tormenting lovers.

I shut the magazine, heaved off the bed, and said, "Ma, I'm hungry. Can I eat something?"

"Why don't you wait? It's only two hours until supper."

I whined, "I can't! I'm hungry! Please!"

Huffing, she rose from the chair. "OK, I'll make you a hamburger and a glass of juice." She shuffled out muttering about how "those damned kids don't give you a minute to rest!"

"Why don't you wait till supper? What's the matter with you?" my father said crossly.

I glanced at the cover of the stag magazine that I had just perused, with its illustrations of a man and woman fighting off gigantic vicious rats in a bamboo cage while their Japanese captors stab at them with bloody bayonets. He not only reads dirty magazines about Nazi sexual perversions, I thought, but wants to deny me food. "I'm hungry," I offered sullenly. "What's wrong with that?"

"Nothing. But you know your momma works hard. She's resting here, why don't you let her rest up a little? She just made you lunch a couple of hours ago!"

"None of your business!" I blurt out. "You don't care about Momma. She don't love you!" Lately I was increasingly unable to contain such little speeches. He stares at me, hurt and angry.

"Who do you think you're talking to, mister? Huh?" But he doesn't rise from the bed. He is quick to anger but slow to act. I have learned that I can go far with him and get away with it. He is a coward.

In the kitchen she is rattling pots, making a big fuss out of the preparation of a hamburger. Smoke spreads through the house carrying the stench of burning meat. Appetite lost, I enter my room, stretch on the bed, luxuriate in the clear glimpse of clean blue sky above the rooftops. It seems as if I have been forever in this bleak, anonymous room in the Bronx, staring out the window, secure in the knowledge of food about to be eaten but with no heart to eat it; at odds with my father, whom I have just injured emotionally, stirred by feelings of lust and guilt at my identification with the torturers of my mother's childhood, terrified by the thought that in the real world of the Holocaust it was one such as I who could have been shackled to a real wall and burned by a white-hot brand. And now I felt a wheeze flutter in my chest, my breath coming with difficulty. Kitchen smoke floated into the room, slipped past my nostrils and lips, tickled the wheeze. My breath came more and more labored.

Panicked, I sat up, gripped the sides of the bed, and struggled to catch my breath, to no avail. I stood up, paced back and forth. "Oh, no," I whispered aloud, "I'm getting an asthma attack." I had had it bad since the age of five when my mother gave birth to a dead nine-month-old girl and started hitting me. "Mom," I gasped, "can't breathe!"

"George! Sheshi! Abie's having an asthma attack!"

My father shuffled in, followed by my brother, who kept his nose buried in a comic book. He looked up briefly, grinned, and returned his attention to the opened pages.

"Whatzamattah," my father said with reluctant compassion. "The asthma's bothering you again?"

"George, let him use your spray," my mother ordered.

"But Mash," he protested, "you know that spray is for me! You gotta have a prescription!"

"To hell with prescription. What does it matter! Look, your son can't breathe. Give him the spray before he collapses!"

"Acchhhhhh!" He shuffled off to fetch the spray.

"Here, Abie, try this," she said when he returned, snatching the spray from his hand and putting it to my lips. "Inhale." She pumped three bursts of phenobarbital-laced drug into my mouth, then again. I sat on the edge of the bed leaning forward, eyes closed, holding the medicine in my lungs for as long as I could. But when I exhaled I still felt wheezy, blocked.

"Maybe we should try steam," she said. So they stationed me over a sink filled with hot water, and with a towel draped over my head like a satanic hood to catch the rising steam, they chanted: "Breathe! Breathe!" like voices in a ritual. But it failed to work.

I staggered back to my bed waving away the proffered spray, which made me dizzy, pushed past my mother, and collapsed. They gathered around in concern.

"Abie, how are you feeling?"

"Bad," I reported, gasping, barely able to speak.

"Should we call a doctor?"

"Call."

My father went to the bedroom to phone Dr. Siegal. Minutes later he returned. "Siegal will be right over. He almost couldn't come. Said he was busy out on call. But I told him it's bad." Then he stroked my head.

Their voices grew solicitous, the touch of their hands and voices more gentle. "Here. Loosen your belt. Unbutton the shirt. We'll open the window a crack." They undressed me and laid me down on the bed like a virgin on an altar being prepared for sacrifice. "Let's get the shoes off," said my father, and he removed my shoes. "Why don't you take off your pants?"

"No!" I pleaded. I didn't want Dr. Siegal to see me in my underwear; didn't want him to bend over my undressed body with a needle, like a Nazi torture-master or a satanic high priest bending over the bound and naked victim. I would receive him uniformed in clothes, a soldier on a battlefield. Only victims were shorn of their clothes; soldiers died with their boots on.

In pictures of Jews murdered by Nazis, naked corpses lay piled in pits. I first saw such pictures in a book in the Grand Concourse branch of the public library, which I often frequented as a quiet place to study and dream. I discovered the book in the children's section of novels, clearly out of place, misshelved, and there, I felt, especially for me, a sort of omen. I was not yet old enough to check out adult books. It's funny how despite every effort at its censorship a book will always find its way into the hands of those whom the prohibition intends to protect.

A picture showed three ovens. A kind of conveyor belt ran into the mouth of one, on which stretched a naked corpse; beside it a thin man dressed in striped pajamas and with a cap set at a jaunty angle peered intently at the camera. In another photo a pale bearded man on his knees with hands tied behind his back peered expressionlessly at the camera as a revolver was held to the back of his neck by a Nazi. In the next photo the man is on the ground, executed, and the Nazi grinning.

There followed photograph after photograph of naked corpses piled up in pits and on wagons and arranged on the ground.

In one such picture I caught the curve of a beautiful breast, looked more closely. There was a matching breast visible, equally voluptuous, the pair belonging to a shapely body spread pinwheeled on the ground, head flung back and mouth agape. The soft, pretty face was not skeletal like the others. I could imagine the woman alive, developed an erection. Eyes closed, envisioned my fingers cupping her breasts, penis grazing her lips, and that as I embraced her she lay warm and satiny against my clothed body, stirred to life, her head of blonde hair nestled in the nape of my neck. I pinched her nipple, gently but firmly, just as was done in my father's mags, and her pelvis arched with desire. This might have been my mother had she not survived. When I opened my eyes, saw that she was dead among others, anonymously, her teeth jutting from her limp jaw, her legs twisted unbecomingly in the open pit, my erection shriveled instantly. The book in my hands was not a window into the boudoir of my awakening sexual life but the graduation album of my mother's childhood education in the numbing and grotesque finishing school of Nazi atrocity.

Shocked and ashamed, I shelved the book in its misplaced spot, but also noted the adjoining call numbers in order to return to it. For months thereafter I stared at the picture of the woman in the pit. I skimmed novels and browsed history books for other evidence of tortured or murdered Jews. I found references to rape and the barbaric infliction of unbearable suffering on Jews in history after history. Jews were boiled alive, had molten lead poured into their orifices, were pulled apart by horses, were crushed, whipped, pierced, had eyes plucked out, limbs severed, tongues torn out with red-hot tongs, were nailed to crosses, burned at the stake, fed to wild animals, had their intestines removed by hand, unraveled, and nailed to a post, were impaled, flayed, skinned, sliced, sawed, and smashed. The things that could be done to a human being were endless, each more horrible than the last, and they had all been done over and over to Jews without hesitation, and though my mother somehow had been plucked alive from this maniacal human destiny she was a ridiculous exception, which only increased the inevitability that I would someday join this procession of historical victimhood. And I knew that more than anything in the world, I wanted not to be Jewish.

It was important to me to remain dressed at all costs. I would refuse to sleep in underwear, insist upon wearing pajamas, even at the height of summer. Every moment of my life felt like that preceding a torturous execution: it could happen at any time and I must be ready to meet it with dignity. My parents could not understand but tolerated my quirky dislikes. For instance, I hated the beach, refused to go to it. The unclad bodies on the sand reminded me of corpses heaped in pits. In many such pits the ground was sandy, like a beach. To this day my heart gets a jolt at the touch of sand. I approach sand with a feeling of intense aversion, a deep sense of distrust, sometimes even nausea: death-fear.

I could be brought to tears by my mother's insistence that we remove our shorts to walk along the shore. Furthermore, I felt perplexed, confused by the sight of so many clearly delighted people running about naked in the sun, shrieking and laughing in their colorful bathing suits and diving unrestrained into the rolling surf, while I stood pale and anxious, unable to move, praying for escape and angry at my mother for placing me in such an insoluble and intolerable predicament. One should not remove one's clothes in public but be prepared to run, fight, or hide at any moment.

I could have been an unfortunate fish washed ashore, gasping for breath just inches from the waves. Shallower and shallower came my breath, and with air slipping away, my chest collapsed and expanded with greater and greater exertions, like a pocket accordion in the hands of a polka musician; farther and farther receded the faces and voices of my parents, whose anxious remarks arrived from a great remove now, and a feeling of profound sadness settled over me, their preoccupations and threats seeming to matter less and less the nearer I drew to death, and that seemed a real possibility now:

I was close to blacking out.

Survival panic set in, and with great irritation and impatience I shrugged off their worried hands, swung my legs over the side of the bed to a sitting position, and leaning forward gave free vent to my physical predicament, the sheer impossibility of breathing.

It was as if I could draw deep gulps of air but couldn't release them. My lungs had lost control. I chanted in a frenzied monotone: "Can't breathe, can't breathe . . ."—a mantra to the mute impartial spirit of personal witness that seemed at such times to hover hidden in a corner of the ceiling (or my consciousness), an angel of History recording these events, my suffering, on a handheld motion-picture camera, relaying images of me—distorted in a fish-eye lens, like some character in an episode of *The Twilight Zone*—up to God.

I heard the knock at the front door. Enter the fastidious and arrogant Dr. Siegal, a slender, energetic elder with a hawklike face and a distinguished head of white hair. The Kaufman family's perennial physician, he had not only delivered both my father and his brother Arnold, but treated my grandfather for his heart condition and my grandmother for cancer. We were all under his care, which usually involved many injections that were supposed to be painless but weren't, despite the vaunted speed of his delivery technique.

The needles were attached to long calibrated glass tubes, and to be stabbed by them was a form of torture to which I was more or less resigned. I was good-natured about it, understood that it was for my welfare. He allowed me my dignity when administering the shots, did not require me to drop my pants all the way but just enough to allow his quick jab, the pushed-in medicine, and then a fast swipe with a cotton swab saturated in alcohol. It was all done in a very manly way, usually with my father looking on. If possible, he let me take shots in the arm, a rare privilege. I had received such injections for as long as I could remember, but lately I was getting more than a usual amount; so much so that Dr. Siegal now and then mentioned the possibility of extended hospitalization.

He set down his familiar black leather bag on a chair and opened it.

Out came the rubber tubing of the blood-pressure monitor and a stainless steel stethoscope. He rolled up his shirtsleeves. I knew the drill. "So, Kaufman, the asthma's getting to you, huh? Which Kaufman is this? Let me guess, don't tell me. This is Alan."

"You've got a memory there, Doctor," my father said with a note of cautious jocularity in his voice, a tone he reserved only for a privileged elect of those who were either college-educated, successful business owners, or just plain wealthy. His awe also extended to persons in the military or any whose occupation involved an element of danger, such as a policeman or firefighter. Common people such as his own peers, blue-collar workers who earned a wage at an average job, were treated with a mixture of condescension and ridicule.

Dr. Siegal's worthiness in my father's eyes gave him an almost mythical air.

I believed in him implicitly, obeyed him blindly. He sat next to me, said, "You can't breathe, can you?"

Hoarsely I whispered, "No."

"Well, don't worry. You're going to be fine. I'm gonna listen to your chest and give you a shot and if that doesn't do the trick we'll take you to the hospital, OK?"

Reluctantly I nodded. "Hos-pi-tal!" I gasped. "I'm . . scared."

He nodded. "I know you are. But if the injection fails to work, we might need a more powerful drug and to monitor your condition. I know you understand what I mean."

I nodded. It felt wonderful to be addressed in this way. I felt so proud that he thought me worthy of respectful dialogue, that he felt comfortable using such words as "monitor" and "condition," as though I were grown-up enough to grasp their meaning, which I did, though only vaguely. The cold disk felt over my bare skin, on my back and chest. With a depressor he flattened my tongue and peered down my throat, waving a pencil-sized flashlight around.

"By the way, those tonsils are about ready to be taken out," he said ominously.

"Can't it wait?" my mother asked anxiously.

"Not too much longer." He removed a tiny bottle with minute writing on the label, thrust a needle into it, and drew off the necessary dose. "OK," he said. "Can you give us the view from behind?"

The others in the room moved in restless anticipation, then became perfectly still. The stillness magnified the sudden calm and the compassionate, almost benevolent resignation for the dilemma illness had placed us all in; for here I was, precisely as I dreaded to be, a virgin sacrifice of sorts readied for my piercing by a long steel sharp object, the hypodermic ritual knife of modern science, wielded by a high priest of medicine; here I was, stretched young, tender, innocent, on the bed prone for the offering, and the others were gathered about me waiting, only lacked hoods to complete the picture, and I forgave them as I came to my knees, jaw and shoulders squared, still barely able to breathe but determined even in these hideous circumstances to retain my soldierly dignity. Tugging down my pants to just below my buttocks, I laid down flat on my belly, clasped my eyes, and gasped, "Ready!"

It took time but I did not shout. The cold swipe of alcohol-bathed cotton signaled the end, and then, I began to shake.

"This is a reaction," Siegal announced to the room. "I've given him a big dose of adrenaline. It should do the trick."

I lay there trembling, my raised hand locked in spasm, and then a sweet feeling of relief flooded through, followed by ecstatic elation.

"You look better, Abie," my mother said.

"Yeah," said my father, removing a cigar from his pocket. "OK if I light up here, Doc?"

"Not a good idea," said Siegal with distaste.

"Oh," said my father with mock regret. "Ex-cuse me, ex-cuse me. I didn't realize. I didn't realize."

"He looks good, that Abie," my mother chirped.

"Yeah, much better, much better," my father added, a little irritated, the cold cigar protruding from the corner of his mouth. "So, uh, what do I owe you, there, Doc?"

"Thirty," said Siegal crisply.

My father gave him a fifty, which Siegal changed from a fat wad of tightly compressed money fastened by a rubber band. "You know," Siegal told him, "you oughta think about how your smoking affects the kid."

My father looked away, shook his head. It all played out before me in heavenly concordance, a ritual enacted by delightful friends. In particular I wanted to hug my mother around the neck and squeeze her like a beautiful doll. And my dear daddy! So well-meaning! Good, brave Dr. Siegal not only restored my breathing and saved me from the brink of death; he also produced the wondrous elation in me from out of his magic bag.

Perhaps for others, life is this way all the time—natural: the great sense of communion I felt with those assembled in the room, that we were all working together under the guidance of a loving Creator who meant only good for everyone, and that we would never really die, and that great events lay ahead in which I was assured a significant role. I even felt filled with tenderness for Howie, who had flopped into bed, his nose in a comic book. I sought his eyes and he looked up.

"So, how-er ya feeling? Better?" he asked.

"What a good, thoughtful boy," I thought. "Yeah, Howie. Thanks, man. I feel much, much better. In fact . . ." An electrifying chill of ecstasy shivered through my spine and neck, causing my voice to tremble. "I never felt this good in my whole life."

Siegal laughed. "It won't last. You'll be back to normal in a few minutes. Marie and George, I want to have a talk with you in private."

"Can I listen?" Howie exclaimed.

"Just the folks."

I lay there shuddering with ecstasy, my pulse racing and little quivering spasms of pleasure shooting through me. With each breath I seemed to unfurl like a silky flag. When my fingers wagged, they stirred the dense air currents into dance, which I thought I could see.

THE DEATH OF JFK

MRS. SHWARTZ TURNED from her desk with a hardened look in her turquoise blue eyes and a stack of marked quiz papers raised in her hand. She surveyed our faces. "Here they are," she said, her voice full of disappointment. "I'm surprised at the results," she said. "I don't care if you've pulled straight nineties in the past on these quizzes. If you failed this one, you get your parent to sign it. Some of you will have to do that today. It's nothing to be proud about, I assure you."

At her desk, Vickie Cantor began to weep. Then Michelle Hyman joined her.

Mrs. Shwartz softened and said, "You're all so bright. You really ought to do much better. Is something wrong? We can talk about it."

"Noooo!" we muttered as one voice, with lumps in our throats.

When the papers were handed out we sat contritely still as she picked up the chalk, began to write an equation in perfect longhand on the board. Finally, all of us bent to our notebooks with a renewed sense of determination. No one took real notice of the young student teacher—a Miss Longstreet; I had seen her around—who entered the room, shut the door behind her with a soft click of the latch, and strode briskly across the floor.

I would certainly have returned my eyes to my notebook, continued transcribing Mrs. Shwartz's perfectly chalked blackboard notes, but for the expression on Miss Longstreet's face and the way it affected Mrs. Shwartz. Teachers wear certain airs when in school, which they drop in the outside world. In school, they are very much like military personnel on base. Off base, as civilians, they can be found to be very different people. Something in Miss Longstreet's face appealed to the civilian in Mrs. Shwartz, and surprisingly, her ice queen face warmed instantly, grew vulnerable. A concerned, inquiring smile played over her lips. She broke the silence in a voice of unmistakable dread: "What is it?" But Miss Longstreet did not answer outright. Instead, she stopped before Mrs. Shwartz, who put down the chalk in the narrow tray at the base of the blackboard and reflexively, without thought, from habit of bad nerves, delicately rubbed her chalk-coated thumb and forefinger together, like a little girl with sticky hands. Miss Longstreet stared intensely into Mrs. Shwartz's eyes, then reached out and placed a reassuring hand on her arm. I now saw that Miss Longstreet had tears in her eyes, and glistening all down her round cheeks, and a single tear trembling undisturbed on her chin. She leaned close to Mrs. Shwartz, said something in her ear, a whisper, and I would not have thought that Mrs. Shwartz's alabaster face could turn any whiter, but it did. There is a shade of white even whiter then the white shade of a corpse: it is the void produced by the death of a dream. Mrs. Shwartz's face turned that color.

She looked at us—we were all staring at her now—and said in a voice barely alive: "Children, I'm going to leave you here without supervision. I need you to continue doing the work in complete quiet. . . ." She paused here to survey our faces in response to the words "complete quiet," as though to judge our worthiness to undertake such an extraordinary mission, and apparently found us up to the task. "Good . . . I know that you can be counted on. You are a mature and wonderful class. OK, I'm going now. I'll return shortly." And with great solemnity she followed Miss Longstreet, unhurried, out of the room. The door's latch clicked.

Our speculating voices exploded in a pandemonium of questions, laughter, screeches, as scribbled notes crushed into balls, loose-leaf pages folded into fighter planes, and paper clips shot from rubber bands, soared into dogfights about our heads. The frenzy of the Israelites as they fashioned the Golden Calf in Moses' absence must have been like this. The big question was: What happened? We all guessed that it was something huge, really huge.

As we boys stood up at our desks with red, grimacing faces, out-thrust tongues spraying spittle-soaked raspberries, or hands shoved under flapping elbows to produce farts from our armpits, or forcing the same rippling flatulent noise from the squeezed air between cupped hands, from the right side of the room where some of the best-behaved girl students sat, a high-pitched chorus of voices edged with sheer disgust intoned: "You're sooooo immature! That's sooooooo immature!"

Mark Steinberg declared conclusively that the Russians had finally invaded, as revenge for the Missile Crisis. As proof he offered our recent drill: crouching under desks. He suggested that we all move away from the windows in case an A-bomb dropped. Several students actually did. But Michael Brooks, short, squat, wearing horn-rimmed glasses, whose father had just recently dropped dead (absenting Michael for a whole month of class, all of which invested him, as partly orphaned, with a certain worldliness that we envied, wishing our own fathers would cooperatively drop dead too), shouted "Baloney! What happened is, Mrs. Shwartz's kid just had a baby and it musta died!" which we considered plausible but deemed much too mundane for our righteous mood.

It had to be something big, really big! We wanted action, catastrophe, and cataclysm that would rock our worlds and exempt us for the rest of the day, and maybe even the rest of the week, from school. For myself, I hoped that a new Holocaust against the Jews was about to ensue; that now, finally, I would get my crack at living through experiences as terrible as my mother's; finally rate in her eyes, the eyes of history, of life, as worthy.

Arvin Molinas came up with something to equal all our feverish hopes: a UFO has landed in Washington, D.C., and a state of national emergency now exists nationwide! This was instantly accepted as the best explanation.

Oh, how I longed for a national emergency! Emergencies always brought people together. Like funerals. Embittered relations sat together, ate take-out delicatessen, spoke in hushed whispers, and were especially nice, for once, to the children, regarding us with moist eyes, extolling our innocence in groaned whispers.

The big discussion that ensued among everyone (with the exception of Mark Steinberg, who sat alone with his arms crossed and a tight-lipped expression on his face, still holding fast to his theory of Russian invasion despite its categorical rejection) centered around two issues:

1) Should we obtain weapons, and if so, which? Baseball bats? Kitchen knives? Paper clips and rubber bands?

2) Supposing aliens *have* landed; would this be sufficient reason for the New York City Board of Education—which rarely declared states of emergencies, even for snowstorms or excessive rain—to close school today?

Opinions varied broadly on these issues. Some thought that school would stay open despite the UFO, since Washington is so far away, and the Army would probably contain the menace, capture the aliens, and take them to be studied. Others said that alien war machines had already reached the New Jersey state line and that if we were smart we would get our hands on some guns, camouflage our faces, and commence guerrilla-style actions immediately.

The thought that in such circumstances our parents' typical caution and authority would hold no sway whatsoever, that in effect, we, as freedom fighters, would operate entirely from our respective homes, ducking in and out of rubble to shoot it out with slimy, insane-looking aliens, was too exhilarating for words. Even Mark Steinberg had come around by now to our view of things and was eagerly explaining to Arvin Molinas, a science buff, how to make a bomb strong enough to blow up an entire building out of wet cornflakes, sugar, and yeast, all kept in a sealed bottle under the sink for a month or two. He had read about this in a U.S. government manual, and had two such bottles hidden at this very moment under the kitchen sink at home, and which his parents—a teacher and a lawyer—knew nothing about.

Then the door opened. All noise stopped as if a switch had been thrown. We scrambled madly back to our desks and sat there with clasped hands extended stiffly on our desks and chins raised in a posture of obedience so still, our faces mashed so flat by good behavior, that we resembled test pilots strapped into cockpits, with faces and bodies crushed by abnormal G-forces. Yet for once Mrs. Shwartz didn't appear to notice how completely we had betrayed her trust in us. Her face was sculpted in sadness. She wore the air of one who has something to tell besides which all things are insignificant but who is sorry that it should be so, because she respects our insignificance—regards our petty concerns as our most saving grace: childhood's right—and is uncertain of exactly how to announce to us our imminent entry into the adult world of infinite disappointment, loss, and disillusionment.

We could sense this from her, and for a moment the prospect of a day off from school, even a week, didn't seem quite worth the price of the ticket. And for the first time I understood that it was too late—something truly irreversible had occurred that would affect me forever in a tremendous way. Was it aliens? Martians? The thought was sickening. Or had God Himself appeared on earth? What would *that* mean? That we'd have to be good all the time now? The end of life as we knew it?! But how, in such a world, would I fulfill my dreams of becoming a writer? Does Paradise on earth need authors? I knew in my heart that it wouldn't. I would be reduced to a brainwashed angel in a white shirt flying around singing "Holy! Holy!" A mere foot servant of God's majesty.

I liked best Mark Steinberg's explanation. Suddenly it seemed the most logical. In fact I was certain it must be the right one and, turning to Stewie Shliefer, a slovenly pot-bellied hot dog vendor-in-the-making with a mop of hair falling in his dopey face, whispered: "It's definitely the Russians landed," and he nodded in agreement. In fact, around me a lot of voices had begun to whisper: "The Russians" and "It's the Reds" and "Khrushchev declared war."

She took her seat with great dignity, looking utterly drained, her face the dirty-brick color of murdered dreams. She seemed to wonder— almost aloud, from moving lips that produced no sound—about her qualifications for the task at hand. And then, drawing a deep breath, she began in a lifeless voice: "Children . . . I have something terrible to tell you. . . ." The unoiled iron bearings of our movable desks squeaked as we leaned forward to receive the blow: "Children . . ." she said, and again, as though to remind herself that we were only that and no more: "Children . . . our President, John Fitzgerald Kennedy . . . is . . . dead."

Brows creased into puzzled frowns throughout the silent room. Here and there, a soft gasp. But it was Stewie Shliefer who best expressed what was in all our hearts when he shouted: "Awwwww! Is that all!? I thought it was something serious! No way they're going to let us out of school for something diddly like that!"

For an instant the old fire flared in Mrs. Shwartz's blue-green eyes. But no, it was only an ember and faded. She gaped at him in listless silence. By that look alone we understood, as much as by any official proclamation of the Board of Education, that no more classes would be held that day. Then she drew herself upright, inhaled and exhaled, said: "Good. I was concerned that you wouldn't take this well. But you're OK. I'm glad you're OK." I felt a pang of pity for her. This was something clearly of great importance to her; we just weren't the ones to share it with. It was grown-up stuff. Who cared?!

Minutes later we were on the streets, instructed to return directly home and turn on our TVs. I toyed with the idea of not returning, convinced that my mother's self-absorption would escape even this important event. I really did see her as inhabiting a dimension separate from the rest of us in which she dwelled time-trapped in grief for her murdered childhood, and mourning for the other, less-fortunate victims of Hitler, and so was unaffected by whatever dominated the lives of others. The isolated safety of America enshrined her in a kind of sorrowful embryonic fluid in which she could float, detached, against a backdrop of canned television laughter. But I went home, following other students up the hills of 171st Street to the Grand Concourse, a small, strangely silent procession of school kids, colorful in ski parkas, backpacks, and woolen caps, noses rubbed red by the harsh November frost, and dropping off, one by one, to our respective streets and buildings with barely a wave goodbye.

I also couldn't ignore the opportunity to immediately rush home and tell them all about it; I regarded my parents as the most ill-informed creatures on the planet, brothers to the bushmen of New Guinea, and to the aardvark. Certainly they gave every impression of being so.

But she knew. I don't know how. With that unfailing nose for trouble of hers, that must have gotten her through the years in hiding from the Nazis and spared her from the death camps. She knew. The TV was on. She stood on her feet before it, wearing around her head a rag tied into bunny rabbit ears, a faded old pink muu muu decorated with turquoise roses, and blue rabbit-fur house slippers several times too large for her feet. She is wringing her hands in the thin grayish apron tied at her waist, her startlingly beautiful eyes brimming with tears in a face tinged purplish with high blood pressure. She repeats aloud to the air: "Oy a *charbon*," which is Yiddish for "What a catastrophe," the same exclamation that she used to greet my chronically failed math tests. But the greatest proof offered to me of the significance of the moment was my father. He was not sleeping his inviolable slumber of the dead before rising at seven o'clock to begin preparations to work his night-shift job at the main branch post office downtown at Thirty-third Street and Ninth Avenue. He is up. Seated in the armchair, a cigar in his mouth, eyes fixed in a poker player's assessing squint, weighing the odds. They aren't good. A pretty bad card has been dealt America to tell from his face, which contains, unbelievably, a trace of emotion. The card is worse than bad. The whole farm's up for grabs. Worse even than that, to tell by his expression the country is playing for its shirt.

And for the first time it really hits me, and I fall to the sofa, mumbling "Ho-ly cow! Ho-ly cow!" both stunned and delighted that our family belongs to something bigger than the tragedy of our homelife: a national tragedy! Hurray! And now Howard walks in. Also just got out of class. Takes in the situation. Says, amazed, "You know!"

My mother looks at him tearfully. "Of course we know, stupeed. The whole country is in shock!" And as though to seek corroboration of that fact, our eyes return to the TV screen, and there in fuzzy black-and-white is the hound-dog face of Walter Cronkite, who in order of national importance is second only to Kennedy and Ed Sullivan, and he is speaking in a casual, un-TV-like way, as if there were no difference between his on-screen world and our off-camera lives. No difference. As though people in the TV world die too, which seems impossible since everyone in television and/or Hollywood is seemingly touched with immortality, and those who report the news are above what they report, yet clearly Cronkite here is shaken. He might have tears in his eyes. He speaks in broken sentences, as though unsure of his information. The picture jumps back and forth between a hospital ambulance loading-dock and Cronkite with headphones in some kind of makeshift office.

And there is Eric Sevareid, another pillar of televised transcendence, haggard now, a cigarette smoking from the side of his mouth, rubbing the heel of his palm into the socket of his eye with the self-importance of someone used to being watched, his manner affected, like the bookie I once saw on 170th Street who burst into tears as he was talking to his partner—someone named Sal or Sol—about his girlfriend cheating on him. I was just three feet away when I overheard. Just as Sevareid was now doing, the cuckolded bookie inserted the heel of his palm into the socket of his eye and screwed, once, to the left, removed his hand, shook it in the air as though to dry it, and then inserted and screwed again, once, to the right. It was really very touching: I felt embarrassed for him, as I did now for Sevareid.

Cronkite was holding up better.

My mother, though, had lost it completely. She seemed to live in a world without news coming in or going out. She had nothing new to report: the worst had already happened. Six million Jewish lifetimes ago. Her first lifetime and the six million kept going, but with nothing to report. There had been gas chambers, ovens, mass graves, children burned alive. Once a partisan gave her a cigarette to puff on. She tried it and gagged. She was hungry. She hid in a chicken coop. German soldiers came. They didn't look in . . . If they had . . . And so on. This news was broadcast, I sometimes thought, on a radio signal known only to the dead and their survivors. And, of course, to me. My existence was the most current news she had; though she didn't seem very proud of it.

I was such a disappointment. Low math grades.

She seemed so convinced of the tragedy going on around us that I became persuaded too. I began to cry a little, to rub the heel of my palm in the socket of my eye, bookie/Sevareid-like, and to say, "God, how could that happen?" though I hadn't the slightest idea of what it all meant. I looked to my father for answers. "Pop," I said, "Pop, this is pretty bad, huh?"

"Sure it's bad. The President's been assassinated. What d'ya think, it's good? Of course it's bad."

I nodded. "But what d'ya think? You think there's gonna be trouble?" I hoped to hear him say that we would all move down into bomb shelters in the countryside, where we would each be issued a Winchester carbine with fifty rounds of ammo, unlimited food and water, and warm clothes. After the Russians dropped the bombs, we would leave the shelter to find most of the population gone, eliminated, blasted out of existence. And like the lone survivors of a nuclear attack in an episode of The Twilight Zone, we would return to a city fully outfitted for habitation but with all of its dwellers gone. The hero of Rod Serling's story went nuts with loneliness, but I knew that I would do much, much better. I already had my eye on a Wilson first-base mitt in the window of Dogel's Sporting Goods on Townsend Avenue that I was planning to loot. To handle the boredom I'd read comic books, assemble models, and go fishing.

"Trouble," he said, without taking his eyes from the screen. "What sort of trouble?"

I thought about it. I didn't know. "War?" I guessed timidly.

"War?" he said uncertainly. "What kinda war?"

"Listen to the two of you," my mother interrupted. "Don't talk war, or God forbid it will happen." And then, just like that, she broke down and cried inconsolably. "Oh, the Nazis are still killing," she moaned. "He was so young! Look at Jackie! Look, George, look at her face. Poor woman. Oh, my God, look at her dress! Look at the blood!" and she just sobbed after that, while my father and I sat numbly, glancing first at her and then at Jackie on-screen as she stepped from Air Force One, the blouse and lap of her suit dress spattered with John's fresh blood.

"I'm going out," said Howard suddenly.

My father gave him a look. "Going out? To where?"

"To the schoolyard. To play basketball," he said, his hand shooting to his horn-rim glasses with a nervous, defensive gesture I had seen him use when cornered by a bully's demands. "Just to play," he added.

"Let him go, George," my mother said with deep fatigue. "What does it matter? He's just a child. He doesn't have to see this." And then, in a whispered aside to me: "He takes after your father. Not too much going on upstairs, if you know what I mean. . . ." She tapped her head with her finger. "He doesn't understand. But you take after me. You're sensitive, which is a sign of intelligence."

"Yeah," I said, "I feel pretty bad about all this. He was a young guy, that Kennedy. . . ." I broke off to ask Howard as he exited, "What's going on in the schoolyard?"

"Game with Zeke and Jack"

"Almalech?" I asked.

"Yeah, the Hook," he said, curving his fingers near his face to imitate Jack Almalech's prominent nose. "Wanna come?"

"Leave him alone," my mother jumped in before I could answer. "Go play in your schoolyard. You're not too bright, you know. Your president has just been killed and you go to play basketball. . . ."

"Wrong!" my brother interjected with a television game-show squawk voice, and, grinning at me, "We're playing punchball. Are you coming?"

"Nah," I said with heavy heart, "I wanna watch," and nodded at the screen.

"Sure," she said. "Your brother has intelligence. He cares."

My brother chuckled at my regretful smile, rolled his eyes, and left.

Just at that moment my father leaned forward in his seat and said with irritation, "Will you two clam up so I can hear?" and turned up the volume. The footage had just returned from the lab, Cronkite was saying, and in a few seconds we were going to see the tragedy replayed.

By now we knew, he said, that a suspect had been found, was in custody, had been identified—authorities give his name as Lee Harvey Oswald—and Vice President Lyndon Baines Johnson has been sworn in as president. "In the shock of the aftermath, the response has been one of virtual . . . I see we have the footage running on-screen and here is what we have as the motorcade is rounding the bend . . . there! The President is struck, and then it looks . . . there! A second time! Connelly has . . . I guess slumped is the right word to describe this terrible scene . . . and Jackie seems to be crawling away in confusion. Those of you out there in the audience who are combat veterans will attest, I think, to the powerful instinct to find cover under such conditions, that is live ammunition hitting the car, and . . . there's a secret service man . . . and another. . . ."

Tuned in not to regular programming but a kind of extended interruption of our regular viewing, a kind of news flash that has kept going for decades, a kind of commercial for the history of our ruin, I could not have found the words to describe what I felt as I watched—privy from a bird's-eye view—President Kennedy's head blown apart and Jackie spattered with his brains and crawling to escape, because I did not yet know the word *obscene*.

Something extremely dirty had happened. As though an angel had been soiled by excrement before the throne of heaven, a victim of hidden malice. I was aware of the whole nation (with a few exceptions like Howard) seated with tearful faces and craned necks before TVs; aware that time had stood still, we were frozen in anguish, and on spontaneous and troubling holiday to witness an act of filth that was History.

"Is this History?" I asked aloud.

"Sure, sure," said my mother, quiet now and watching the screen with a stony expression.

I had expected History to mobilize one's entire existence and turn dull routine topsy-turvy: barricades manned in burning cities and flags raised over conquered domes, the sun behind you, always behind you, silhouetting your figure in gallant profile. I wanted to be chased, hunted, to attack and counterattack, to stealth, shimmy on my belly, dart from alley to alley—but here we were sitting through History on the plastic-covered seat cushions of an installment-paid Castro convertible, crying or worried yet unthreatened in any visible way, and History seemed altogether tame.

"Was the war like this, Mom? Was it like this? Did it feel like this?"

My mother looked at me strangely. "You know, Abie, in the beginning it felt a little like this. With Hitler? Yes. With those damned Germans. It felt like this. Like a clock ticking, like everything was changed and ruined. Like there was no turning back. No one then wanted to live the future that was about to come, but what choice was there?"

"Is the future gonna be bad, Mom?"

"Whatever it is," she said, "it won't be as bad as what happened to us then. . . ."

I was irritated to be denied a future as traumatic as her past had been, for nothing less than a world bent on manufacturing corpses on an assembly line, as she had once described it to me, could justify the complete termination of school. And I wanted everything to change completely. To tear down whatever world had made us the way we were and start it all up again, fresh, because the world as it was made me uneasy.

And then she added, with a sour expression: "But it's not gonna be very good."

It troubled me in a way for which I then had no words: that I lived in the same world that had hunted my mother and put millions of people like us into ovens. How could it be that after such an act the people of the world had not joined together to burn their flags in a big pile, and tear down their cities, and change the names of their countries from France and Italy and Germany and America to exotic and indescribable ones like Zibberkadoo or Apalop or Ningalling? Why would they not abolish all recognizable forms of human culture—from government to school—as essentially failed and corrupt and instead let us all just roam freely doing as we could, being what we wished, enjoying ourselves and having great adventures? It confounded and irritated me, for instance, that before the war, before war came along to interrupt her education, my mother had gone to school. To think of what followed, the horrors that had stalked her, made me want to scream out in Mrs. Shwartz's class: "All this school stuff don't mean nuthin' because my mom went to school but that didn't stop the Nazis from coming to get her! How come no teachers didn't stop the Nazis from trying to take her!" Just as now Mrs. Shwartz had been unable to prevent the murder of the President or do anything but sit, like us, and helplessly spectate.

If they could hunt my mother and shoot and torture and burn six million people and even kill John F. Kennedy who used to be a PT boat captain in the U.S. Navy, what could they not do to me, to all of us?

Who needed school? We needed guns. Who were they? Nazis. Nazis. Nazis. Nazis then and Nazis now. What was the use of passing math in a world where they ran things? I could believe in a world run by Kennedy and Mrs. Shwartz, but they weren't in charge. We needed to tear it all down and start from scratch, beginning with the TV set and the sofa and Walter Cronkite—even he and Eric Sevareid, behind their seemingly impenetrable armor of waves and light, could be affected. We needed a new world.

I was living in a world that was running on a lie that everybody pretended to believe in. I despised them for it. They had no limits to what they would endure, to what was unacceptable. To murder six million Jews was acceptable, but for me to talk out during silent period in class was a punishable offense. What kind of world was that, that killed innocent babies and handsome young presidents and still made you go to school?

Dry Goods

MY MOTHER HIRED an old Jew to give me Bar Mitzvah lessons. Mr. Unger didn't look like a rabbi to me. I knew him as the one who came to the door of our apartment peddling all sorts of "dry goods"—sheets, towels, pillowcases, underwear—which my mother bought in huge quantities on a regular basis. It seemed that he was always at the door, handing big packages to my mother that filled the little rooms of our dingy Bronx walk-up with the smell of camphor and factory plastic; or else he was engaged in long minutes of arithmetic calculation in a grubby little notebook held together with a hundred rubber bands that took him forever to remove before he could leaf to the smudged page inscribed with my mother's name.

She worried herself sick about paying him off. "Oh, gosh. I don't know what to do Abie," she said, whispering in the empty apartment as though fearing the presence of spies. "That damned Unger's coming over for his money and I'm broke. Your father didn't do so good at his poker last night and I don't have what to give Unger. Abie! If he comes to the door, open it and tell him your mother's sick and had to go to the hospital," which I'd do with relish, glad to be enlisted in the service of my poor mother's pride, like the proper hero that I was. When he came, I opened the door and stood there scowling at him. He met this undaunted. Roly-poly and five feet four inches tall, I wasn't very intimidating to look at. He said simply, "Where is your mother?"

"Not here."

"She's coming home soon?"

"She's in the hospital."

"Oh. What's the matter? Her kidneys again?"

"Yeah. Her kidneys. Try again next week."

"Of course. Tell her I'll be back." And to me, he confided: "She owes me some money, you know."

Trying to enlist me in his cause. I must have looked like an easy touch. But I was loyal. My gut a knot of hot anger. And if I didn't yet look tough, I was learning from local schoolyard thugs how to seem tough; leaning out of the door, I fixed him with my lusterless masturbatory gaze and said, "She's not here. Now *scram!*" Which made no apparent impression upon him whatsoever.

He looked at the badly scratched glass face of his tarnished gold watch. "Maybe I try back in an hour, huh?"

At this my gorge rose with a fury that frightened even me, and without my having to say a word he backed off. He smiled with disappointment in a manner meant to stir my empathy: all the more offensive in that it succeeded. I felt a little sorry for him that he'd come so far only to leave empty-handed, and he tipped his hat and again checked his watch, both at the same time. I shut the door with a vague sense of guilt, and of loathing for him, me, even her.

She peeked out of the bedroom door, hand covering her mouth. "A *charbon!*" she said, "So, is he gone? I'm so embarrassed!"

I nodded wearily, my worldly job well done, a little man who has just defended his womenfolk. "You can come out," I said. "It's safe."

Hurriedly, she shuffled out in pink rabbit-fur house slippers purchased from Unger, hugging close an Unger purchased-on-credit quilted turquoise-colored housecoat, one hand flying to her head to adjust the Unger installment-plan babushka wrapped around her face. "So, was he mad?" she asked in the voice of a little girl.

"No. It's OK. He'll be back next week. Everything's OK, I swear. He didn't mind."

"Oh, I bet he did," she sighed heavily. "What can I do? Your father's so illiterate! We're so damned poor. You shouldn't know from it," and I thought bitterly: "You're right. I shouldn't know from it!" But I knew from it, I knew from it. It seemed at times like it was all I knew or would ever know. I hated the very fact of Unger's presence at our door. No mother of any of the other boys I knew—not Mrs. Auria or Mrs. Razumny or even Mrs. "Juicy Lucy" Morales—struck deals with such unsavory types. No other boy, I felt sure, had to intervene in such a way on behalf of his mother. It made me feel extremely sorry for myself. The experience had not been so terrible but I blew it up to Dantesque proportions until it became in my mind one of the great heroic rescues of our age: Unger, a sneering, smoke-expelling demon from hell with fiery red eyes and long crooked fingers like the Wicked Witch in *The Wizard of Oz*, and me, a veritable Sir Galahad of the slums, my limp gray T-shirt converted into spit-polished armor. In my fantasy, my last words to him, uttered in my best tough-guy dialect, expanded to become an epic speech against the evils of installment plans and the virtues of mothers.

In one of the great back-stabbings of this century, this man became my Bar Mitzvah teacher, invested by God and my mother with total power over me.

He began the first session: "There is no point or the time. You won't learn Hebrew, or what means these words," and opened a decrepit old book to a page of enormous-sized Hebrew letters. He pointed to one that looked like a Chinese calligraphic sketch of a piano stool. *"Aleph,"* he said. "Say it. Aleph!"

"I thought you're not teaching me Hebrew," I protested.

"I didn't say I wasn't teaching. I said there was no point because you weren't learning. But I'm being paid, so I do. When we're done you'll know your *haftorah*. God knows a great Jew you won't be, but you'll be a Bar Mitzvah. That is the least you should have. Tell me, you are circumcised?"

Shame burned in my cheeks and ears. "Sure," I gasped.

He slapped my knee: *"Nu!* At least we don't have to go through that again, huh?!" and laughed. And then he said, "You know, with some of the *goyim*, the Yugoslavs, for example, they have the circumcision when they're thirteen. Did you know this?"

For weeks after, I lay awake nights in a sweat trying to imagine how it must feel to face such a thing. I tried to imagine how it would feel to see your father among the celebrants as the knife chopped at your pecker. At dinner, as my father bent to his *chav* soup, slurping up the green broth, my heart filled with despair to think of him as a Yugoslav clapping his hands and slapping his heels in dance as the blood ran down my thighs. "How could you?" I wondered with silent bitterness. "And I see that the thought of it hasn't dented your appetite either, has it, my father?" And so on.

Unger had a gift for brushing aside my truculence to reach the scared, insecure boy inside. He offered instruction to my hidden fear rather than to my emerging, somewhat unconvincing voice of hoodlum bravura. I responded to his questions in a humble little-boy voice of abject ignorance. The tremor in my throat betrayed my unworthiness. Hebrew letters swam before my eyes. My heart pounded in the House of God, a temple constructed of the fat black characters of an ancient, obscure alphabet. They hinted at a civilization to which I belonged but that was, effectively, without meaning for me. To its representatives in my own household it meant less than nothing.

To my father, Judaism meant a towel on his head serving for a yarmulke on Yom Kippur as he stood in the dark kitchen dressed in underwear to light candles for his dead father. For my mother, who endured the Holocaust, it meant Nazi torture and death, pure and simple. I gained my best glimpses into the emotional and spiritual contents of the culture to which I belonged in the occasional Yiddish they spoke when they didn't want me to understand something. The language struck me as instantly humorous, but the sound of it contained, paradoxically, the distillation, the very essence of sorrow. And yet it was effortlessly intimate, a familiar language. It spoke from the tongues of an invisible, ancestral family gathered around a table spread with gastronomic delights, lit by candles. Yiddish patted me on the head, pinched my cheek. The sound of it assured me that I was a good boy, automatically assumed as much. All that mattered was that I should be healthy and happy, it said. "Eat, eat," it urged, pressing sweets into my hand and pulling my earlobe when I sneezed, to ward off death.

Even the detestable Unger was drawn closer to me by it, and me to him. When he spoke an occasional word of it, he seemed to soften. Once, as he spoke a few Yiddish words to me, I thought I could see that he was not at all at home in the air we breathed, that his whole being contained the longing for some other place from which he was exiled. What place was that, I wondered? A country? A town? A family? Yiddish was like a map of the place. It contained the physical geography of a place that even I yearned for though I had never been there.

But Hebrew evoked from me no such response. The black letters stood before me like iron gates, refusing entrance. I wasn't sure that I wanted in, afraid of what lay beyond. The prayers bored me, especially their translations into English. At least when voicing them in Hebrew I could think of them as magical incantations, the Jewish equivalent of Ali Baba's "Open sesame" or of Captain Marvel's "Shazam!"—believe that their utterance would endow me with magical powers. But when I saw what the words meant, my heart fell. Over and over, Bless God this and Bless God that and King of the Universe this and Lord of the Universe that, and how unworthy I am and how glorious is He, and I thought: "What's He done so great that people wanna say this kinda junk about Him all day long in some synagogue? And what's He done for me that's so great? It's lucky I got born at all with what happened in the war. If the Nazis had got their hands on my mother, I wouldn't even be here!" And so on. I needed proof of a miracle. I never thought of my existence as that. I would have been more impressed if the doorbell had rung and a stranger in a checked sports jacket handed me the keys to a brand new El Dorado than by the fact that I had been born despite the best effort of the vilest force ever known to mankind to kill my mother and prevent my existence.

"Aleph," he said. *"Beit. Gimmel. Daled."* His frail finger with thick horned nail and soiled wrinkled knuckle moved from letter to letter while my bored insides shrieked and my brain teemed with visions of the incredible schoolyard events that were passing me by: touch-football extravaganzas, near-naked blonde babes showing cleavage on the fenders of Mustangs and GTOs, epic games of Ring-a-lee-vio and Hot Peas 'n' Butter.

I could have wept with frustration. Instead, with hunched shoulders and a stricken look, I rasped: "Aleph. Beit. Gimmel."

Sometimes, though, a gleam of comprehension, almost mystical, would shine through. Suddenly the characters of the words would melt into pronounceable sounds that contained a meaning: *Baruch Atah Adonoi Eluhainu . . .*

Bless the name of our God . . .

Our God . . . We beseech you . . .

I belonged to that *we*; was entitled, expected even by this invisible *we* to learn such words of prayer and to make a transition from boyhood to manhood. If only I could meet this *we*, this spectral contingency whose expectations I was required to satisfy. Was Unger their emissary? But he addressed me with such disdain; it was so apparent that he despised me, my life, the way I lived, that I was certain to fare even worse with his superiors. I knew that the *we* were Jews, but did just any Jews qualify? Jews like my classmates Arnie Razumny, Mark Steinberg, Stewie Schlieffer, Arvin Molinas? My teachers Mrs. Shwartz and Mrs. Adler? Were they the *we*? Was my Uncle Arnold with his ten kids, four of them in jail, the *we*? Or my Aunt Ray with her dyed black hair and false teeth, who fancied that she looked like Elizabeth Taylor—was she the *we?* Or had the true *we* been slaughtered in Europe? Were we here only an outpost of lonely Americans performing the old rituals in an essentially meaningless context and fashion for the sake, effectively, of nostalgia?

I could not have said so much in so many words, but these were the questions I felt without possessing the language to voice them.

I don't believe that Unger would have cared in any event to answer. He led me through my haftorah with the rough, unyielding skepticism and mistrust of a ranch hand convinced of the innate meanness of wild horses. I needed to be broken, led to water and made to drink, with an iron hand and with vigilant checking of all impulses to bond, share, exchange, discover, or otherwise weaken before the task of my humiliating subjugation to custom. Sometimes I interrupted the dry rote learning to ask a sincere question. He didn't quite bat it aside but yelped his response with impatience and a demeanor that regarded from my type all signs of genuine interest in things Jewish as aberrational at best. In this way my lazy memory plodded to Jerusalemic redemption. When some months later I could recite my haftorah without glancing at the book, my arrival was greeted without fanfare. After crossing a mighty desert I had entered an empty city without a single well containing water.

Perhaps only by then could Unger take pity on all my questions that he had left lingering unanswered in the air. It is not that he failed to respond with words addressing my questions and all the necessary details. These he provided as the need arose and time permitted, impatiently. But it was the questions within the questions I asked that he had failed to answer, refused even to countenance. The same question contained in all my many different questions; the inarticulatable yearning for love I felt, for a certain tone that was missing from his answers, the deeply satisfying tone of shared visions and assumptions of an unqualified membership in a fellowship of love, justice, and truth, of mutual admission of yearning for God's redemption—this tone was missing from his answers, and at the heart of the questions was yet a further, deeper question, one addressed to the mystery, a question that could be summarized as the essence of a single word: What is a *Jew?*

Perhaps it was in deference to this unanswered question that for months hovered so painfully between us that he one day brought to the house, along with the usual study books, something which he sprang on me with an air of glee, as though rewarding me with the treat of all treats. Perhaps he did so because he had been to the house so many times and had begun to understand something of the sheer vacuum in which life had forced me to sink thirsting roots; perhaps he saw as miraculous the survival, even the very existence of the mysterious "what" question that lay at the heart of the many questions in soil so completely devoid of nourishment—from the sight of my father dressed in Unger layaway boxer shorts and house slippers shuffling in to say hello reeking of aftershave and leaving behind white trails of freshly applied Argo cornstarch spilling from the armpits of his short-sleeve T-shirt, to my mother who concealed her flaccid refusal to practice her faith behind a fawning and excessive humility that at times bordered on ceremonious hypocrisy.

For whatever reasons, of his own volition, even at his own expense, Unger produced from within his coat's deep pockets a comic book version of Charleton Heston's *Ten Commandments* movie and said with a touching display of forced enthusiasm: "You like comic books, I notice, no? So. Do you know the story of the Exodus?" Before I could tell him that I had seen the movie, Unger explained the story of Moses, how he was spared from mass murder to become a prince of Egypt and then the great man of God who took the Jewish people to the Promised Land.

The illustrations and story line couldn't compare with even the average Marvel comic book, yet when he was done explaining I was moved to such emotion that I had tears in my eyes, which Unger acknowledged by nodding with satisfaction. To my amazement, Unger reached over with his grubby hand, pinched my cheek between two cold knuckles, and jerked my head around. "So, you like Moshe Rabeynu, huh Avraham?! You're a good boy, Abie, a good boy, and God will do right by you! You'll see, *boychik*. I promise!"

S C U M

I EXPERIENCED MY first wet dream on a Sunday night after reading a Dick Tracy comic strip on the front page of the Sunday edition of the New York *Daily News*. In the strip a grotesquely deformed criminal named Squiggles accosts a woman in an alley with a knife; something about the disarray of her clothing, the loose strap slipped from her shoulder, the hoisted hemline of her black miniskirt revealing firm white cartoon-illustrated thigh made me feverishly excited. It was all I seemed able to think about for the rest of that day.

That night I dreamed I had sprung up from between two automobiles in a supermarket parking lot, knife in hand, and forced a woman pushing a shopping cart full of groceries to her car to lie down on the blacktop and "do it" with me. I stretched atop her and groaned, groaned, with a sweet feeling of white-hot release melting my loins, as though I were sweaty under blankets in bed, needing badly to urinate but too lazy and sleepy to get up, and so I just made in the bed and no one cared, not the woman or my parents or Dick Tracy. When I awoke from that dream I seemed to be living out the sweet piss-in-bed pleasure, helplessly gripped by the strangest, most wonderful sensation; but when it ended my amazement eroded into worry and then fear and I threw off my blankets expecting to find piss-drenched sheets.

Instead all I found was a strange white jelly on my thighs and smeared on the sheet. What the heck is this, I wondered. Was I gravely ill with a secret disease?

I knew only that I must conceal it from my parents, that to leave it would produce an encounter over something so inadmissible as to be extraterrestially obscene, something contained in me, that alien jelly, the euphoria that its explosion had produced from my body and which I must protect them from.

I had never known such blissful relaxation, but its unholy by-product was the queerest substance—like nothing one would ever find openly displayed in decent, normal society.

I knew vaguely that it was called "scum" by my peers. I leaned close to my window to examine it by moonlight, rub a little between my fingertips. It was slippery, oily. How terrifying. Suddenly all air seemed to have been sucked from the room by a great vacuum. I hoped that God was not watching this, was instead preoccupied in some more interesting corner of his Kingdom than Wythe Place in the Bronx. My heart pounded with guilt. I tore the sheet off the bed, tiptoed to the bathroom, gently ran the faucet, and rubbed out the stain with water and hard soap.

Then I carefully unloaded all the dirty wash from the hamper, placed the sheet at the very bottom, and stuffed down the other dirty wash on top, so that it would lie hidden, this strange obscene substance from my body, under soiled clothes and underwear, the secret filth of my innermost being.

The next Saturday a group of us boys from seventh grade got together to hang out. Among us was Jeffrey Spieler, with his friendly, horsey face and a Rudy Vallee haircut, which gave his head an odd tilt. For much of the afternoon we sat on the steps of a building on the Grand Concourse, discussing masturbation. Spieler was an authority on the topic, did it apparently all the time. He masturbated, he said, every day and sometimes all day. He thought he may have broken a world's record for the number of ejaculations he had managed to squeeze from his penis in a single afternoon but didn't offer an exact number count. "Just until I was rubbed raw and even saw blood," he said.

When finally I confessed that I had never done it but told about the experience I had had, he and the others all said in voices weary with the commonplaceness of it: "Wet dream." Spieler, the evident expert, expressed surprise that it had happened to me only recently and just once. He had his first, he said, in fourth grade. I was amazed to think that a fourth-grade boy could already have such an easy conversance with obscene mysteries of the sexual netherworld. Apparently, though, it wasn't all that obscene: a wet dream like sneezing, masturbation little more than blowing your nose—or your dick, as it were. Everyone did it, according to Spieler, or had done it.

"Even Mr. Young, the shop teacher?" I asked skeptically.

Sure, Spieler replied, with perfect confidence. Mr. Young was the vulture-faced gimp-legged dean of the ninth-grade boys, who purportedly hanged troublemakers upside down in his closet and beat the flats of their naked soles with a steel ruler, like a cruel Turk. "Sure he beats his meat. Of course. Even President Johnson pulls his own crank."

That pretty much settled it for me, imagining Lyndon on the potty with his big gray suit trousers down around his cowboy boots, stroking away.

The field narrowed now to the only possible exception on the face of the earth, my father, but after some reflection I decided that his exception still held. He was just too out of it to do anything so interesting.

And just why did only boys masturbate, not girls? Of course, Spieler knew: Girls experience sexual desire only occasionally, whereas boys are constantly hot, so jerking off is a way to get instant relief. Also, girls don't have much sexual feeling. But no sooner does a guy "cum" then the testicles or "balls" produce a new load of "gysm" ready for discharge.

To assure a solid supply of "pecker juice" one should eat lots of eggs, Spieler added. We all took mental note of this. Spieler was a veritable mine of information. He even knew a boy in summer camp, he said, who could twist himself into a pretzel and give blowjobs to himself. All of us grumbled with admiration. Such was the way of the world: always there was one just a little more fortunate than oneself, or, as in this case, a lot more fortunate.

I jerked off at every opportunity. They weren't many. I needed the bathroom undisturbed for a reasonable length of time in which to lean with my head against the tile wall, the plumbing pipes pressed uncomfortably against the small of my back. Eyes closed, I began to rub myself slowly up and down, up and down.

Invariably, though, someone tried the cut-glass doorknob. "C'mon," snapped my father, "I gotta go!"

I gotta go too, I thought sarcastically, we're just not going to the same place.

"A-bie!" my mother's high histrionic voice shrilled through the closed door and the doorknob jiggled. "A-bie, what are you doing in there? Come out!"

My hands then snapped into rapid two-fisted motion, one-two, one-two, like a twin-piston engine, until the desired uncontrollable heat convulsed my loins and sperm shot spattering over my thighs, hands, the dingy floor tiles.

Then, in a heartbeat, with a big handful of toilet paper, I scrubbed scum off of everything, unlocked the door, and exited quickly past the intruder with averted eyes and a squeamish smile. In time, I got quite good at this.

Masturbation sexualized the whole world for me. I either approached life with full balls or empties. When they were full they needed to be emptied. When they were empty they needed to be full again so that they could be emptied.

I ate lots of eggs, encouraged my mother to make them. I need protein, I informed her, lots of protein, the more the better, to get big and strong. I thought that my mother had no reason to suspect my real motive. There was a lot of truth in this for a boy my age. I *did* need lots of protein to grow. Secretly, though, I knew that very little protein reached my thirsty bones and muscles; instead it was channeled to my balls from where it shot pointlessly onto the floor.

Nonetheless I was willing, really any day of the week, to trade personal development for pleasure. And scum was my little secret—only I knew of my secret life of spent protein, the incredible and lavish waste of it, billions of unborns sopped up by white-petaled toilet-paper flowers, and in fact I dreamed of reaching legal age when I could move out and jerk off as I pleased, safe from interruption within the confines of my own residence.

Somewhat prophetically, I envisioned manhood as one long succession of masturbations extending over years with breaks only to consume protein, and I looked forward to such days with a kind of feverish eagerness. By then I would not even have to convert the eggs into sperm but would just ejaculate whole hard-boiled eggs through the engorged tip of my adult pecker.

It would sometimes occur to me that my mother and father were not stupid, that they knew what I was up to in there for up to a whole hour on some Saturdays—a day when I felt particularly ready to blow unless I got some relief. I sat with my pants around my feet, head tipped against the tiles, my crank in my fist, and a dreamy, expansive smile on my lips as my glazed eyes regarded the door behind which one or the other of my parents stood, commanding me in a voice of oddly muffled irritation, almost hesitant with distaste, to "come out of there already. It's been over an hour!" and me thinking, if not in these exact words, So what if they know? It's good.

For are we not all born of the animal kingdom, come here in sweet togetherness? The thought aroused me even further. My blood-swollen member grew so leaden and stiff that only several straight hours of incessant stimulation could provoke it to spew its splendid sap.

I was trapped, too, in a weird downwardly spiraling dilemma from which there seemed no escape. The more I masturbated, the more I wanted to masturbate, and the more desensitized I grew to the touch of my hand, the harder I had to pump my fist and the less pleasure I felt.

It got so bad that I had to use two fists going full guns at increasingly more incredible speeds to where they became just a blur while my whole body stretched across the toilet seat stiff as a board, from my heels mashing into the grimy floor tiles to the hospital-white walls supporting the pressure of my exploding head. My face was flattened by G-force on the salt flats of pleasure. I must have looked, upon the approach of orgasm, like an abducted astronaut subjected to weird gravity experiments by his Venutian kidnappers. My entire pear-shaped frame trembled so hard once that my foot, gripped by its own independent life, leaped out and shoved the entire sink off its base just as I came, howling with a stubbed toe. The experience of peak pain and peak pleasure was indescribable.

Certainly, my mother knew. Her voice through the door adopted an insinuating tone that was at once aloof and damning. The whole morality standard of Eastern European Jewry was in it: the impecunious scathing, spiritually repulsed voice of dynastic rabbinical bloodlines, the great minds of little ghettos and *shtetls*, the spirit kings of the teeming metropolis, from Maimonides to Martin Buber.

To their stern disapproval, speaking to me through her voice, all I could do was shrug. It felt too good to stop. I was alone with myself, fantasizing about love embraces with calendar girls. Was this so terrible? I honestly didn't think so. Some part of me felt deeply, profoundly ashamed at the thought that God had a front-row seat to my sordid goings-on. But at other times as I approached the white light of ground zero, my jaw grew limp and a pink tsunami wave of joy drowned me; then I felt OK with God, realized that he understood my loneliness and suffering, and I smiled warmly as raindrops dappled my cheek and nose, opened my eyes and saw that I had shot sperm all over myself, even had some on my eyelids and my hair, rocketed by the sheer force of my two-fisted propulsion method, and the angels sang as I wiped myself clean with toilet paper.

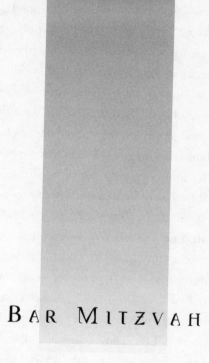

BAR MITZVAH

NOW MY BAR MITZVAH lay only two months off. The anticipation was killing me. Mr. Unger, the tutor, force-marched me through my paces. Gone were his lingering disquisitions over the meaning of this or that word of my haftorah, the portion of scripture I must read on the appointed day. My memory was a lazy, slothful beast that he felt he must beat senselessly until it learned to dance. My clumsy mental legs came to move in time to the music, an anxious look on my face. It wasn't an especially long haftorah but nonetheless I panicked. From those of my classmates who were Jewish I came to understand that a good several hundred invited guests would be present, hanging on every word of Hebrew from my mouth, so I had better get it right. Besides, the rewards made it more than worthwhile. Gifts and money would rain down on my head at the conclusion of the ceremony. At Jeffrey Spieler's Bar Mitzvah a professional clown wearing a yarmulke fashioned animals from balloons while a not-bad orchestra played fox-trots for the old folks. Spieler's take was a cool two grand, of which fifteen hundred dollars went into a bank account for college and five hundred he got to blow. As he told me this sitting on a stoop on the Bronx Grand Concourse, my eyes popped out of my head. "Two thou-sand! Yer kiddin'!"

"Nope!" he said, his gentle, horsey face shaking charitably from side to side. "Two thousand. If you get any less, you've been screwed."

I couldn't get that sum of money out of my head. What would I do with two thousand? Probably I could get my family out of our crummy apartment once and for all! I could afford a bicycle. A Wilson catcher's mitt. A phonograph. Levi's jeans. Converse sneakers. H.I.S. corduroy slacks and plaid shirts. Penny loafers! A purple nylon football jersey! A helmet and shoulder pads! And a year's subscription to *Fantastic Four* comics. I lay on my bed dreaming, head pillowed on my folded hands, a jazz piano tinkling cool and sad on the radio, and my mother clattering dishes in the kitchen. Life seemed so good. I had been disappointed by my parents in so many ways in my life, but this involved God— not even my parents would dare to mess with Him.

The date of my approaching Bar Mitzvah became widely known among my fellow students, as I intended for many of them to be there. I even considered extending an invitation to Mark Steinberg.

Mr. Unger was less than enthusiastic about the approaching date. "*Katzenkopf!*" he grimaced. "People who hear you are gonna say, 'What kind of *shmuck* is that Unger, what sends a boy to his Bar Mitzvah with a haftorah sounds like praying with a mouth full of *kugel*.' Not 'hashman!' '*Ha-sho-mai-yim. . . . Mai-yeeeem!*'" His dingy finger tapping the book frantically. And then Unger fell back in his chair, studied me with an all-over, weary, groping-at-straws look, and said as though probing for forbidden mystery, "Your muther is from War-shaw, yes?"

"From Paris. Her parents were from Warsaw."

"Ah, the parents were from. Yes. And de fadder, de fadder is also from Warshaw?"

"No," I said with deadpan resignation at repeating these facts to Unger for the thousandth time. "He was born in America but his parents came from Russia." And at this, as always, he grew especially alert, and asked hopefully: "From Moscow?"

"No," I said, "from Minsk."

His reaction to this was identical each time. "*Ach!* Minsk. These were not very educated people, yes?"

"No," I said, only too happy to mock and condemn my father and his family going back a thousand years if required. They were no kind of family to me, the Kaufmans, and I was ashamed of those few with whom my parents chose to stay in touch: Uncle Arnold, Aunt Fagel, Aunt Ray, some of Arnold's older sons, and Barbara and Jean.

Unger's face nodded sleepily. "Minsk," he repeated. "From Minsk. Not so much going on up here," tapping his temple. "So, you must try harder because you have less to work with." And as I leaned over the book, determined to try harder, he added: "These were the poorest of the poor from Minsk. But also, many great rabbis came from there. Maybe there is hope, Avraham. Begin." And he listened while the village simpleton and the Great Rabbi struggled for my soul. The simpleton won each time.

Whenever I asked my parents for details about the coming event, my father would increase his concentration on whatever lay before his eyes, a television show or the *Daily News* or a bowl of chav soup, and say: "I told you, you're gonna have the Bar Mitzvah. Now, let it go. What more do you need to know? On the day it happens, you'll see."

This explanation served for a while. But as the date approached and I failed to see any arrangements being made or my parents energized to perform anything but the usual mind-numbing routine of work, sleep, eat, and work, sleep, and eat, I began to fear the worst.

"So," said Spieler at school, his kind face cast in a look of hurt, "when do I get my invitation?"

I said, "I told you, the Bar Mitzvah's on January 12. What else you gotta know?"

Spieler, flabbergasted, expressed his exasperation in a series of sharp trumpet notes blown from his big horsey lips, spraying spittle everywhere. Tears of disbelief welled in his eyes. Then he laughed so hard that he keeled over from the waist, clutching his ribs and staggering around the corridor. When he was done preparing the ground to introduce the point he was trying to make, he delivered it red-faced in a squeaking voice pitched to shatter glass: "You mean you don't got no invitations to hand out? You're gonna explain to everybody? You explain what's the address and the time and the place 'stead of giving them an invite? And what about the map on the back that's gotta show how you get there? You gonna draw them a map on a piece of loose leaf? . . ." Here he gasped for breath, barely got out: "You gonna draw for them . . . arrows?" and gave up trying to speak, his face purple with mirth and tears rolling down his cheeks. Spieler was very persuasive.

I couldn't wait for the clock to strike three. The distance between school and home seemed like a continent to cross. To make matters worse, my parents were short on cash, couldn't spring for car fare; I had to trudge home. Luckily it was a beautiful blue-sky day with big mountain-range cloud banks of thickly ridged white puffs cut by impressive shadows. It was so unseasonably warm that the snowfall from the entire past week ran in the gutters like brook water, and the dog-piss and feces-stained snowdrifts seemed to shrink before ones very eyes. My galoshes sloshed home down the thawing curving wide and endless streets of the Grand Concourse, my parka slipped down my shoulders, and my schoolbag swung from my back. The whole way I fumed, avoiding groups of kids who waved at me to join them. I threw up my hand and marched on. My fists clenched from time to time and I emitted a loud "Oh!" of sheer frustration. I did my best to keep out ugly thoughts but they raced by anyway, and sometimes they cradled my brain with the teasing confidence of a magical imp, kept me riveted on scenes of hideous revenge that left me feeling sick and ashamed. But on I marched, undeterred, to discover if indeed my parents, who were guilty of disappointing me so many times in the past, were also capable of disappointing God. I refused to believe it possible, even as I sensed an irreversible turning point in my relations with them, which frightened me even more into hoping that the outcome would prove different than the one I most dreaded. But if they couldn't afford to give me car fare this morning, how would they afford to throw a party in a big synagogue for more than three hundred people, and afford the balloon-tying clown with the yarmulke or, more important, my big cash gift in honor of becoming a man? Surely they didn't plan to usher me into manhood penniless. That had to be the reason they were so short: saving every cent for the big day.

But my heart just wouldn't buy it. My pace increased. I half walked and half ran all the way home. Took the three steps of the front stoop in a single clumsy bound. In the dark lobby punched impatiently at the elevator button. Rode the clattering pea-green lift up to the fourth floor. Entered the apartment muttering furiously to myself. Stopped. Listened. No one in the kitchen. They must be lying down in the bedroom, where they spent most of their waking hours, with breaks between for him to work at the post office and her to clean, do the laundry, shop, cook.

I huffed into my room. Howie wasn't home yet. Threw off my things. I was breathing hard. Placed my hands on my hot cheeks to feel. Closed my eyes. "Take it easy, take it easy, take it easy," I repeated to myself. Expelled a long breath. Came my mother's voice: "A-bie? Is that you?" My heart lurched angrily. Why didn't she ask if it was Howard? Why always if it was me? As if he wasn't worth checking on but close tabs had to be kept on me. Or worse still: She had been lying there waiting especially for me to come home. What did she want from me? Why would she be waiting for me? She has a husband. Go bother him with your waiting. Go wait for someone else to come home, not me! I wanted to shout: No, it's not A-bie, it's Alfred Hitchcock! Watch out when you wash up! Never know who's on the other side of the shower curtain!

I kicked off my shoes. With two loud clunks they struck the floor. "A-bie! Don't make so much noise! The neighbors will have us evicted!" That was the last straw.

I threw myself on the bed, clutched the pillow, and sank my teeth into it, and as I chewed the freshly laundered cloth I growled under my breath: "Goddammit, you better not go back on your promise! You said I'd have a great Bar Mitzvah! You told me that all the way back when I was ten even. You better not change your mind! I don't care what your excuse is . . ." and whined softly, "Oh, God, please don't let them do this to me, please, please, please . . ." But it was no help. I had no choice but to face them with my question. I didn't want to know the answer. I didn't want there to be a question or an answer, just the event done as it should be, as for anyone else. And me to stand crowned by God, family, and friends with a fat wad of checks in my breast pocket.

My fingertips bumped on the cool hard beige-colored pimples of the bad paint job that covered the walls of our living room, found the fluted plaster molding around the bedroom door, and rested there. I put my hand on the molding opposite and hung there crucified, my arched back and big belly thrust into the dim bedroom, which reeked of farts and perfume. "Pee-yew!" I said. "Pop's really givin' the gas to the old troops. You need a gas mask, Mom."

They were lying there side by side, dressed in underthings, their hefty legs like white worms turned at vulnerable angles. Thin pale lips of light seeped through the gray slats of the venetian blinds. It wasn't a big room. Just enough for the queen-sized Castro bed, the green vinyl upholstered reclining chair patched with masking tape, a Panasonic console TV, dresser bureau with a mirror that once swiveled before it broke. A few framed pictures from their wedding hung on the wall: her in a satiny gown that ran down her body like melting ice cream and ended in a big cream-colored puddle of melted dress around her feet, and him in a Fred Astaire suit glaring at the camera with piercing black eyes, beetle-browed like his movie hero Tyrone Power, whom everybody claimed he looked like back then. He did. A little. A picture of me and Howie, aged two, with long hair like girls, dressed in identical blue button-down sweaters with a white stripe banding each sleeve, and dark little-men's pants and grown-up looking black shoes. I have my arms around him and neither of us seemed to mind. A couple of real chums. Back then they dressed us like princes. Nothing too good for us. I even remember my mother asking my opinion about what shirt to buy and what color of clip-on bow tie, and I had opinions about it that she respected, and she made the purchases. For years she told that story. But with time Howie and I more and more took a backseat. My father's wardrobe grew more and more fancy as ours became lousier and lousier. He brought home hundred-dollar Italian shirts, calf-skin Italian loafers as thin as a hanky, even a gray fedora in a box so elegant that it looked even better than the hat inside. By contrast, he sought cheaper and cheaper solutions to our clothing problems. "There's no point in getting you kids nice things," he'd say, one eye squinting stonily above a wreath of smoke from his cigar. "You ruin the nice things we get you, and you outgrow the stuff so fast that by the time we get it home from the store already it doesn't fit."

More and more it seemed that when we needed something, my mother's answer was: "We'll have to see how your father does at cards tonight." He was quite the cardplayer, apparently. He played a game with us: his feet could use a massage after standing on them the whole night in the post office. "Straightening out the feet," he called it. "Abie, Sheshie, come in here. Who wants to make a quarter straightenin' out me feet?" in that fake Irish brogue he adopted whenever making an uncomfortable request for personal attention of any kind—when speaking about himself. The voice of Victor McLocklin, a big manly soldier of an actor always angry, drunk, or making sappy sentimental speeches on the battlefield, a big pugnacious sensitive lovable dope. Is that how he saw himself? In that McLocklin brogue: "There's a quarter in it fer ye! Come and git it!" Sometimes Howie took one foot, me the other at the foot of the bed on our knees, his big callused foot in my hand held like an enormous sandwich, flexing the top part with the toes, back and forth as he groaned: "That's good, Abe, that's good, Shesh, that's good," and for which we each got a quarter that he then offered to double, triple, even quadruple over a few hands of cards. Sometimes we played. Need grabbed my heart. A whole dollar spun out of a quarter! "Sure," I said, "sure," somehow convinced that this time luck would ride with me;

I might even win at blackjack. A ten. "Hit me," I said. A six. I thought. "Hit me," I said, swallowing hard. I peeled back the corner of the card. A king. "Hee, hee, hee, hee, hee," his laughter followed my dejected penniless exit from the room. "Hee hee hee hee hee!" But always he gave me the quarter back. The humiliation of my defeat was reward enough for him, the stunned, sad, helpless look on my face as I winced, my sheer incapacity to play, a naive innocence that perhaps he had lost, liked to be reminded of.

He watched televised boxing matches with an intent quiet concentration. We all crowded around the set. My mother asked, "Who do you bet on?" "Uh, Carter, Carter." "Is he doing good?" "Uh, not bad. Not bad." Who lost. And my father growled: "Ach! Acch!" in disgust. "A charbon"—a catastrophe!—my mother said nervously. "Did you bet a lot?" He answered in Yiddish. A number. I recognized the Yiddish number words. "Finif hundert und svansik," and so on. She looked like someone had brought the heel of a heavy shoe down on her forehead, between the eyes. Her face sank into disbelief. She whimpered something back to him in Yiddish. He responded in Yiddish with a fatalistic air that barely concealed his own worry. Brow clammy with sweat.

The apartment grew darker, as though a hand covered both the sun and the moon. Our close quarters became a coffin. We sat at the kitchen table with my mother. We sat and we waited. My father rarely came home now. Working double time. Went to see if he could borrow money. On Saturday. We're up, waiting for breakfast. Nothing to eat. The clock ticking. Ten o'clock. Eleven o'clock. Usually by now he's home. But he worked overtime to make a few more bucks. And then he went to see the loan shark. "God help us if he says no, and God help us if he says yes," my mother said. I don't understand. "The interest, stupeed!" she groaned at me. "Do you know how much interest they charge, that lousy loan shark? And if you don't pay up in time . . ." She stopped, looked down at her hands. Made a decision. "Nothing. Never mind."

Howie and I jumped out of our chairs. "Whatdyamean, nevah mine? You gotta tell us! Tell us! Tell us!"

"You don't want to know," she said chillingly. But of course now we *really* wanted to know! "What is it? What? What?"

"They'll break his legs," she said simply. Something so unexpected that Howie and I looked at each other like, "What? Break Pop's legs?" I asked, unsure of what I'd heard.

"Who else?" she snorted, disdainfully.

Who else indeed? Gangsters will break the legs of my father. Those unbearably white worm legs turned at vulnerable angles, exposed in underwear on the bed. Those feet that Howie and I straighten out for a quarter. I tried to imagine how such a feat could be accomplished, the look on my father's face as his bones snapped with a sickening crack. My own legs grew weak as jelly and my stomach flip-flopped. I pinched my nostrils closed and said in a gagged, breathless voice: "The perfume's not helping, Mom. His farts are too bad. You need something stronger."

"Shaddap the two a you or I'll give it to ye both but good," said my father, talking on his turned cheek with his eyes shut as though fast asleep. He's not. Just lying there. They liked to lie down. Were never on their feet if they could help it. Sometimes we all four lay on our beds, like lazy seals slumped on rocks, whiling away the afternoon, doing nothing, time passing, neither bored nor restless, our systems stupefied with excess food and inactivity. It nauseated me to think about it. So tried not to. Just lie there. The Kaufmans at play.

"Dad . . ." I began slowly.

"What is it? Make it quick. I gotta get some sleep before I go to work tonight. The both of you slept, didn't you? So let me get my sleep."

"What is it, A-bie. Your father's tired," my mother added, to show who's side she's on if a fray broke out.

"How come we don't got the invitations made up yet? How ya gonna invite three hundred people without invitation cards?"

My father's face screws up sarcastically: "Three hundred . . . people . . . ? Where do you get three . . . hundred . . . people? What are you crazy? Or what."

"Oh, no!" I moan.

"What are you oh-no-in' us for here?" my father snapped angrily. He turned over to face me, head propped on his fist, his elbow turned my way, covered with a raw pink-scaled outbreak of psoriasis. "Are you payin' for the Bar Mitzvah? Or just getting? So until you pay, just be happy for what you get."

"Your poor father," my mother jumped in, her voice a clarinet introducing a new motif. "He owes so much out there, we're lucky we have what to eat . . ."

"But I don't want to hear that!" I shouted. "I'm sick and tired of hearin' that! This is my Bar Mitzvah! This is God you're screwin' around!"

That brought my father to an upright sitting position. "Screwin'? Who you talkin' to, mister, with that dirty mouth . . . !?"

And suddenly I saw it all getting away from me, and said, hands up in a plea for peace: "No! No! No! Please! No! This is my Bar Mitzvah! It's supposed to be a happy thing for me and Howie . . . ," amazed at their readiness to do battle with me even over an occasion as holy and as profitable as my Jewish coming-of-age.

I grew choked with tears, caught spinning down the disappointing drain yet one more time, compelled to mediate the successful denouement of my own Bar Mitzvah, and torn by an angry sense of complete disgrace as yet another deathblow was dealt to my hopes of enjoying a normal childhood in any way. "So, just tell me . . ." I sobbed. "Please just tell me what *will* be there, OK? Is it gonna be in a shul? Will it have that at least?"

My parents grew furtive.

"Uh, yeah. Sure. Of course."

"Which one? Can I ask that? The big one on Fordham Road?"

"No," said my mother, her voice stepping forward like an official spokesman for the two of them. "We're going to do it in the Mount Eden."

I started. "The what? Did you say the Mount Eden? Tell me you didn't say the Mount Eden!?"

Her lips pursed with ruffled pride as she addressed me in the formal, aloof tone that she adopted whenever compelled to disappoint me.

"And what's wrong with the Mount Eden? It's a Jewish shul. Mr. Unger knows the rabbi there. He said we can have it for a small contribution." I saw reality and was ready to forego the Buckingham Palace–scale coronation that I had envisioned, as long as the reception was respectable.

"So, what hall did you rent for the reception?"

She glanced icily at my father and muttered in French: *"Il est fou, tu connait?" Il est* this and *il est* that, and so on, as he shook his head in agreement. "It will be there in the shul. They have a little dining room. We'll bring a cake. A bottle of wine. Say a toast. And that's it! We don't think anyone's going to come anyway. Your uncles in Caracas and Paris can't fly here just for a Bar Mitzvah. Your Uncle Arnold has no time or money with that crazy wife and kids. The others you know, Fagel, Barbara, Jean, Al, ain't worth inviting. You'll be lucky if Barbara doesn't end up stealing the few bucks you *do* get." And after a pause my father added, "She's a klepto, that crazy nut!" and said again in the shocked silence that hung in the air between us: "A goddamned klepto!"

I couldn't speak. Parted my lips, came out nothing. Instead, everything seemed to be sucked back inside of me. The doors and shutters of my heart slammed shut. Grief caulked every seam of my soul. My brain was sealed behind a wall of shame. If you had slashed me with a butcher knife, I would not have bled. I was not shattered—I was demolecularized into another dimension so sad that those who inhabited it had unlearned language and spoke in silences to an earless world. A world in which those with normal hearing were the deaf while the deaf listened to silence like a symphony. Also, the visible world was a lie; only darkness was true. Only night.

I returned to my bed, stretched on my side, lay on my cheek, waiting for night when I could come out, as children wait for first light to go out and play. I would come out and grieve. My form of play would be to perish a little bit more and a little bit more with each new moon. I felt a hand on my head. Didn't turn. The love contained in that hand pressed my head gently into the pillow, like the warm weight of a cat. The hand belonged to my father.

"Don't feel bad, Abe. You know your mutha and I love you more than anything in the whole world. Don't you know that, ya dummy?" He said "dummy" with such affection that I wouldn't have minded him calling me that, in just that way, for the rest of my life. Still, it stung a little, made me feel stupid. *Dummy. A-za. Shvantz. Stupeed. Stoopie.* All the nicknames they gave me. On and on. Rivulets of tears sprang from my eyes, trailed down my cheeks. I opened my mouth, tried to speak. Air fluttered against a canopy of thick mucilage, made a sound. I closed my mouth. I wept.

"Don't cry, Abie. You're making me feel bad over here, you know that? Abe! You think I don't want you to have a big Bar Mitzvah like them other kids? But what can I do? You know, your momma and I don't got that kinda money. If I had it, Abe, I'd spend it on ya. I swear! The biggest Bar Mitzvah you ever saw. You know what kinda Bar Mitzvah I had? Nuttin!"

"Sure," cooed my mother mournfully from behind him. She circled the bed to sit at the far edge, near my feet. "It was the Depression. They didn't have what to eat. And what do you think I did when I was thirteen? What did I have? Do you know where I spent my thirteenth birthday?" She began to sob. "I should live so, George. We were hiding with me and my mother and my aunt and her husband, the four of us in a chicken coop by this *goyisha* farmer who we weren't so sure we could trust. We paid him so much not to give us away but who knew, and don't you know, I should die if I'm lying, on my birthday the Germans stopped at that farm and were snooping around, may they rot in hell, and I almost *kocked* in my dress from fear. We heard their voices. Talking to the farmer, right outside the chicken coop! Ten feet away!"

"In German?" I asked weakly, my curiosity piqued. How, I wondered, did a German soldier speak with a French farmer?

"Who should live so, in German? That filthy Nazi spoke French better than the Frenchman! And translated for the others. What do you know? You should have heard them talk between each other: *"Achbf! Achbf!"* her jaw snapping open and shut disdainfully on absurd guttural sounds in imitation of German-language words.

I sighed, oddly satisfied. At least my deprivation made some sort of historical sense. I could even see it as heroic. At least I wasn't hiding in a chicken coop or eating potato peel soup and listening to Roosevelt on the Depression-era radio. I sighed and said, my head a touch headachy, "It's awright. I understand."

"That's a good boy," said my father, stroking my head. I closed my eyes like a pleased kitten.

"You got a good head, you know that? A good head!"

"What do you know?" said my mother, her voice remote, distant-sounding, her mind perhaps still back in the chicken coop.

When Howie came home I broke the news to him. He shook his head. Not in disappointment but in amazement at my unfailing naiveté.

"You mean you expected different? When are you gonna learn? They got a poor people's mentality. They think like poor people. So, they're poor. They'll never change. When are you gonna wake up?"

Once or twice before the Bar Mitzvah I presented a last-minute possible game plan to them whereby with the right investment of energy and a small outlay of cash they might yet manage to garner thousands in gift checks. I cited the example of Jeffrey Spieler and others. I explained about sending out as many invitations to as many people as they could think of. But they didn't know that many people, they protested, laughing nervously and shaking their heads at my entrepreneurial desperation. My father, seated at the dinette table dressed in boxer shorts, T-shirt, and house slippers, freshly shaved and powdered with cornstarch, his thinning wet hair combed into a pompadour, even his flaring purple psoriasis calmed into a soothed-looking pink color, and speaking with a full mouth as he tried to masticate his finely cut rib steak and lumpy mashed potatoes with nerve-sensitive, poorly maintained teeth that were rotting out of his head: "You know what you can expect from your Uncle Arnold?" He tore the center out of a slice of Wonder Bread, tossed the crust aside, and stuffed the white bread into his mouth. "*A sac mit nuff!*"

"What's that?" I said.

"Mash, translate for him, willya? I got a mouthful here."

"It means in Yiddish a lot of nothing," said my mother, coolly spooning food onto a plate for me.

"Aza," said Howie, "why don't you give it up? Don't you see they don't get it?"

"Hey you, dummy," barked my father, "mine yer own business or I'll *klep* that stupid head a yours."

To which my brother smirked and mumbled: "Yeah. Right."

My efforts were not entirely fruitless. At the last minute my mother had twenty elegant-looking invitations made up by a local printer and gave me ten to hand out at school. Spieler examined the gold lettering on pale blue card stock and grunted: "Not bad." Sniffing, he pocketed the invite. The other ten my mother and I sat up late one night personalizing and slipping into addressed envelopes.

"These cost me some money, don't ask," my mother moaned as we worked. Her tongue sliding out of her mouth—small, spade-shaped, and lined with blue-purple veins underneath—filled me with pity, and love. The fine down of light blonde hair lining her upper lip. The downturned, humbled slant of her eyelashes bending over the glue flap of an envelope as she licked and sealed, her eyes waiting to look up but trapped in the function of her mouth, shy, too embarrassed or well mannered, or afraid, to look up.

I stood to my feet, circled the table, and hugged her. As always, her head, frizzy with reddish blonde hair tied back by a rag, ducked tortoiselike between her shoulders, a nervous involuntary reaction of defense, perhaps against Nazi blows.

I said: "I love you, Mommala," but her cheek still waited for my lips to leave.

"Don't you know your father and I would do anything for you and your brother, stupeed?"

A week before the big day we were taken into Barney's Big Men's Shop on Fordham Road to be fitted for suits. My father led us to the Husky Boys department. It was staffed by a middle-aged balding man with untrustworthy eyes and an air of absolute certainty about the quality of his goods. I liked his clothes: a millionaire playboy blue blazer with shiny gold buttons, gray slacks, oxblood loafers, and, over a pink pin-striped shirt, a blue-and-gray striped tie. It made him look like Hugh Hefner, the publisher of *Playboy* magazine, whose photo I had glimpsed while sneaking a peek at this month's centerfold in Al and Lou's candy store. And he had a suntan. His bald pate gleamed like bronze. I wondered where he got such a tan in the Bronx in the dead of winter. We tramped in shaking snow off our galoshes and tracked up the floor right up to the counter where he stood. On his bronze face, his smile lit up like a white bathroom.

"What can I do for you?" he asked with unnerving gentleness, in a voice so soft we strained to hear. Maybe, I thought, we're too loud, and glanced anxiously at my father and brother. My father was switching a toothpick from side to side in his mouth. It made a noise like *tshik tschik tschik* as his lips drew back to allow the wood splinters rotation, the noise of wet flesh peeling away from soggy gums. And my brother was going: *"Brrrr-rrrrrrr! Brrrrrr-rrr-rrr!"* Every inch of him huddled into his coat and his eyes rolled wildly behind his horn-rimmed glasses. By contrast, the hush in the Husky Boys department was like that of a monastery.

"I need a couple suits for the boys here," said my father in his finest imitation-gangster voice.

"All right," said the salesman, gliding away from the counter and sailing down an aisle of circular racks containing pinwheels of suits in a variety of drab blues, grays, browns, and blacks, with an occasional cream or green leaping out at the eye. My heart sank. When we caught up with the salesman I noticed that his name tag read: ALBERT NAYLER.

"Mr. Nayler," I said in a high chorus boy voice, "do you have Nehru suits?"

Immediately my father plucked the toothpick from his mouth with a violent gesture and gaped at me, aghast. "What are you, crazy? You ain't gettin' no Nehru suits for no Bar Mitzvah!"

"But, Daaaaaaad!" I whined. "Everybody at school got Bar Mitzvahed in a Nehru suit!" Which was a lie. Only one had, Zeke Graber, but I figured it was worth the gambit. Of course, it flopped. My father gave me such a look as would swat a fly dead on a wall and returned his attention to Mr. Nayler, who waited with a discrete air for our spat to terminate so that we could return to the real business at hand.

"Yes?" he gently inquired. "Yes. Well, what sort of suit do we have in mind?"

Resentment rose in my gorge! "We" indeed. That I would have to wear the suit or how I felt about it counted for nothing.

"It's for their Bar Mitzvah, Mr. Nayler," said my father. "So, something with good taste and a size bigger than what they are now, so later we can let it out a little. They're growing so fast I'll have to throw the suits out in a month."

Mr. Nayler smiled politely, hands clasped at his waist the way we did in chorus class at school. "They're big boys. I bet they eat a lot."

"This one," said my father, jabbing at me with a finger, "this one don't know the meaning of the word 'stop.' So, whatta ya got for them?"

"Here is a smart double-breasted with flap pockets and matching pants." Said Nayler, laying it out: "Here is houndstooth check . . ."

My father cut him off. "No houndstooth . . ."

Annoyed, Mr. Nayler's face flushed. "All right then," he said, his voice suddenly high, and with trembling hands he returned it to the rack.

"How about a nice black?"

"No," said my father.

"A gray wool!"

"With these two? It'll be filthy in an hour. Nah. How about a burgundy? You got a burgundy? The mother said she likes burgundy. Let's try burgundy on them."

"You mean," said Mr. Nayler, "maroon."

My father smiled with a sarcastic snarl: "What's the difference, chief? Maroon. Burgundy. Just as long as it's not red or purple. And no Nehru suits!"

"Of course," said Mr. Nayler, whom I liked suddenly; for an instant his eyes sought mine for empathy and found it. I winced in understanding. He raised his eyebrows.

"Well. I'll have to check in back for your 'burgundy.' That's a special color."

"Wine," said Howie. "Mom called it wine-colored."

And I could hear her voice right there in the store, see floating above the sea of suit racks her flushed high-blood-pressure face and French lips pursed reverently as she said: "A nice *wine*-colored suit. So gorgeous!"

He returned with two enormous identical wine-colored suits so repugnant to me that I clutched my father's sleeve and pleaded in a low calm voice: "Pop, please, I beg you, don't make us wear that, please, I beg you."

He shook my hand off with an irritated laugh. "Are you crazy or what? Leggo a me. What d'you care? It's for one day; you don't have to wear it after that."

At which point I did a kind of dance: my torso collapsed at the waist, my head, shoulders, and arms flung forward like a puppet whose strings have been cut, and shuffling backwards with little geisha steps I whined: "It won't be for just one time! It won't be just for one time!" the downbeat falling on the word "won't," and returning to my original position, repeated the tantrum dance again. To no avail. We were ordered to the dressing room to change into the suits, which were two sizes too large.

Without pants' cuffs or sleeve cuffs and with our hands and feet swallowed by dangling tubes of maroon-colored cloth, we were led by a somber Mr. Nayler to a raised platform before a giant triptych mirror in which I could see myself from every possible angle. A short, stubby, balding man with a deadpan face and a tape measure looped around his neck came out from behind a heavy curtain with pins in his teeth and a chunk of chalk in his hand. He began to measure me and stick pins into the cloth and make short slashing chalk marks, and the whole time spent in my wine-colored prisoner's uniform on the scaffolding I felt as though I was being readied, on the eve of my execution, for a pine box.

On the night before my Bar Mitzvah, my father went to his night-shift job as usual but promised to return early for the ceremony. Howie went to bed, and my mother and I stayed up late, pouring over the snapshots of the dead in her special valise full of photographs. It lay open between us on the bed. I felt so much hope on the eve of this important occasion, more hope than the world had in itself to fulfill, given the desperation of my hope.

"You don't know," she said, "how I prayed for this day after the war. To see a son Bar Mitzvahed! This would be my answer to Hitler!"

I smiled. "Are you proud of me, Mom?"

"Proud?" She stopped, choked with emotion. Tears rose in her during the silent, perfectly still interval. And then she sobbed with tears in her eyes. "Of course I'm proud. Did you think I ever dreamed I would live to see this day, when I was hiding all those years from the Nazis? Any new day brought a death warrant. There was a price on my head. I was a Jew. Do you understand? Thirteen years old, your age, and they wanted to kill me!" The floodgates burst. She cried. I waited, used to her tears. I looked around me at the drab, aqua-colored walls and chintzy furnishings from Castro's and Macy's and Alexander's. Beyond the imprisoning slats of sealed venetian blinds was an air shaft in which the bedroom window across the way framed the fleshy white leathered figure of an old crone who sat there in her slip day and night, in all kinds of weather, ghostly behind a pane of sooty glass, motionless and staring at God knows what. I remembered photographs I had seen of Hitler's Nazi empire, the mass torchlight rallies of pale, wild-eyed faces spotlighted against pitch-black night, the leaping light from the flames spurting in their lustrously manic eyes. Crowds of these faces, in the thousands and tens of thousands and millions, with demonic formations of black-uniformed robotic SS goose-stepping right off the page, and of Nazi chieftains, always laughing with hyena grins of absolute certainty. I had seen austere, terrifying, massive buildings of Nazi administration, and Nazi battle formations of tanks and bombers and SS soldiers confidently inching forward in the face of machine guns, and, again, the leering grins of soldiers tossing a border gate aside. And convening heads of state—Roosevelt, Stalin, Churchill—meeting to discuss ways to overthrow the madmen, and the pictures of the camps, the ones I found more

and more of in the Grand Concourse public library in books and magazines, my silent air of respectful shock upon first encountering the walking corpse gaping at me through a camera lens, asking me: Are these, my
eyes, real to you? Are these, my bones, real to you? Does your heart
admit to the possibility of such things? What does your mind make of
such a world in which people can do this to other people, without the
interference of anyone, God or man? And, slamming shut the book each
time, returning it hurriedly to its place on the shelf in a panic, stuffing it
back, not wanting to see it anymore or ever again. I returned to the
novel section: Ernest Hemingway, Thomas Wolfe, James Jones. They
were safe, their easy world of sad stone angels and disillusioned fighting
men in love with the nurses of their wounds. It was difficult to connect
the grainy pictures of the Nazi past to my mother, flabby with purple
scars across her belly, scars she was fond of showing me from the emergency cesarean of my difficult, life-threatening birth. It was hard to see
the victory over Hitler in this stuffy Bronx bedroom with steam pipes
knocking and footsteps creaking overhead and the neighbors' raised,
quarreling voices through the paper-thin walls and the old woman's
ghostly stare at an alley wall; or to understand how I, in a Barney's Big
Men's Shop maroon-colored husky boy's suit, with poor grades and bad
hygiene and flattop crew cut gawking ugliness, could be an answer to
the horrors of the past. But she said it with so much conviction, so much
absolute conviction, that I believed her and rose and said good night and
kissed her on the top of her frizzy head, which ducked tortoiselike
between her shoulders, and plodded out to strip off my pants and lie in
the dark, listening to my brother snore in the next bed and wondering
at the poverty of God's miracles.

He roused us in his usual way: four iron-hard fingers jabbed into our
sides as we slept, surprising us out of our dreams into anguished wake-
fulness and sleepy cries of "Doooon't. Noooooo!" When we were much
younger, I sometimes wept. Now I threw the blankets off and rolled
out, coming to my feet with an angry shout: "Don't do that! Stop!"
which made him laugh. "Hee-hee-hee! Hee-hee-hee! Mash, come in
here and take a look at their faces."

"How dare you?!" I cried, something I'd heard recently in a movie and liked. "How dare you?"

"How dare I?" he asked darkly. "How dare I? I dare! And I'll dare you right in your ass if you don't get dressed . . . !"

"Geooorge," crooned my mother, wiping her hands on a dish towel. "Be nice. It's the boys' Bar Mitzvah day. *Rachmunis.*"

"I can't believe you can wake us that way. Why don't you just shake my shoulder?"

"Because you don't get up. That's why."

Which was true. Ten attempts could not stir me. I'd hear and feel their efforts to rouse me as from a great distance, and calculate the cost of ignoring their summons, and return to sleep, not finding the price very high.

"Besides, my father woke me and your Uncle Arnold that way. If it was good enough for us, it's good enough for you."

"Get dressed, please stop, before you both give me high blood pressure."

We tore open packages containing new white dress shirts, then donned the maroon suits and slipped our feet into brand new loafers from Thom McAn's. That discomforting sense of not knowing who I am came over me, as if new and different clothes could rob me of my identity without replacing it with a substitute. Fully dressed, we stood before our parents, who made us turn around as they muttered in admiration at the nice job the tailor had done and the good taste they had shown in their choices. My head was filled with expectations of big money. "How many people you think'll come?" I asked hopefully.

"Nobody's gonna come! Your Uncle Arnold will come with Aunt Ray and a few of the kids, that's all."

"But what about all those invitations you sent?"

My mother glanced guiltily at my father. "I feel terrible," she said.

In response he got his hackles up. "You feel terrible? Why should you feel terrible? What, is he paying for all this? Why should you feel terrible?"

He looked at me stonily and said, "We threw 'em away. We spent our last dime on the suits. We're in hock up to our necks. If we sent out all those invitations, who has money to feed so many people? We didn't mail 'em."

"What!" I gasped. "What!? You . . . threw . . . what . . . you!" and a cry of rage for how they never failed to surprise me in ever more despicable ways roared from my lips, an inarticulate howl of absolute despair that froze everyone in the room, and I threw myself against the wall and began to pound my head into the plaster, grunting *"Uhh! Uhh! Uh!"* and trying to decimate my skull, to drive a dislodged spike of bone through the gray, pound's-weight of sickening disbelief. My father sprang from the dinette table, threw his arms around me, pushed me out of the kitchen, into the living room, shouting: "What are you doing? What are you crazy?! Stop that! Stop that!" and threw me into the plastic-covered sofa cushions where I collapsed in a crying mass of shattered nerves.

A small, cheerless synagogue.

Faded, threadworn, velvet coverings here and there tossed over finger-smudged wood worn smooth by the weight and touch of more congregants than it was ever meant to accommodate. Since it was a Saturday morning, a few old men stood in the pews with prayer shawls on their shoulders and yarmulkes on their heads. Mr. Unger was up in front, assisting a man whom I took to be the rabbi, to move a lectern into position. The service had not yet begun. When Mr. Unger saw us in the rear, lined up in a row with abashed faces, he rushed over, pumped my father's hand, saw the shopping bags filled with things for the reception, and said to Howie, whom he didn't like: "You. Go put those in the kitchen back there." He asked my father, "Shnapps you brought?"

"The best! Manishevitz!"

Mr. Unger smacked his lips and rubbed his hands with, I thought, exaggerated anticipation. Nothing that we had brought was all that wonderful. A dry-looking honey cake from Friedhoffer's Bakery. Two bottles of cheap wine from Met food stores. Wax cups. Paper plates. Plastic spoons. Napkins. With these we would celebrate the triumph of

Jewish survival over Hitler's tyranny. My eyes were still red-rimmed with crying, my normally robust cheeks quite pale.

Mr. Unger noticed. "*Nu, Katzenkopf.* What's the matter? You caught flu on your Bar Mitzvah day?"

"I'm all right," I croaked, through a wan smile.

"And your haftorah you remember?"

I nodded vaguely.

"You see," said Unger to my parents, "a Jewish scholar I made from your sons. Both smart *yingeloch*, but with your Abie I'm twice impressed."

"Sure," said my mother. "His *zeder*, may he rest in peace, called him Little Einstein."

Unger leaned past my father's shoulder, whispered something, my father nodded. They stepped to the side. Tightly folded money changed hands. Unger said, overly loud it seemed, "And a little something for the shul? Very nice! Very nice!" More money handed over. The rabbi and a handful of congregants nodded with approval. "Please, Kaufman family, take seats. We will begin soon. You are expecting many guests?"

"No. No," said my father quickly.

"No." Surprised, or maybe unsurprised, Unger nodded with a sour smile and led us to our seats, near the front, a place of honor.

Suddenly, from the street entrance came loud, nasty, grating laughter, a machine gun spray of sinister snickers, scuffling, shoving, protests, threats, and Uncle Arnold entered with his herd of juvenile delinquent kids. My heart sank with shame. He was as tall as my father but without the symmetrical boxer's build. His dramatically sensual face was handsome and ruled by conflicting passions, but an absurd pompadour, jutting like a unicorn's horn from his head, spoiled it. His good looks were further spoiled by layers of fleshy decay. Bags underscored his prominently bulging eyes. He had narrow shoulders, long arms with massively veined hands and a protuberant potbelly. He wore a silver sharkskin suit, the tie loose at the unbuttoned collar of his pink silk shirt. Gold gleamed from his fingers, wrists, and tie. His shoes were so

pointy that he could have kicked a cockroach to death in a tight corner. His voice boomed with the swaggering insolence of a Mafia chieftain: "Where's my brother!?" as though he and my father were the
Romulus and Remus of an Imperial empire and not a cab driver and a
postal worker from the Bronx without eight completed grades of education between them.

They called each other by nicknames. Uncle Arnold was Sam, my
father was called Ushkie. No one kept their own name around Uncle
Arnold. His eldest son was called Bugsy. The next oldest, Harvey, was
called Jake. Dennis was called Louie. Keithie was called Mouse. And so
on, ten of them in all, with jeering grins, cuffed ears, slapped heads, crim-
inal-mischief eyes that went dead and life-threatening from time to time
(perfect ovals of dispassionate knife-thrusting and trigger-pulling and rib-
splitting mayhem), with scars over their mouths and cheeks and broken
noses and tattoos, a moiling, scuffling, shoving mass of mugs moving
along in a pack. Bringing up the rear was Aunt Ray: tiny, wicked, col-
lapsed-cheeked face of mascara-whore eyes and scarlet mouth almost
buried in a mink fur coat, her hair dyed blue black, a diamond cluster glittering from her knuckle, batting false eyelashes at the congregation a la
her heroine Elizabeth Taylor, whom she sought in every way to emulate,
right down to her stormy marriage to Arnold, which she compared to
that between Taylor and Richard Burton. It was hard to imagine that the
wolf pack disporting around her had come from such a petite frame. So
much trouble, like the incarnated golems of her discontent. A kind of
black cloud followed her. Something almost occult. I thought she was a
witch, once told my mother so, and she said that Aunt Ray was a
Galiciana, a Jew from Galicia, the trashiest of Jews, and might even have
Gypsy blood in her veins. She passed her afternoons in the kitchen com-
plaining on the telephone, to anyone who would listen, of Uncle Arnold's
endless misdeeds. Otherwise she smoked, gambled, and practically lived
in the bingo parlors. She never shopped, cooked, or did laundry. Her
children grew up around her, a dirty, neglected litter of unhappy criminals. They were in and out of juvenile halls and detention farms. Already
Harvey was famous, his photograph published on the front page of the

Daily News as he lay on a sidewalk in Castle Hill projects with a knife wound in his side, stabbed in a rumble with the Puerto Ricans.

Uncle Arnold and his family were, without exception, the most horrifying racists I had ever met. Had they not been born Jewish they could probably have formed their own vital component of the Ku Klux Klan. "Dem niggahs!" he liked to say, almost sing really. Race hatred was a song in his throat, vibrating from the deepest recess of his innermost being. They could talk about "dem niggahs" tirelessly. What Arnold and the boys did to them and vice versa, and what they'd do next time they got their hands on "dem niggahs."

His racism sickened my mother. "You should not talk that way!" she'd say sternly. "The first American soldier I ever saw after the Liberation was a black man! I was so starving and he gave me his K rations to eat! What do you know? Skin and bones I was, and he was such a nice gentleman! He told me I was going to be all right! I was so afraid! Shame on you, Arnie!"

And Arnold laughed along with my father, who quipped, "Yer lucky we let you into the country! We don't like no 'ferners' round here," in the fake Yankee accent of those who undoubtedly said those very same things to my father's immigrant parents, both of whom came from Russia. But my mother was adamant.

Once, down South, as we travelled to Florida by Greyhound bus to visit Aunt Fagel, the driver stopped in a small town, in the dead of night, to take aboard a handful of blacks who struggled aboard with children and suitcases. They headed immediately for the back. One had a sleeping baby in her arms. My mother leaned over to my seat, said: "Abie, get up and let the woman have your seat," which I did as other white passengers glared angrily and an old woman with a sharp-featured face and cold blue eyes behind wire-frame spectacles shifted irritably in the seat next to my mother and said with a southern twang, "You shouldn't teach your boys to make accommodation with people of that color! Let them learn to be gentlemen to their own kind," to which my mother crisply replied: "Mind your own business, thank you!" Which filled me with exulting pride for a short while, until the long miles began to get to me, the endless swamp South ticking by in the eerie headlights' glow and the broken-line center stripes and the evil eyes burning through me from the silhouetted turned heads of offended passengers, even though there was some message of peace for me in the sweet sleep of the baby and the occasional upward glance and grateful smile of the mother; my brain raced with the horrible vision of the bus brought to a sudden lynch-mob halt, the windshield filling with white hoods, torches, and the flicker of a flaming cross and the old woman's nasal twang: "Here's the Jew that give his seat to the colored! Take him out and string him up!" and the white sheets advancing with ropes and whips.

"There's Sam," said my father, huffing to his feet with difficulty. He liked to seem spry but wasn't. Already arthritis nagged his joints.

"Ushkie!" Uncle Arnold roared. "I brought the whole *mishbuka*! Where do we sit?"

Mr. Unger reached him first, pumped his hand as his sons watched leering and scowling, and asked them to take their seats in the rear. Immediately Uncle Arnold took offense. His eyes bulged with indignation. He looked around with hands spread, his cuff links glinting. My father tried to calm him down while his sons stirred ominously, and Dennis, otherwise known as Louie, stepped up to Arnold coolly, gave Mr. Unger a savage smile, and leaning into his father's ear whispered something; at the same time his hand moved subtly near his breast pocket, which slightly bulged.

"Get your face out of here, ya piece of shit!" Arnold rumbled, and Dennis stepped back.

"For the love a Mike, Sam, sit where they ask . . . ," my father pleaded, and turning with a big finger aimed like a gun barrel in the general direction of my cousins, he growled: "And I don't wanna hear no lip outta you wise guys, you hear! Keep your noses clean or else," to which they responded with jeers and snickers. Aunt Ray was up front, her lifted hand displayed against the Ark of the Covenant, showing off her rock-sized diamond ring to my mother, brother, and anyone else who was interested.

Finally, everyone was in their seats. A few of my cousins had drifted out; their voices could be heard by the front steps raised in jeering and vicious complaint. The rabbi, a short, humpbacked old man in a rumpled blue suit, stood on his feet with great difficulty but his voice rang sharp and clear as a bell. He thanked God that with so many assembled guests of the two Bar Mitzvahs, there was, for the first time in a long while, a *minyan* in the shul, and this, he said, looking all the way to the back of the room and directly at Uncle Arnold, this is a great *mitzvah*, he said. For if it is true that no Jew can pray without a *minyan*, it is also true that no *minyan* can pray without its Jews. Every Jew is that Jew who is needed to make a *minyan*. It does not matter what kind of Jew, any Jew is welcome! All the Jews here today are welcome. And what is a Jew, asked the rabbi, intertwining his withered fingers and resting them upon the podium. What is a Jew? Is a Jew someone what is born to Jewish parents? I say no! It is not enough. A Jew is one born to Jewish parents who calls himself a Jew! And is such a one then automatically a Jew? Again, I say no. He is a Jew because he has chosen to practice his Jewish faith. Our two Bar Mitzvahs, with the help of their wonderful parents, have made their choice today. . . . And so on.

I felt quite proud. And also quite warm; so much so that I began to squirm. At first I thought it was my nerves, but then I noticed that others similarly had flushed faces beaded with perspiration, and as we stood and prayed and sat and listened and prayed and stood up-down, up-down, and the Torah was removed from the cabinet, hefted on the shoulder of one of the congregants, and borne around the room for us to press the fringes of our prayer shawls to and kiss, it seemed to grow hotter and hotter in the little shul, until people were openly mopping their brows with handkerchiefs and wrestling loose the knots of their ties. Several times the rabbi halted the ceremony to ask if maybe a little window couldn't be opened a *bistle* to let in some air, and then me and Howie were called up to read and I felt a little faint as I read, the letters seeming to spread at their edges and melt into each other, and when I picked up my face, sweat dropped from my nose and splashed onto the opened scroll, and Mr. Unger muttered: "*Katzenkopf!* Be careful you don't make dirty the Holy Torah!" dabbing irritably at the stained parchment with the edge of his prayer shawl, and then it was Howard's turn and as he read I swayed, not with holy spirit but in a kind of near-faint, and in the meantime I saw my father glancing at the entrance with a puzzled and angry look and utter loudly: "What the hell are those crumbs up to in dere?" and he could finally contain himself no longer and haftorah or no haftorah, months of hard work or no months of hard work, and regardless of the fact that this moment would occur but once in our lives, he stood up and rushed out, and in truth who could blame him? Were I not assigned by my faith to stand there at that moment pouring sweat before the Ark of the Covenant, on the threshold of assuming manly responsibilities for my Jewish faith, I would have charged out to join him.

Seconds later his voice cried out: "You goddamned dummies! What the hell are you doing in here!? Turn that off! Are you nuts?" and I heard him coughing and gagging. Now I did go, leaving my brother in mid-sentence, and was met at the entrance with a blast of heat and gas smell emanating from the kitchen. My cousins stood about on the steps laughing nervously. Now Arnold came out. They had turned up the stove to maximum heat, left the door of the oven open, and when it was hot enough in the shul to bake a chicken on the altar, they turned off the stove and turned on the gas jets, their intention to either bake and gas us all to death or else blow the whole shul to smithereens. For a moment I caught their faces in profile against the dead winter trees and cheerless gray Bronx sky, their long, lean, snarling, scarred, handsome faces sporting real and affected nervous tics; some had Ray's blue eyes, others took after Arnold with brown eyes, but all their eyes were hard, staring, opaque disks of meanness under their felt stingy brim fedoras and sharkskin suits with narrow ties, waiting defiantly for consequences of the bad kind to befall them, almost with a sense of gleeful disdain. And then Arnold was upon them with fury, chanting in a slow, steady, quiet voice of contentment: "Son . . . of . . . a bitch . . . son . . . of . . . a . . . bitch . . . ," his big, stiff, close-fingered hand hard-slapping every-where and his sons scrambling over each other to escape, regrouping on the icy pavement where they stood with offended yet gentled eyes, not really mad, some even smiling in an odd sort of maniacal way, holding their cheeks, a few of which bore the visible imprint of his hand. Astonished, I returned to the shul to rejoin the ceremony.

My father was right: No one came. Not one of my schoolmates or any other relatives. I barely heard the rabbi's loud *"Ma-zel-tov!"* or paid attention to the short speech he made. As the elder twin by four minutes I was asked to speak a few words about what it meant to be a Jew. My lower lip twisted with fierce deliberation. I looked out at the small room of scuffed, aged wood, almost like milk crates with benches on them, and the old Jews bent in the pews, and my mother, tearful, in the front row, and my father standing with Arnold in the rear, heads bent together, whispering as they looked my way pretending to listen, and I looked at Howie beside me who couldn't wait for this to end so he could go as promised to Jahn's Ice Cream Parlor on Fordham Road for an ice cream pig dinner with Arnold and his family, and where we were promised by my father to be permitted to order each the kitchen-sink platter of twenty-eight assorted flavored scoops, and I said, even maybe meaning it a little, "I come from a poor family and so my pocket is empty. I got no checks to show for this day. But my heart is filled up with love for all of you. That's what it means to be Jewish."

"From your lips to God's ear!" cried Mr. Unger.

And the congregation said together: "A-men!"

SCARS

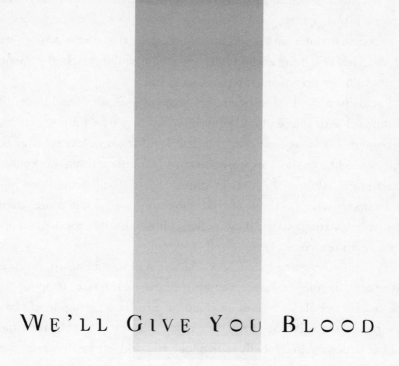

WE'LL GIVE YOU BLOOD

ON COLD FALL weekday afternoons after school, when sunlight-drenched buildings carved the sidewalks into shadows and gold, when the dying leaves blazed like canopies of rustling fire and the soft-voiced poet of the wind spoke of belonging to a great and beautiful plan designed in heaven, one was happy to walk along in the gift of the living city with its mighty skyline and cheerful sky wheeling overhead. Approaching the schoolyard was akin to drawing near to the thronging pedestrian main street of a great fair, where brightly colored shirts and hats weaved a shouting tapestry of play. The loud bounce of basketballs on tar clanged-clanged like broadswords.

In schoolyard games kids competed for their place in a great hierarchy; some of the heroes I knew from a distance. The broadest rungs of this pyramiding schoolyard aristocracy belonged to boys of average athletic prowess, boys neither ungenerous in disposition nor excessively coarse in manner, and it was into their games that one might hope to be chosen if one hung around long enough, if only for lack of someone better to make up a team.

I actually prayed *not* to be chosen, even as I stood around under the backboard with a look of groveling hope. To play was, for me, extremely painful. I was fat, soft, and winded. I didn't know the rules of the games and had so short an attention span that after a thousand hours of coaching by skilled and patient professionals, I still would not have understood what a three-second violation was. Half-court games pushed my stamina to the limit; getting chosen for full-court was a possible death sentence.

Typically in a game I would wheeze and huff up and down the court, asthmatic, flapping my arms, catching elbows in the face, tripping over the balletic tangle of bodies engaged in exhilarated struggle. If someone passed the ball to me I not only failed to catch it, but the rock-hard rubber struck me in the belly with a loud *ping* and left a painful red mark that I clutched at with my soft, pudgy hand. I tried to ignore the pain, fought back tears, and ran so hard downcourt in pursuit of the pack that I turned my ankle and sprawled facedown on the broken-glass-strewn cement, skinning my hands and my knees.

As I enacted this private, painful drama on the empty part of the court, my team, with one man short, suffered a reversal at the crowded end. They passed my way thundering like cavalry, flowing around and past as I stayed on one knee, emphatically waving a skinned hand to demonstrate the medical emergency that kept me glued to the spot. Finally, a time-out was called and one of the boys yelled in a cold, skeptical voice: "What's going on there, Alan?"

"I hurt myself," I called back in the high, timid voice of a badly injured little boy of no possible consequence.

"So, you're in or out?"

And, huffing to my feet, I said: "I'm out! Sorry! I'm hurt," and limped off, to the utter disgust of the other boys.

I quickly gained the reputation of a soft, unreliable little quitter. To be poor at a game was unfortunate, but to show no heart was despicable. I had no heart whatsoever.

I was content to sit out games by the fence, watching the heavily muscled horde sweep past, back and forth, as the orange sun sank low over the roofs. At dusk I returned home with a sense of failure, injured, and cursing my fat body and cowardly soul. But each afternoon I returned. There was nowhere else to go.

Often, between games, as teams warmed up, I took my turn; snuck onto the court to try a few ungainly shots. My fatty chest flopped and belly wobbled. I tried to jump and shoot at the same time like the other boys. I tried to dribble. The boys snickered. Some openly laughed. I had learned to accept derision without responding, afraid of escalation or retaliation. The world was divided into killers and victims. Nazis and Jews. Tough boys and sissies. I knew my place. I was the sissy son of a Holocaust survivor, a born victim.

In my mind there was no difference between a victim and a survivor. Both had suffered ultimate forms of degradation. Only chance kept one alive, killed another. I was the child of one who had been ultimately degraded by an unstoppable display of strength, of brute force and a willingness to use it. This essential fact haunted me, for I had neither force nor a willingness to use it.

The other boys had hard, sinewy muscles; I had soft, white-skinned baby fat. The other boys wore the accepted uniforms of schoolyard aristocracy, including Converse sneakers, Levi jeans, nylon football jerseys, and reversed golf caps; I wore bargain-basement polyester *shmatas* that no self-respecting Bronx boy would agree to wear. They wore their hair slightly long; I had a buzz-saw flattop crew cut. They could rattle off the names of baseball players and batting averages; I knew the name of the Marvel comic-book Nazi supervillain responsible for the death of Captain America's sidekick, Bucky: it was the Red Skull.

But of all the things that separated me from the others, attitude was the greatest problem. I didn't really want to play sports—only to be accepted, liked, and to become so proficient at sports that my father might feel love for me, even respect me as an individual. Sports was the only thing that American boys appeared to respect, so I played them. But I hated the pain. At heart I was a bookworm with a head full of fantasies, plundering books, novels mainly, to gain a sense of life's possibilities and escape the lack of options around me.

In a physical contest, I didn't care if my team won or lost. I lacked all competitive instinct and had a sense of self-worth so meager that it didn't matter to me which team I played on, considering myself equally useless to either side. Most of all, I feared the suppressed anger seething just below the surface of play that occasionally erupted in an outburst of words, fists, dagger-sharp elbows, slamming torsos, and the knocked heads of a brawl.

Over disputes in games I had seen boys cracked across their skulls and fallen to their knees, faces painted with blood. I saw tripped boys hit the ground and roll in agony, clutching exposed knee joints and writhing with shattered cartilage. I saw boys pound each others' faces with bare-knuckled fists over some controversy about rules, and one leave the other behind on the ground comatose, even near death, head smashed by a baseball bat. I saw ambulances come, police. I saw knives pulled, a gun. One boy fell from a roof, another was run over by a waiting car in an act of vengeance. Violence was the rule of thumb around the schoolyard, the games repressive substitutes for murder; balletic forms of symbolic homicide, and I had neither the grace nor the attitude to successfully, if only symbolically, slaughter an opponent. Even the terms used to describe the besting of another stank of the charnel house and the abattoir: an opponent was *slaughtered* or *butchered*, in a game of one on one; the loser got *killed* or *smashed* or *destroyed*.

The great sports slayer of the schoolyard was George Auria. It intrigued me that this boy was pointed out to me by several of the best students in the school as its great scholar. Yet in the schoolyard he was adored as Prince Brutus Derocko, in homage to his uncanny athletic prowess and his sheer gift for malevolent mischief and brutal indifference to bodily injury, his own or another's. In school he dressed like a law student in pinstriped shirt, paisley tie, corduroys, and Clarks, his thick neck stretching the seams of his collar. He walked on the balls of his feet like a Native American pathfinder. His powerful hands, hanging leisurely at his sides, seemed to radiate a ready capability, his thick arms aching for a football to carry, a hardball to pitch, a basketball to shoot. He was a natural, everyone said, as great as Jim Thorpe.

On one of my weekly excursions to the Grand Concourse library, where I had by now acquired a big beige square-shaped lending card with my name and address typed in next to the word BORROWER, I found a book on Thorpe, who was described as the best all-around athlete of the century. The resemblance of Auria's legs to Thorpe's kept me spellbound in the aisle for a good quarter hour, my jaw slack and shoulder pressed into a shelf as I eagerly ingested the surprisingly slender, shapely legs with slightly convex thighs and roundly swelling calves; legs that could run like deer downfield in a football game, pick their way with high-speed panicked grace over tumbling bodies, slant off vicious blocks into sudden portals of daylight, glide effortlessly, with not a single soul behind, into the endzone.

To be George Auria was to always compete at a remove on the field, court, or diamond; in the breakaway moment to reveal God-given gifts solo; to be like a commandment, your decisive prowess a prophesy. Even those with whom he clashed seemed, in the instant, to pause in homage to his genuflecting body's violent prayer.

At the time we first met, his already accumulated scores from all the sports he played, if manifested as food, would have fed the earth's population several times over, every day, for a hundred years. To cap his perfection, he wore gold-rimmed wire-frame spectacles, like Mark Steinberg, that favored son in my homeroom who, besides earning high grades and captaining the school's punchball team, also on occasion encroached upon my coveted title as the best writer in the class by turning out a gifted composition, for which I hated him. Meeting George gave me perspective. For what was a Mark Steinberg beside a George Auria? A fake. An over-privileged posturing little dwarf! George Auria lived up to his title of Prince. He had the natural dignity and savage modesty of an unpresuming mountain lion. I had sought for, but failed to find, an American image in which to remake myself—a mentor whom I could admire. Now I had one. And this messiah of American boyhood bore the same name as my father: George! If he was born for my veneration, I was born to found the religion for his worship.

Yet, it was he who made the first approach. It took place on a basketball court as I huffed around dribbling the ball of an older kid who sat in a corner of the yard observing me through eyes slit like a wildcat's, as though pondering whether or not to have me for his lunch.

I was on the lookout for danger greater than his as I played, glancing back over my shoulder at the schoolyard gate for Danny Dougherty or Brian Moran or Big Gus or Larry Speaks or, worst of all, Butch Brunet—psychotic and violent men with criminal records who haunted the yard and who were capable on any given day—on whim alone—of taking a life. Also I scouted for some of the lesser predators who might come along to make life hell for me, like Billy the Barrel, who from time to time ordered me to stand in a shadowy corner and hold his balls, whereupon I'd place my hand over his fly and wait, cheeks burning with shame, for the words that would set me free: "Awright—get the fuck outta here. And you a say a word a this to anyone, I'll blow your fuckin' father's brains out in the bed where he fucks your mother. . . ." Which I believed. People were shot in the Bronx all the time.

The coast now seemed clear enough to enable me to attempt, pathetically, to execute some of the difficult moves that I saw performed so easily everyday, like jump shot and "snatching" a rebound. But even dribbling was difficult for me. I bent to the ball, slapped it down, chased it as though it were a chicken, but regardless: it wouldn't submit to my control or move in the direction I intended, making it impossible to travel on the court. My only viable play move was to get the ball and quickly pass it off, before I was called for a traveling violation or had it stolen by a defender, and of course I dared not shoot. Then, suddenly, there he was, adjusting his wire frames with a casual gesture that filled me with envy.

I was pretty shocked to find myself standing face to face with him. He had penetrating eyes and angry red boil-sized pimples on his face and neck. He wore black sneakers inscribed with white stars and the word CONVERSE. His jeans were faded and the Levis tag had shrunk to a small, wrinkled red spot. It was so cool! Draped from his powerful shoulders was a purple nylon football jersey emblazoned with a big white number 88 and the words STUYVESANT HIGH SCHOOL—it must have belonged to his older brother, Mike, who was starting freshman quarterback for the school. Wrapped around his wrist, a red calico bandanna held it firm against sprains. From his back pocket a crushed all-weather golf hat hung out.

"You're in Mrs. Shwartz's class," he said.

"Yes," I said, brain racing furiously.

"I'm George Auria," he said, "and your name is Alan, isn't it?"

"Yes," I said, surprised.

"You're new in the neighborhood? Just moved in?"

"No. I been here a few years."

He smiled. "Well," he said, rubbing his hand over his chin and mouth in a sagacious manner that reminded me of an old prospector in a film about the Gold Rush. "That's pretty new."

The observation stung my feelings. I resented the lingering suggestion—after what seemed to me more then sufficient probation—that I was still a newcomer, still an outsider. I could tell that he caught the ill-concealed hurt in my eyes, a flash of resentment, that he added to the score of a measure he was taking.

He continued. "You seem interested in learning to play basketball. Would you like me to show you how?"

At this my pride flared, surprising even to me, and I issued a complete lie that I could tell failed to fool George. "My father showed me already."

Again the old prospector's thoughtful stroking of chin, and he chuckled. "Well," eyelids fluttering with the delicacy of the observation he was about to make, "that may be so but it don't seem to have done you a lot of good."

"No," I said with a sigh of relief. "No. You're right. I stink. It's hard to learn. I'm too fat and slow."

He laughed. "Well, lose it."

"But how?"

"Run. Play a lot of ball. You'll lose it. You'll see."

"Ya think?"

"Sure. Here. Let me show you a few moves."

"OK."

We tossed the ball back to the slitty-eyed wildcat, who slinked off, and used the ball that George brought: a brand new Wilson.

He must have sunk a good three hours into the demonstration, his patience was monumental. He drilled me over and over until I understood the basketball basics and made me repeat them a hundred times: pass, catch, dribble, shoot, rebound, layup, defend, press, steal, block, over and over, my face pouring perspiration, heart pounding, legs and arms quaking with fatigue, and still one more time and again . . . but when it was over I had made my basic start as an athlete and the effect on my spirits was dizzying. I'm sure I walked straighter, and some of the cloudiness was now gone from my eyes. With a gaze cleared momentarily of shame, I could bear to look at George as he spoke to me, didn't turn away every other second and gape down at my sneakers, nodding my head like a disciplined flunky. My lungs burned, my breath wheezed, but I had hope. My presence in the schoolyard on a beautiful autumn day made sudden, tremendous sense: I belonged, this was my schoolyard as much as anyone's, I had every right to be here. Having George there helped, of course: nobody dared fuck with us. By myself, I was nothing, but his friendship meant status. We parted with a handshake.

"Well," he said, chuckling modestly at my effusive gratitude. "Heh-heh. It's probably gonna be a while before you learn it well, but you got the hang of it. Well, take care. See ya around," and carrying the ball, he took off with that slightly pigeon-toed walk on the balls of his feet, one capable hand swinging freely as he went.

The next day I couldn't wait for school to end. Instead of going straight to the schoolyard and hanging around under the backboards dressed in my pathetic school clothes, I rushed home to assemble from the poor materials at hand a costume suitable for an initiate of the George Auria Church of Perfect Being.

I rolled the cuffs of my fat-boy Lee Wranglers and cut out numbers from an old piece of cloth and sewed them to a sweater that my mother assured me was ready for the trash. I even cut off the tops of my high-top sneakers to make them low cuts, like George's, for which my mother gave me several slaps and shrieked about what an idiot I was, didn't I know how expensive those sneakers were, my poor father, how hard he worked to afford those things!! (In the meantime, kid-glove Italian loafers at eighty to a hundred bucks a pair continued to fill up his shoe rack in the closet.) I stole and wrapped one of my father's embossed silken handkerchiefs around my wrist. For a hat there was nothing to do but hope and pray that I could afford to own one someday. I no longer worked at a stationery shop now that Captain America, Spider-Man, The Fantastic Four, Doctor Strange, Green Lantern, Hawkman, Daredevil, Thor, Conan, and my entire comic book collection had gone to the ovens when my mother had tossed them into the incinerator. "Where are you running like a crazy *meshugener?*" she called as I charged out the door. "Don't forget to do your homework!" But homework was the last thing on my mind now: under the backboards, the look in my eye grew less evasive, more direct. I now desired to be chosen into games.

My game had not improved that much, but my attitude had changed. I now cared whether or not the side I played for won. I remembered the names of my team members. I huffed up and down court without falling, and if I was yet unable to do more than hop up and down flapping my arms and shouting "Here! here!" for a chance at a shot, which no one gave me, at least I did so on the side of the court where actual play occured.

Still, all too often I was made aware of what a long, painful road I faced, like when Butch Brunet suddenly appeared, forced me to follow him into a building, lined me up against the mailboxes, and drove his fists into my gut. I knew that more hard times than good times lay ahead for me when Danny Dougherty and Brian Moran flanked me at the Four Doors, a school exit on whose stoop the bad kids often hung around.

Moran was a cold-eyed killer who spoke in a raspy voice barely raised above a whisper: "Do you have ten cents for me, Alan?" he asked, scanning the roofline reflectively.

"No, Brian. I'm really sorry. My mom's got broke again and can't gimme no money."

He cupped his hand to his ear. "Did I hear you say no?"

"No. I mean, yes. I'm busted."

"Do you know what is going to happen to you?"

"No," I lied.

"Danny, tell Alan what is going to happen to him . . ." And just at that moment a squad car's siren whooped. Two patrolmen got out with a great slamming of doors and hands resting on pistols. They sauntered over.

"All right, what the hell is going on over here? Moran, you looking to get sent up again, aren't you? And you, Dougherty, I told you I don't want to see your mug around here." He looked at me. "These two animals bustin' your chops?"

I looked at Moran, then Dougherty. "No," I said. "They were just talking sports with me."

Moran smiled at that.

"Yeah, like the kid said. Sports we were talking here. Football!" and Dougherty laughed. "Hike! Hike!"

The patrolman warned them, returned to the car, and drove off.

"I like that: talkin' sports," said Moran.

"If I had money I'd give you some, Brian, but I swear to God I'm flat broke. No kidding."

He encircled my shoulder, his blue snake eyes and beer breath just an inch from my face. "You know . . ." he said, turning suddenly to Dougherty, whose face seemed abstracted, planning some crime. (Their talent was to make the simplest act seem larcenous. Just standing there thinking was, in Dougherty's case, a felony. His smiles were homicides.) "I like this kid. I mean it. I like what he just did. Serious . . ." He turned back to me. "You done me a good turn. I don't forget. . . ."

He was vain enough to think that I had acted either from loyalty or from a personal code against squealing, when really I only feared his retaliation in the event that I got him into trouble. As for not forgetting favors, the very next week he was back, scanning the roofline with sky-blue snake eyes, wistful, murderous, shoulders slumped, an air of sadness about him as he cleaned the dirt beneath his fingernails with the seven-inch-long blade of a folding knife.

One day I received a nickname, a sort of pregame initiation before my first football game. I had hung around so long and faithfully that eventually I was noticed. The community of the schoolyard was alerted to my presence. It was almost by collective decision that I received the name, though the one I got was decided by Tommy Dedorian, a stuttering mountain-sized Greek with a rich crop of curly black hair and shiny olive skin bursting with greasy pimples. In the schoolyard he was known alternately as Da-Da-Da Dorian for his speech defect, or more simply the Fat Greek. Usually he traveled in an entourage of several cronies, including two identical twins, cousins, all inveterate gamblers who spent their days and nights at the racetrack, losing big. They were all in debt to one loan shark or another. To raise funds they scalped tickets at sporting events, shot pool, dealt drugs, pimped whores, or fenced hot jewelry. Sometimes they committed burglaries. They were all wonderful football players, too. Autumn in particular was a fine time when they turned out in a big happy mob, decked out in brand-new sporting goods, sneakers as white as vanilla cupcakes, shiny new jerseys in bright colors and still creased from the packaging, jeans that hadn't yet seen their first wash. They wore lots of gold chain jewelry, particularly Tommy, who jingled like a belly dancer when he walked. Then there was Bernie Shuman, who had only one testicle; Come-Down Dorkis; Connie O'Conner; and Bobby "The Face," who was given the name in honor of his incredible ugliness. Mike Auria also appeared, smaller than George, wiry, more springy, his sharp-featured

face keen and sensitive, wearing a Stuyvesant High School off-season
football team gym shirt with reversible sides that I would have sold my
mother into slavery to own.

The sun was sinking over the roofs, and a soft chill was in the air. No
wind. Shirtsleeve weather. Dry ground conditions. One by one the
streetlights arching overhead blinked on, and their radiance flooded
the whole schoolyard. Better playing conditions did not exist at Yankee
Stadium, except for the broken, glass-strewn cement. Along the fence,
men began to gather. Here and there they stood around talking, and I
saw money changing hands. Tommy Da-Da-Da Dorian was the big
center of attention, a kind of organizing emcee of the coming event,
the nature of which I hadn't the slightest idea. With a lump of regret in
my throat, I tried to leave. It was time to go home, late: supper already
being set out on the table.

"Hey, you!" said Tommy as I started to leave. "Where ya going?"

"Gotta go home," I said. "Time to eat."

The group of boys around him laughed. "'Time to eat,' he says. Hey,
kid: What's your name?"

"Alan."

"Hey, Alan, you know what's the Greek word for *cunt*?"

I stiffened, alert to the possibility of violence, looked around for
George. What did I think he'd do? But at least he was a possible ally, a
known quantity and had shown kindness. Tommy uttered a word that
sounded like "Moony." "Hey!" he called to the boys standing around.
"From now on this kid's name is Moony! I see anybody call him Alan,
I'll personally kick his ass! He tried to g-g-get out of a g-g-game with
Tommy Da-Da-Da Dorian. He's a cunt, and cunt will be his name in
Greek! Moony, get over here. You stay and you play football until I tell
you otherwise."

I started to protest. Not to be home for supper was unthinkable. I
was being forced against my will into a life of crime. "I can't," I repeated in a flat, low voice.

"You *can't*! What do you mean you *can't*? You mean you *will*! Or else I
will kick your *ass*!"

I saw George standing near. "It'll be all right," he said. "You should play. It's what you've been looking for."

"But I can't play! I'm no good!"

"You gotta start someplace," he said.

I nodded, close to tears on a night certain to hold much suffering for me, no matter which way I turned.

The school building loomed medieval in the gloomy gathering dusk, the boys milling about before the choose-up began, wearing pregame airs of fatalistic solitude. The presence of Tommy and his gambling cronies assured that big cash stakes were on the line for some of the participants. Along the fence, gambling had stepped up, and the men, some of whose sons were among the players, waited with keen antici- pation, their fingers looped through the fence links, turning their heads to chat with one other from the sides of their mouths. It would have thrilled me to discover my father among them.

I saw George and Mike stroll over to a stocky, balding man with a pug face who rubbed his big grizzled chin the way George did, and knew that he must be the father. He clapped George on the back, grabbed his arm and shook it with tender gruffness, and then laughed a low *"Haw Haw! Haw!"* that carried all the way to me. Mr. Auria had quite a pair of lungs. I thought I could hear him talking, carrying on really, at the level of a shout, while George and Mike glanced around in sheep- ish embarrassment. But clearly he was proud of his boys.

The choose-up was about to begin. Referees were picked from among the spectators. It was hard to know if they were impartial observers or ringers planted by the Fat Greek. I scanned the fence for signs of my father and mother: all clear. But with a sinking heart I knew that every passing second brought them closer to a furious appearance. By now I looked forward to playing and to hell with the consequences. I would not even mind injury, would court it even, if that came. George was right: this was a chance. It felt right.

The cloud-heavy night sky, tinged fiery red with the last light of the sun, looked leaden and portentous. I was a new recruit on the threshold of his first battle in a real war. The players looked as though they were cast from iron ore. George and Mike and a few others performed warm-up exercises; I tried to follow suit. The look in George's eyes had grown odd, distant. I did not yet know how to recognize the killer instinct of the born athlete. He had grown almost animal-like. His breath came in loud snorts. Great wads of phlegm were coughed up, spit. Clasping each others forearms, facing off, players slammed shoulders with loud grunts. A boy I recognized as Pat Pacello suddenly broke into a frantic run in place, then stopped, and then started again, his figure charcoal gray, leaden, strange. Players assumed three-point stances and snapped off the mark. A pigskin spiraled at bullet speed through the spotlit sky. A boy named Louis Morales zigged, cut left on a dime, then zagged back, went long, and near the opposite endzone leaped, snatched the ball one-handed out of thin air, and slammed into the wall, fell, and jumped to his feet without a pause. He trotted back on springing calves, like a high-powered gazelle.

Then Tommy Da-Da-Da Dorian and Mike Auria stood face to face with the referee between them, a tall potbellied man with a cigar and a fedora too small for his head. He tossed a coin in the air. Mike called "Heads!" It came up heads. He laughed and shouted: "George!" George stepped over to Mike's side and stood behind him.

"Fuckin' shit," Da-Da-Da Dorian grumbled, "two Aurias on the same side. I should get the next two chooses."

"Go ahead," laughed Mike.

"And you gotta take Moony," Da-Da-Da Dorian added.

Mike looked at me without enthusiasm. But to my amazement, he said: "OK, Moony," and he called to me: "Moony, come over. Stand with us." Astonished, I joined them.

"Gee," I said to George, "I'm sorry you had to take me. I promise I'll do good!" But George didn't answer. He was breathing hard. He stared through me and looked away. Then suddenly, he murmured: "Oh, shit. Look who just walked in." A big man with powerful arms and thighs and a neck like a fire hydrant lumbered into the schoolyard. Tommy the

Greek shouted: "Doobis! Get over here! You're with us!" Then he said to the ref: "I'll also take Schuman. And they can have Pacello." He looked at Mike Auria. "So? You want Pacello?"

"Of course," laughed Mike. "Hey, Tommy, you fat tub! Why don't you just gimme Morales, take whatever else you want, and we'll make our teams. I wanta get outta here sometime before tomorrow." Da-Da-Da Dorian glared at Mike Auria: "You watch your language, OK?! I'll tub your mother's ass on Delancey Street, you talk that way to me!"

And George chuckled stiffly, "Heh, heh!" and rubbed his chin with a pained smile.

"Hey Tommy!" called Mike. "I hear your mother gives head to off-duty bulls behind the stationhouse on Kingsbridge Road with a loaded gun shoved up her ass," and George chuckled, "Heh, heh," and rubbed his jaw, the pain in his eyes gone crazy, but the other players waited motionless, and up and down the schoolyard fence the gathered men listened quietly, four heads deep on the sidewalk, shoulder to shoulder, taking measure of the team captains, their spirits, and Tommy—more to please the crowd than genuinely stung by Mike's remarks—lifted his fist, sprung his middle finger free like a switchblade knife, and jabbed it in Mike's direction as he spoke in a low, glowering voice: "OK, motherfucker. You wanta play like that, we'll play like that. I thought this be a nice game maybe for fun, maybe make a little money, but you want blood, we'll give you blood." Then, suddenly, his great arms exploded skyward and he did a kind of war dance step and shouted to the roofs, which listened closely: "You want a blood game, you got a blood game!" And his team shouted, "Tom-my! Tom-my!" and "Yeah! Yeah!" and the men along the fence called out: "Kick their fuckin' asses! Kill the motherfuckers!" and it must have been close to seven o'clock, my family gathered around the supper table talking angrily about my absence, the punishment in store for me, while I trotted with my team to our end of the field and with them kept a dignified silence before the jeers, threats, and epithets hurled at our faces.

Pat Pacello called a huddle. We stood in a circle, heads bowed to Pat, who hid in the center on one knee. My team members were quiet, breathing steadily, and I recognized that each and every one of them was in a cold rage.

"Well," Pat said, looking all around at our faces. "Is it Louie? Or what?" And no one spoke to allow Louie to say what was in everyone's hearts. Louie said simply: "The Bomb." Then Pat looked at me. "Moony. You go on the line and the first person you see, run up and throw yourself down in front of their legs. Do you understand? Throw yourself on the ground in front of their legs." He glanced at Mike and said: "It *might* work." Mike grimaced doubtfully but held his peace. "On three," said Pacello, and the huddle shouted "Break!" and clapped once in unison.

We lined up. I looked at the man before me: the giant, Doobis. Heart pounding, I squeezed my eyes closed and prayed. "Please, God, please help me do this, please." For my own personal safety I had no thought at all. We could have been on the brink of plunging as a group over a cliff and I would have gladly followed. I simply could not believe my good fortune to be among such heroes. "Please, God," I whispered, "please."

I heard, "Twenty-three . . . sixteen . . . three . . . ," and all around me bodies rumbled into motion. I charged as fast as my fat legs would go, straight at Doobis, and just before his bone-crunching rush I fell to the ground, arms covering my head. It seemed as though he must have simply leaped over me, that's what I thought, because as I fell I looked up and saw what seemed to be Doobis outlined by the night sky in a graceful leap, and then I heard Pacello calling, "Go! Go! Go! Louie! Catch it! Catch it, motherfucker, yes!!" and then he was jumping up and down, squealing "Mora-les! Mora-les!" and downfield in the end zone I saw Louie Morales flip the ball casually to the outrun defender, who received it with mingled astonishment and anger. And then Pacello ran up to me, offered me a hand, pulled me to my feet, and shouted, "Did you fucking see Moony cut down Doobis?!" and noticed that Doobis also watched all this unfold but from the ground, and hands clapped my back: "Nice play! Good block!"

I suppressed the loud *"Aw-right!"* that wanted to erupted from me, the urge to jump up and down shouting "Yeah! Yeah! Awright! Awright!" for it was the first time in my life that I had truly tasted victory. Instead, comporting myself with solemn pride, I returned to the huddle.

I sought out George's eyes, but he didn't meet my look, absorbed in something far away.

"Nice work," Pacello said to everyone gleefully. He looked at George. "George!"

George grunted: "Yeah?"

"Me and you, end sweep, left. Take 'em out."

George nodded grimly.

"Moony," said Pat. "Just try to knock into Doobis, that's all, just knock into him. On two. Break!"

We lined up. Doobis stood above me, legs poised to charge, big hairy paws with taped fingers swinging expectantly. I got down into something like a three-point stance. Heard: "Chicago! Eight! Green Bay, Two!" Something heavy like a baseball bat smacked the back of my head and I fell to my knees, stunned; and then a colossal knee into my head smashed my nose and blood spurted down my shirt front. It was as though I were locked into the gears of a machine gone out of control, battering my head again and again. Then I was free of it, staggered to my feet gasping "Uh! Uh!" blood all over my hands, barely able to see through my tearing eyes. I thought I could make out a mass of bodies that seemed to be moving downfield in slow motion, with George Auria at the center and Pat Pacello just behind him with the ball in one hand and the other hand resting on George's shoulder, and then George's head vanished and several bodies seemed to tumble down together, including Pacello, and a gain of about twenty yards had been made.

"Abe!" my father's voice startled from behind.

I looked around. There he was, glaring, a cigar in his mouth, hands pocketed, his shirtsleeves rolled.

"Get over here! Now!"

"But Pop!" I pleaded.

"I said get over here now!"

"No!" I said. "I can't! The game! We're winning!" He made a motion as though starting forward to attack me, then stopped and said: "Mistah! I come in there to get you, you'll wish you wuz nevah been born! Now, get over here!"

"OK," I said sadly. "OK, wait." I went over to Pat Pacello, who was trotting back with George. "Pat! Pat! I gotta go," I said, ashamed. "My father, he's over there." I pointed.

Pat saw, nodded, put his arm around me. "Don't worry about it. I saw Earl. We'll put in Earl. Nice job!" George seemed to see me for the first time. "Nice job," he said, and smiled.

Mike Auria drifted over. "What's a problem?"

"Moony's gotta go," said Pat. "His father wants him home."

"So what?" said Mike. "Why don't he stay and watch his boy play? He should cheer him on!"

His words stunned me. To hear the words of my heart from another's lips.

"Abe!" my father called in a gruff, warning voice.

Mike seemed to understand my whole life in an instant. "Yeah," he mumbled, "Sure," then looked at my father and shouted, "Awright! Pipe down! He's comin'!" and said, "Nice job, Moony. Uh, Alan. You wanna be called Alan?"

"No," I grinned. "Call me Moony. I'm gonna make that into a name I'll be proud of." It was a response worthy of my poor cremated comic book superheroes. And as I trotted off, "Hey! Hey! Moony! Where you goin'?" roared Da-Da-Da Dorian. "Whatsamattah, little cunt. Scat-tah! Had enough? Scattah!"

"Nice friends you hang around with," my father said, marching off in a hurry to leave the place. "They got big mouths, your friends. I'd ough-ta go in there and shut a few of them up. Next time, I will!"

Naturally, at home I was hit, despite my explanations and the blood all over me. As he shoved me over the sink to soap my face, she struck my arm with a wire hanger. I gagged on my sobs and gasped for air. The pain was all over, I didn't know where to go. When it was done I was forced to sit down to a dinner of noodles and beef and to finish off the whole plate. It went down my throat like a dirty mop. I was then sent to bed, barred from watching my favorite show, *Car 54*. But I didn't care. I lay with covers to my shoulder, thinking of the team down there clashing heroically with the dark forces of Tommy Da-Da-Da Dorian, praying that my side, *my* side, would win. It felt so good to belong to a side that believed in me and that I could believe in. I remembered our quiet dignity as the other team jeered, the businesslike way we went about our touchdown without responding with loud words or insults. It was so much more powerful to respond with successful acts than loud threats.

Naturally, the next day I was unprepared for school, had done no homework, and my thoughts were far away, on George Auria, on what Mike Auria had said, on the way it felt to send Doobis flying against the starry sky. It was a clear act of violence, but no one had been harmed; I hardly felt my fall to the ground, nor, from the expression on his face, had he felt his. Only his pride had been hurt, while mine had just been born.

EYES

SHE HAD EYES as nurturing as Bambi's mother, and long brown hair that hung down to the small of her back, worn loose. No ribbons or clasps. Sometimes, though, she wore it pushed back with a flower-ornamented braid comb. Her small, slender, triangular face with a pert, perfect nose and full-bodied, moistly parted lips brought to mind Susan Richards, the Invisible Girl of Marvel Comics fame and the pretty, petite blonde wife of Reed Richards, the elongated man and leader of the Fantastic Four, which was my favorite comic book in seventh grade.

With no trouble at all I could envision Miss Stein in cobalt-blue tights adorned with a number 4 in a white circle, hands out-flung and eyes wild, expelled from the impact of an exploding fireball hurled by her angry rebel brother, The Human Torch.

Miss Stein was the first female whose physical charms combined with something other then my masturbatory fantasies to produce an effect in me. She had brains. She had a soul that had been touched by my compositions. Her soft brown eyes shone with belief in me. Her slender figure with hydraulic breasts moved in a paisley minidress that hugged her like a sheath as she lectured on *The Snows of Kilimanjaro*, a short story by Ernest Hemingway, her favorite writer. Immediately he became mine. She was from Michigan, Hemingway's home state, come all the way to the Bronx to lead me on the path to literary fame.

As she lectured she held the chalk pinched between thumb and fore-finger, with her pinky slightly raised above and away, as though chalk contained potent and soiling ingredients that she must avoid too much contact with. That is how I imagined she would hold a penis. Words flowed pink across the green blackboard. The pink chalk was her own brought from home, wherever that was. Manhattan, probably. And a gold ankle bracelet on her leg. She had someone. This sent a certain electrifyingly illicit charge surging through the exchanges of our eyes. I did not look anyone else in the eyes at that time, couldn't have. Feared to. To look into the eyes of a schoolyard thug brought instant pain. To look into the eyes of my twin brother, Howard, was to see his disdain for me. To look into the eyes of my mother was to see the hunted little Jewish girl clinging to her life in Hitler's European kingdom of death, and the madness it had left in her produced my sheer hopelessness at receiving normal treatment at her hands. To look into my father's eyes was to see fear and defeat masquerading in the pool hall hustler, card shark gangster attitude that he affected. He played out his low self-esteem in the drafty bowels of the main post office on Thirty-third Street and Ninth Avenue, where he spent his waking life in night-shift work: mail-hauling undead ghoul of locker-room poker, french fry/scrambled egg platters at three in the morning in the Cheyenne Diner, Italian loafers in which his feet froze in winter, and pool games in the Penguin Billiards Parlor on Jerome Avenue. At this time of my life, looking into eyes was unprofitable, dangerous—on a subway or a bus, riding to school, I could be killed for looking into the wrong eyes.

A sudden, rage-contorted face, a violently brusque: "What you looking at, motherfucker!?" and "You lookin' at me, man, you lookin' at me?" by a knot of tattooed muscles in a white T-shirt with a stubby finger jabbing at its own slablike chest: "Lookin' at me, man? At me?" No, I wasn't looking at you. Please. I was too tall, clumsy, dirty, poorly dressed, penniless, friendless, and hopeless to look anyone in their eyes.

Only, when you looked away, I *did* look at you. Caught you as you were rising to leave or glaring at someone else, or absorbed in clothes on a rack. You wouldn't notice my staring, I had it down too well, so practiced in avoiding notice as I noticed you that I could anticipate the loci that your eyes would reach if your head moved, before it actually did, a feat of intuitive physics that I had developed to protect myself from any impression you might get that I was looking at you.

I was looking, but you didn't know. Except for Miss Stein. Miss Jean Stein. She knew. She welcomed my seventh-grade looks. Her brown eyes deepened, darkened, yielded, enveloped my looks and held me like warm arms or firm thighs and did not drive me away.

Sometimes my eyes lay down in her eyes like a puppy's head in its owner's lap. Made a place where I could rest. I wanted to cry there. I did, once or twice. Her eyes shone full of belief in me. Calmed my spirit. I grew older in her eyes, behaved like a gifted young gentleman.

If the shadow of disapproval ever crossed her eyes, I would stop my misbehavior instantly. In all other classes I earned either mediocre or else completely failing grades. In her class my lowest mark was 90, but more often it was 98. I received 98s from her in English and in composition. On report cards slashed bloody with red-ink minus signs and the words "Poor" and "Misbehavior" and "Disgrace" appeared her warm blue 98 beside the words "Brilliant writer!" and "Magnificently creative!"

In her eyes: the Michigan woods of Hemingway's youth. In her eyes: noble coming-of-age, honor, campfires, railroads, hobos, and the valiant disillusionment of soldiers at war. In her eyes, the gin-swarthy dangers of safari, in her eyes the dust and heart-stopping cheers of bullfights, in her eyes cold carafes of wine in a drafty garret, while writing great books and dressed in bulky sweaters of yarn unraveling like afternoons whiled away in cafés with others struggling to wrest glory from the world of literature.

When our eyes met I entered through her iris into a tiny, shimmering portal of light that became a room containing a desk on which lay a notebook, a quill pen, an ink pot. She sat me into the chair and instructed me to open the book, an immense book containing all the writings of the world since the beginnings of human civilization. The first available blank page faced the last handwritten entry of Ernest Hemingway's career. Leaning over my shoulder, her sugar-cinnamon-flavored breath on my cheeks, she whispered, "Now, begin. I will be with you always as you write," and, straightening up, she fanned her long hair over my head like a protective canopy and placed her small, warm, delicate hands on my shoulders. As I wrote I had a lovely erection which pulsed with anticipation of the relief that would be mine when I had set down all I had to say and earned her praise.

My manner, however, changed when I entered another teacher's classroom.

All through the day I would be focused on the bad smell rising from my unwashed ass, the sweat-and-soil reek of unlaundered polyester clothes. Universally known as "B.O., baby," all through the day I focused on the people-repelling smell, ashamed, laughing in loud flat-top crew cut, bulge-eyed guffaws: "Haw! Haw! Haw!" and with clown-red lips distended in jeering anguished disobedience. All day snorting, laughing disruptively, whispering and chattering ceaselessly, ashamed, so ashamed, and my fingertips sliding through my cuff to tunnel under my shirtsleeve and worry the oddly comforting, bizarrely fascinating wormlike meals of hanger marks left by my latest beating at home, and brain fatigued after a sleepless night up with my mother in the old, now-familiar routine that followed every one of her wire-hanger-wielding frenzies of temper; on the bed facing each other across an open valise filled with snapshots of all the relatives and friends whom she lost to the Nazi war, me searching in their sweet, friendly, happy, dignified, somber faces for a hint, a premonition of the grisly end awaiting them: nothing. And at three in the morning, while my mother's face grew red

with high blood pressure and tears as she pressed her lips to the snapshot of a dead loved one, the future opened before me like the jaws of
a horrible worm that grew into a tunnel black and yawning with unpre-
dictable outcomes, and I shivered, shot through with paralyzing fear.
How could one know where one's actions could lead? Maybe it was best
to keep perfectly still, forever, and anger no one.

But when I entered her class, exhausted, driven, out of control, I
regained my poise and the only real sanity that I knew in a day.
Suddenly my painful relations with my fellow students didn't really
matter so much; my mother was not a monster but only a sick woman
who had been through a terrible experience and didn't know any better; my life not a crapshoot in a neighborhood ruled by the savage code
of schoolyard gangs but a purposeful sojourn by a sensitive young
writer in a painfully struggling blue-collar world and from which my
emergence would someday be part of my glory, as Hemingway's beginnings in Michigan gave birth to his legend.

I didn't notice that I smelled. Neither did she. My pale blue polyester
shirt became the open-throated blouse of a Romantic poet. I felt handsome in her eyes. She circulated through the room with nimble steps,
like a young girl. I stared at the shadow-shaded gentle hollows of her
dimpled knees. My imagination raced. A euphoric chemical lit through
my brain like a fiery torch, setting me ablaze with a thousand profound
things to say as she handed out our graded compositions. She had them
hugged against her breast, as though she didn't want to part with them.
She pried them away, read the name on top, snapped them back against
her breast, went to the next student, pried them away, and handed one
down with a serious smile and a word or two of encouragement or con-
gratulations. Once or twice, though, her face clouded as she handed
down the paper, and the one she spoke to nodded with a look of genuine remorse. It was a venial sin to cause such a woman to give one a
low grade. One would have to be depraved in the extreme to disappoint this angel.

The longer it took to receive my composition, the better the grade I
knew I had received. Finally, everyone had theirs except me. She kept

it hugged tightly to her breast, spread her legs rather wide, and said: "Class! Class!" to calm our chatter. All faces turned to her. "Alan Kaufman has received the highest grade. A ninety-eight." They glanced my way respectfully, my aptitude for creative writing by now well known to everyone as the only saving grace in an otherwise disastrously floundering specimen of very early adolescence. "I want Alan to come to the front of the room to read it for us."

Heart pounding, amazingly able to exchange my typically shit-eating grin for a quiet smile of confidence, I shambled up to her and she said, "It really is wonderful. Did you know when you were writing it that you were imitating the flowery style of a nineteenth-century author? Was that a conscious, deliberate decision on your part to write like that?" This before the quiet, rapt audience of my fellow students: my very first author interview.

"Yeah, I guess," I said. "I been reading a lot of Alexander Dumas and Arthur Conan Doyle, so yeah, I guess I tried to write like them."

Her eyes grew lustrous. "You're a real writer," she said. "That's what a real writer will do. Copy other writers in order to learn how to develop his own style. It's something that we all can learn to help us develop our own styles. You read a lot, don't you. On your own, I mean?"

"Yeah," I shrugged. "Yeah, I guess. You know: Dumas, Hugo, Twain, Conan Doyle, James Jones, Norman Mailer, stuff like that, but my favorite writer is Ernest Hemingway!"

She smiled furtively, in secret understanding with me. "You have a lot in common with him. He was also tall like you." She handed me the composition to read aloud. "Do you mind?"

"No. Sure," and I began: "The boat bearing Sherlock Holmes to Hawaii passed through a fierce storm . . ." and so on, while the class listened with interest. I had them!

In fact, when I finished they applauded, and when the bell rang many crowded around to congratulate me, tell me what a great writer I was.

I watched them file out, until only Miss Stein and I remained. "See you, Miss Stein." I grinned, bleary-eyed, and yawned.

She rose from her desk, came over, and touched my forehead with cool, tight fingers. "Are you all right? You seem a little flushed, a little sunken-eyed, like you haven't slept much!"

My eyes averted hers, and I heard my voice say: "Nah, I'm OK. I just wanted to say thanks for the good grade."

"You really are a wonderful writer," she said. "I hope that you never give it up."

"Me?" I said fiercely. "Never! I'll be a writer till the day I die. I wanna win a Nobel Prize."

She didn't laugh. She said, "Are you still having trouble at home?"

I shook my head no. "You mean 'cause I look tired? I went to sleep late, that's all."

"Uh-huh," she said, in a distant, watchful tone of voice. Could tell that she wasn't having any of it. "Does your mother like your compositions?" she asked.

"Yeah! She's a French Jew. You know, we're Jewish. She was in the Holocaust. They read a lot of books in Europe. She speaks seven languages too, including English."

Miss Stein looked surprised and I thought a little disappointed by my closeness to European origins of mass murder, and suddenly I saw it—what I hadn't seen before—the gulf between us. And then I knew that it had always been there. She was an American through and through. I was a Jew. How would I ever be Ernest Hemingway?

But just as quickly as it yawned before us, the gulf closed, and we were on familiar ground again, me giving my impression of the Kilimanjaro story, she pressing me to read his other books on my own, particularly *The Sun Also Rises*. "You'll like that, I can tell," she said, as though to say: "I know all about what pleases you, how you feel inside, what excites or bores you; my recommendations come from my deep knowledge of who you are and my respect for that.

I promised to check it out of the library that afternoon. As I left, she called out: "Alan?"

"Yeah, Miss Stein?"

"Your mother had a bad time during the war?"

Surprised, I said in a small voice, "Yeah."

"OK! Thanks! Bye!" And though she never mentioned it again, I knew that she knew. And it was there, between us, contaminating my chance to be like her, a pure American, unbridled, Huckleberry Finn, ribald, innocent, punting my raft down the river of human error, triumph, and misdeed. The dark chariot I rode bore the heraldic emblem of humanity's betrayal of the Jewish people, the dirty secret of my disorder, a certain knowledge that as a Jew I was never safe for very long, could never really blend into a crowd. I was an object of hate, of mass annihilation; people of my stripe ended up, diploma or no diploma, Nobel Prize or no Nobel Prize, not running yachts out of Cuba but as a naked corpse pretzel-twisted on a trolley poised to be fed to the flames.

Still, I tried as hard as I knew how to make believe. I escaped into Ernest Hemingway. I could be a Hemingway as long as I kept my eyes fixed on the pages of his book, as long as I could imaginatively reconstruct his adventures in Paris, Spain, Africa. I could feel safe—my problems were of the self, not of jackbooted Nazis crashing through my garret's door to shave my head, dress me in striped pajamas, tattoo my arm, starve me, work me to the bone, beat me without stop, and shove me— in a walking coma—into a gas chamber, and toss my corpse into a furnace.

As Ernest Hemingway I had a head-bandaged battle wound; I had a pretty English nurse for a girlfriend; I wrote little stories that were admired in Paris, city of my mother's birth, betrayal, and expulsion; I drank a lot of wine—wine stained all my clothes, all my experiences, all my memories; I wore a beret and a World War I uniform; and I boxed. That would impress my father, the would-be boxer. I conquered literary Paris for my mother. My parents would have loved Ernest Hemingway.

It was Hem they should have had for a son. In my reveries I was Hemingway and it was lovely. I had good women lovers with boyish hips and short hair who called me "Poppa," and I had knowing friends who I took cold-stream fishing for trout and pike and who disparaged "kikes" as they baited their hooks and made me chuckle. And in his books men who were not kikes died as gallant soldiers in wars, yes; but he lived, he didn't die but re-created their experiences in steely prose and had great fun while doing it and making fun of "kikes." And though my guts churned with rage at his hatred of Jews, I lay on my bed with his books and a notebook and a pen. I read a few lines from *The Sun Also Rises* and words flooded into my mind, like blood from an opened vein, and I wrote them down. I overlooked the word *kike* or the fact that his hero despised a Jew named Robert Cohen. When my eyes saw the word *kike*, they closed and opened elsewhere on the page and read on. Then I read further and paused, inspired to copy down an interrupting flow of words. A new masterpiece to show in class.

Then I lay with my eyes closed and my hands clasped behind my head, thinking of how Miss Stein's naked corpse might look in an oven engulfed by flames.

THE RIVER

FROM THE THREE-STORY-HIGH platform of the elevated subway I could look down over 170th Street, packed with shoppers, the streets all lit up like a carnival with glass signs writ in neon script. Blood-red fender lights flowed through the 170th Street underpass beneath the Grand Concourse, an invasion of space microbes, and I could see Yankee Stadium far down Jerome Avenue—even thought I heard the faint sound of a distant roaring crowd from the old ballpark.

"Is that possible?" I asked suddenly. "Is it possible I heard the crowd at the stadium all the way over here?" and Mike Auria said, "Sure," and I smiled.

I was listening to that sound all on my own tonight, my own person, my own man, out on adventure with a great bunch of schoolyard guys:

George, Mike, Louis, Erik, Earl. We were heading to the Hudson River!
For this I was going to get it but good when I got home, was anxious
about staying out as late as I knew I'd have to, but dressed in a wind-
breaker borrowed from George and a cool river hat belonging to Mike
made me feel braver. And Mike had given me a cigar and matches, too,
that he claimed were necessary tools of survival for Bronx river rats.

Here was the same 170th Street I'd seen from up here but always in
the company of my father on the way to Dr. Siegal's office to get medicine for my asthma or shots for my allergies, always oppressive with
him: stood up here, looked out at the same zigzagged green and red
neon and big plate-glass windows filled with shoppers bent over produce counters, or diners in car coats supping in the delis and lun-
cheonettes, and big cakes exchanging hands in the window of
Friedhoffer's Bakery, the same world but different now, as though
revealed through parted curtains and presented elevated upon a stage
and a voice saying, "All this was made for you, and whether you're with
your parents or alone, you'll be all right—there's no mystery about it.
This is the world in which human beings live. You are a human being.
You belong."

And just then the train pulled in, rounding the corner like a clattering caterpillar in a blaze of molten blue electric sparks, and we stepped
aboard and were incredibly well behaved, probably because of Mike,
who exuded a gentle air of authority and seemed to anticipate our every
crazy urge, studying our eyes constantly, and when he thought he
caught a glimmer of mischief brought his face up close with a kind of
frenetic Groucho Marx expression and sang, soothing singsong: "Yes!"
and "Moo-ny the Gi-ant, going to the river!" with the crazed look in his
eyes.

It took the wind right out of your sails.

And George slumped by himself on the narrow two-seater bench
near the conductor's booth, sulking or dazed and bored. Always hard to
tell with him.

Louis Morales, Erik Cohen, and Earl Dupreen on their feet, hanging
from straps, engaged in normal conversation.

Mike Auria with his benign, shrewd, watchful eye on it all. Knowing how easily we could slip into high-spirited, good-natured, boys-will-be-boys pandemonium. And leave behind us a wrecked subway car without too much effort, though there wouldn't be a lot to break. Windows to smash. Tear down signs. Work a knife into the upholstery and spill out its guts. Trash the fire extinguisher. Tug the emergency brake. Spill passengers to the ground, off their legs or out of their seats. A few busted lips, a few broken heads. So easy.

But, we're good boys. Mike sees that about us. We're basically good. The subway rocketing north into the high-number streets. At Fordham Road we disembarked and caught a bus that careened in the dark Bronx night through the cheerless streets of Kingsbridge—big Irish neighborhood, brick walk-ups with dusky courtyards and taverns with windows painted black against intruding eyes. Half-Moon Bar. Kilarny Rose. Blarney Stone.

"Here," said Mike. We got off.

"Where are we?"

"Broadway," said Mike.

"But how can it be?" I asked.

"Broadway's the longest street in the world and runs all the way to Yonkers. You don't believe that, look it up in *Ripley's Believe It or Not.* Yes!" and danced over to George, who was sullen-faced, and sang in a mock singsong voice: "Bru-tus De-Rocko! Bru-tus De-Rocko!" to which George groaned, "C'mon Mike! Cut it out!"

Mike desisted instantly.

"So," he said, with mild irritation at his brother's peevish mood. "Do we show Moony the Columbia C, or take him upriver to see the Ax Man?"

George looked at me, considered, said: "Nah. I don't think it'd be good to take him climbing up the C at night. We'll take him north to the Ax Man!"

North! The sound of it thrilled me. And immediately the others grew nervous with anticipation, and big Erik Cohen said: "Uh-oh! The Ax Man!" and shrieked like a female victim in a grade-B horror flick.

Mike Auria laughed. "Haw! Haw! Haw! Cohen knows that the Ax Man's up there right now sharpening his tools for cutting off punk heads."

"Hey!" Cohen glowered, pretending offense. "I ain't no punk!"

To which George drawled dryly, "No, but your mother pulls daisy chains for the Marine recruits at Quantico," and we doubled over imagining Mrs. Cohen in an apron on her back on a barracks bunk bed, covered with semen and beer, like the whore Tra-la-la in *Last Exit to Brooklyn*, a book we'd all read in secret bathroom masturbation sessions and kept concealed under mattresses and in closets.

We were at an El that looked exactly like a Lexington Avenue elevated train but wasn't: tall dark spidery girders, and tracks winding above a cobblestone paved avenue.

"Where is this?" I asked.

Mike Auria circled my shoulder with his arm, like an older brother. "Look, Moony," he pointed.

And I could see it, just hadn't known where to look. A dark mass of rock, a slip of water glittering with shore lights and moon reflections. A river. The mighty Hudson! Until now I had only glimpsed it when crossing back into New York from visiting relatives or shopping trips to depressing Jersey with my parents, as the bus nosed off 95 into the jammed traffic of the Holland Tunnel, really just the mouth of the harbor more than actual river, and narrowing into the north to become what I now saw a magnificent glimpse of.

"No! Let's go there!" I cried out, beside myself. "Let's go! Oh, my God! Look at that! Oh, my God!"

And Mike Auria crowed: "Yes!"

And Louis answered: "Ee-yew!"

"The river fever has bitten Moony in the ass! Hee! Hee! Hee!"

And George drawled dryly: "Well, I still think we better not climb the C tonight."

And Mike sobered up immediately. "Yeah, George is right. It's only Moony's first time," and asked an invisible audience in a wee-voiced aside: "Isn't that why we call him the Prince? Prince Brutus DeRocko?"

"Prince! Prince! Prince!" chanted Erik Cohen. And to all this the tall, sallow, somewhat depressed-looking Earl Dupreen did not offer or add a single word.

We took the bus then, up Henry Hudson Parkway. A long ride of sixty more blocks up into areas with big trees, tall, ritzy condominiums, and houses with big-spread lawns. We're in the country: 250th Street! I'd never been so far on my own. This was the mysterious North! The bus pulled into a circle and the driver shouted: "Last stop!"

Last stop!

Is this still New York City? On the last stretch of bus ride I kept glancing in disbelief at Mike's watch, noticing that the time was now past nine o'clock and we had still not yet arrived, and I did a little math of the kind that I was good at, the arithmetic of fear, and realized that I wouldn't be home earlier than midnight, probably later, this the latest I had ever stayed out without permission; with each passing minute of prohibition-violating time I was like an astronaut piercing the blackness of unexplored deep space, forward, forward, stretching the fabric of my outlaw freedom to its absolute maximum limit, and with it, the level of my abuse. So that it made me feel sickened and joyful at once to be here. And where we disembarked now from the bus had the appearance, even the feel of an unknown galactic unexplored cosmos, with its fairways of shadow-soaked grass and facades of colonial-style houses looming ghostly and white out of the gnat-miasmic evening.

The air was so fresh here that it tasted sweet. I smelled the unmistakable fragrance of an enormous body of water nearby.

"Where is it?" I asked anxiously. But no one answered. Single file we proceeded down what seemed like a country road of nice houses, turned off sharply into a melting mass of trees and unpaved road, and glanced up at a cloud-mottled sky that glowed silver compared to the ground-level pitch darkness. Then we stopped. Mike fumbled with something in his pocket, and a match flared. Inserting a cigar between his lips, he puffed it to life, as I had seen my father do. One by one the others lowered their faces to matches and stoked their own cigars to life. Then I had mine glowing too, like a hot coal just a few inches from the tip of my nose, and Mike said: "Stay close. We're heading into Ax Man country. If you get lost, find your way by the light of your cigar. Keep it in your mouth, get it good and hot, and head in the direction it's pointed." He chuckled. "Just like your own dick."

We commenced walking, slowly, feet crunching leaves fallen early from their trees, heralding the approach of autumn, my favorite season. Gradually, my eyes adjusted. And miraculous things came into view suddenly, such as a mansion with a pond in front of it containing a fountain shaped like a flying goose and nearby an actual cannon such as was used in the Civil War and I whispered, "Wow!" and George went *"Shhhhh!"* and along we walked, my heart pounding though cheered by the stalwart numbers of our coal-like cigar tips floating in the pitch dark, and we came upon a fenced enclosure with a skull-and-crossbones warning sign that bore the words DANGER! ELECTRIC FENCE! The fence was topped by Buck Rogers ray-gun-type cathodes. A white cinderblock house of some kind, eerie as a poltergeist, seeming almost to float above a black pipe from which thick liquid oozed into a brackish pond, and Mike halted, stooped, lit a match, and leaned close to examine the ground. He looked up to the circle of our concerned faces. "Ax Man," he said, showing us a deep, enormous footprint, and blew out the match.

"Maybe," said George dryly from a little ways off. "Or maybe one of the sewage plant workers made that print."

"Yeah, sure," Mike huffed defensively. "Did you see the size of that print? You know the Ax Man wears shoes that size. It was the Ax Man!"

"OK, OK, so it was the Ax Man. So what?" said George with a bored air.

Then suddenly he was gone, melted into the foliage behind him, and his voice called back, already receding fast: "I'll meet you by the barge!"

"Idiot!" Mike muttered "Good riddance."

But I felt uneasy at losing him. Now I'd have to entrust my own protection to others about whom, really, I knew little, and none of whom inspired me—excepting Mike—with the kind of awed faith that I had in George. But we continued walking. I followed their cigars. And when they accelerated to a pace that I felt unable to sustain, I let them go, with heart pounding, and just followed my own cigar. Mike was right. It led me to the river. And there, I knew, I could not get lost.

Near the river it was amazingly bright, refracting a full moon glow over the trees of the eastern embankment and lights from the cliff-top homes and buildings of the New Jersey Palisades, though I didn't yet know them as the Palisades, still unaware of their name. To me they were nameless prehistoric cliffs; I half expected screeching pterodactyls to launch from them in lazy circling arcs. And to hear the boom-boom-boom of prehistoric native drums. And to see a Mark Twain Mississippi boat paddle by. And a raft with a little tussle-headed barefoot white boy on it and a black man with a torn shirt punting them along. But instead of these things I saw a tugboat pushing a garbage scow and drew a deep breath of excitement.

From far away I heard a rumbling sound and saw way down the shore the shape of a freight train drawing near. So I sat down, put my bottom into the molting, damp leaves and rich black dirt—I didn't care—and folded my arms about my knees and just puffed on my cigar—big smoke clouds trailing from me like a locomotive or a steamboat—and absorbed the whole spectacle of cliffs and river and train in the moonlight, and felt grand for the first time in my life.

There is no other term or better word for how I felt, and I knew that I was going to be all right. I think that until that moment I had never really been sure, but now I knew; and not just all right, better even than that. I would do grandly—I could think of no better word—and since I was an official outlaw of the family—at this late hour there could be no turning back—I considered the possibility that when the others rose to return I might remain behind and somehow live off the land. I hadn't the slightest idea of what that would entail, had heard the phrase once in a movie, a western I think, but it came to mind now and I considered the possibility with cool confidence and in so doing experienced myself with a new kind of regard. For an instant it occurred to me that I liked myself. The idea of me being here at this late hour, facing punishment and yet risking all anyway to adventure beyond the crocodile moat of my parents' choke hold, made me like myself. For a moment I almost seemed to hover, absorbing the scene and chuckling with appreciation. So many times before I had felt myself removed from the action, hovering detached, yet could only feel, at best, a kind of savage pity as I saw myself beat up in the schoolyard or beaten or berated or mocked at home, but now I felt a high regard for myself. I saw my own possibilities and liked them.

The train took a while to pass, but as it did I seemed to watch tableaux after tableaux of my possible future life flash past, projected on the doors and sides of the big freight cars. I saw myself a writer, traveling, living in cities, writing, sometimes working as a field hand in the country or as a ranch hand on the plains or on a boat of the kind pushing the long flat scow upriver, but whatever I'd be at I'd always be moving, eternally on the move, restless, homeless but well, and fiercely lean and soft-spoken and without a single attachment to family or friend of any kind, at once a friend and relation to everyone and no one, a drifter writing about drift in the big drifting landscape of America.

I got up. Kept moving. They were down there, silhouetted by the tides, a small fire going, by the glow of which I saw George.

"Hey!" I called. "Hey, George!"

He looked up, cupped his hands to his mouth, and shouted something that I could not hear.

"I can't hear!" I called back. "I can't hear," and so another figure came running up the shore to me. Mike made his way over the stepless frame structure of an old trestle bridge whose stairs had rotted away; he thumped heavily on the floorboards, hopped nimbly over the gaps, and climbed up to my perch.

"Here, follow me, Moony," he shouted as he approached. "We'll cross the tracks," and he led me down the slope. It was rough going. I mostly made it on my butt, which struck a few sharp-edged rocks along the way, and I cried "Ow!" which made Mike laugh gleefully. "Hee-hee-hee-hee! Moony the giant! Goin' to the river!" But I could barely catch my breath to laugh. At some especially steep points I was going on pure faith alone. I said, "I'm stuck!" and Mike said "You're OK! Let go!" and so I slid, fast, but always I was OK. And then we were down. The solid ground felt good to walk on. Gravel crunched underfoot. We marched between tracks, watching for the approach of trains.

It could be that the river, the Hudson River, along which thriving Native American tribes once lived, all the way north to Canada is still inhabited by the spirits of those betrayed and murdered peoples, for I felt suddenly nativelike, with spring in my step and balance in my posture and an uncanny sense that I had been here before, lived here even, and that the boy in front of me, no more than a dark shape now, was in fact my hunting companion and fellow warrior. But then suddenly we were transformed, virtually mid-stride, into immigrant railroad laborers heading back to work camp, penniless and lonely. And yet as we drew near and I could clearly make out the faces of George and Earl and Erik and Louie gazing pensively, fixedly into the fire, we were anonymous river-rat rail tramps just off the freight from Montana, stopping by for grub in a hobo jungle.

Food was cooking. Hot dogs sizzled on sticks and buns were toasting. From his pack Mike produced a big bag of marshmallows that he tore open and extended to each of us. Our hands grabbed, which Mike noted with some satisfaction. "That's why I didn't tell you animals about it on the way up. I figured you would have killed me for a fistful of marshmallows. Haw, haw, haw! Yes!!" Wild eyes rolling in his Graucho Marx face.

"Maybe we'll still do it, for a fistful of dollars," George drawled. "You got money on ya, don't ya? Wit that job you got after school in the electric shop. You got money, hey gringo?" His voice become that of a Hollywood Mexican bandit: "Maybe we cut off your stinking head and feed it to the dogs, gringo pig."

Mike tittered grimly. "You probably would, you psycho. And you got these loons here to help."

Lit from beneath by the flames, our faces looked mighty evil. But in fact it was hard to stare at the fire for too long before one's skin felt scorched, and once turned to the cool dark relief of the river we just looked like good kids.

I stared with quiet, secret fascination at the blazing heart of the fire, the almost jewel-like embers, wondering how hot is hot and were the ovens used by the Germans to kill my people as hot as this. Hotter, probably. To reduce so many people per day to ashes. And still parts of the skeletons remained, had to be broken down with sledgehammers and then ground into powder that they dumped over marshes. Read about it in a book. Wild shit. Found the book upstairs in the adult section of the Grand Concourse public library.

I looked at my hand with new curiosity. This smooth, soft, slightly pudgy hand in that fire, I thought: first the blistering skin, the popping veins, and the roasted meat turned black to charcoal, and then only the white bone remaining, the skeleton of my hand lying among the fire's jewels, removed and pulverized into dust and dumped unceremoniously by slaves, themselves doomed, into strange marshes, and no one ever to know. I shut my eyes at the pain of that thought, turned away and drew a deep breath of Hudson River air.

So far from Europe here. Pretty lucky, I thought. Where a Jewish boy can still pretend to be a native American with confidence. Pretty lucky, I nodded to myself, and looked up at the sky, freewheeling with a blaze of starry constellations. And my thoughts asked of the sky, "But God, how could you let that happen? Especially to the babies, God, what did *they* do wrong?"

I had read of how babies in the hundreds of thousands were gassed, shot, or simply thrown alive into the flames. A million children in all butchered. I hadn't even realized that my eyes had closed again. They snapped open to escape the image in my mind of a beautiful infant pitched with frenzied eyes and a howling mouth into an inferno.

"God," I whispered aloud, shaking my head. "No!"

"So," said Mike, clapping my back roughly, snapping me back. "How do you like the river?"

"It's great," I enthused sincerely. "It's the greatest place I've ever been in my own whole life. Thanks, Mike, for bringing me here. Really."

"You're gonna catch hell at home though, huh? Oh well. You're a big boy. You can take it."

My face dropped. "Yeah," I nodded, swallowing hard, "I can take it."
I didn't want to think about that just now.

"I feel like an Indian brave," I said, straightening up. "I'd like to live out here."

"The Indians used to live here, all up and down the river, before we came in and killed them and drove them off their land . . . ,"said Mike.

"To build condos," said George.

There was part of an overturned barge just a few feet off the beach and George reclined on it, coolly toking on his cigar.

"That's right," said Mike. His arm swept over the river. "This whole area was Indian land. But we bought it off 'em for beads, and then we killed them, every man, woman, and child. They killed a lot of kids. Shot 'em where they stood. And you can still find arrowheads and stuff in the ground around here. I've found some. I have 'em up in the house."

"What about bones?" I asked. "Did you ever find bone? Like dumped human bone?"

Mike made a face. "You mean of the dead Indians? I don't think they dumped them after they were killed. What do you think, George?"

"They had mass graves," he said, and added, "I suppose. I'm not sure."

"They did," said Erik Cohen. "Secret graves, where the army buried them. But those are farther north. You won't find any of that here."

"Sure," said Mike. "The land developers knocked down everything and dug up the rest. This whole area has been steam-shoveled and whatnot, so that people like Louis Morales and his mother Juicy Lucy could take the commuter train to Tappan Zee State Park for a Puerto Rican barbecue picnic. Right Louie?"

One corner of Louis's mouth turned up and for a moment his cheek dimpled in a half-hearted smile. "You got it."

"Yeah," said Erik Cohen. "And so you Dago Wops can commute from your Mafia estates up in Croton to whorehouses on Delancey Street and social clubs in Little Italy."

"And safe houses in Red Hook," added Earl Dupreen. It was the first I'd heard from him all night.

"Yeahhhhh!" growled Erik Cohen. "Where Joey Gallo goes to the mattresses!"

Mike Auria absorbed all this with a slightly irritated smile, but nodded in agreement and said good-naturedly: "*Gum*-ba!" and then again, "*Gum*-ba!"

So they do it here too, I thought. Kill babies. I never thought that the United States would be capable of that. But here, Mike Auria had said it. And George seemed to know about it. I needed no further proof than that. If the Aurias knew of something, then it was so, and if they didn't I figured it must be a lie.

"But how could they *kill* the babies?" I blurted out. "How could they *do* that?"

"'Cause people are sick animals," said George, his back turned to us and face slightly in profile against the cliffs of the opposite shore. "Sick fuckin' animals. This country's pretty fucked up, Moony. Things aren't as good here as it seems. The rich get richer and the poor get poorer."

"That sounds," said Earl Dupreen, in a dry, sarcastic voice, "like some of your father Donald's pathetic Socialist bullshit!"

"Oh yeah?" said George hotly. "Well I guess it's better than some of your father Victor's Alabama Ku Klux Klan nigger-hating butcher shop ignorance."

And Earl quickly retreated into himself, silent, inscrutable, withdrawn to a place so far removed from the rest of us that I couldn't tell if he breathed or not. He seemed so strangely out of reach. So different. Even his face was odd. I couldn't place it within the range of faces that I knew. I wondered at what strains ran in him. He seemed to contain some Chinese. I had seen pictures in *National Geographic* of New Guinea bushmen who resembled him a little, though not quite. I just couldn't place it. And Dupreen wasn't a Jewish name. But there seemed something Jewish about him. His father was from the South, hated black people with a vengeance, yet there also seemed to be in Earl a touch of the black that I'd asked him about and he'd denied vehemently. It was queer. I joked like everyone else that he was descended from a race of Martians whose spacecraft had crashed centuries ago in Tibet.

But also I felt a special kinship with his cultural estrangement. Like me, he was not typical of the neighborhood and possessed the lonely air of a perennial outsider. Like me, he was weak and at the mercy of predators for no better reason than that of difference, and an inability to defend himself. Like me, he had attached himself out of loneliness and the need for protection to George, ringleader of the outcasts, the idol of the schoolyard and the epitome of all that we admired.

Scorched black marshmallows seared our tongues. We blew on the roasted hot dogs between cautious nibbles and washed everything down with great gulps of sweet orange juice. Upshore, the coasts loomed like mountains and closed at a bend into seamless darkness. The smoky fragrance of burning, brine-saturated railroad ties seeped into every pore of our skin, our clothing, and gave us the odor of cured meat. I could live here. Make this my home. Maybe I would. My eyes closed sleepily, watching the flames leap so high that some tickled the telephone wires overhead. I stretched out flat, deliciously weary, with head propped against a rock and the cackling flames in my ears. The unwinding of my nerves released a deep fatigue throughout my body. I was overcome by the first real sense of peace that I had ever known and gave in to it with snores.

"You're snoring," I heard as from a distance, and felt my foot nudged, but I continued to sleep.

It was past two o'clock in the morning when I came home, covered with dirt, reeking of smoke, and my swollen red eyes sullen with indifference. My soiled finger pressed heavily on the door buzzer. No answer. I pressed again. The tumblers unlocked in an unfamiliar order. And the door chain was not on. I noted all this with little more curiosity than a pedestrian waiting for a bus might show for the operations of a work crew painting stripes in the road. I was tired. And grimly happy. At the river I had met myself alone for the first time, and liked the encounter. It made me feel differently about my parents, see them differently. I would not so easily accept their version of me, or their acts of physical retribution for the crime of being me.

But only Howard stood there, fully dressed. "A-za," he said wearily. "Come in. You don't know how lucky you are." I crossed the threshold, fully expecting a belt to land across my face. Instead, he sat at the dinette table in the kitchen and resumed eating a plate of melted ice cream. He stopped to tap a big bucket of Sealtest chocolate ice cream with his spoon. "Get yourself a plate. Pop gave me permission to take it from the freezer before he took Mom to the hospital."

"The hospital!" I gasped.

"Yeah. But he's not there now. He's at work. She's spending the night. We're alone. Get yourself a plate. So, how was the river?"

"How'd you know about that?"

"George's mother called. Man, Pop was mad! He didn't tell Mom. She kept asking: "Where's Abie? Where's Abie?" But she was pretty sick and she stopped asking. Pop told me he was gonna kill ya." He paused with a sarcastic smirk to let this sink in, then said: "Yeah, right. Like he could really give a shit. I don't think he'd care if you never came back."

"What's wrong with her?" I asked, trying to shake off my sleepiness. I went to the dish rack and plucked out a clean plate. It looked so white between my dirty fingers.

"Kidneys or something. I dunno. Here. Use the wooden spoon. Try to leave me a little."

"You selfish hog," I laughed. "I'll leave you my spit in your eye."

"Ass-hole!"

"So what did Pop say?"

"About what?"

"About my being out so late?"

"He said you were looking for trouble and that you were gonna find it."

I shook my head sadly. "But why? I bet he did stuff like that when he was this age. Why does he have to make me out to be bad? I'm not bad! I'm a good kid! You should see what George's father says. He goes "Haw, haw, haw, they're just a bunch of good boys with a lot of crazy ideas!"

"What do you care about what Pop says? You did it, right? You'll do it again. Maybe now I'll get to stay out late too. Anyway, I'm not goin' to school tomorrow. You don't have to either. We got a good excuse. Pop said if we behave tonight he'll give us a treat tomorrow. I think he's planning to take tomorrow night off to stay with us."

"I wish he wouldn't," I laughed.

"Yeah." Howard nodded, barely able to speak with a mouth full of ice cream. "I know."

A powerful need for bed drove me into my room, where I peeled off my clothes, left them in a heap on the floor, and slid deliciously between cool sheets.

Consciousness seeped from me like blood. That I had gotten off scot-free was little less than a miracle. The last thing in my mind before sleep was an image of the freight train and before it Mike Auria's Groucho Marxing eyes rolling as he hissed with charlatan ecstasy: "Moo-ny the gi-ant, go-in' to the ri-ver! Yes!!"

THE UNHOLY ALLIANCE

AS A JOKE, some eighth-grade students, Erik Cohen and Leslie Rudner among them, decided to run George Auria as an independent candidate for student president. Overnight, campaign mottoes scrawled in blue Bic pen on sheets of torn loose-leaf paper appeared posted in places intended to solicit gasps and laughter: the topmost reach of the lunchroom's central column; the door of the dean of students, Mr. Young; sinks in the boys' bathroom; and the door to the second-floor girls' bathroom.

They read:

George Auria for G.O. president
Makes you want to brush with Pepsodent.

Signed,
The Holy Alliance

I wanted to join the cause, but when I asked Erik Cohen about it during recess, he grew evasive, shrugged. "I'm sorry. The Holy Alliance is a secret organization. I can't betray the cause," and turned away with a sad smile of regret.

Infuriated by rejection, wanting more than anything in the world to belong to some secret organization, and committed to the cause of a dark horse candidate whose idea of a good time was to throw water balloons from his homeroom window onto the heads of passersby, I decided to form my own independent campaign organization called the Unholy Alliance.

My first recruit, Arnold Razumny, immediately saw the importance of the undertaking and agreed to join up. Others quickly followed: Lloyd Markowitz, Steven Rice, Jack Moy, Stewie Schlieffer, Dave Dubinsky, and Seth Pearlman. Very soon, almost fifty percent of seventh-grade boys secretly belonged.

The core of the leadership, myself, Rice, Markowitz, Moy, and Razumny, shaved time from study periods for our clandestine work. While our deeply absorbed classmates cracked books, we hunched in stairwells, manufacturing the paraphernalia necessary to conduct a covert guerrilla political campaign. Our objective was not merely to win the presidency for George Auria, but to do so through means of terror.

Like most marginal splinter groups, we sought to exceed the worst excesses of our parent body and in so doing win their love and admiration. Our organizational efficiency was impressive.

Jack Moy, an overweight Chinese boy who ran an illicit candy store and stationery supply outlet from his 007 briefcase, agreed to hike his prices by a dime for the sake of the campaign, the proceeds from which he'd secretly funnel to subsidize our network. Moy also agreed to act as smuggling go-between among the different classes, distributing illicit flyers from his briefcase.

Steven Rice, a fanatical amateur chemist, took charge of producing stink bombs, which he concocted from a blend of ammonia and lye. His investigations into ordinance led to the creation of a highly explosive device assembled from moist cornflakes fermenting in a sealed jug that was capable of blowing an entire building such as Wade Junior High to smithereens.

Lloyd Markowitz, our expert on psychological terror, volunteered to produce disruptive and offensive noises at critical times, such as making hand-generated noise farts at special assemblies and the like. Razumny tailored arm bands from loose-leaf paper and bearing the logo I personally designed: capital *A* superimposed over capital *U* and the whole ringed by a circle. More important, by dint of Razumny's obvious acquaintance with the dark forces of human nature—he was a particularly sick kid—he was to be our Minister of Perversion, his job to goad us on to ever more obscenely senseless acts of destruction.

I was a kind of leader and didn't press hard to be one, but I was everywhere at once, now making posters, now taping them up, now helping out Steven Rice with his experiments in explosives, now covertly scavenging through the desk drawers of Miss Kintish, our jovial and accommodating homeroom teacher, for pins to fix the armbands to our sleeves. The speed with which this enterprise degenerated into the prototype of your typical extremist fascist movement was simply astonishing.

It started as a joke: a Jewish member of the Unholy Alliance—namely me—passed around a note in class that read: "Kill the Jews!" Seeing that it registered shock, others, Jew and non-Jew alike, followed suit.

"Nothing is sacred," we muttered to each other and sputtered with laughter.

Soon notes bearing the evil inscription "Kill the Jews!" were flying around the room.

Then it escalated.

If Miss Kintish left the room for a moment, the Unholy Alliance erupted in cries of "George Auria for G.O. president!" and "Kill the Jews!" The Jews among us, in particular me, Razumny, and Markowitz, chanted the loudest.

A few of the Jewish girls in class were at the point of tears over this, especially Barbara Millman, who stammered angrily: "But how can you . . . but you're . . . how can Jews . . ." etc. etc. We were happy to greet her protestations with stupid leering grins such as Brown Shirts must have worn when challenged by their own mothers about the decency of shoving a pregnant Jewish woman down the stairs of a Jewish milliner's shop in prewar Berlin.

We leered and grinned and increased the rate and volume of our chants until Millman and at least a few others rushed from the room, and when Miss Kintish came back in there, raising her hands to ask "Why?" behind her stood the red-faced girls, indignant. We answered Miss Kintish's hands with self-satisfied silence, and with one ominous eye kept trained on Millman and the others. Just in case they got it into their heads to go over Kintish's head.

We knew, though, that they wouldn't.

We were wrong.

They did.

I was the first called into the office of Mrs. Wexler, the school psychologist, a thin, sharp-featured woman with a nervous demeanor. Her anxious, somewhat angry, heavily mascaraed blue eyes framed by dyed black, chemically treated hair with brittle gray roots, were either in constant motion or else at a dead stop, during which she fixed you with a look of horrified amazement. I stood in her office, my first visit ever to a mental health worker, uncertain of where to sit or what to do.

"Sit there, please," she said, really pissed. "There, in that chair."

I sat.

She flipped tartly through a file, the tip of her tongue caressing her two front teeth, exposing the tongue's blue-veined underside, which I found grotesquely intimate, like being shown someone's skid marks. A good disciplinarian, I felt, would conceal all trace of their human physicality, like Nazis. No Jew, I felt sure, ever saw the underside of an SS man's tongue, for how could one have seen the big blue veins embedded in the raw-looking purplish flesh and not known that the Nazi was little more that an imbecilic human posing as a God. Surely the Jew could have slain him with his bare hands on such a pretext, instead of marching with shaved and lowered heads through the gates of annihilation.

She looked up at me. "I don't understand," she fumed. "Will you help me to understand. Help me, will you please?"

"Sure," I said, abashed, "but can I just ask you something?"

"What?" she said icily.

I was going to ask if I stood to be expelled from school, but the tone of her voice deterred me and I said, "That's OK, forget it," and, crossing my leg, I sank back in my chair, shoulders slumped and eyes hooded with gangster-style, self-preening arrogance such as I had seen Mafioso's display in the interrogation rooms of the television show *The Untouchables*.

"So what can I do for you?" I asked while insolently examining a fingernail.

"Your records say that you're Jewish. So are a few of the other boys. So, what . . . how . . . can you feel . . . can you hate . . ." she swallowed hard before saying it: "Jews?"

I laughed. "I don't hate no Jews, Mrs. Wexler. That's just stupid jokin' around, that's all. No one means it."

"No, yet I understand that you and the others have formed an organization called the Unholy Alliance that patterns itself after the Nazis."

Now I really had to laugh, to see the silly goofings of our warped brains treated so seriously by this silk-bloused educated professional with bright red cherry earrings.

"Yah, waaaaaaal . . ." I drawled Gary Cooper/George Auria–style, and rubbing a hand, old-pardner-ranch-hand-like, over my mouth and jaw, "Heh-heh, yeah, waaaal . . . I don't . . . it's just stupid goofin', ya know. How can I be a Nazi? My mother was in the Holocaust and stuff . . ."

Her eyes bulged from her head, and with a drained expression she carefully closed the file folder like an infant's coffin lid and looked at me as though we had just suddenly found ourselves face to face in a strange motel room with no idea of what had brought us there or what to do next.

"Your mother," she slowly repeated, "was in the Holocaust. . . . In other words she . . ."—and added for her own clarification—"she was there, she's a survivor."

"Yeah," I shrugged. "Whatever, yeah, I'm . . . she was there. So I know all about that Holocaust stuff, OK, and I know I'm no Nazi, believe you me, it's just crazy kid stuff, takin' it to . . . you know . . . the limit."

"A Jewish boy chanting the words 'Kill the Jews!' in a classroom is not crazy kid stuff! Membership in secret fascistic organizations is not crazy kid stuff. Don't you see how terribly, terribly wrong, wrong, wrong . . . ?"

I didn't hear the end of her sentence, the word "wrong" echoing in my head, each repetition unhinging a little more of a solid-steel gate that I had not even known existed in me. The room, her face, the desk lamp, the painting on the wall of a flying man playing a violin to a winged cow over the roofs of a little village, all clicked into sudden, spectacularly sharp focus, as though someone had made in my awareness an abrupt adjustment to an internal telescope through which I'd been peering for my whole life in frustration, and been able to discern only the blurred shapes of things so dimly that even outright blindness was preferable.

I had always suspected that something was terribly wrong, but to have an actual trained professional say it outright was riveting. My heart raced excitedly. Contrary to fearing expulsion, I glimpsed for the first time the real possibility of rescue from the insanity of my home life. By a stroke of luck, everything seemed to change, and forever. In a flash I saw that once the welts and bruises on my arms were discovered, for years to come I would probably live in institutional dormitories as a state ward; envisioned intensive encounter sessions with teams of psychologists in the cheerful sterility of counseling offices that smelled reassuringly of ammonia and talc. I would make friends with fellow patients my age, together climbing slowly but surely from out of the pit of our scarred minds into rainbow-colored mental health. I would stand a chance to live a sane, productive life, predicated upon a reasonable version of reality that I could feel good about.

I now grasped that the key to this new life lay in my complete honesty before Mrs. Wexler. Clear as day I saw, grasped, that within this new future I could truly develop my creative gifts as they were meant to be cultivated; supported, encouraged, and guided by impartial loving professionals whose job it was to assist unfortunate, severely abused children like myself to find their way back from the lonely torture of the lower-middle-class, blue-collar struggle to live, into a land of milk and honey.

"I'm going to call your mother, Alan," she said, and I burst into tears of the most profound relief that I had ever felt, for I now could see the whole marvelous chain of events to come: the two women, Mrs. Wexler and my mother, together deciding to give me the chance that I deserved; my father rejecting the idea outright, but my mother's overriding love carrying the day.

"Yeah," I nodded happily, my throat gummy with mucilage and face shiny with tears. "Yeah, of course, go call her, talk to her . . ."

"Yes," said Mrs. Wexler, handing me Kleenex tissue. "Blow your nose," she said gently.

I complied with a noisy, baby-elephant toot.

"Why don't you take a few minutes to yourself before you return to class. It's going to be all right. I bet there's a lot of things for us to talk about. We're going to begin that process, Alan. We're going to work for wellness. We're going to learn to love ourselves."

I shook my head, face pinched with relief as I struggled against the new flood of tears called forth by her therapeutic, healing words. No one had ever spoken to me that way, but instantly I recognized it as something I desperately needed. All I could do as I shook with sobs was gasp, "Yes, yes," in a choked voice

When I entered Miss Kintish's class—after ten minutes spent in front of the boy's room mirror, bent over a sink, alternately crying and splashing cold water over my puffed face to ameliorate the effect of tears, and then watching myself cry again with a sweet feeling of hope, relief, gratitude, and splashing more water, torn between letting it all come out and calming myself—I had wrestled my emotions down to a wan-faced, sniffling, melancholy smile as I shuffled past Miss Kintish, who followed me with saddened eyes. The class became abruptly silent; every head in the room turned, following my steps to my desk. I felt at peace, but to them it must have seemed that I had returned from a KGB torture chamber in the basement of the Kremlin.

"Welcome back," said Miss Kintish with a half-hearted smile. One could tell that she found the whole business too preposterous for words. "They're bright kids," she had been overheard telling Mrs. Wexler. "Just bright kids with a lot of energy and bored with this school."

"We're talking about city government," she called out to me. "Want to join us? It's a real scream of a subject. Almost as interesting as home economics."

The whole class burst into laughter at Miss Kintish's splendid irreverence.

All except the other Unholy Alliance ringleaders, who scrutinized me with narrow, accusatory looks, angry at me for having gotten them into such a mess. Rice leaned impossibly far out of his seat, limp blond hair falling into his angelic, triangular face. "So what happened?" he demanded, but I was too broken to speak and felt a million miles away from him, Miss Kintish, the class—already transported in the vise of dramatic change to another world, my destiny guided by forces too powerful for me to do more than submit to with a numb and grateful smile.

Of course she was home when I returned, as always, clattering soap-sudsed dishes and apparently in a good mood, over the sound of running tap water singing "Pigalle," a favorite French tune that summoned up images of GIs and French girls strolling down boulevards with arms about each others' waists, past tanks and artillery emplacements along the Seine as Nazi howitzer shells fell around, and the sentimental wheeze of an accordion groaned in the dusk.

At the sound of my entrance she hurriedly finished off a dish, wiped her hands on her apron, switched off the tap, and called, "A-bie! A-bie!" in a shrill, histrionically amused voice.

"Yeah," I replied, hang-dog.

In her reddish, flushed face, her blue eyes glittered with a hard diamond brightness. She was either pumped full of medication or else having dangerous visions. I couldn't tell which. Either way, my stomach warned of trouble. "A-bie, I got a call from your Mrs. Wexler at school."

"Oh, yeah?" I said, struggling to smile, braced for the assault.

Instead my mother laughed a hard, stubbornly fierce sort of laugh. "She said that you and the boys are going around in school saying "Kill the Jews." That you boys have made some kind of fascist club."

Again she laughed. "Do you know what this Wexler said? She said, 'Mrs. Kaufman, your son Alan is an admirer of Nazis.' I told her: 'Do you know who you're talking to? A woman who spent five years of her life hiding from the Germans! I lost half my family,' I told her."

My mother's face grew indignant. "Can you imagine the nerve? Who is this stupid woman?"

"She's the school guidance counselor," I said.

"Imagine the nerve," she went on. "So what is this guidance she counsels?"

"Psychology."

"Ha! She's the crazy one, not you. She told me she thinks that you need psychiatric help. I told her that she's the one who needs the help, not you. Then she said again, 'Your son admires the Nazis,' so I told her: 'And I'm Hermann Göring!' and I hung up on her! The nerve! Why do they hire such nuts to be with children? I don't understand."

"But it's true," I said.

"What?" she said, our presumed conspiratorial understanding interrupted and her eyes narrowing with suspicion. "What are you saying? What is true? That you admire Nazis? *You* admire Nazis? I should die in my sleep and your father should drop dead on the spot if *you* admire Nazis! What kind of thing is that from your stupid crazy mouth to say?!

You make nothing like sense . . ." her English disintegrating as it always did under extreme duress.

"No, not the Nazi stuff, 'course I don't admire no Nazis, but it's true I need psychiatric help. I gotta agree with Mrs. Wexler. She's right."

At this, she seemed to implode, her confidant aura sucked through a hole created by her sudden clasping hands. Then her hands began to talk their own obscure silent patois, like an insect's feelers, to slide across the top of each other, then get sucked back under and reappear again, move as on a circular conveyor belt of anxiety from which there was no getting off or way to stop the machine. Then her lips spoke, very fast, pleading with me not to feel what I was feeling, since no member of her side of the family, the Juchts, had ever seen a psychiatrist. My father and she did not believe in them. I must not want to see one or it will stand on my "records" as an eternal black stain! Then she diagnosed my true problem: only thing wrong with me was I was spoiled! I didn't need a psychiatrist, I needed a father who would take me across his knee like her father had, never mind how tall she was, and give her a good klep such as she would never forget for the rest of her life . . .

And so on.

I listened calmly, with patience, and when she finished said, "But I *do* need psychiatric help. I'm not right in the head. I always feel crazy. Mom, please, maybe you can call Mrs. Wexler back and ask what we should do. Please. I'm askin' ya."

"*We* do?" she laughed angrily, her face astonished. "Me ask her? Not on your *life*."

And within me the frail bridge that supported the opposed cliffs of my brain spilled my identity into a gorge, and I began to cry, and as I cried she spoke like a lawyer delivering his summation before the tribunal—a tribunal I imagined as the ghosts of the Six Million. I envisioned them as having appointed her, by dint of necessity, as their representative among the living, and I wondered what they thought of their ambassador from the world of death, of her relations with her son, of me? Did they feel pity, shame, sadness? I cried, for I felt so hopeless as she railed on that none of her brothers had ever seen a psychiatrist, no one in her family!

"Sure, on your father's side," she said, "are a few who should be in Bellevue in a padded cell, but I hope you don't take after that side!" No, I took after her own side, she said, and over her dead body would she let this Mrs. Wexler ruin my future! "Imagine," she gasped, "to have such a thing on your record! No college would ever take you. And no one would want to hire you!

"You have troubles, you come to me! What kind of troubles do you have? You have troubles? Look at you, so fat you can hardly fit your pants, that's how much good food you eat! Do you know what I ate when I was your age? I was lucky for a potato, we were so hungry! We ate the potato skins *raw*."

She began to weep, red-faced, her blue eyes round circles of painted stone. "What do you know from trouble? My cousin Charlie, a little boy—a beautiful child!—they took from the potato sack where some prisoners had hidden him, opened the oven door, and threw him in . . ." and the vivid image of Charlie's skinny, naked, grimy little body weakly wrestling in the powerful sweaty arms of a crematorium worker, and the watching Nazi's voice snapping like whip steel: "In with him," and Charlie's eyes and mouth oval with wild terror for the roaring tongues of flames waiting hungrily to lick his pale white skin.

I am weeping now for Charlie and no longer care about myself. She is right! What do my troubles matter compared to such things, what real suffering have I ever known? A few welts, bruises, and so forth. I was born to witness my mother's suffering, not my own, and to remember her memories at the expense of my own life.

I felt so small, ashamed, a stupid kid living a privileged life who parodied the worst horror in human history through school antics more worthy of the Three Stooges than a son of the Holocaust.

She's right, I thought. Mrs. Wexler is nuts. Whatever hope of rehabilitation that I experienced in her office was the selfish daydream of a frivolous clown. It was for my mother to decide my future. I had no power to assert my needs against so much monstrosity, so much death.

"You're right," I said thickly. "She's crazy. I don't need no psychiatric help. I'll be OK. I'll stop kidding around in school, you'll see," and I walked past her into my bedroom without another word and lay down on my bed with my jacket still on.

"Don't put your dirty feet on the bed!" her voice shrilled into me.

I swung them to the side.

And fell asleep.

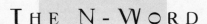

THE N-WORD

I CALLED THEM just plain "kids." But others called them *shvartzer*, coon, jiggaboo.

I felt sick inside when they said it; while everyone around me cackled and grinned evilly, I offered a remote half-smile and lapsed into silence.

Still, I was scared of blacks. My impression was that we were at war with each other. My father and his friends recounted tales of epic fights with black gangs in the movie houses and public parks. In their accounts, they'd be sitting around, minding their own business, when a swarm of "coons" would appear and one of them "said somethin'" to my father and his friends, and I'd say, "What? What did he say?" and Harry the Eagle or Teddy or Uncle Arnold would laugh uneasily, "Heh-heh," and repeat my question aloud: "'What did he say?' I don't remember. He said sumptin. What does it matter what he said?" And the next thing they knew they were "mixing it up," and as many "coons" as they took down still more kept coming, a veritable army of them, jumping from the balconies ("like apes from trees"), wielding baseball bats, zip guns, shivs, but though my father and his friends were armed only with their bare fists, they always won. The "coons" were routed. Order was restored.

These days, though, they were losing the war, they said. Coons everywhere. This friend was held up, that relation recently stabbed. On a subway. Coming home from work. Fer krissake! Goddamned coons.

My mother also didn't like this talk. She didn't laugh. She snapped at my father and his friends: "You should be ashamed of yourselves, talking like that in front of a boy his age. You'll teach him to grow up racist like you. Alan, put your hands over your ears. Don't listen. Those people are human beings just like we are. . . ." And someone—my uncle or father or one of the friends, the boys from the "old neighborhood"—snarled: "Don't you believe it, kid. They're goddamned ignorant subhumans is what they are . . ." and my mother glared so fiercely at my father that he felt forced to say, "OK, OK! Tone it down a little, ya dummies! The kid don't gotta hear all of this," though later in the bedroom, as he slipped off his sharkskin pants behind closed doors, I heard him shout: "So, good! So let 'im grow up racist! Who the hell are you to tell me what's what? Go back to that goddamned Europe of yours! This is America! And I don't like no niggahs! Period! You like 'em so much, go live with 'em on a Hundred and Twenty-fifth Street and Lenox Avenue. You'll be singing a different tune, I can tell you that!"

I always wondered how she felt hearing her own husband speak like the Nazis who'd tried to kill her during the war: maybe, secretly, it thrilled her.

The next day my mother would tell me that he should be ashamed after what Hitler did to us, but I should understand that my father wasn't in Europe, doesn't understand, comes from low, uneducated, ignorant Americans: "Not too much going on up here"—tapping her head with her finger—"if you know what I mean," and I would wonder how she could have brought herself to marry a man who held such opinions, after what she herself went through, hunted by racists for five years, how?

Still, enlightened though I felt myself to be, in league with my mother against hate, a true son of persecution, I feared blacks. I could not penetrate through the differences of skin color and features to the human beings inside.

There were a few who attempted to make a home for themselves in the local schoolyard, but inevitably they disappeared, driven out by an unspoken prohibition that loomed the instant they set foot in the yard.

Sometimes one came in and played with a haughty, angry kind of pride, regardless of what anyone thought of it—stood there with an expression that just dared someone not to choose him into the game, and was chosen in. He might even play fabulously well, we might even, by mid-game, be grinning and slapping each other's asses, and one of us might say, "We're down here pretty much every afternoon. Come back!" but he didn't, as we knew he wouldn't. Too much of a chance.

Blacks lived in the neighborhood but I didn't know where they played. On the streets, walking by myself, a group of approaching black kids froze my heart in ice. As I passed them, a shoulder might get thrown into mine, or an elbow slammed into my arm painfully, or a hand shoot out to lightly slap the back of my head, but I kept walking with a savage expression on my face of completely neutralized emotions: a zombie who might or might not explode in murderous rage, who did not feel the shoulder or elbow or slap, who responded to the violation by pretending total invisibility: a self-defeating response, since their blows came in the first place precisely because *they* felt invisible; but also an inevitable one because I felt too afraid to make contact. Contact might lead to death.

Even my mother had told me again and again that to meet their challenges squarely would result in my certain death. "No, no, Alan. Get away. If you say anything to blacks, they'll kill you on the spot: stabbed or shot. Run if you have to." And my father: "They don't just fight you one on one. They stick together, you know what I mean? You start up with one of them, they bring their friends, their brothers, their cousins, their fathers: the whole goddamned tribe will be over here looking for us. So don't start with them. It's the best policy."

Yet how I envied them! For who could I count on in a fight? No one. It was customary in the schoolyard to keep out of each other's quarrels. You were truly on your own. By contrast, the alleged solidarity of blacks seemed to make them invincible. There was never just one, even if only one stood before me, jeering an insult. Behind and around him hid an invisible, invincible array of badass brothers at his beck and call, ready to rush to his defense, right or wrong, on the given signal, whatever it was.

Sometimes on an empty street a black kid bopped past and sneered "Honky!" and I whirled, and so did he, and there we stood face to face, and I looked him up and down and thought: "He's not that big, I bet I'd stand a chance," but all I said was, "C'mon, man, I'm not trying to start with you. Let it be," and as I walked off with the sound of his indignant "Fuck yous" boom-boxing my ears, I'd increase my pace to a near run, afraid of the battalion of black fighters already sliding down their poles like firemen responding to a four-alarm.

The rift was just always there. I neither added to nor subtracted from it: couldn't.

I could not see any more of their humanity than that they walked and talked like us.

My eventual reflexive numbness toward them helped salve the sting of bodily hurt and injured pride that I experienced when, in passing them, they raked me with a spray of insults, peppered my head and body with blows. Their whole moiling passage of violence was a warning barrier of pain and possible death.

James Miller and Gregory Laughinghouse, the only two blacks in my eighth-grade class, were exceptions.

James was big, pudgy, effeminate, with aviator-style gold-frame glasses. He sang Supremes tunes in a high-pitched mock Diana Ross voice. His favorite was "Baby Love." The girls liked him and I felt easy around him because clearly he had no thoughts of violence. And he liked me for liking him. I could look him in the eyes. It was pleasant. A nice person dwelled there, a soul with whom I had things in common: a similar sense of humor, enthusiasm for James Baldwin's *Go Tell It on the Mountain*, and a shared hope to someday live in a world where laughter, deep feeling, culture, sadness, beauty, and intelligence would more than amply sustain us without racism, bloodshed, or hate.

He wanted to be a fashion designer; I saw nothing wrong with that. He obsessively drew women in brightly colored psychedelic garments on sheets of loose-leaf paper, with Venus colored pencils. He drew pictures of the Supremes over which he traced the group's name in a lavish script, underscored by a flourishing scroll for emphasis.

"Baby love!" he sang on line in the yard at recess, as we waited to go back to class. "Oh, baby love—oooh—ooooh—baby love!"

I laughed. So did Maria Fernandez and Barbara Millman and Lloyd Markowitz. Since we all took French together and were all failing at it miserably, we formed a kind of sympathetic coterie. We were also in the chorus and tried to persuade James to join—he had such a fine singing voice—but he wouldn't hear of it. "Uh-uh!" he'd snort, limp wrist waving disdainfully. "And get my butt whupped by that nasty teacher, Mr. Arena!? Forget it. I'm here to be educated, not degraded."

The other black student whom I could safely experience was Gregory Laughinghouse. In many ways he was the exact opposite of James: tall, broad-shouldered, a powerful athlete with a straight-A average and a dour, sullen expression. He claimed to be part Cherokee Indian, walked around like a coiled spring, but one knew somehow that he wouldn't permit himself to explode no matter how badly pushed.

He did not associate with the other blacks in school and hung with us whites only by dint of being in the same class. Also, like me, he aspired to be a respected scholar-athlete with an appetite for lunatic mischief, a gutter-tough schoolyard wild man who could by turn excel at knee-scraping touch football and also grasp Walt Whitman's poetry. I used my stories about crazy schoolyard stunts to penetrate Gregory's defenses and awaken friendship. Stories that made Gregory alternately laugh and shake his head in wonder at what a "crazy white guy" I was.

I sensed that he too wanted to be crazy. But Gregory had reined himself in too rigorously. He was not spontaneous. The grooves around his mouth held his smile in check like a bridle. His piercing brown eyes contained the hint of a plea for rescue and apologized for their lack of feeling. He studied harder than anyone I have ever known. Even in school, at breaks, he was at it. No respite. The high grades rolled in as if off an assembly line. He wore his achievements like a shop apron. His forehead gleamed with entrapped light, the sweat of ceaseless reflection.

His father, he said, was an important man in a bank, a former college football player who had worked his way up from nothing to make a success of himself and open the doors of the world to his son. The key was to study hard, brutally hard, till your fingers ached and your eyes blurred.

To Gregory I confessed my misery over earning mediocre grades in all my subjects but English and chorus, and his brow furrowed gloomily. "What do you expect? Instead of whining, why don't you go right now, right this minute over there, sit down, and do your homework? Start now!" But I didn't want to. Preferred to whine. I wanted to be advised. I wanted to change the tone of my voice to an insincere imitation of a ne'er-do-well in need of help, and appeal to his experience. I wanted to do these things because I genuinely admired him and also because he was black and being this close enabled me to change the equation that haunted my street and home life, of Them against Me. He was on my side. Concerned about me. And as he talked I could watch the different, subtle inflections of mood expressed in his face change from anger to contempt to mirth to happiness to suspicion to compassion to boredom to sadness to weariness to indifference. He became human. In his face up-close as he lectured me on my poor academic performance, the faces of the black kids I had encountered on the streets attained some kind of fuller dimension in a general way, at least to the extent that I could imagine them as real human beings.

Gregory disliked James Miller, though he never said why. The feeling was mutual. James avoided him. Both James and Gregory seemed to
occupy a similar place in the racially divided school—a kind of limbo
found on neither side of the fence. Blacks and Puerto Ricans were on
one side, whites on the other. And James and Gregory were on a third
side of the fence, seeking their reflection in a white mirror. Either they
sought it in our faces or in a fantasy world of Parisian haute couture and
white commodified soul music, or in a crazy white guy, pre–Ivy league
mindset of sports, pranks, and passionate humanism; regardless, the
process was transforming them into phantoms.

As eighth grade wore on, Gregory felt increasing disaffection with
my epic schoolyard stories. A mysterious irritation had set in. He met
me with long tirades about racism. "But Gregory," I said, "you and me,
we're not racists, we're not into that bullshit. We're not part of that."

Lately, with his encouragement, my grades had shown signs of actual improvement. He was becoming a kind of role model for me. When
I confided to him my desire to become a writer, publish a book some
day, he scowled, and the next day showed me a small chapbook of
poems that he had printed up himself in a limited edition of fifty. "Don't
you see? Don't think about it, just do it. That's your problem—talking
without doing. That's what my father taught me: What good's the talk?
What do you have to show?" And in this way his father, without my
ever having met him, taught me.

But now a change had come over Gregory. I don't quite know how
to describe it. He was more snappish than usual. I told myself that it
was me. When he chose to avoid me in the lunchroom, or chose to
evade my approach at recess: it was me. My whining, needy character
was to blame, I told myself, my shaky and sickening sense of self. And
he was fed up, I told myself, with my stories of racist blood relatives and
disaffection from the brutality of schoolyard life.

One day, when we hadn't spoken for weeks, I cornered him on the
street and asked him what was wrong. Before he could speak, I quickly
answered my own question, outlining all my faults and weaknesses,
while his face grew gloomier and gloomier, and his mouth set tight as

a clamp. Suddenly he shouted: "Man, Alan, you fucking self-centered bullshit guy! It's got nothing to do with you! Nothing!" He began to talk, rapidly, angrily. "It's this white motherfuckin' world, and you're a part of it. I am nothing to you, man, just some Fred Flintstone or Mickey Mouse cartoon! No one looks at me like I'm human! You know what that feels like, Alan!?!?"

Stunned, I shook my head to indicate that I didn't.

"Thank you!" he sighed, relieved. "At least your big mouth's not gonna pretend to know that! Because you don't! You never will! But I am tired of being a black man! What is black? That's some word, a white word. I'm not black. I just am! *You're* fucking black! Your whole mother-fucking white race is black! But I'm just me! But no one's— I haven't seen myself in anyone's eyes for . . ." he choked up, lost his ability to speak.

The pity is that as a Jew I knew exactly what he meant. But when I tried to speak, he cut me off with an angry wave of his hand. Anyway, I could not have put it into so many words—it was only a feeling that I had in which, for an instant, I felt myself able to step into his skin, sneeze as he sneezed, stretch as he stretched; to cross my leg as he would in the sheltering privacy of his bedroom at home and slowly, thoughtfully, scratch the bottom of my foot, fantasizing of sports glory and meritorious attainment at some honorable profession, and also wonder how to get into the panties of such and such girl in class, tor-turing myself with that for a while. My mother, Mrs. Laughinghouse, is in the kitchen preparing dinner, and though I am feeling well for the moment, also I am dreading to go to class, to see white eyes that telegraphed: "Black, black, black, stay back . . . warning . . . danger . . . tree climber . . . monkey . . . King Kong . . . white-woman-raping homi-cidal pimp carjacker . . ." Or simply glaze over into blindness that denies even your corporeality, and so, just to survive, having to pretend that it's not happening, act as though everything were normal, and sometimes succeeding at it so well that for a time everything did seem normal, until some word overheard in the schoolyard or class—nigger, coon, jiggaboo—or the curling scornful smile on the lips of one who you know to hate your race, or else something read in a textbook or seen in a movie, snaps you back to the massive all-pervasive conspiracy of shadows assembled against you, in an effort to make of you a minstrel shadow.

And now in my heart, resentment flared, human resentment, a poison-tipped dart infecting my blood, liver, mind with an inimical form of spiritual fear, because as I returned to my own body, Gregory appeared more and more to be bloated with hatred, his movements rigid, his eyes not so much revealing pain as unbudgeably, suicidally convinced that no pain existed in the world but his own; that the treachery of the way required a kind of inner stoical numbness to serve as guide, to the exclusion of all others, and I could tell that it was leading him now, past my plea for mutual regard and friendship, to a hell of his own making for which I could not be blamed. "OK," I said with a plainly sad but fatalistic air. "OK. I don't know what to say except that I didn't make this fucked-up, racist world. It's not my fault. I thought we were friends. I guess I was wrong. Take care," and walked off heroically into my stained future without looking back.

Thereafter, we didn't speak to each other. We sat on opposite sides of a room.

I still hung out with James Miller, and we two drew quite close. So much so that now and then he would throw his arm around my shoulders. Sure, we were becoming real pals, though his constant singing of "Baby Love" finally got on my nerves. The odd way he walked sometimes inexplicably troubled me. I couldn't name what was wrong, if anything was wrong, and in many ways I preferred James to Gregory as a friend. James spoke often and openly about his home life but without self-pity: dead father, working mother. I could easily envision every inch of James's house, the way he described it, right down to the yellow lace lamp shades and the smell of pork chops that he said clung to the air, permeating everything. I could see James and his mother in their living room watching Diana Ross on *Ed Sullivan*, James snapping his ringed fingers, shaking his shoulders from side to side and his head bobbing Diana Ross–style as he sang: "Ba-by love, my baby love, ooh-ooh-ooh-ooh, my baby love . . . !" and throwing up his long fingered hands to exclaim: "Oh, I do love her!" which his mother no doubt took as a hopeful sign of future interest in girls. Hard to tell how a boy should be at that age, or any age really, with no father around. And she is supposing that he is normal, though she's secretly uneasy at the fact of her wondering in the first place. I did not wonder. I did not know that such a thing ever existed to wonder about. And then one day, queued outside the school for a fire drill, a guy named Howie Mazer broke ranks with his class and sidled up to me to watch James Miller, dressed in psychedelic shirt and elephant bell-bottom trousers such as Diana Ross wore, put on an outrageous and hilarious performance of "My World Is Empty Without You, Babe," which had the whole class in stitches except for Gregory, who stood off to the side, dourly looking away, and Mazer leaned into my ear, whispered: "How come you hang out with that homo? You want him grabbing your dick someday?" and I glanced at him nervously though still smilng at James's performance and said, "What are you talking about? James is no homo!" and he said, "No?" pug-nosed with this sardonic, confident air. "You wanna make a bet on that?" And I said, "What are you talking about?" and he told me that the other day he was downtown near this place called FIT or Fashion Institute of something-something and he saw James Miller hoofing down the street with this Puerto Rican twit and they've got arms around each other and James leaned over, gave his friend a big wet kiss that turned Howie Mazer's stomach sick with horror, and I looked at James and said to Mazer: "You mean he does it . . . with guys?" and Mazer said angrily: "Damned right!" and suddenly I'm angry too, thinking of all those times he threw an arm around me, though I still can't quite believe, homo or no homo, that it was anything more than genuine friendship—in fact I'm sure it never was—and yet I chose, perversely, to believe the opposite, knowing that it was wrong yet unable to reverse it, and snickering evilly and loudly in full view of James, Mazer and I commenced exchanging slurred words like "homo" and "fag" and "queer," a hand covering the mouth and blurting out the slur in blurred speech, followed by theatrical coughs, sputters, and shrieks, and James has stopped performing. He stands there watching us. I see the pain in his eyes but feel unable to stop, even when he sheds his first tears. Soon his round cheeks are glistening with two bright ribbons of sorrow and his hurt eyes—grown round and questioning—are fixed dead on my eyes, but I avoid looking at him for more then a second, and blurt it out: "Fag!" and Mazer said, "Homo!" and with one hand adjusting his gold horn-rimmed aviator-frame glasses he said in a voice grown quite suddenly hardened: "Well, baby, you can call me fag and you can call me homo, but you can both kiss my ass in Macy's window!" and spinning around, thrust his big ass at us, and fire alarm or no fire alarm threw open the door to the school and walked inside.

It's a few days later. We're in the same SP class, in full view of each other through the day, yet I didn't see him. When my eyes passed over his location they perceived a featureless shape cut out of space by cosmic scissors. When he answered a question in class, it came to me as over a radio, on a special program devoted to the history of civil rights in America: static, scratchy, badly recorded by an archivist of broken dreams. When he burst into his flamboyant Supremes skit in the tarpaved schoolyard as we waited in line for the gong announcing the end of recess, I hung my head in anger, feeling mocked. I hated him, felt betrayed by his "dirty secret," muttered: "Fuckin' homo," and the words "Fuckin' nigger" queued right up behind it, in line for expression, though from that I refrained. I wouldn't allow myself, I thought, to degenerate into that. After all, I'm a Jew. Son of a Holocaust survivor. Have come to grasp the nature of persecution, even within myself. Whether or not you feel that ugly feeling, I told myself, you just don't allow yourself that ugly feeling. You shove it down under the heel of a hard boot in your heart. You say: It doesn't exist, and just don't feel it, and eventually it won't exist. Because you're a Jew. Your mother was hunted. You've been beaten up, called names. You know what it means. So you don't do that to blacks, even if your father says it, even though a part of you wants to believe like your father: you crush that part, you gut it completely. Nuke the shit. You don't say the n-word, ever.

But it's different with a fag, I told myself. That's not a race thing. That's not a thing the Nazis chased down and shoved into gas chambers with Jews, is it? Nah! It's not like you had fags and rabbis and little Jewish babies all asphyxiating together. They probably didn't even have fags in Germany. And mentioned one day to my mother: "They got a fag at school," just like that. I wanted to run it by her. See her face color with crimson indignation. Expected to hear her say: "They should not allow such a thing in school," and me to laugh heartily in agreement. And we could have had a good talk about what a shame it was. Instead, a shelf was jarred in my emotions—a plate crashed angrily to the floor. She said, coldly: "You should not call such names to homosexual people. You know, the Nazis persecuted them, just the same as Jews. They had them at Auschwitz. Sure. Don't talk like a vulgar gutter filth. I curse the day we ever moved to the Bronx. You used to be a nice boy. I don't know you anymore."

The next day at recess, as James imitated Diana, I muttered: "It's your fault! You scared me with your arm around my shoulder and shaking your ass like that. I got scared. I got scared . . . ," arguing with his ghost in my mind, even as his living, feeling self performed before me, which I ignored.

And so, a few days later, because a special late-morning assembly had been called, those of us with a free period on our hands were welcomed to spend it as a study period in the big auditorium before the official assembly began. I had the time, and tests were coming up, so I went there. Normally, we're not allowed inside, the doors kept locked. To be there when it's empty was a treat of sorts.

It's a typical school auditorium, with three sections of scarred mahogany-colored wooden seats ascending amphitheater-style to the foot of a large stage covered by drab green curtains. I slipped quietly in through the unlocked doors, spotted in the first row a supervising teacher reading intently in a book. Here and there the hunched shoulders and heads of students deep in study. I circled around to the left section, scanned the rows for a good place to sit, and saw James. Quietly, I took up a seat where I could enjoy a good view of his face without giving my presence away. From the high arched windows a column of weak gray-white light fell over him, mildly irradiating his gold frame glasses. He raised a hand to scratch his ear and the big, silver ring on his hand glinted.

His long fingers scratched slowly, his brow furrowed with concentration. Yet James was relaxed, and his face seemed indifferent, serene, composed, reflective, and kind. The theme of empty wooden seats repeated around him with a kind of somber and austere beauty, like hand-carved waves, and, against the backdrop of the dark green stage curtains, his face looked so calm and intelligent that I wanted to call his name and smile and nod at the mutual consensus about human goodness that I felt must be implicit between us. Only, it is not. I am the barbarian who wronged him from savage ignorance and I didn't know just how to set it straight. Instead of asking his forgiveness, I sank into self-loathing. Instead of praising the miracle that has allowed me to see his full beauty and poise, I muttered, "God, what have I done? What have I done?" and let my shame place him forever beyond the reach of friendship.

In the future our eyes met, but his gazed blankly without noticing while mine shrugged above a timid half-smile that didn't contain a single morsel of feeling or information. And in this way blindness to each other became so automatic a condition that on occasion we would bump shoulders in the hall and I would realize only hours later that it was him.

Gregory Laughinghouse yielded one day not long after this to my pressure to join Lloyd Markowitz and I for a few games of after-school basketball over in Lloyd's neighborhood in Mount Eden, about a fifteen-minute stroll down the Grand Concourse from Wade Junior High School. But during the walk we became immersed in debate about everything under the sun. Our two-hour-long pedestrian forum had us frequently pausing to sit on stoops where we shouted and gestured passionately about whether or not the war in Vietnam was right or wrong, whether or not the Beatles music could be classified as music, who is the best tight end in the National Football League, whether or not it was OK to say so and so at school had nice tits, and if not what should

one say and what were honorable as opposed to dishonorable inten-
tions toward a girl: What was one looking for, sex or company, a good
time or a good fuck? For instance, I got along with Barbara Millman real
good, she was like a friend, but every so often I had this thought of getting into her pants, and what if I tried? Would that ruin the friendship?
And besides, she was kind of ugly. But I wouldn't have minded "doin' it"
with her once, just to see. And Gregory asked: "See what?" and I got hot
under the collar, but Lloyd laughed: "It's natural to want to, between
men and women. That's why they can never really be friends." At that,
Gregory exploded: "Bullshit!" His parents were good friends! The best
of friends! Better friends than most men are with men. And as he talked
I tried to imagine my parents as friends, and couldn't, and then tried to
imagine them having sex but couldn't see that either: they were like
neutered Pilgrims performing passionless rituals in a monotonous
monastery where time and purpose had become as meaningless as pinwheels waiting for a breeze.

On and on we argued, having fun, but Gregory's intensity lent it a
certain edge: he was remarkably explosive, majestically opinionated,
and without a trace of humility. This was a Gregory that I had not seen
before. His tight-lipped demeanor unlocked, he blurted out a continuous narrative into which our questions dipped like ladles. Clearly he
had thought about much in what I began to imagine as a strange, somewhat sad solitude. He had absolutely no doubt about the correctness of
his views and had the information to back them, whereas Lloyd and I
stammered, hemmed, and spit around our somewhat flamboyant, spontaneous assertions. Clearly, neither of us had given a moment's thought
to very much outside of ourselves.

By the time we reached the schoolyard it was well past five o'clock,
and over the dun-colored brick roofs the dusk's descending sun hung
like a fiery bronze disk, tingeing the edges and corners of the world
with harsh gold, and we were all spent emotionally and intellectually.
Discussion with Gregory was exhausting and neither Lloyd nor I had
emerged right about anything.

We shot a few hoops half-heartedly, Lloyd appropriating the ball from a chubby little silent boy who stood watching us warily with his arms at his sides and his head hung slightly. Noting this, Lloyd teased Gregory: "He's scared of you," and Gregory stopped with the ball placed between his hands for a jump shot from the foul line, and his jaw tensed as his teeth champed on the big muscled bridle of his inhibitions, and then he simply walked over to the boy, extended his hand with the ball balanced on it, and said: "I'm sorry. We're just a little crazy today. We should have asked for your permission." And the boy nodded with evident satisfaction and accepted the ball. Gregory looked angry with himself. "I'd never normally do that!" he snapped. "Takin' someone's ball! Never! It's from hanging out with you crazy white boys!" "Hey!" I interrupted. "What do you gotta get into that white guy/black guy stuff for?"

He glared at me, his eyes almost crossed with angry disbelief. "Why? Why? Because it's true. You're white. I'm black. Nothing's gonna change that!"

"Yeah, but that's insulting," I said. "Why you gotta always drag race into this? That's your problem. You don't look at people; you look at their color. Don't look at my color, man, look at me, who I am."

Gregory said coldly: "I'm looking. And I see *white*, spelled out in big capital letters."

And now anger jumped into my throat, put a catch in my voice. "Shit! I don't like that, Gregory. How would you like it, how would you feel . . . ?" A kind of dark, angry smile of mischief crept into my face, and Lloyd, guessing the point I was about to make, said: "Don't say it," and I didn't. I stopped. "Forget it," I scowled. But the imp was out now, and as we strolled around the yard debating again, Lloyd and I glanced at each other wide-eyed and chortled with secret mutual understanding, which Gregory noticed after a time, his jaw muscles bunching and eyes faintly cross and he said: "What's up?" and Lloyd glanced at me, with a look that said: "Go ahead. I'll stand behind you on this, but I won't say it," and so I tried to adopt a casual, good-humored, jaw-rubbing congenial style reminiscent, strangely enough, of a Southern small town sheriff, and began with a soft chuckle: "Heh-heh," which Gregory responded to, his shoulders tensing, and I said, "Wellllllll . . . you know, the question is how sensitive do you get? Like I get sensitive about words like whitie and Jewboy and kike," and Gregory interrupted: "But you think it was funny that you used to go around in gym saying 'Kill the Jews!' even though you're Jewish, so I guess you have a double standard." And I said: "Double what? What's that mean?" and fiercely, almost as a challenge in which I sensed, for the very first time, his intense dislike for me, he said: "It means hypocrite. You say one thing and do another."

"Well," I said, speaking past the flush of hot, angry blood that rushed into my face and neck, "I guess if I'm a white boy and a hypocrite that you must be an Uncle Tom phony nigger," and I did not even feel the punch that landed squarely on my jaw. My head just snapped, and I stumbled back though I did not fall, stood there stunned as much by what I'd said as by the shock of the blow, while already he was well on his way across the yard, the back of his pin-striped Arrow shirt a sturdy V, and I shouted, though with difficulty, in a kind of garbled voice that grew clearer, louder, and more anguished with each effort: "That's right, coward! Go, don't stay and talk. It's just you and how you feel! *Punk!* God damned . . . punk . . . fuckin' . . . god-damned . . ." and my voice trailed off into a whispering sob.

"Fuck him!" spit Lloyd. "He's got a fucking nigger attitude . . ."

But I shook my head weakly, though emphatically, from side to side as I slid to the ground to hold my head. "No, I shouldn't have done it, I shouldn't have done it. It just came out of me." And Lloyd said: "Sure, what do you expect? Those people got an attitude. He had it coming to him." And I said: "No, no, no, that's all wrong, It's all wrong. It's sick. Really sick. Oh, shit. He'll never forgive me. I know it. I know it," gasping the words, even as I felt a faint glimmer of hope that he might.

"He never will. I know him. I know him."

He never did.

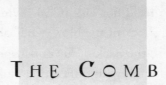

THE COMB

MY MOTHER HAD a long-handled comb that she claimed reduced the explosive high blood pressure in her head when raked across her scalp, and once, when she entered our room after my father had gone to work, she asked: "What did you do with the comb?"

Howard looked at me in disgust, shook his head, and returned to his comic book.

"What comb?" I asked.

"The one I use for my blood pressure. How many times have I told you not to touch my things!"

"What are you talking about?" I smiled angrily. "I didn't touch your goddamned comb!"

The word "goddamned" set her off. Talking to herself, she went to fetch a belt from the closet to hit me with. I shouted, as I heard her rummage for the belt, "You touch me with that, I'll wrap it around your fucking head!"

She knew I meant it. I had grown too big to hit anymore, easily. So she switched tactic. I heard the bathroom door bolt shut. Howie looked at me. I said: "What the . . ?" and Howie shrugged.

"Fuck her," he said. He read.

In my window, brown alley walls and golden lights. Drawn shades like luminous parchments awaiting a wise word. I felt gripped with a sense of excitement at the retreat that I had caused. Suddenly I heard the loud thump of her body collapsing to the ground, followed by a short, soft moan, and then another. My heart raced. This is it, I thought, I've killed my mother, she's dead, my liberation has come early, the true adventure is about to begin. Howie didn't even lift his face. "Did you hear that?" I gasped. "Howie, I think she's fainted! Or worse!"

"So? So what?" said Howie.

"What are you, nuts?" I shouted, throwing off my covers. "C'mon. Get up! Something's happened! Get up!"

Reluctantly, he followed into the foyer. I stood before the locked bathroom door. Pressed my ear: listened. "Mashala, Mashala!" I rattled the doorknob. Listened again. "Mashala! Can you hear me?" my voice sounding almost like that of a husband, and she uttered a weak moan from the floor.

I turned to Howard. "Oh, God, Howie, maybe she's dying in there."

Howie shrugged. "So let her die."

"Asshole!" I snarled indignantly, and rattled on the doorknob. "Mashala, Mashala," and for a moment the strangest sort of a smile crept over my lips, and a feeling of a malevolent, mischievous, insincere presence inhabited me, as though this were all a sort of game, a form of fun. Then, just as suddenly, it vanished. I was back to myself again, able to believe my own panic.

I must calm my voice, make it seem older than it really is, I told myself. Tried to imagine whose voice to emulate. Not hers. Certainly not my father's. In comparison with other adults, they often seemed so childish. When I spoke to other kids' parents I beheld adults and felt like a child, but at home I spoke to my mother or father and faced a child and felt like an adult and became so enraged at my misfortune that I turned on them suddenly, violently, with abusive words and ranting accusations. And there she is now, I thought, my misfortune lying on the floor. This was no time for the anger I felt, or to pity the perpetual anguished turmoil in my gut, or to resent my unhelpful brother standing behind me, whose indifference, much as I would have hated to admit it, steadied me. To bolster myself, I thought of Ward Cleaver, the puzzled but unflappable father in the television comedy *Leave It to Beaver*, and managed a fair imitation of his personality and speaking manner.

"Marie," I said, my voice lowered several octaves to my version of Ward's hollow bass, "Marie, you had better get a hold of yourself, and come to your feet. If you're really that sick, you'll need to see a doctor and there's no way for that to happen while you're locked in. So come, open this door and we'll take it from there. . . ."

"You're such a shmuck," chuckled Howard. "Just leave her in there. What do you want, for her to come out and beat the shit out of you again? You're practically begging her for it. Leave her there. At least while she's in there you're not getting hit."

"Yeah, sure!" I exploded. "I should go lay down and watch TV while she dies on the floor. You're such a creep!"

And at that moment I heard the lock unbolt, the door opened. Out she stepped, walked up to me, slapped me in the mouth, and then again.

"In your mouth, I give you. There! And there!" Her blue eyes gloating crazily. "Yes, that's good," and raising her hand to strike me again as I stood there stunned by her betrayal, my eyes filled with sudden blinding tears, the figures and planes around me dissolving into a vague, trembling impression of blurred shapes fissured by the sharp report of her voice: "That is what you get for using filthy words! Wait till your father hears about this. You're gonna get it but good!"

And my voice erupted from my throat in a kind of high, thin scream:

"But how can you hit me? I'm trying to help you, why should you turn on me, I'm good, a good son, a good boy . . ." and so on.

"You're a dirty-mouthed imbecile like your Uncle Arnold: a real disappointment, believe you me. I thought you took after my side of the family, but you're no Jucht! You're a Kaufman, through and through!

I groped my way to my room, stood hunched in a corner, face to the wall, shaken by the utter hopelessness of it, though what "it" was I found so hopeless I could not have said exactly, and I could hear Howie's bedsprings squeak as he threw himself onto his bed, and heard the pages of his comic book flip as she ranted in the next room: "My head is going to explode if I don't find that comb. . . . *Boo hoo hoo hoo . . .* Why did they take my comb? God, why did you curse me with monsters like that for sons, wasn't it bad enough that I had Nazis, you had to give me two like those two? . . . *Boo hoo hoo!*"

I sank deep into the darkness behind my eyes, which gradually assumed the shape of a cave's mouth in which I could see her twelve-year-old pretty elfin-thin face pinched with hunger, shuddering in tattered military-style clothes too large for her, shoulders covered with a blanket, arranging her pallet on crates marked DYNAMITE, as big husky partisans with guns slung over their shoulders stamped in and out. It was snowing outside, but there was no blanket over the cave mouth, the dark interior lit by a single lantern that remained on as she lay down shuddering and covered herself with the blanket, and now the cave mouth assumed a human shape opened operatically wide in song, within it the face of the curly headed handsome Italian boy Mario who would sing to her on spring days his favorite song, "Santa Lucia," and I could see where the hanging flesh at the back of his throat gradually became the hangman's noose of a gallows in the town square, in the valley below the mountains in which the partisans fought, and two SS men dragged Mario up the steps. Just before they threw the red blanket over his head to signify his Communism, his mouth opened in a terrified shout that gradually softened and became the oval of my mother's eye as she sat with a belt in her hand and I stood before her singing "Santa Lucia." The song echoed from the roof of my mouth and the back of my throat out into the world, though not quite perfectly, and so the strap lashed me buckle-first across the arm and my singing mouth became a screaming mouth became my gaping mouth now sobbing and all I could utter was: "Oh . . . God . . . Oh . . . God . . ." and my shoulders shook, and she appeared in the room, went to the window, threw it open, and announced: "I'm going to jump!"

My arm extended, hands open-fingered, head shaking from side to side, but my throat was too locked for any sound to escape, and Howie said: "So, go ahead, jump!" and I looked at him in horror. She leaned farther out.

"No!" I managed to shout, and rushed over, grabbed her, pulled her away, my hands sinking into the unfamiliar, soft, scarred flesh of her belly's many surgeries, and immediately she sought to free herself, not to attempt death but to escape intimate physical contact. Normally we never touched each other, except for her to beat me, or when I planted a kiss on the top of her head, which made her shoulders hunch and her head duck in distaste.

And just like that, she was all right again. Completely all right. It only lasted for a few minutes. She said calmly that she would not be able to survive an entire night with such blood pressure in her head. I tried to reason with her. Let's go to the hospital. Let's call Dad to come home. But she refused all options. So I'll go down, I volunteered, find an open drugstore, buy you a new comb. And, strangely, this option she found acceptable. It was past midnight. I was fourteen, had never before been out alone this late in the streets of the Bronx.

"Wanna come?" I asked Howie nervously.

He looked out the window, considered, said "Forget it," and went back to reading his comic book.

I dressed hurriedly, received in hand from her five dollars and a note with the name of the comb type: Max Factor Maxi-Teaser. "But make sure it's the right color, it looks like— I don't know, what is this . . . brown . . . like your brother's glass frames . . ."

"Tortoiseshell," I said.

"Is this what it's called? Such a crazy language, your English . . ."

As I stepped out into the street, the weak light of the streetlamp seemed to announce my presence to any predators lurking about. Otherwise the street was totally dark, the humped shapes of cars lining the curb and the hard planes of the building shadowed in against the distant night sky. Two blocks away, the shopping center on 170th Street looked shut down: rows of dark storefronts, the streetlamps casting a golden light over the discarded boxes heaped at the curbs. I hadn't any idea of how I would find an open drugstore at this hour around here. So I began to walk in a blind haste, my huffing breath loud in my own ears, emphasizing the drama of my predicament to myself.

After traversing a few blocks I felt more comfortable with the night. I saw that I was as obscured as anyone else out there. There was a kind of ghostly, drifting anonymity to walking out alone this late, and a sense of calm detachment settled over me.

I felt myself to be an observer, or an angel, sent by God to earth to see my daylight world by night, how peaceful and lonely it was as I slept, how empty of anything good or bad, a kind of deserted warehouse awaiting the arrival of workers to buzz it back into life. For me alone the neighborhood would not perform its night rituals. It was only prepared to show itself fully to a big audience. But it gave me a few signs of life. Someone returning perhaps from his job hurried past with head lowered and a newspaper under the arm. Would he come to my aid if I were attacked? I wondered. And knew that he would not, that I was completely on my own out here.

As I passed the big empty lake of darkness that was the schoolyard, I thought of my bed, the room's cozy yellow glow, but it was not safe there for me—I had been driven out into this dangerous, inhospitable, companionless night to search like a fugitive ghost for a comb, and I hunched my shoulders, felt my face harden, my soul shift from tears to numbness, and for the first time in my life I could truly imagine what it must feel like to be a man. This is how it is to be grown up, walking the lakeshore of shadow, your back a little bent under the night, clinging to walls and windows of closed shops, stopping with a resigned, wistful sadness to endure the crawling steel caterpillar of the overhead subway as it screeches into the station, slashing the silence with its matter-of-fact calamity of noise, long blue strings of electric fire dripping from its wheels.

This is what it's like. A desolation within oneself perfectly matched to the desolation without. I finally saw the argument for getting good and stinking drunk. When there's nowhere to go but walking and no one home to greet you, booze, I imagined, could make you feel like home's anywhere. Give a kind of meaning to being lost and alone. I don't know why I felt this, had never drunk before, yet felt in me something very big and exciting awaken at the thought of booze, an eagerness to explore the world with booze in hand, the last tie between me and the people in that little apartment snapping, and I thought: Booze is the magic potion that someday can take me to the farthest regions of the earth and make all my dreams come true.

Along Jerome Avenue I saw, here and there, aprons of light spread before lit windows of shops. One was a liquor store, and I stood outside viewing the extraordinary variety of products on its dark-hued shelves, a thousand different labels, shapes, and prices—a real arsenal of potential future courage—and knew that with one of those fancy fuel cartridges loaded in my chamber anything was possible. Another closed store was a men's clothier. I admired the many kinds of adult clothing that would someday hang on my frame as I barreled along with a confident smile, the hint of expensive whiskey on my breath, and preceded, like Thomas Wolfe, by a reputation as a great novelist. But in the next moment I was sloshed on cheap table wine like Jack Kerouac, dressed in plaid flannel shirt, tattered jeans, work boots, standing in the doors of freights rumbling through vast fields of high golden corn while somewhere far off in the big cities my books were stacked high in bookstore windows and people queued up to buy them.

Yeah, I thought, nervously wrinkling the five-dollar bill in my pocket, tempted, almost, to set the ball rolling into motion this instant. Why not trick the future into happening this very moment, buy myself a big jug of table wine, grab a subway up to the Hudson River railroad tracks north, jump a freight Canada-bound, see what happens? Why not have a revolution right now?

But my thoughts rushed ahead to visions of harsh, jagged-edged trestle bridges and abandoned mills, and the hidden encampments of heartless men with murderous eyes and how it would feel to come upon such men alone, with no one to know where you are. Would I be butchered in my sleep, my pockets rifled of pennies and my corpse rolled into the river lashed to a rotting section of railroad tie? Under the moon of America I sensed that many forms of murder lurked about. My mother's tales of horrible killers, Satan worshippers, malevolent drifters, filled my head. And the depth of my fear filled me with shame. Studying my reflection in the window, I saw that I was beginning to possess the size and build of a powerful man, but I knew that my heart was yet that of a timid, frightened child.

On Mount Eden Avenue I found a drugstore open for business. Behind the counter stood a pharmacist in a white smock, his deadpan face watching the door.

I wondered why he didn't sit at this late hour. Just stood there and waited. Strange. But I soon realized that I was the strange one, red-rimmed eyes tired with crying and cheeks streaked with dirty tears; glimpsed my own pathetic face in a makeup mirror as I tried to explain in an urgent and querulous voice the exact sort of comb I needed, but which he didn't carry. Sorry.

Thunderstruck, I stood there. It couldn't be. Didn't he have something like it? Yes, but not in tortoiseshell, and not that brand, and the handle's slightly shorter but it does pretty much the same thing. Did he know, I asked, if there were any other drugstores open around here, and he shook his head: not till Fordham Road. OK, OK, I'll take it, I said, my grubby fist holding out the crumpled bill, my face in the makeup mirror desperate.

When I came home, she was asleep. Howard too. I sat in the kitchen with the lights up bright, gaping, exhausted, at my reflection in the window. My face seemed so sallow, gaunt, yellowish, my head wafer-thin. I was hallucinating with fatigue. It was past two o'clock in the morning. The satiny paper bag containing the comb crinkled in my hand. My neck was so disproportionately narrow compared to my wide shoulders and my chest was somewhat flabby. I needed a lot of work before I'd be the kind of man to hit the road alone and write big books. I'd need to look different. That would give me the confidence I'd need. If I showed a strong face to the world, they'd be tricked into thinking that I was strong inside, and eventually maybe I would be.

But there was nothing I could do about it now. I felt ferociously hungry. So, gingerly, I removed cornflakes and sugar from the closet, milk from the refrigerator, a bowl and spoon from the dish rack beside the sink. I filled the bowl with cereal and emptied close to half a box of sugar into it. Splashed in a little milk. And spooned big sweet spoonfuls of solace into my mouth.

When I had finished the bowl, I filled it again, emptied in the remaining sugar, and repeated the slow, comforting ritual. Then I just sat there, growing sleepier and sleepier, though not sleepy enough to want sleep, but just gazing at my reflection in the kitchen window, my imaged face crisscrossed by fire escape ladders like my mother's surgical belly scars, only steel. I felt in the sad defeated Bronx tenements of my muscle and bone that I could just sit at this dinette table for an eternal night, just this way, neither moving nor speaking, and with the bagged comb at my elbow and the others asleep forever, it wouldn't be so bad to just sit and wait, and sit and wait, and pass one's life this way.

VIRGINS

A TITSY GODDESS shed her coat in a doctor's office. Underneath: naked love.

Man oh man oh my God will you look at that, grunted my friends, shifting on the couch, sweating, amazed. Nipples hard, the blonde reclined under the doctor's pimpled, hammering ass, her wet black lips moaning O, O, O, O, O. All this time I'm thinking: So what?

Then: sudden jump cuts in frame, a number 8 in crosshair sites, and now she pumped her head up and down, up and down, up and down, my friends cheered, the doc's johnson clutched in her wicked mouth. Then, clasping red nails jiggled his rocketing semen all over her face.

Now *that* held my interest.

So I watched on in envious silence. We all did. Then the lights blazed on. No one moved.

In walked Earl's pop, Vic Dupreen.

That's how it began, my falling-out with innocence, the loss of my virginity. A look-alike for the actor Warren Oates, Vic casually removed and folded his black horn-rims, pocketed them, and said, "What you boys doin' home? Don't you have school today?"

"We cut," said Earl glumly.

"What you got my projector out for?" He shut it off. "What you watchin' there?" He tugged a length of film from the reel, the corners of his mouth bunched in a tight smile. "It's not even my best one. You oughta watch *Pumpin' Pups*, it's a lot better than this junk. Ever see a dog fuck a woman, Alan?" And he's not kidding.

"No," I blushed.

He looked us over. "Whatssamattah? You boys never got any poon-tang?"

No replies.

"Virgins," he uttered in disgust. "Why, at your age I was up to my balls in ass!" He glared at Earl. "Well, I can understand them, but I'm damned disappointed in you! Why are you hiding from me? What's your daddy for if you can't let him help you on a thing like that? You ashamed?! It's nothing . . . just . . . what d'ya call it there at school: Just *hygiene!* S'all. Why, I'd a taken you down to that cathouse I go to . . . the one I took your stupid brother for his eighteenth birthday, don't you remember, Earl?"

Earl shrugged.

"It's a good house. Clean girls. I'd a gotten ya laid," Vic railed on.

I just sat there, floored by the whole improbable scene: that here in the Bronx a grown male—who hailed from Humphreys County, Mississippi, the son of pig farmers, no less—should speak openly of sex to his own son! Now he looked back at me. "Alan, I'm taking you and Earl and George there—yes *you!*—to a house, a cathouse, a good one. I'm gonna change this sorry state of affairs, you hear me boy?"

"Yes, sir."

"You boys scrape up ten bucks each, meet me here Saturday, front of the house. Ten o'clock in the morning. That way we'll get the girls fresh. Later they'll be all wore out." He looked gravely at Earl, said in a low voice: "Tell your mother we're going to the racetrack to play ponies that day."

Earl nodded, familiar with the alibi.

Victor surveyed our faces: "We all makin' sense here?"

We nodded, sniffling.

"Well, then, get the hell on out of here and let me to get some sleep." Then he flipped out a fiver, tossed it on the table, said to Earl: "Now go get me a cold six-pack and Chesterfields."

And our asses scrammed out of there.

It's tough to greet your mother's eyes when you plan to visit a whore.

"What is the mattah with you, Abie?" she asked. "Your face, it looks funny. What are you thinking of?"

A whore, Mom. I'm thinking of a whore. Of course, I didn't say. But all that week she sensed something was up. Mothers know.

George dropped out but agreed to lend me some bucks on Saturday morning. All that week weird sensations snaked through my loins—that garden with its death tree of forbidden fruit, in which Satan tills a sinister soil—and I felt an imminent sundering from some primeval innocence, admission to universal woe. Yet this gave me terrific satisfaction. For after the whorehouse, I told myself, no longer will I remain a naive child cut off from the realities of life; I'll be a man equal to the secrets of his mother's suffering under Hitler. Sexual knowledge tasted of death. I could not have said so much in words, but I sensed it with intense fear; felt sure to be fundamentally changed in some catastrophic way.

"You should see the nice chicken your father and I bought from Louie the butcher," my mother informed that Wednesday. "I'm gonna make some nice meal for Rosh Hashanah," and startled, I spit: "When's that?" and she said, trembling: "Saturday."

My spoon clattered angrily in my soup plate. She recoiled, startled. "What are you doing? You break my plates! Stupeed! Oy, a *charbon!*"

"Forget it!" I howled angrily. "I'm not blowing my weekend for no stupid Jewish holiday."

"Shut up that filthy mouth of yours, *putz-kup!* How dare you! The Nazis almost killed me just so you could speak that way to me?! You'd better be here on Rosh Hashanah, and how, mister!"

Then it was my father's turn, in his boxer shorts, to threaten, bribe, and cajole, to no avail.

"No way! Shove that Jewish holiday shit!" I exploded as their faces paled. "I'm an American! I don't celebrate no Rosh Hashanah! Thanksgiving and New Year's, that's my holidays! Unnerstan? Unnerstan?!?!"

But of course, no one did. And besides, the real truth was I just wasn't going to be robbed by Jewish history of my trip to the whorehouse.

Come the day, the only others abroad were dignified Jewish families strolling to synagogue. The air possessed that ascetic, archaic, and deflating quality of stifling sacredness so endemic to High Holy Days. I scorned the solemnity of the worshippers grinding life to a standstill; doubled my pace, a demotic force of inexorable self-will. Under George's window, called up five flights. He thrust out his head. "Got that ten bucks?" He nodded, threw it down in a sealed envelope weighted with a stone. "So long, sucker!" I waved. His face receded with a grin.

I hurried along, lonely in my new empowerment, patting my pocket with my hand, both sickened and thrilled. For this was to be my Bar Mitzvah into damnation. By this single stroke would I fathom the hidden motives of the world.

At the rendezvous point, Victor Dupreen sat behind the wheel of his big Pontiac, engine running, thick exhaust blackening the air. A cigarette twitched in the corner of his mouth. "Get in," he ordered.

I slid in next to him. Then Earl appeared, sat behind his father.

"Where's George Auria?" asked Victor, a little offended by his absence. "I invited the son of a bitch, didn't I?"

"He couldn't make it," Earl weakly offered, shifting in his seat, "but with us there's enough money."

"I don't care jack shit about the money," snarled Victor. "I in-vi-ted the boy to come get laid, not give me no goddamned money. I'd a paid for the fucker if he was broke. Is that it? He broke?"

"No," I said. "He got the money. He just don't want to pay a woman for no sex."

Victor's bloodshot eyes narrowed into slits in the rearview mirror. "A big saint, huh? Well, you tell your friend I ever catch his saintly syphilitic ass up in my house watchin' my fuckin' private porno flicks, I'll blow his haloed ass right off the goddamned planet!"

"Yes, Mr. Dupreen," I said as his hand slammed the gearshift and we pulled out of the spot with a squeal of burning rubber.

The house was downtown, and I sank back in the vinyl seat cushions for the long ride. En route I cringed at the sight of more decked-out Jews strolling to prayer; counted myself lucky to have the kind of nut-case family I did, so unobservant of their Jewish roots that I had no obligation to God whatsoever but to eat guilty roast chicken and lie with hair in my teeth about where I'd been.

"What a joke Judaism is," I thought jeeringly, without conviction. "I'll never feel about it like those fuckin' suits do, dressed up for what?" Ran a smoothing hand over my white T-shirt and jeans and inspected my high-top black-and-white Converse sneakers; then peered numbly out the window at a journey without return, for every street ticked off beneath the tires marked my last time passing over as a virgin.

I felt so sick.

We reached downtown: Second Avenue off Houston Street. Before a gated grungy building with junkies lounging on the stoop, Victor jumped out smiling: "Here it is!" Earl was solemn as we ascended in the elevator, sourly scrutinizing my attire, timidly checking his pop's face for mood swing. "Couldn't you do better than that?" Victor snarled. "Dungarees and sneakers: that's not fit dress for this kind of establishment. This is a clean and classy operation. Earl, what kind of fucked up deal is this? I'm not sure they're going to let you in. We'll have to see what Birdy says." And for the benefit of my puzzled face, Earl added: "The madame. Birdy's the madame."

Madame! A realization that such things as I had only heard about from smut novels did actually exist, and that I was about to experience it firsthand, seemed to corroborate history itself, the terrible things my mother had seen in Hitler's Europe. The reality of brothels proved the lunacy of war.

However, for a brothel I had envisioned a mansion with a big veranda, like down south: not this dingy Second Avenue tenement. Whorehouse meant that literally, I'd thought. I'd never heard of a whore apartment or a whore flat. So, here was something else: Reality did not resemble the stories about it.

Victor paused before the door for one last-minute inspection: my attire had raised his hackles. "You got money?" he snapped "At least let's see it."

I flashed the ten.

"OK. Be polite, do what you're told. And don't eat all the goddamned potato chips. Leave something for the next guy. You too, boy."

We nodded, two good soldiers. He knocked.

A woman who could easily have passed for one of our mothers stood there, head crowned by a big orange bouffant, dressed in a matching tangerine-colored muumuu. On her feet were turquoise rabbit-fur house slippers.

"Hi, Victor!" she sang happily, a mother glad to see a son.

Victor responded in a warm, respectful tone: "I brought you some business, Birdy. Virgins!"

She clapped her hands with delight. "Virgins! Oh, how nice. Come in, boys, come right in, make yourselves at home." We filed in. She slammed the door, shut several locks, including a floor-to-door police lock. Once she had us inside, her eyes hardened by degrees. She said to Victor: "I'm surprised at you. I like having the business, but to bring in boys dressed in blue jeans and sneakers . . . is that all you think of me, honey?"

He leaned over, whispered in her ear.

"Oh, I see," she said. "And this nicely dressed one is your boy?"

"Yes it is, Birdy. My very son; so now make him a man."

"Well, all right then, I'll tell you what. Why don't you go get a burger or something and leave these two pups up here with me. Come back in about, say, an hour. They'll be done by then, I think."

After he left, she handed us each a blue poker chip in exchange for our ten dollars. She led us into a kind of waiting area: comfortable chairs and a coffee table spread with nudie magazines. The radio played "Lay Lady Lay" by Bob Dylan. Two men dressed in drab suits sat facing us. Pistol grips peeked from under their jackets when they stirred, and one had a badge clipped to his belt. They were police detectives, bulls on the take who'd already received the bread part of their bribe and now waited for the pussy. But they were drinking, and in no hurry. "Hey, Birdy!" one of them called out, shitfaced. "Birdy, come in here! Bring in some more beer! And for these two here. Give 'em each a beer."

"No beer for them," growled Birdy, indignant. "They're under legal age."

"Aw, g'wan, Birdy, give the beer fer krissakes! What, we gonna arrest ya?"

She laughed elegantly. "You heard. I'll bring 'em both in some nice Cokes and potato chips. How'ze that, kids? Good by you?"

"Fine!" we chimed in together. "Great!"

She returned with potato chips heaped in a dirty cut-glass bowl. A curtain divided the room. The music on loud. We all had to shout to hear ourselves. Earl spoke with the bulls, who were interested to learn that we were virgins. They wanted to help us along with the induction, impart their experience. But each seemed at a loss about what to say. "Virgin," one kept repeating over and over. "A virgin, huh?" and nodded profoundly. His partner filled in the ensuing silence with: "Just don't be nervous is the ting. Dat nervousness spoils it. Just relax." The other bull looked queerly at his partner: "You sound like you're the fucking whore. What're you, the ho'? Relax my ass. Who gives a fuck? What, you wanna fuck 'em yourself, I tink. I tink you got a pussy under those pants a yours," and so on.

Then, suddenly, the curtains parted and a man in shirtsleeves with his hand touched to his horn-rimmed glasses hurried out. A moment later, the most beautiful woman I had ever seen in my life, naked in high heels, stepped out, looked around, said: "Who's next?"

As one facing a summary execution, I followed her lonely, lovely back through the curtains, into a room outfitted with a bed, a sink, a window, and a coatrack. I stood off to the side, at the end of the room farthest from the bed, unable to bring myself to look at her. "My name is Michelle," she said to my lowered eyes.

I nodded with a stiff smile. "Hi."

"Hi," she responded, in a fur-stroking voice. "And what's your name?"

"Alan," I croaked.

"Hi, Alan. You look French, you know? Are you French?"

"My motha, my motha is French," I offered, horrified to have even mentioned her in such a place.

"That makes you French," said Michelle. "How exciting."

I didn't want to touch her, or be touched. I wanted to go home. But Michelle moved right up on me and placed her palms flat on my chest; her perfume filled my head, and she asked: "Do you have the chip?"

Wordlessly, I handed over the chip. She leaned down, slipped it into her high heel shoe, the blue disk against her pale white ankle. I unlaced my sneakers, hoping my socks wouldn't smell; they did, their stench unmistakable. Quickly, I sat down on the cold floor, peeled them off. All this time, Michelle watched. I dared not raise my eyes or acknowledge her stare, but could feel it on me, hungry.

I climbed to my feet, tugging my T-shirt around my shoulders.

"Take it off," said Michelle.

I pulled it over my head, dropped it onto the pile of my clothes. How strange to see the same dungarees that my mother washed, ironed, and folded, lying now on the floor of a whorehouse. Ashamed, I stood there in my briefs.

"Take it all off," said Michelle, running a small spade-shaped tongue lasciviously over her lips.

"All of it?" I asked, surprised.

"Yes," she said. "All of it."

Suddenly, from the other side of the curtain, the bulls, who had listened to every word, exploded in laughter.

"Ahh ha ha ha! Did you hear dat!? All of it? All of it! Ha ha ha ha!"

"Hey!" cried the other, gasping for air. "Hey, Mrs. Whore! Should I take it all off? You bet, Mr. John! All of it! Ha! Ha! Ha!"

I felt crushed. "Don't mind them," said Michelle softly. She led me by the hand to the sink, where, against the backdrop of their laughter, she lathered her palms, and reaching down, cupped my genitals in her hand and gently soaped them. "For hygienic purposes," she explained intelligently above their voices. "This protects you and protects me." I nodded that I understood. But my genitals didn't, hung cold, ashamed, shrunken with dread inspired by the derision of the police. I looked down at them peevishly. The time had come! I'd practiced for this over and over in the bathroom, in fantasy. Fuck the police! Please, don't crap out on me now! But they played dead. Just as my emotions pretended not to feel. Yet my brain's function seemed sharper than ever, ran on, multivoiced, cacophonous. "Come," she said, after she had towel-dried me with terry cloth strokes so tender a corpse would have moved its hips. She drew me to the bed, laid me back. "Relax," she sighed. "You're a cherry? Are you, honey? A cherry!"

"Yes," I said in a small, weak voice. "A cherry."

"Hmmmmm," she hummed with sincere gratitude. "How delicious! Don't be nervous, hon. Just pretend that you're doing it with your girlfriend."

My eyebrows knitted crossly. Having no girlfriend, how could I pretend what I've never done before? I tensed up. But her persistent lips moved down my chest, stomach, played over my thighs with light teasing kisses. Then, unbelievably, she took me into her mouth. I lay there, ashamed, sure that God was shooting me from heaven with a Bell & Howell 8-millimeter movie camera. The film would be shown in Hell at my trial.

Suddenly, I asked: "What high school'd you go to?"

She looked up, surprised. "What?"

"Uh. You know. What school did you graduate?"

Michelle studied me with a chagrined half-smile. "Whatsamattah? Doesn't it feel good?"

"Yeah. I guess. Maybe we should talk a little."

"Talk? Sure. What ya wanna talk about?"

She brought herself to a cross-legged position and so did I, facing each other. I kept my eyes trained on hers, though they strayed down to her breasts and nipples, which I found pleasant to look at. The sight of her vagina, though, I found positively terrifying, a small pink mouth speaking soundlessly from a devilish beard.

"So, this is what you do for a living?" I began stupidly.

"Right now it is. Uh-huh."

I nodded. "You don't seem though like . . . like a . . ."

"Like a whore? You can say whore. I'm a whore. But I'm also a college student. I'm taking my degree in biochemistry. I'm just doing this to get through school."

"Really?" I said brightly. "No kidding! I knew you was intelligent. I could tell you got brains. A . . . a co-ed. Right? That's what it's called? That almost makes me in college myself."

She laughed. "It's a nice way to get your degree."

"Yeah," I laughed. "Yeah. So, what are you, sophomore?"

"Junior," she said. "Another year to go."

"I like that. A junior."

"You're so impressed. Do you want to go to college?"

I nodded. "Sure. So my big success will prove that Hitler didn't win the Holocaust. Something like that. My mom was in the war." It was the most important thing I could think to say about myself.

She gazed at me for a long time. "You're really scared, aren't you?"

I shrugged. "Wouldn't you be?"

Then her hand pushed me gently backwards and she climbed on top, moved down, but this time I kept my eyes fixed on a smudged windowpane that contained both a slip of the alley and a shard of pure blue virgin sky, and there was no resistance left in me, I let her take my soul. She could have it now, I didn't mind. It was too late.

Earl studied my face coldly as I emerged. The bulls were gone. "How was it?" he asked. "It was great," I lied. As yet, I still felt virgin, only contaminated by paid-for sex, a tainted celibate. I thanked Birdy on my way out, and left Earl there, awaiting his turn. A naked black woman in a bedroom door, dressed in leopard-skin panties and tan high heels smiled and beckoned to him. The corridor to the elevator was dismal, a blacked-out naked lightbulb screwed into the ceiling. The elevator stank of urine; I hadn't noticed that coming up, or that the lobby was covered with graffiti. Lust can make a slum seem like a condo, but when that urge is spent, the slum returns.

In the street, I winced at the fierce light and took a big gulp of air, glad that my initiation was over. Told myself that nothing had changed, even as I knew that everything had.

When I saw Mr. Dupreen slumped behind the wheel of his car, cigarette smoking from the corner of his mouth, suddenly I understood his sad air. I now shared his sense of incompleteness. Of having touched my desire with Michelle, only to see it all evaporate into illusion.

"So how was that?" drawled Mr. Dupreen, his tattooed arm flung over the car seat.

"I owe ya," I said, and slid in behind him.

He kept glancing up in the rearview mirror, to catch my attention. His repellent alcoholic bloodshot blue eyes sought in mine for a sympathetic chord, a sense of identification, as though we were now of the same cloth. But my eyes showed intense dislike and he glanced away uncomfortably, and staring at the windowshield asked: "So how's ya mom, Alan. She still having trouble with her health, the poor woman?"

"Uh, she's OK, Mr. Dupreen. I guess. You know, she's always at the doctor for something or other."

"I know, I know. People who been through what she's been through a lot of times are real sick, real sick. I knew a man, had been in Ouchwitz, had the numbers on the arm, the whole thing . . ." When he said numbers my eyes shot to his tattooed forearm, the drawing of the panther. He continued: "And this friend of mine, all of a sudden, out of the blue got cancer, diabetes, heart condition, one thing after another, no visible cause, man seemed in reasonable health. . . ." He shook his head, paused for me. I just sat there. Then I said, "I guess I feel a little ashamed."

And Mr. Dupreen asked, with a trace of irritation: "So what's the problem?"

"Well," I said, gazing sadly out the window, "it's Rosh Hashanah. I'm a Jew. Going to a whorehouse on a high holy holiday . . . it's like a slap in the face to God."

Mr. Dupreen's face screwed up in disgust and he shook his head with a bitter laugh. "You lettin' that Jewish guilt trip work its mojo, aren't you, Alan. But guess what? I know about that: my wife's a Jew. Listen, I took you to a good house, believe you me. Spic-and-span girls. Birdy could be your own mother. She treated you like a son. You had that good time, didn't you? Well, let it go then. Don't get all tangled up in God shit. Man! I spent plenty of time down south around ignorant folks who fried their brains on that God shit, to no good, I can tell you—no good. Jews and niggahs have that in common too: God this and God that."

I flinched at the racist term for black, especially as he was a quarter black himself, though he didn't know that Earl had confided after swearing me to secrecy. As I was Jewish, he no doubt refrained from the term "kike" but would have used it otherwise. He continued, a little angry. Maybe felt that I didn't appreciate his good turn. "It's just a whorehouse. That's no crime. You got whores in the Bible. Always been whores."

I nodded, gazing out the window. "I know. It's just . . . I feel kind of ashamed, doin' it on Rosh Hashanah. It feels like the whole world's just one big whorehouse."

Mr. Dupreen nodded, happily emphatic. "Well, it is! It is! See, now you're making grown-up common sense. You should thank me! You got educated! You got a good fuck and you grew up. The world *is* a god-damned fuckin' whorehouse. Bottom line, that's what you learn from fucking. Most people are nothin' better than whores."

Newspaper blew past and a cup scraped down the sidewalk. A one-legged wino in a wheelchair scanned our windows as he passed through air thick with heat and violence. It looked like a real whorehouse out there, and I felt like I had a whorehouse inside. I knew in my bones: People are nuts. At any time, it could happen again: another Holocaust. I needed to be tough to survive. I needed to touch the most depraved depths, learn to commune with the most sordid aspects of life, because when it came down, no good would be left. I would need to soldier in an ashen world of flames and darkness. I would need to learn to trans-act with the lowest scum on earth, for they would be in charge.

We were back in the neighborhood by noon. I asked to be dropped off near the schoolyard. At the fence I stood with fingers locked into the chain links, sadly, sadly considering the kids playing ball. They seemed so naive. A gulf divided us. I no longer belonged to innocence, was tainted, had sinned. I went home, observing how every inch of familiar street felt to me, now that I had so fundamentally changed.

It was different. I had left faultless; returned guilty. Now wished I hadn't done it but knew it was too late for that. Killing someone must feel this way, I thought. I had murdered my own childhood. I would need to bear my shame in secret from my folks. How could I show a dead child to its mother?

The tumblers clicked. She stood there at the open door in her apron, face flushed with exertion. "Oh, here you are, mister!" she announced to the whole house, hurt. "I thought you didn't want to celebrate this stupid Jewish holiday with us."

I dropped my head, chagrined, walked past her. "I was wrong," I said. Paused in the foyer, sniffed the air. "It smells delicious."

"Of course it smells delicious, stupeed!"

She hurried by, reentered the kitchen, went right to work. Pots boiling. Foods chopped. Ingredients baking. The blender whirring. She had the juicer juicing and the toaster popping too. "Your father is hungry," she explained. "What's the matter with you? Why do you look at me that strange way?"

"Me?" I asked, surprised. "Uh, nothing. I'm sorry. So, Pop's home?"

"Sure he is. It's Rosh Hashanah. He's not going in to work. You're not supposed to. It's a sin against God."

I winced. If so, then what I had done must occupy its own special category of sin, with particularly hellish penalties involved. I swallowed hard and went to see my father.

The room smelled of his soap and water and cornstarch and aftershave surfing to the nose on waves of pungent cigar smoke. He was stretched on the bed in his underwear with hands folded under his head, vacation-style, and the cigar jutting from the corner of his mouth. He hummed along off-key to big band music on the radio.

"How're ya doin, Pop?"

He parodied shock. "What . . . why, what are you doin' here with us lousy Jews, mistah? I thought you don't go in for them Jewish holidays."

"C'mon, Pop, gimme a break, will ya?"

"Give you a break? What about me? Who's gonna give me a break? Who's gonna giver yer momma a break in there, working all day long in that kitchen. . . ."

Certainly not you, I thought.

"To make you food. So you can turn around and insult the Jewish holiday. You know what she went through in the war! What's wrong wit you? You talk that way to a woman been persecuted?" He emitted a growl of deep guttural disgust: "Achhhhh! Abe! I'm surprised at you, you know that? I thought you had more brains than that."

I almost told him. I almost said: Dad, I just been to a whorehouse. I fucked a whore, Dad, on Rosh Hashanah. But I couldn't.

"Why don't you put on Million Dollar Movie," I said. "I think they got a war picture on."

My father looked doubtful. "Wit who?"

I shrugged.

"Take a look in the *TV Guide*," he said.

I looked.

"The Great Escape," I said.

"Ohhhhhhhh!" he exclaimed appreciatively, "that's some movie! With Steve McQueen and Charles Bronson. Go ahead, put it on. Be careful how ya turn that dial, there, ya dummy! Slowly, slowly. Easy does it. That's it. Now turn off the radio, sit over there, and make yourself comfortable. Wait'll ya see the nice food your momma's got for you. You should be ashamed of the way you talk to her! Your momma's a real sweetie, you know dat?"

"I know," I said. "I know"

And there was Steve, in sweatshirt, chinos, sneakers, and baseball mitt and ball, crossing the dusty parade ground under the eyes of machine guns and guard towers, and in the distance barking dogs and searchlights swept the ground. Steve, the Cooler King, walking between two Nazis armed with submachine guns, going to solitary confinement, "the cooler" as it was known. Steve *was* cool. He stepped inside, took up his familiar spot, tossed the ball against the wall, caught it. And again. And again. For days, weeks, even months. If only I could do the same with my life.

What if, though, just one time, he entered, the door slammed shut, and from the air vent overhead, gas began to seep in. Zyklon B. Would he stand in the gas chamber, still, coolly tossing the ball? What if around him were a thousand Jewish people, men, women, and children, hysterical, defecating, urinating, crying, screaming, menstruating, bleeding, vomiting; what if he were naked too? And before the door slammed shut the Germans took away his glove and ball?

FOOTBALL HEAD

BEHIND HIS BACK we called him Balloon Head, also Football
Head. We might also have called him Skull, due to its enormous size,
but Pauli Gicash already owned that particular moniker, so-called after
Vince Skully, the famous sports announcer, which over time local street
usage had shortened to Skull.

Time changed things. I came into the schoolyard a fat little pink
punk named Alan; soon I was nicknamed Moony, and grew into a six-
foot-tall snarling bastard member of the Bronx Huns, our schoolyard
gang and sports squad with a reputation for suicidally zestful violence
in sports. George Auria was our ringleader, and I was his notorious sec-
ond-in-command.

But for Prendivoy, Michael Prendivoy, the one we called Balloon Head, official mascot, trainer, waterboy, and manager of the Bronx Huns, the worst that time could do had already been accomplished by disease. I forget what the disease he had is called—oh, yeah: hydrocephalus—that sends you out into the world at birth with a crippled, limping little body like a malformed baby chick, and a gigantic football-shaped Martian head full of bulging blue veins, and scarred skin so transparent that you fear seeing clear through to a coiling gray lump of brains.

There was a skull there, though, a pretty hard one. And a much thicker skin than one might suppose. I didn't even really like him at all. He was bossy, spoke with this high, imperious voice, ordering you around, demanding things to be his way, and others complying, usually from guilt. And he was more physically adept than you'd imagine. Like when we played snooker in P.S. 64, or Ping-Pong: Prendivoy ruled. He was definitely not helpless. In Ping-Pong he had a murderous serve. Most never got past it. In snooker he'd take you for every cent you had and laugh.

What were you gonna do, beat the dwarf up?

Prendivoy irritated me. He seemed to spot me out of the crowd as some kind of fellow patient or something. He would ask me all kinds of questions about the asthma medicines I had to take to keep playing ball. He angered me once when he said that I was crazy, would have a heart attack if I tried to play football on medication. "That stuff's got phenobarbital in it!" he shrieked, his long, misshapen hands waving jerkily, like a puppet's. "Don't you know what that stuff does to your heart?"

It was one of those uncomfortable situations that I always tried hard to avoid: me alone with someone else who's all involved with my business. What the fuck! Why don't he mind his own B-I-business, I thought; what's he stickin' his nose in my shit for? And I glanced at the doors of the school every few seconds, pretending only to half listen, though his words seared through me like bullets. We were waiting for George to show up with a football for a game of touch.

"Yeah," I said, "sure. Whatever." But he kept on in his badgering voice, like some kind of old lady or something.

"I know about medications, Moony. How long do you think you'd last before someone catches on? Ha, ha, ha! Why, you'll be falling asleep on the scrimmage line."

And I snapped: "Well, fuck it then, OK? Fuck it!"

And Prendivoy's manner changed. He grew cold, seemed suddenly very grown-up, said: "Look, Alan. I'm going to call you Alan for a moment. I'm much older than you think, much older. I'm almost twenty-two. And I'm probably not going to live out the year. Do you understand? People with my condition don't live long. I'm going to die. In fact, I've already lived a few years past the deadline for people with my condition. So I don't care if you take the medicines and play. I've got my own worries to think about. But look at me and look at you. My death makes sense: I've got this condition. But if you die young, will that make sense?" And just then George entered and I rose, speechless, exited into the schoolyard to play, pretending not to have heard what I had just heard.

But, I had heard. About two days later, at dusk, with streetlights and the moonlit windows and the stars all tangled up in the dark hair of the trees, I found myself charging angrily up the Grand Concourse shouting at the top of my lungs: "Fuck! Fuck! Fuck!" I had just returned from a monthly visit to Dr. Siegal, who wouldn't even hear about signing the doctor's permission slip that I would need to play on varsity. This was not even to mention the parental form that my mother would have to sign.

I had my inhaler in hand: reared back and pitched it across six lanes of traffic on the Grand Concourse. It bounced on the windshield of a passing car that weaved, slowed, sped off as another car behind it crushed the inhaler under its wheels. Which didn't accomplish anything. I had a spare in a drawer upstairs. But why, why, why me? Why me? My mind was made up. No matter what, I'm playing for Clinton. Of course Siegal didn't want me to; wanted me a sick cripple all my life, like my mother, or that damned Prendivoy. "I ain't no Football Head," I howled at traffic. "I ain't no fuckin' hunchback cripple dick gonna die anyway! I'm playin' varsity!"

Yet for about a week, to right my sanity, I had to numb out and dismiss the whole matter from my mind. It was just too much to handle.

Strange week it was, too: not a single asthma attack, which was unusual considering the high humidity as we headed into August, the city paralyzed in a sweat bath, the fire hydrant caps knocked off and a white frothy torrent irrigating the hot tar on every street corner of the neighborhood.

By day the whole Bronx looked like one gigantic poor man's cabana for drenched, shirtless guttersnipes and sewer rats who padded barefoot on the streets of shattered glass, like on sand, shaking their stiff-fingered hands with skinny shivering grins on their faces and water streaming off their chins. "Yaaaaaah!" they screeched like alley cats. "Hoo-hoo-hoo-hoo-hoo!"

Only certifiably suicidal, mentally ill people would think on such days of playing full-blown games of touch-tackle football. We played. I must have lost ten pounds a game that summer. We should have died of heart attacks. Our bodies belonged not to ourselves anymore. We had become the pain-inured, flying, hurtling, bloody, crashing, murderous sweat-minions of a cruel, thankless football god. Sometimes that god seemed to be Prendivoy himself.

Though he didn't play, he patrolled our side of the schoolyard, our "bench," where all our personal belongings lay in small heaps side by side, protecting them from theft while pumping his fist into the air howling "Yes!" and "Good play!" and "Fuck!" at mishaps, and calling suggestions that we sometimes followed with good results.

The games were torture, pure and simple. Heart booming in my chest, breath pumping like a crazy squeeze-box in my ears, my head was the pivot for a merry-go-round of snarling, bloody faces swearing to tear my fucking heart out on the snap of the ball. My own team, which tended toward reticence, took up three-point stances with ears pinned back in wild animal alertness. Then Pat Pacello's voice called the magic number that sent us hurtling out of his cryptic numeric prayer into pain as forearms slammed into my face, head, and ribs, and shoulders drove into my gut. Hands latched onto my jersey trying to hurl me down but I slid, crashed, spun, pounded past or through them and managed to place myself at the bullet nose of the end run. We bore through flesh like space capsules for a few yards before we fell in a skin-scraping pile of abrasions on the schoolyard ground.

Then up again and into a huddle, ignoring the thick, viscous streams of cranberry-colored blood seeping down our elbows, knees, noses. No one asked solicitously after your wounds or offered help; if anything, a pain-dazed eye settled on your hurt with satisfaction, its owner emitting a soft, satisfied grunt that you too bleed and suffer for the same senseless, spellbinding cause of crossing an imaginary end zone demarcated by crumpled T-shirts placed approximately forty yards apart, just before the last basketball backboards at the north and south ends of the field. Minutes pass in a kind of stillness segregated at the heart of our fury. We are out of time, bodies in full extension hurtling through the air. Our torsos, ribs, chests, shoulders, and spines are packed with an agonized need for relief through bone-crushing, physical contact, another terminal between which the discharged energy can flow. So much is in motion so constantly that we can land on nothing but cement, which won't absorb the impact but jams it back into your body, intense and rolling. With a grimacing face on the ground until the end of the play, there is a moment of private agony: to be alone with your own dirty martyrdom, clutching the wounded place, surprised into supplication by the force of the earth which rushed to meet you, broke your fall on the altar of God, who hears your private, whispered, teary-eyed prayers beseeching help to stop the hot nerve-smashing pain. Someone trots by, back to the huddle, looks down at you, asks, scornfully: "You OK?" and already you're on your feet as you answer: "Yeah, sure."

And Prendivoy was the spiritual instigator of this. For him our play was his projected manifest rage. It was so obvious: It hurt to be so bent, so twisted out of shape, so ugly no woman would ever look at you— except for pity's sake, the thought of which made me sick, that some one, anyone, could pity you like you were helpless or something. Some kind of helpless cripple. Which he was.

Wham! I rammed my forearm into the flattened nose of the guy lining up across from me. His head flew back and I crunched my shoulder into his throat; could have crushed his windpipe but didn't, though my legs delivered a cyclone of short knee punches as I ran over him and felt my foot step on something soft that gave, which exhilarated me. Up shot my hand—I'm on defense now—and it's like slow motion as it fell in an arc across the quarterback's eyes; he dropped the ball, and Louis Morales scooped it up and ran into the end zone. But I wasn't really watching this, or exulting yet; I was in this quiet, slow-motion kind of stillness at the heart of our fury. I was watching the quarterback claw at his damaged eyes, which I saw for a second, red, slashed, crying—blind. He was reaching for the air, his mouth parted in a desperate moan of anguish, and I thought: "Oh, God, be with this poor son of a bitch in this, his trial on earth," and I laughed. "Hey, Mikey!"

Prendivoy was grinning from ear to ear.

"You got a cane this guy can use? And throw him a begging cup."

And yet I could tell that he felt bad about the brutality. He knew that I did as well. We were both trapped in this strange, miserable world where one feels one thing and does another, pretends to be the opposite of what one most truly is.

A few days later I sat with my back to the schoolyard fence while Prendivoy pitched in to a strike box chalked in red and blue on the walls of the school.

"But I *gotta* play. There's no such thing as I'm not gonna play. I'm playing. I'll die before I don't."

"You're right," said Prendivoy, winding up. It was weird to see this Martian-shaped guy mimic a pro hurler on the mound. But he knew the moves. I sometimes think that buried within every living, intelligent creature throughout the galaxy is the inner configuration of a slide ball ace, that we are born with pitches encoded in our genes. His pitch exploded in the box at surprising velocity and sent a sound like the crack of a carbine echoing through the neighborhood. "You could drop dead just playing right here in the neighborhood. Your heart could stop."

I groaned miserably. "That fuckin' Dr. Siegal's never gonna sign the note."

"Stop whining," snapped Prendivoy. His complete misshapeness made him powerfully immune. He could say what he wanted, and did. I once saw him tell Danny Dougherty, a known killer, to go fuck himself. Dougherty's response was the same as anyone's: his eyes searched nearby for witnesses, and finding some, he spread his arms and grinned as though to say: What am I gonna do? Hit this?

"But you don't understand," I said cruelly. "I mean, it's not somethin' that's ever gonna happen to you." He looked at me, but instead of hurt, his eyes were full of understanding.

"So go to another doctor," he said. "For every doctor who says no you'll find another that says yes." This information astonished me. I had assumed that medicine was a monolithic cult of pain-inflicting priests, all known to each other, all bearing the same diagnosis; it hadn't occurred to me that two doctors might have two different opinions. I had thought, because of the high regard that my mother and my culture held them in, that doctors were gods. Prendivoy was telling me they weren't.

"Believe me," he said, "I know."

He wound up, pitched. The ball boomed dead center and scurried back into his hands like a glad pet. He scooped it up. "Look in the phone book," he said. "Yellow Pages. A thousand of 'em. All after your money. Tell him what you need: watch what happens."

My head dropped and my bottom lip drooped with low self-esteem. "Forget it," I said. "Where'm I gonna get twenty dollars for a fuckin' doctor?"

A moment later a crumpled twenty landed in my lap.

I gaped at Prendivoy. "Mikey . . . what the fuck . . ."

He laughed that high-pitched, maniacal blend of willed mirth and acerbic skepticism. "You make my heart bleed!" He placed his hands over his heart. "Poor Moony. O poor, o poor Moony! Boo hoo hoo! Boo hoo hoo!"

I scrambled to my feet. "I'm goin' to look one up right now and call!" and rushed out of the schoolyard with Prendivoy's mocking *boo hoo hoo* careering in my ears and nipping at the heels of my pride.

I found a Dr. Kaplan. He had an office on the Grand Concourse. I dressed up in slacks and such. My mother asked, "What's the occasion?"

"No occasion," I lied, "just wanna feel . . . you know . . . like everybody else. You know. Kinda normal-like."

"Praised be God," said my mother.

"Yeah," I said. "Whatever . . ."

Though he was right across the Concourse, only half a block away, it was a journey across an ocean to a strange country. I felt ashamed, guilty, but also proud to be taking an adult action on my own, the first positive, wordly transaction on my own behalf.

His office was in a big new high-rise. I entered from the street, down three steps, between rows of hedges. I rang, stepped into a deco interior, sterile furnishings as for a television talk show set. I felt as though my actions were being filmed before a live audience. But no one laughed or clapped. Reproductions of Peter Max prints on the wall. There were lots of music magazines. Judging from the issues of *Rolling Stone* and *Cream*, I put his age at under forty.

"Mr. Kaufman."

He was eighty-five if a day. His head looked like a Q-Tip: a ball of cottony white hair supported on a stick neck. The face seemed almost incidental. But his voice belonged to a young man. And his step was springier than mine. Shoulders slumped, I dragged my feet into his examination room.

"Sit here," he said, waving me into a wooden chair.

He sat in another chair facing me.

"Say *ah*," he said.

I *ahhhed* as his tongue depressor coaxed my tongue out of the way for his eye to have a look.

"You had tonsils out. How old?"

"Five," I said.

"Good job they did."

Slipped his cold stethoscopic disk beneath my shirt.

"Breathe. Now cough."

I did both.

He stepped back, scrutinized me, said: "What is it? Asthma?"

I nodded hopelessly, my covers pulled.

"Since when?"

"Five."

"Five. Same as the tonsils. Any connection?"

"I don't know," I said. "You're the doctor."

"Yeah," he said bitterly, "I'm the doctor. So, I could use a few hundred fast ones to pay off my annual dues to the yacht club. So I find a coupla poor immigrants—where's your folks from, son?"

"My mother's French."

"Father's American?"

"Yeah."

And nodding he said, more to himself: "Sure . . . sure," understanding something he didn't share with me, and then continued. "So I cruise my patient files for a victim, and there you are: five, needs his tonsils lopped off. That'll pay the bills. So, how was it? Horrible?"

"Yeah. Petty much. I sure screamed when they held me down and stuck stuff up my nose and down my throat, and then I passed out from I guess it was the ether . . ."

"Let's call it by its name: torture. It was torture. They tortured you in the name of medicine, a little boy, and you developed asthma. Unless someone's been beating you up at home all these years?"

"No!" I said emphatically.

"Of course not. Look," he put his hand on my knee, gripped it, "asthma is a psychosomatic disease, OK? Whatever the cause is. I don't care what anybody else tells you. You can beat it. It's in your head. So, why did you come here?"

"I need a letter," I said, hardly daring to believe my good luck, afraid the room was going to change into Dr. Siegal's office.

"What kind of letter? What is it for? School?"

"Yeah. Football team."

His hands were already at a drawer, pulling out a pad of stationery and a pen. "What position do you play?"

"I'm going out for tackle."

He nodded as he wrote, seemed to know exactly what to say. Tore it off the pad. Handed it to me. I read it, my smile lit with glorious disbelief. It said that I had been examined and found fit to play all high school sports, especially football.

"What about your mother?" he asked offhandedly, but I could tell he would listen closely to my answer.

I hesitated, stammered, not wanting to lie but not knowing what else to do. "She agrees," I finally managed to say.

"Well," he said, "if she doesn't you can always find someone with a good handwriting to forge her signature. Look. Don't let them force you into thinking of yourself as a sick person, OK? Not your mother. Or your doctor. What's the putz's name?"

"Siegal," I said.

His face flushed. "Solomon Siegal? I know this shyster. He's been living off the poor Spanish up in the South Bronx for years. Fuck him. Don't let them stop you. Understand? Do as you wish. And throw away that asthma medicine. It weakens the heart."

Then the strangest thing happened. Instead of feeling encouraged I found myself defending my mother's point of view. "What if I got an attack?"

"Try to calm down."

"But what if it happens in a game?"

"Just keep playing."

"But what if I choke, can't breathe?"

"So, choke."

I shook my head, laughed. "I like that." I chuckled. "I like that a lot, what you said. Just choke, huh? I like that. Yeah! Fuck it! So I'll choke. So what? At least I'll die playing football."

"Right," he said. "Look, I'm old. So I can tell you this. Something happens to you, they want to sue me. So sue me. I'm worth a couple a million. I've had a good life. Now you go have a good life. And stay out of doctors' offices. They make you sicker than better. Go get 'em. Score one for the Gipper. Hup! Hup!"

I charged out so elated that when I stopped walking I stood on Fordham Road, two miles away, dazed as to how I'd gotten that far. And realized: the money! I'd forgotten to pay him! Frantic, I phoned.

"Yessss," he answered, leisurely.

"It's me," I explained, "I forgot to pay you. I'll bring you the money right over."

"Listen, Alan. Where are you?"

"Fordham Road, sir."

"Look around. Do you see a sporting goods store around you?"

My heart was pounding. I knew what the sweet son of a bitch was going to say. I just couldn't believe it. I dreaded to breathe, to spoil it. "Uh, yeah, right across the street. You got Modell Davegas."

"Do you have a pair of cleats yet, Alan?"

"Uh, yeah. Crappy ones. My friend's. He threw them out."

"Go buy yourself a good pair of cleats, Alan. Lineman, you said? Get high cleats, for the ankles. You'll need the support."

I played hard after that. Real hard. I broke my ass playing. Before, I was restrained by the fear that when it came down to the wire I wouldn't have the doctor's note, or my mother's permission, and so what's the use of trying?

But I was going to play now, no matter what. I knew that nothing would stop me. I had Kaplan's note. The rest was bullshit. I wouldn't forge my mother's signature either; felt too sure, too strong for that. When the time came I'd just bulldoze her into signing. I would will her signature onto that permission slip.

Everyone noticed the change in me. Only Prendivoy knew the truth. The exchange between us was brief, curt. He paused in his pitching-in as I passed, asked, "So? Did you find a doctor?"

"Yeah, Mike," I said. "Thanks. It's all worked out." And boom, his

Spaulding echoed like a bullet in the yard. I headed for the high-pitched hammering of halfcourt basketball, where I played with the pure, clean savagery of a white-hot flame, beautiful to see but scorching everything I touched, a fluid, graceful form floating to the hoop with an orange sun balanced on my fingertips. I dunked the light. I left ashes in my wake. Teams fled the field in mourning. My purpose had been found: I was the slayer of worlds. Even George. Even George went down that day. Tripped on his feet, fell flat on his ass with an astonished grunt. The complaint in his voice surprised and amused me. He refused my extended hand. His voice rumbled. I didn't hear the words. Just saw his slow-motion nostril-flaring: laughable. His visage bully-faced as he swaggered to the foul line for a throw-in. I remained silent. When the ball was in play again, it tried to sneak past on my left. My hand flicked out, scooped it up, laser-beamed it through the hoop for an easy score. All summer it was like that. I didn't even feel the disdain. I was even patient with my parents.

Every morning, rain or shine, up at six.

"Why so early?" whined my mother as she scraped scrambled eggs onto my plate. "You're a growing boy. You need your sleep."

I was fifteen years old, six feet one inch tall, and weighed two hundred pounds—solid, hurtful sinew and bone. A kind of light lit my face. I was a saint of pain. A bastardized natural-born rabbinical *tzaddik* of the gridiron. I lived only to open holes: liberator of halfbacks and fullbacks, a pass-blocking knight, an end run cosssack of the cross-body takeout.

On the early morning fields of DeWitt Clinton, I consecrated my body to perfect service. I lived most fully between the end zones. This was my synagogue, the ten-yard stripes like empty pews on which a few seagulls squatted. George perfectly understood my devotion. He respected it. "This is the way you do a three-point stance. Forget the schoolyard stuff. Don't rest too hard on your knuckles. Watch." His swiping hand knocked my arm out and I fell on my face. I understood. I leaned back on my heels to compensate and he shoved me on my ass, ramrodding his palms into my shoulders. So, I nodded: not too far forward or back, but solidly planted; I understood, and as his grabbing hands tugged me every which way by my sweatshirt, I was unbudge-able. He said: "You've got it. That's just right."

We practiced pulling out. The arm flung outward, the step to the side across the path of opposition, and a bone-breaking charge straight down the yard line, over anything in the way. I saw how much of it was chore-ographed. When done well, nobody got hurt. Bodies thudded with pre-destined, almost balletic beauty. I saw that to play well was holy. And in the brief breaks we allowed ourselves, George confided: "The school-yard's a loser way of life. A lot of guys are never gonna get out of there." And I nodded gravely, grateful for this astonishing confidence. "You just gotta have discipline to get out. No matter what you wanna do, it's a question of discipline. Football will give you that. You'll learn how to take pain. Taking pain is the most important thing that you can learn in life."

And so on. I soaked it up, hungry for wisdom of any kind, prepared to believe. I was ideal fodder for a fanatical cult that venerated homicide, only such things were yet unknown to the Bronx. Had George placed a machine gun in my hand and ordered me to assassinate the president, I would have done so. I was the perfect drone, trained to absorb pain, grateful to suffer for some higher cause. Luckily, happily, I was com-manded only to play tackle for a high school football team. I was safe from my own wish to self-immolate on the pyre of a worthy cause.

As the end of summer neared, Crazy Al, owner and financier of the Bronx Huns, had the idea that we should turn semipro. George and I were intrigued, though we had reservations about jeopardizing our amateur status playing for money against beer-guzzling behemoths. Still, we couldn't resist the idea. Finally we succumbed. Fuck it.

Crazy Al sprang for purple team jerseys emblazoned with white num-bers and the words BRONX HUNS. Prendivoy was elected coach and trainer. A game was arranged against the Kilarny Rose Crusaders from Kingsbridge Road.

Prendivoy was beside himself. All that week he drilled us in a loud, hysterical voice. Power turned him into a little Hitler. Louis Morales even went around with his hair slicked over his forehead and a black comb under his nose like Adolf's brush mustache and said, "Who am I?" We laughed. "Adolf Prendivoy!"

And yet we let him run us ragged. Knew what a good time he was having. Our blindness was his blessing. We couldn't see the forest for the trees—a gift he wanted. Victory. I think that our flushed, sweat-beaded faces, earnestly toiling with life and death against the backdrop of brown brick tenements, following his commands with sightless obedience, blasted a hole in his ironclad cynicism, through which his surviving innocence could run for daylight. He even dropped the tyrant role: didn't need it. We were willing, unwitting angels in an Eden of ignorance. I couldn't see beyond the sweat drop on my nose. Psychologically I dwelled where yogic swamis aspire to reach through constant purging of self: I breathed in the grime, hopelessness, and stench like the deathly perfume of the Ganges.

The hammering in my chest paced me through my shame of mortality. Living every instant in the fear of death, I strove through action to become a god, with absolute faith. Every block was entered in a ledger, every forearm rammed in someone's face, and spilled blood added to the sum. I was earning my liberation into the future through competitive maiming. Prendivoy made a chariot of our hubris. We pulled him, gloating in our wake, the freak demon of our glory-hunger.

On the day of the game against the Crusaders, a sweltering Sunday, we met down in the schoolyard, a milling purple horde, our scabbed elbows and knees taped and Ace-bandage padding everywhere. We were ready for business. Sunscreen smudge blackened our features like war paint. Our frenzy mounting, we became incapable of speech. Several times, frothing at the mouth, Louis Morales left the mooring of concrete underfoot and exploded his Converse sneaker at the backboard-supporting basketball pole, shrieking an insane war cry: *"Eee-yew! Eee-yew!"* and then drove his padded forearm into the brick wall, eyes bulging from his ecstatic head. It wasn't put-on lunacy either. This was real.

Pumped, Crazy Al bounced around the yard in a Weissmuller Tarzan delirium, muscle-stressed arms Olympic pressing the sky, and shouting *"Ah-bay!"* so loud that windows slammed closed a block away. The meaning of the summer was clear now: we had trained for apocalypse. It had come. Suited up for Armageddon, we strutted before our school-yard god of war.

Prendivoy never looked more like a crippled dwarf. The scale of his deformity was horrific. Yet we wished for nothing more than to bend our animal spirits to his will, make our healthy bodies his instrument. He was the physical incarnation of our inner grotesqueness. We didn't really exist: Prendivoy had imagined us, hellhound minions of his affliction. We longed to snap, tear, crush. To drag down and devour our prey in a swel-ter of tackling bones. It was clear to him: he moved our waves around like electromagnetic dust. We made ball-snapping, grunt-charging configura-tions of destruction. We clapped in the huddle, barked "Break!" and mowed down invisible foes. Then Prendivoy took the lead at the head of his purple troops and led us shouting "Ah-bay, Ah-bay!" to the Jerome Avenue subway station, while doughy corpse-faces watched deadpan at windows, lifeless eyes unable to express a goodbye or wish us luck.

It united us, this unresponsiveness of our environs. We prided our-selves as warriors of desolation. The more comfortless our existence, the harder, more brutal we'd become. The Spartan runner of legend held a vitals-gnawing fox beneath his tunic; we clutched a manhole cover to our guts. It neither killed nor nourished. It simply kept the lid on our rotting souls.

We danced in the gutters, a merry procession, a carnivalesque caval-cade of shadow-recessed faces caged in facemasks and Plexiglas, our shoulders and thighs armored too, and Prendivoy spun in circles with his arms raised and limp hand flapping in rhythm, a carton of Tropicana O.J. held aloft like a stein of grog, chanting

Bronx Hun, Bronx Hun
The Kilarny Crusaders
Are Low Scum

Prendivoy led us in a rapture up the El stairs and onto the open-air northbound platform just as the No. 4 Woodlawn rumbled in and we got aboard, a riot in progress, passengers rising and changing seats to avoid us, and the conductor came on warning us to pipe down but we chanted louder, and whatever transit cop was aboard knew better than to interfere. What the fuck. As long as we kept our mob scene confined to one car and did nothing more than bang fists against the dented sides of the car, what the fuck, and so we pulled out of the station, our challenged but unbroken elation a victory chant over the crumbly brown tenements' Appian way of television-antenna roofs stacked the whole length and width of the dismal summer-infested Bronx.

We got off at 205th, near Clinton, and swarmed down through the beltway trees and marched past the fenced-in, shut-down arena of impending autumn gladiatorial battles. To the field: a cleat-pocked, neglected, semipro charnel house with dust bowl clouds sweeping over it like a drought-stricken Oklahoma plain. We could see the beefy figures of the Kilarny Rose Crusaders in shamrock-green jerseys and helmets, white pants, and black cleats, dream figures, phantoms, unreal, and our sudden chanting appearance pronounced the blessing over their imminent funeral.

Massively muscled, heavily pimpled dray horse calves burst out of their scrimmage pants as they warmed up by running head-on into one another from a distance of twenty yards—just smashed full-speed into a crash of their pads, and bones, their grunts that of bulls felled by surprise blows from an ax. And then, jumping to their feet, they took their places at the back of the line and did it again.

Four of their biggest linemen made a tank charge, armored-cavalry-style, down the length of the field. There was a rusting four-man sled without the requisite tackle dummies. Fuck it. They hit it. In tandem they rammed and drove it downfield like a brakeless wagon careening down a long, suicidal slope.

It's always strange before kickoff. From the sidelines, Prendivoy's voice squawked encouragement. Otherwise it was silent, the hot day settling in for a long sweltering stay, not a single bird in the sky, all ducked into shadow and shelter. Just us crazies suited up for mayhem listening to the loud astronaut sound of breathing in our helmets with a sense of unreality as the ball sailed off the kicker's toe and our bodies jolted into motion tentatively, then with greater assurance, and finally moved with adrenal rushes to crush the bodies in our way.

I found my target: tall, rangy, hard-boned, all unforgiving muscle. His cool, resentful, Black Irish face and hostile eyes seemed to scorn me at the moment before contact, but I'm sure I surprised him as my helmet drove into his ribs and plowed him under like so much dirt. And to be sure he understood, I rammed my forearm into his head, a sort of hello that he acknowledged by jumping to his feet almost instantly and shrieking, "You're fucking dead. Fucking dead."

To which I replied, "Only when I shove it up your mother's cunt."

And sure, he came out swinging, as was to be expected. And I suppose that's how they figured it'd go. Just a typical ugly grudge match. In a way it was my job to set up their expectations for George to dash. I only made the cut; it was George who would operate. I opened the service; George would lead it. I offered prophesy, but George would deliver religious miracle. We were setting the ground for Lourdes all over again. This tested the unwitting converts, plumbed their depths. They were good candidates for the Messiah of their own annihilation.

On the kickoff, George held back, trotted to the side, away from play. This was a habit of his on the first play of every game. He wanted his gift to be a surprise. He understood how it would seem to them the first time he rushed. How he would come to them as out of a buffalo-sized cloud, the figure of a phantom fullback death angel carrying a skull like a pigskin and airborne over their astonished heads on his way to the Promised Land.

I met my dance partner at the scrimmage line. He stood over six-four and weighed a minimum of 270 pounds. I guessed his occupation as slaughterhouse worker, one of the pig-eyed grunts with chainsaws who dismembered freshly slain gentle-eyed cows and sometimes found a still breathing steer among the dead and—what the fuck—sliced off its legs with that high, biting engine whine. Laughed at the scream from the dying throat. Sliced off another leg. This guy looked like a real contribution to his community. The helmet shoved his dull brow down to the bridge of his nose. I could tell that he couldn't wait to get out of here, go slam down ten or fifteen brewskis. A strong reek of alcohol wafted off his breath. He was drunk. Numbed out and uncontrollably angry. I liked that. First play off the scrimmage line I didn't know what happened, didn't follow the play. As I took my stance, I grabbed a handful of loose dirt, and on the snap I threw it into his eyes. As his hands shot to his face, I drilled my head between his legs and drove him backwards, his hands still clawing at his cage, and with a wrenching lift, all thighs on my part, sent him over with an earth-shuddering crash.

I immediately felt bad about the dirt, wanted to grab him, shake him, shout: This is not me! I don't even know who I am! I want to be George Auria, but I have to be different so I pretend to be George's dark side! I'm only a make-believe version of George's dark side! That's who threw dirt in your face, not me! I don't normally do stuff like that! I learned it from Danny Dougherty!

"Gee, I'm sorry," I said, standing over him, hand extended to help him up. "You OK?"

But there are forces in life that, once triggered, don't know how to forgive. I noticed that his eyes were green: it was hard not to, his eyeballs pressed to mine. I never saw a man move so quickly from prone to upright. Dirt speckled his irises. He said: "I'm gonna kill you, you sack of shit, I'm gonna rip your fucking heart out."

I just nodded: "Yeah, OK, sure," but only halfway believed him.

Then, suddenly, the whole foundation of my personality seemed to collapse. I felt not an ounce of conviction in my right to live. My will to kill turned to mush. I just wanted to be home in bed curled under a blanket reading Ernest Hemingway. This guy was too real. I couldn't stand that I had hurt him, in effect had invited him to kill me. And he had just given his RSVP, returned on thick, bloodied lips. I had no choice but to go through with the party: after all, I had invited him to it. I turned, and he shoved me hard, but I only stumbled and continued. "You wait, punk-shit, you just wait!" he bellowed.

Chagrined, sickened, disheartened, I returned to the huddle. "Nice block, Moony," said Pacello. "Looks like the goon-o has it out for you."

I nodded with a lifeless smile, glanced over at George.

Action had revealed his true nature: he waited to receive his orders as patiently, as perfectly obedient, as abstracted as the Angel of Death. His god was the quarterback. He had no suggestions to make. Breathing hard, his eyes gaped blindly out of the cage of his face mask, no real expression in them. The play Pat had in mind was to give George the ball. That was also his overall game plan. Even Louis Morales, always pushing Pat to pass long, the infamous bomb, nodded vigorously when Pat said: "Hand off to George and sweep left on three." The team shouted "Break!" and with a bounce we jumped to the line.

The end zone shimmered like a hazy desert mirage. It was so hot that I saw wavy lines of baking heat rise from the parched ground, against which the opposing linebackers and safetys moved in slow motion, like jackals prowling a waterhole on *Wild Kingdom*. My friend showed no reaction when I offered a warm "Hi!" Sick to my heart, I took the three-point stance, hunched over, arm thrust out, ready for pain.

As he pounded through me, an experience akin to getting stomped by a pack of rhinos with a grievance to express, I felt a dull sense of remorse at the way my life had gone. Happily, George's run wasn't off my end, so all I had to do was keep green-eyes tangled up, which seemed to content him. His knees pummeled my helmet with enjoyment, and the forearm that he rammed under my chin in a neck-snapping, head-lifting invitation to observe my own behind, actually seemed fond of me. I thought I detected a note of regret in his eyes when play ended.

I don't remember anyone ever more wanting to spend time with me than him. As I limped back to the huddle, he called: "See you back here in a minute."

"How does it look your way?" asked Pat.

"Great," I said. "Beautiful."

"OK. George off Moony's tail, on seven. Break!"

I felt George's hand on my back for a second, then a kind of wind pulled my jersey, like a sucking vacuum, and I knew that green-eyes had been there just an instant ago, because I had personally gone out to greet him with a friendly handshake of a block, which caught him by surprise high up, where his face used to be, but then George moved off my block and the next thing I knew green-eyes had completely disappeared under George's cleats. I searched the ground for green-eyes but couldn't see him, unless that strange discoloration on the grass was him, and sure enough it was. Oh well. There was nothing to do but stand around and cheer as George dragged five Crusaders into the end zone. They hung off him like the skinned pelts of slain bears. Prendivoy clapped and danced on the sidelines, ecstatic. Crazy Al howled *"Ah-bay!"* and we chanted *"Ho!"* The Crusaders stood around looking hostile, puzzled. I guessed we seemed too rag-tag to pull off what we had already achieved less than five minutes into play. I could tell that they chalked it up to a fluke, though their respect for George was already apparent.

But it wouldn't matter how many of their men keyed on George, he found the end zone anyway. And when we were three touchdowns ahead, we threw three more to Louie Morales, who caught them one-handed, or twisting like a marlin through the air, or nose-diving to the equator with an astonishing disregard for his own well-being.

It didn't matter that I had no heart for the game. No one seemed to notice. I did my job. Green-eyes wanted to make it personal. I let him. It was an abusive relationship. We had long since forgotten the source of our quarrel. By the third quarter the violence had become habitual. I wish that I could have been the victim. That it would have been me, not him, with the mashed nose, blackened eye, dislocated finger, sprained ankle, and crushed nuts. I even offered to find a protective cup for him in our spare equipment. But he insisted on acting as if he were the batterer, and not vice versa. Stood there spitting teeth and blood, insulting my mother with meaningless adolescent invectives, his fury like a mask. I could tell that, behind the mask, his physical being wept for its own destruction, but I didn't let on. Instead, after every play, I slunk back to the huddle with slumped shoulders and a look of shattered self-esteem. As his body dismantled and his team went down in flames, he watched George as though from afar, some distant mythic hero performing heroic deeds with no connection to his own life. That we ran off his tackle for more than two hundred yards was not something that he seemed able to connect with himself. In his mind, he was winning as long as my face looked ashamed. And that it did, quite naturally. It was so weird. I felt grotesquely vulnerable, a Jew, someone to be kicked, humiliated, tortured, and gassed. He seemed to sense that in me, and went for it. At one point he even shouted: "I'll kick your hymie ass when this game is over!" and I snapped back quickly: "I'm not Jewish!" and he gloated "My ass!" This as we're getting off the ground. And from then on, no matter how much punishment I meted out to him, still, I felt like the punished one, the victim. Reality was insufficient evidence to contradict this feeling. He lost at the level of play but won at the level of feelings.

When the game ended, he hobbled off, sneering, gloating, as though his team and not mine had won by six touchdowns. I could not even explain to the others why suddenly I felt so shattered. They whooped and pumped their fists in the air, as Prendivoy led them on a victory jog around the field, but I walked behind at a sad remove, head hung low, shuddering, glancing over at the Crusaders bench to see whether or not my psychic executioner continued to jeer.

It filled me with despair to realize that no matter how well-muscled, how martially outfitted, how inured to pain, how ready to inflict hurt, how outwardly tough or victorious in sport, inside I was still a plump, soft, white, defenseless, helpless Jewish child shuddering naked before a flaming pit filled with corpses, awaiting the bullet that would send me to join them in the abyss, my melted fat to snap and sputter with that of my slain people.

Two days later, Mike Prendivoy died. I first heard it from Louie.

"Holy shit!" I exclaimed ingenuously. Really, I didn't care; I was more excited by the news of a chapel service that I was welcome to attend. It was a chance to really feel like I belonged. Just another good old American kid going to a goyish funeral, like George and Pacello and Morales. Inside, my sense of being different because Jewish was like a dull persistent ache.

The service was at four that afternoon.

The weird sight of all of us somberly decked out in suits drove home the fact that someone we knew had died. Uncertain of how to behave or respond to my own shock, I looked to George. He was cool and pragmatic, trying to work out with his brother Jake the best bus route to the funeral home. Earl Dupreen was there, moody, withdrawn, dressed in a charcoal-gray tweed suit that appealed to my eye. We walked together to the bus stop, in the long procession of Bronx Huns mourners. Crazy Al was up ahead, inconsolable. Jake had his arm around Ah-bay and supported his head on his shoulders as he cried, a grown-up thing that none of us would have done for each other. When the bus came, we filled its empty interior. Then Earl leaned over and said softly: "Hike," that's all, just like that, and to my horror I found myself chuckling against my will, and Earl counted off numbers like a quarterback, softly, with that sinister halacious grin: "Twenty-three, forty-two, hup, hup." Each time he said "hup" my belly flopped with hysterical tension, and suddenly, unbelievably, eyes filled with tears, clutching my gut, I was bent double laughing. Jake looked grimly my way and said: "What the fuck's that stupid giant laughing about at a time like this. . . ."

And yet even as he said this a slight, almost imperceptible grin infected the grave set of his mouth, and George allowed a sacrilegious, delicious chuckle to rock his frame, just once, then clamped down on it and said gravely: "Fuckin' sick animals," and yet the very saying of this brought a smile to his lips. Crazy Al, who saw it all, smiled savagely with hatred and hotly warned: "I better not see anybody making fun of my friend Mikey or I'm gonna get very mad," and of course not to take him at his word would have been tantamount to suicide. And yet I couldn't seem to put a lid on it. My laughter was like a penis in erection and death was a pair of teasing lips. The more I tried to stifle it, the harder I laughed.

Earl didn't help. He was perfectly capable of setting his face in this Buster Keaton mask of petrified feeling while muttering the most hilarious shit. This time, though, all that was needed was a single word, like "hup" or "hike." Or he jiggled his head in a parody of weak excitement and exclaimed in a teeny voice: "Touchdown!" Of course I could see Mike Prendivoy's unreal, Martian-sized skull set down by a referee on a yardstripe and a big, bleeding, soiled hand spread taped fingers over its countenance. His head snapped on the count for a round of extraterrestrial, supernatural, postmortality gridiron play. And by now even George couldn't contain himself, or even Mike, whose suppressed laughs exploded with spray from the pressure-cooker of his mouth, and Louie's voice crooned with angry admiration, a shamed refrain: "Moony, Bru-tus, Ja-ake," and so on, a roll call of the damned, for whom nothing was sacred, not even the death of a good friend.

The bus disgorged us in front of the chapel and pulled out with a snort of disgust. It was a dismal-looking white building with tall oak doors; inside all gloom pierced by electric flowers and a gold-plated crucifix. The weird thing about the chapel was he was laid out right there in the rotunda. The transition from the street to his corpse-white face was instantaneous. One minute we were doubled over with beet-red faces on the pavement, the next we were gaping stupefied at the waxen makeup job of a third-rate mortician. I felt nothing that I could tell; a sort of numbness if anything. I had expected from death a more stupendous result.

Instead I noted the resemblance between the grains of pancake makeup discoloring Prendivoy's cheeks and my mother's occasional lousy makeup jobs. George's head was next to mine, Louie's next to his, our conjoined mugs a corona of shabby, sniggering vitality to a dwarf's death mask. His minions in life, we were his mockers in death.

In fact, we all grew quickly bored with Prendivoy's extinction. Already it seemed perfectly natural that we would never see him

again. Personally, I felt little regret about it; I was more curious about
the printed funeral cards depicting Saint George slaying the dragon
on one side, and on the other Prendivoy's name, dates of birth and
death, plus a corny Christian prayer that I forbade myself to read for
fear of being contaminated with Christian doctrine. My sense of
Judaism was so shaky that I feared any influence could creep in to
steal my mind. My soul was a quivering, exposed nerve, grateful for
any shelter. I'd get all choked up if my eyes strayed over any sort of
spiritual literature. An accidental reading of some words in a Jehovah's
Witness magazine like *Awake!* could send shivers through my system.
So, I avoided the prayer. But I could not fail to study the picture.
What does it mean, I wondered. Why was this considered worthy of
religion, this slaying of a dragon by a knight? Why did the goyim
regard it as holy? Didn't God pity the dragon? An ugly dragon, like
Mike Prendivoy.

Earl leaned close, mumbled: "Run to daylight!" I choked with vomi-
tous laughter.

Al's hand slowed my shoulder. "Not here," he snapped. But I couldn't
stop. An elderly woman appeared and introduced herself to George.
Still laughing, I tried to duck behind Earl's back as she shook hands all
around. It was Mikey's mother! Damn!

"I'm so grateful to you boys for befriending Michael. He spoke about
you all very often. It meant a great deal to him to be with the Bronx
Huns. You must be Louie. And you're George? Oh, he had special
praise for you. And is there an Al? A Big Al? He loved you very much.
And a Mike . . ." She touched her hand lightly to her forehead with a
look of distress. She was very pale. "Oh, my, I don't seem to remember
any other names . . . forgive me. We're glad that his ordeal has ended,
but nonetheless, it's very difficult to lose a son. He was my son, regardless of how he looked. . . ." She began to weep. The laughter continued, unabated, to flow from my mouth. I was beginning to panic. I
didn't know what to do. I could suppress the sound of it but not forever. The effort it took to contain it constricted my face into a pressur-
ized mask timed to explode.

A man in a somber suit ushered her away, and, as a group, the Bronx Huns expelled me from the chapel onto the sidewalk, where I stumbled sideways into a big Pontiac and collapsed against the fender with a sound almost like crying.

"Sick," George groaned. "Sick fucking animal," and his face dissolved in helpless mirth. One by one they joined me, my laughter a virulent, viral strain of disrespect. Only Al refrained. Stood to the side, resigned, to grieve alone. From the corner of my eye I watched his heartfelt, lonely vigil. By now I was almost separate from my stomach, lungs, mouth, and eyes; could function normally in every respect but for the panting, jackal, gleeful noises exploding from my chest. We commenced to walk along at a strolling pace as a group, still bellowing laughter in an uproar, otherwise as casual as you please. Fucking Earl was like a sinister firestoker, prodding at our embers with his poker face, inciting us to cackle, pop, and wheeze. Any reference would do at this point.

"First down!" he tossed off indifferently, and we collapsed in a row against cars, like mobsters gunned down in a massacre. Crazy Al stood by in silent witness. Then we moved on.

By now the laughter was a bestial life-form of its own with a will independent of ours. It was merely using our hapless bodies to vent itself. Some convulsive, mocking, belly-laughing demon force had entered us to turn our grief to travesty. It boarded the bus home with us, where, for an instant, it appeared to subside. We all disengaged our eyes from each other, to gaze with quiet, hopeful solemnity out the window at the dreary, passing gray Bronx landscape. I don't remember who was first to resume laughing, me probably, but it was like a chain of dominoes, we all went down. Crazy Al's disappointment and sadness could not have been more complete.

Off the bus, back at 170th Street, at dusk with a gentle out-of-season rainfall pattering around us and a lavender-colored sky ripening above the strip of lit shops, he studied our grimacing, crying faces, shook his head, and walked away. This, oddly, snuffed our laughter instantly. The moment he vanished from view, so did the beast of our mirth. His sudden absence was the sword that slayed the dragon. Our laughter could not exist without his genuine bereavement. Strange that it worked so. We glanced with weak, astonished, questioning looks at each other. I felt a sudden pang of voracious hunger. "Jeez," I said, "I'm fuckin' starved."

We went to the Greek's. Ordered up big cheeseburger platters. Once Earl tried to resurrect the monster with a mumbled: "Hup!" but nothing. We were strangely neutral. The humor rang flat, hollow. George snarled. "Why don't you fuckin' stow it?" Earl's face retreated between hunched shoulders. Not a single snicker escaped our lips as we passed around the ketchup.

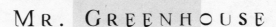

MR. GREENHOUSE

I HOOFED AROUND blindly searching for the room where the creative writing class was scheduled to meet. Finally, I saw a cryptic sign: CW/101. Found the place. A nice, big, spacious, ground-level mahogany-paneled room with tall black-trimmed windows facing onto the parkway that ran past DeWitt Clinton High School; all serge-colored hedges, embankments, and slopes that rose to dense woods. I imagined that New England must display grand hues and contours like this, or the Michigan woods. Hemingway had one hand laid on my shoulder as I swashbuckled through the door, and Jack Kerouac had his hand on the other. But once through, I stood nakedly alone there, Alan—fledgling writer—and yet still felt fine.

A smattering of faces. Seated on the edge of his desk, a man dressed in tweed jacket with patched elbows, corduroy slacks with flaring cuffs, and suede Hush Puppies—uniform of a genuine man of letters— stroked his smart, short-cropped, literary beard. He had a soft face, searching sad blue eyes that studied me tentatively. He said: "Hey. Welcome . . . do you know where you are? Is this what you're looking for? Do you know that this is creative writing? Are you looking for Mr. Greenhouse? Ronald Greenhouse? I'm Mr. Greenhouse. Are you a writer? What year? Let me guess: Sophomore. Sophomore? What's your name?"

"Alan," I said awkwardly, blushing. "And . . . uh . . . yeah. Yeah. To all your questions. Yeah."

"Yeahhhhhhhhh . . ." he crooned hiply. "Oh, yeahhhhhhhhh," and I noticed his very cool paisley tie. A smile came to my face. I relaxed. Said, "Yeah," nodded, and took a seat.

Mr. Greenhouse glanced at his watch. "Few more minutes," he said. He gazed at me intently. "Yeahhhhhhhh, oh, yeahhhhhh," he crooned, and I stirred uneasily. "You look like a writer with the capital 'W,'" he said. "Anyone ever tell you that?"

I swallowed down a hard lump of shock. "No," I said, barely able to utter the words, "nobody."

"Yeahhhhhhhh, oh yeaahhhhhh," crooned Greenhouse. "Oh, yeah, ba-by! You got that Thomas Wolfe–Hemingway–Kerouac–John Steinbeck look. 'Kaufman': sounds like a famous writer's name. Oh, yeahhhhhhh. I'm glad you came. Real glad. What brings you? Do you write? What does it mean to you? Think about it." He glanced at his watch, rubbed his hands, said, "Another minute we'll start," and just hugged his elbows again, waiting and gazing into space, freeing a hand to stroke his beard.

In the meantime I stared out the window, where everything had suddenly snapped into hallucinatory focus, and my brain couldn't keep apace of its excitement in trying to absorb Mr. Greenhouse's words. *So, I wondered feverishly, that is it? I am anointed? So quick? Years dying of hope that someday the world will recognize my gifts and now I walk into the right room where this high literary priest declares my mes-*

sianic legitimacy strictly on the basis of . . . what? Feeling? Intuition? What the fuck? Has he trained so many writers that, like a good boxing coach, he operates on an unerring sense of crude material, spotting winners in the trash pile the second he's laid eyes on them and knows? Why not?

I looked around me. To my left, a skinny guy with pasty skin spread with jam-colored acne.

To my right, a crazy hippie-looking guy with frizzed hair, wire-rim spectacles, ratty army jacket. Looked kinda stoned.

Over there, this black guy much older than his high school years.

They don't seem like math brains or law-school-bound academic pedigrees. I feel comfortable here. In them I recognize a quality I think I share: a kind of masturbatory slow-stroking of time with the nimble, unhurried psychic fingers of language that can master any moment and explode into a pulsing *ooooooh*-sighing release of shooting verbs on a page. And I found myself nodding my head and thinking, Yeahhhhhh, this is cool. My very first discovery and proclamation of hipness.

We all wrote like we jerked off: behind a closed door of mind. In secret shame, covering the spew of our quickly moving pen with a cupped hand and, afterward, all spent, secreting the stained page away, dirty handkerchief of soul confessions and private dreams, and, as with the handjobs, this sense of celestial criminal mischief, that God is watching right there in the bathroom, peering over your shoulder, alternately shocked and amused at these little baby Genets.

Bad boy! To utter such forbidden things as one might, in a grab for truth, set down, then quickly cross out behind the cupped hand, before God can see and censor. Yet with a hunch that God of course sees what is anyway and is moved to mercy (though he feels me in other ways undeserving), because undeniably the writing sizzles. Plus: I'm the kid of one of those precious few who survived the Holocaust. Born historically maimed, psychically jammed—privileged by my ultimate crippling—to filter truth through the fractured lens of my paranoid, paranormal imagination.

Greenhouse just leaned up against his desk, all casual-like, stroking his beard, absorbing my face, the others. I didn't mind his studied gaze, it being partially the bait for being there: a safe place to look at people I could understand, and to be seen and grasped in turn. I could stare straight back at him, the others, without consequences.

Eyeballing anyone that way, on the street or a subway, could get you killed in the Bronx. But in here was refuge, where we were free to visually imbibe one anothers' humanness. This I understood. Looked closely at the black guy, saw that his countenance was both young and old. Imagined him as some sort of James Baldwinesque ghetto genius. Couldn't wait to read what he wrote. Or any of these guys. What did they write? How? I shuddered. How did I write? How would it sound to them? Yet it didn't occur to me that I wasn't a genius—I only wondered whether or not they'd grasp the power of what I had to say.

Greenhouse began. A list was passed around. Once our names were down we were officially enrolled. That made me happy: here was something no one could take away. Safe haven. The next concrete step into the future. Greenhouse, clearly, was a literary man, first I'd ever met. And already he had laid on my shoulders a mantle of sorts; knighted me with a promise of future glory. I watched to see where he placed the list and, more important, how he handled it. His soft, well-manicured hands showed proper deference as he slid it carefully into an oxblood-colored leather satchel. I listened with satisfaction to the click of its gold-plated fastener. My enrollment among immortals was secure.

What is writing? he asked. It is words put down on paper. And again, for emphasis: It is words put down on paper. It is something that we do, again and again; a big river of words that we set flowing and wade into to fish for deep riches, dig?

We all nodded, except Fred Henry. He raised his hand. His voice was scratchy as an old Victrola, had an oddly pleasant voicebox remoteness. Enunciated his words in a slow, self-indulgent drone. I thought I saw in his face a wise old granny coupled with the shrewd and deliberate sensibility of an artful businessman. "But writing," he said, "is more than that. It's craft." I glanced around, alarmed at the apparition of a word I didn't know. Greenhouse stroked his beard.

"What's your name?"

"Fred Henry," said the black youth.

"Fred Henry," said Greenhouse. "Fred Henry, yeaahhhh! Great name. Great name. That's a writer's name, ba-by! Fred Henry! Yeaaahhhh! And what is craft? Anyone know?"

The frizzy hippy guy raised his hand and answered with a stoned smile: "It's making words sound right."

Greenhouse stroked his beard, brow furrowed in astonishment.

"You know," he stammered, "you guys . . . this is one amazing dude! One pretty amazing group! What is your name, my man?"

"Joey Goldman."

"You got that anarchist look, Joey. Jewish?"

Goldman nodded.

"Socialist?"

"Just me and my mom. My father's dead."

"Hey," said Mr. Greenhouse, "if you're not part of the problem, you're part of the solution. Dig?"

Goldman laughed, and shook his head, puzzled. "Not really."

Greenhouse pursed his lips and rubbed his hands together. "That's cool. That's cool."

"Craft," he said, "is to throw out your lace doilies. Dig? Like, to make the meaning of writing real clear, take out all that fancy stuff, change the facts to fit the story, not the story to fit the facts. Just leave in what communicates the maximum thing you need to say. You know, like putting out all those lace doilies on a dinner table maybe looks hip, you dig, but what's it for? Ornament. Writing's not about looking good. It's about saying something exquisitely meaningful."

"Excuse me," I said, raising my hand. "What's a doily?" The question seemed to throw Greenhouse for a loop. He was at a loss for words, finally settled for, "Like, you know, a napkin. A fancy napkin. What your mother puts under the ashtrays and candy dish."

"You mean those cloth things?" I frowned. "But what's that got to do with writing? They're, like, to keep furniture from getting scratched up, right? What's that got to do with being fancy or not?"

"Well, who needs them?" Greenhouse parried.

"The woman who put them there," I said.

He frowned, stroked his beard. Then his face seemed to light up. "Yeahhhhhhh," he said. "*Wwwwwooowww!* That's genius, dude! Do the Zen literal shtick! I love it!"

And so on. Forty-five minutes later I left less enlightened about what writing is but ten times as determined to become a writer, and blessed now with the absolute certainty that I could accomplish my goal within a foreseeable time.

It was an agony to return home from school that first day. In the space of just a few hours I had already found a new understanding of myself. My cheek rested against the cold trembling windowpane of the bus, glass ghosts of reflected trees and buildings and streets rushing by, and the bus wended a slow way home. Thankfully, the immense Grand Concourse was riddled with endless stops, and at each one a clamor of bundled-up, *kvetching*, groaning and shrieking shoppers, elderly women mainly, got on with their bundles and net bags.

But already I was leaving the place forever, could see my surroundings from the perspective of imminent absence. I was hardly capable of remaining in the moment for a single instant without a painful sense of melancholy. Even my street, Wythe Place, seemed transformed, at once older and newer than I'd recalled, like Fred Henry's face; the air was charred with the stench of exhaust, a sense of inevitable defeat, but also of having never really been experienced by a single human inhabitant. A wilderness unexplored.

I had no proof of my impending escape to a better life than the bitterly stubborn set of my heart and mind: I would get out if it killed me. Paused at the stoop of my building, reached down, ran my fingernails over the cheap pebble-studded cement. Remember the feel of this, I told myself, don't ever forget the feel of this.

I set her up for my approach like a well-positioned shot. Kept a low profile all through dinner: politely answered their sparse, disinterested questions about school. I did my best to appear satisfied by my lot in life, my face a pink glow warmed by the tinkle of cheap silverware against chipped soup bowls, the grinding scratch of serrated steak knives sawing through pot roast against badly scratched dinner plates adorned with cheap machine-stamped scenes of bucolic rural seventeenth-century life.

I looked at my father's bowed head, thinning hair baldly displayed as he spooned big forkfuls of mashed potatoes into his mouth. Then he sat up straight with a jaw full of roast and with his neglected, greenish teeth chewed gingerly, his lips smacking like an old sea salt and me struggling to suppress an urge to shake my head in bewildered disgust, asking instead: "How's the meat, Pop?"

"Good, good," he said, and offered no more. Naturally. He never spoke. He ate. And answered in clipped phrases, his air polite, distant, a manner less warm than that of a bus driver greeted by a boarding passenger on a gridlocked city street.

"How was Taft?" I asked, turning to Howie, who ate with clear relish for the food but with little use for the present company. Taft was his high school.

"Good, good," he said curtly. *Slurp, chomp, chomp. Smack. Belch. Gulp, gulp, gulp. Clang. Tinkle. Clack clack clack. Belch. Gulp. Slurp. Chomp. Chomp. Chomp.* It took a lot to make me scream. An accumulation of such moments. A month's worth, say, before the cork popped and the rage flowed. My mother in her pale blue *shmata* housedress with overheated face shuttling back and forth from stove to table, refrigerator to stove, to table, to cupboard, and then, when we were fully larded down with victuals sufficient to feed the army of the Potomac, she climbed back up onto her crucifix, slipped the nails like pegs back into their respective stigmatas, and asked: "So, how do you like that meat, George? That's some meat, isn't it?"

And my father—*slurp*—without lifting his head from his soup bowl—*slurp*—with soup dripping from his lips—*slurp*—asked—*slurp*: "Mashala, why don't you sit down already to eat? What the hell's the matter with you?" in this irritated voice of hypocritical concern that turned my stomach. But I let it all slide, impelled by my great metaphysical purpose: liberation, to perform on the playing field of destiny.

I contained the spoked wheel of truth in my heart—wiped my lips with a napkin and carried my plate to the sink. And still, a small, sweetly surrendered voice wondered: How can they not notice how tall, powerful, and graceful you've grown; how have they failed to note the gradually emerging shape of genius in your face? Why do you continue to be an ignored child in their presence, one who should be seen but not heard?

I rinsed the dishes with Lux soap and warm water, dried my hands on a gravy-stained dishtowel, and sauntered into my room. Flipped on the radio. A song by the Monkees. The loosely vibrating guitar twangs transformed my room for one brief instant into a hippie commune. It was the Summer of Love, but in the Bronx much of the Digger life was still but a distant, unreliable rumor; an advertising gimmick glimpsed in the pages of smuggled issues of *Playboy* to promote and sell rock and roll, which I didn't even like. Musically I was not even a throwback, did not inhabit the human sphere. Listened to such stuff as Ferrante and Teicher's piano rendition of the theme song from the movie *Exodus*. Judy Collins singing "The Patriot Game" was as cutting-edge as I ever got.

I had to wait for my father to leave; four more hours to go. But I didn't feel like going inside. Laid there for a full hour shaking my crossed legs, watching twilight slowly leech the light from my window as it turned from powder blue to gray to black and the bloated alley decomposed into night.

Around seven or so I wandered into their bedroom, where my father, already showered, powdered, and shaved and dressed in boxer shorts and a freshly laundered white shirt, sat in the cockpit of his La-Z-Boy recliner, shaking his leg nervously, a cold Dutch Masters stogie wedged between his pressed-together lips, eye squinting in appreciation at a Shirley Temple dance routine on the Million Dollar Movie's televised presentation of *Poor Little Rich Girl*.

With his silver-flecked, squared-off sideburns he looked like a dignified sea captain whose own essential apathy was the last vessel under his command, and he was having a grand time steering to nowhere. Old films were his favored islands in these empty latitudes, particularly those of Shirley Temple, whom both my parents proclaimed as a child messiah of show business. The miracles of Shirley's talent were boundless. Just now she was tap-dancing down Depression sidewalks with a tall black man dressed in rags.

"Look at dat girl dance. Will you look at dat? Mash! Take a look at dat!" said my father with manly awe.

My mother's voice rose to protest the tone of his voice, which cast doubt upon her status as a true believer in Saint Shirley: "What do you think I'm doing here, silly?! Gosh! Don't you think I know what a gifted child she was?" Her lips pursed with reverence around the words "gifted" and "child."

"What are you getting upset about? I know! I know you admire her. I'm just saying will you take a look at dat girl dance? She was a genius."

He broke the word into syllables: "Geee-nyooos," exaggerating them for more powerful emphasis.

Howie was stretched across the foot of the bed, his face near the glowing screen. "You know," I said, "Howie's gonna die of radiation poisoning watching that close."

"Azzzzz," my brother said acidly, "why don't you go shove it somewhere?"

"Shmuck-face!"

"Hey!" snapped my father, glaring for some reason at me, as though I were crossing the boundaries of what is permissible. "Why don't you watch those mouths of yours or I'll give ya both a rap you won't forget."

My hands flew to my chest in protest. "What did I do?"

"I'm talking to both of you. Sit down and shut up."

So I sat in the chair that stood between his recliner and the bed, the worst, most uncomfortable spot, reserved for the latecomer, and watched Goody Two-shoes do that hoodoo on my parents, wishing like hell I could get them to praise me with equal enthusiasm, just once. Anybody out there with an inch of ability was Shirley Temple to them. They had boundless awe to give away to the little celluloid girl, or anyone really, except for Howard and me. I didn't even bother to show my writings to them! Why would I? Or talk to my father about football, how much it meant to me. He was too busy admiring others while failing to present me with something to admire. No wonder at times like this I filled up with rage for the unshared exaltation I had known, all that solitary joy in myself beginning to rot, big warehousefuls of lonely self-esteem gone to mold.

I closed my eyes, listening to her prodigious baby voice make my own chance for success seem ever more remote. With such parents as I had, what could I grow into but crippled, emotionally scarred, hobbling on life's stage in a flea-infested gorilla suit, singing "Good Ship Lollipop."

The long evening groaned on to the Victrola-scratchy dissonant trumpets and saccharine dialogue of Shirley Temple's unremarkable world. And at nine o'clock he rose from his cockpit to suit up for life on the ground. And it was sad, the reluctance with which he donned his clothes.

His absence began to be felt even before he left, a genuinely painful sundering from the cozy warmth permeating our bones. With a familiar sense of dread my eyes fell on the frosted, black window. I could never bear to imagine what it must feel like to step out into such bitter night, alone, travel all the way downtown to a job that sounded like sheer torture to endure. All I knew of his job was the ailment it left him with: painful arthritis in his hands and feet from *schlepping* big mail sacks and dragging around on a cold steel deck dressed in inadequate shoes. Why didn't he wear thick-soled work boots instead of calfskin Italian loafers, I would ask, but he'd shake his head and growl with disdain: "Naahhhh. I don't like them." So, he limped and already couldn't fully close one hand, but at least he looked good. In his own mind, anyway.

None of us ever felt right about saying goodbye. It was the moment when I experienced the most love for him, his leaving.

"Goodbye, Pop," I'd say tenderly, my voice Shirley Temple sweet. Everyone became solicitous, like characters in one of her flicks.

"Bye, Dad," said Howard.

"Pleeze, George, wear the earmuffs tonight. You'll catch walking pneumonia," and leaping off the bed, she went to the closet, found them, and clapped them over his ears. Radio to pilot: Runway cleared for take-off. The rummaging of his hand in his pocket change, searching for exact subway fare, was like the switching on of engines. Then, my mother guided him out of the hanger, rushing ahead, stood at the side of the landing strip, snapped the signal flag, and, wheezing asthmatically, his rekindled cigar pumping thick, viscous clouds in his wake, he lifted off into the night.

"Please, Mom, sign it," I began. "For once in your life don't gimme a buncha trouble about this. I want it bad, Mom, real bad. . . ." I stood in the door with the form in my hand. It was permission to play football for DeWitt Clinton High School. She was in bed, propped up on her pillows with a cold wet rag on her brow. She didn't look so well. Howard was in our room, on his bed, reading comics. The new issue of *Spider-Man*, probably.

My voice was low, imploring, soft. I parroted the reasonable voice of a middle-aged, middle-class Jewish businessman, the kind who owned and ran haberdasheries up and down 170th Street or along Fordham Road. I figured that since such a voice could persuade my mother through the years to blow our tiny clothes allotments on chintzy wine-colored suits, it might work to trick her John Hancock on a parental release form. However, the fatigue in my voice was genuine, my sheer exhaustion at anticipating this moment. "Pleeze, A-bie, don't bother me now. I don't feel good. My lou-zy blood pressure is getting to me."

"You should see a doctor," I countered irritably. Whenever something important to me came up, it had to yield before her medical emergencies. All my life it was: "Abe . . . don't aggravate your mother. You know what a sick woman she is;" and, "Abe, not now. She's going into the hospital to be operated on next week. Give it a rest."

"But it can't wait, Mom! You gotta sign it tonight!"

"What is it?"

"It's permission for football"

"To play? Are you crazy? Did you see that story in the paper, that poor boy in Idaho whose neck was broken in the football? Forget it! I'm not signing your death warrant!"

Amazingly, I didn't blow. I nodded, expecting this early rebuff. I pressed on, in a world-weary tone, with Yiddish empathy born of experience with infinite sorrows and bittersweet joys. "I know, Masha-la, I know. You don't want me to get hurt. But I'll be safe. They wear top equipment. The coaches are great. One of them used to play for the Green Bay Packers, Mom, the Green Bay Packers! Can you imagine it, Mom: Your Abie, coached by a Green Bay Packer! . . ."

"Greenberg Pecker? What is this Greenberg Pecker? Your stupid American football? I'm not impressed! You want to impress me, tell me you'll get tutoring for your lousy math. Tell me you want to graduate like Ruth's son Kenneth from M.I.T. I don't care about your Greenberg Pecker."

"I understand, Mom," I nodded unctuously. "Sure. The education thing. Of course. That comes first. Natch! Natch!"

"What means this, 'natch'? This is English? I never heard such a word. 'Natch.' This means something?"

"It's just slang," I grumbled.

"Well, speak English. Mine is not so good you know. I wasn't born in this country, thank God."

"Mom, please." I held out the paper as if to say: Do the decent thing, the only thing possible in this situation.

My face wore the expression found on the face of Timmy's dad in the television show *Lassie*, when father is explaining to son why the horse with the broken leg must be put out of its misery, while Lassie sits by, cute, whining.

"Please," I said. I thought I saw her relax, a shadow moved off her face as though she'd decided to give in. Then suddenly her face darkened, she ripped the rag from her brow and swung her legs off the bed. Furious, ignoring me, she pushed past, her house slippers slapping on the floor, entered the bathroom, and locked the door.

I heard water run. Gargling sounds. A nauseated retching. Soft moans. More tapwater. Again, retching. Then: nothing.

"Mom." I tried the door. "Mom." No answer.

Enraged, I slammed against the door, in which a crack suddenly appeared.

"What are you doing, you idiot?" she groaned.

"Don't you idiot me!" I howled. "Come out there and sign this god-damned note now or I'm gonna break down this door!"

Suddenly the door flew open. Quickly, she stepped out and smacked me smartly across the face. "There," and again, smacked me, declaring with evident smug satisfaction: "And there again. And here another, in your dirty mouth," and hot tears sprang to my eyes. I didn't try to cover my face, didn't really feel the slaps so much as my outrage and fear at how quickly the ground was evaporating under my feet. She went back inside and lay down. No cold rag now. Her face unnaturally flushed. Beet red. Burning. Just a pen in her hand, I thought, just a simple, mind-less flourish of her wrist.

I removed the pen from my pocket, tiptoed to the side of the bed, and attempted, gently, to slip the pen between her fingers. Her arm recoiled, a look of mock horror in her eyes. "Stupid. Get away! What are you doing? Get away!" and heard my father's voice echo in the room in French-accented imitation of this protest that she issued whenever one of us attempted to embrace her: "Get a-way!"

"Just sign," I said grimly. Then, at the top of my lungs: *"Sign!"*

She jumped off the bed.

"Sign, goddamn it, sign, sign, please, I beg you, I warn you, goddamn sign!" and threw form and pen on the bed.

"I can't," she said. "You have asthma. Dr. Siegal won't give permis-sion. You want me to get into trouble with the authorities, stupid? What if something happens to you? I'll go to prison! Not you! Me! And if I get into trouble I'll be deported. I'm not even a citizen."

"I got a doctor's permission already," I said, weary.

She looked genuinely surprised. "What doctor's permission? How do you have this?"

"What does it matter? I got. Just sign. You're free. If I get hurt you're off the hook, OK? No immigration problems. Nothing. Just me with a broken arm. OK?"

"But why do you make me sign this if I don't want? I don't want to!"

"Because it affects me. You have no right not to sign. It affects me. It's what I want, not you. You have no right to say no."

"I have no right? I'm your mother! That's my right! Did I survive five years of Hitler to see you get hurt? Is this why I nearly died on the operating table when you were born? Gosh. Poor Dr. Luchinski. He didn't know if I would make it or not. I have the right! You, you don't have common sense. You have no brains, you and your stupid brother both. So I have the brains for you. That's why I don't sign. I know you'll get killed. You weren't meant to play football. You take after my side of the family. A *klutz* with two left feet. Football is for the *goyim*, not for Jewish boys. You should study hard for college, not waste your time getting good and hurt. Idiot! You'll break your back and then see how you like to be in traction. O gosh! Do you know what it's like to live in a wheelchair? No one will ever want to marry you, believe me, pretty girls don't like to go out with crips. And for what? To be like that crazy friend of yours, George Auria? For this you would risk sitting in a wheelchair for the rest of your life? Such a good-looking boy. So young."

"Sign," I said.

"Give me already to sign. I'm sick to argue. My heart doesn't feel good. You know, A-bie? I think my heart gives me trouble sometimes."

I didn't know what to say. I watched as she signed, then grabbed away the form.

"Thank you," I said stonily, and went to bed.

Later she came in as I drifted off to sleep. I couldn't pry open my eyes. Sleep was dragging me by the heel, an undercurrent to which I surrendered, but I heard her voice as I sank down: "Don't be mad at me, A-bie. I want you should do good in the football. Oy, I'm sick, A-bela. . . ." She was crying, whimpering like a frightened little girl. "I'm scared. My heart don't feel so good. I'm scared, A-bie, I'm scared."

But I couldn't wake up.

The next day, it started. I hardly understood that I was in high school to learn.

I went directly to the school library, checked out *The Fire Next Time* by James Baldwin, *For Whom the Bell Tolls* by Ernest Hemingway, *The Grapes of Wrath* by John Steinbeck, *Sometimes a Great Notion* by Ken Kesey, *The Naked and the Dead* by Norman Mailer, *Invisible Man* by Ralph Ellison, and this crazy dog-eared paperback anthology about existential philosophy titled *Man Alone*. What drew me to it was the inclusion of writers whose names I'd seen bandied about in newspaper book reviews: Kafka and Dostoyevsky. I figured I'd need to know about them if I was gonna make it as a great writer. In a sense at Clinton I completely broke away from the rigid parameters of school routine and made a fundamental decision to exchange knowledge of the officially taught topics in the classroom—math, history, science, social studies—for the secret knowledge of novels covertly read and dreamed over in class.

It was the beginning of the great daydream that was to become almost a permanent and sometimes chief component of my inner life for the next twenty years. The world past my nose could not compete with the world behind my brow, which was directly fueled on an almost perpetual basis by novels hidden on my lap or sandwiched between the covers of my loose-leaf notebook. While around me my fellow students strained together to grasp and achieve command over Pythagorean theorems, the causes of the aurora borealis, the basic principles of Keynesian economics, and the subtleties of legislative lobbying in the Congress and the House, I was Roberto lying in the arms of Maria on the night before the blowing of a Fascist-held bridge, explaining that all of life can be lived more richly in the space of three days than most people have experienced in the course of a lifetime, and, had wiping the sweat from her brow, asked if the earth had again moved for her during the lovemaking. Already, that first day, I could not contain my word-greed, embarked on the ultimate escapist trip of projecting myself into the shoes of imaginary figures from novels, ultimately experiencing their lives and feelings and even corporeal realities better than I was able to experience my own.

In the pages of books I wore flannel shirts and jeans and rugged Carolina work boots and stood dreamily on the shores of ice-cold white frothing river rapids in Kesey's northern Oregon, remembering my bachelor-day trips by Indian motorcycle across America while behind me my gorgeous young belly-sweet wife flirted with the hippie brother who was going to seduce her into betraying me.

In the pages of books I lived in the electric Ellison lightbulb-lined basement of a gutted ghetto tenement, crazed like a deluded, delirious, and magnificent messiah of mounting rage against honky racist society while mourning the death of my right to an average sort of self in a social order bent upon my persecution and subordination. I went to sleep a man and awoke a cockroach. I fought in war and died in an alley with a knife in my gut. I gave breast milk to a starving migrant worker in the manger of a freight car in Dust Bowl days of California. I wandered the length and breadth of the land, the whole world, and imagined my own life through the imagined lives of others, my raw hunger and loneliness for literary existence inseminated into the womb of novels where I gestated, evolved, and by the end of each text was born anew with an agonized gasp of pleasure and regret. I said goodbye to the characters I had come to know better than my own family, better even than myself, though some residue always remained and often amplified and resonated over time with new meanings, feelings, pleasures.

This was only the beginning of high school, yet already I cultivated the new, detached posture of defiance toward expectations and duties of the life around me that was to become the hallmark of virtually my entire life to come, mostly with devastating results. I began to live a life separate from the life of the world; became more than a devouring reader of books: a beast of prey whose game was print.

I didn't just read them, I mauled them. I was cruel. Covers fell off. Pages ripped. Food spattered the words—beverages, snot, sputum, semen, even blood from a bleeding cuticle. I reacted violently to interruptions of these dream states. Hot anger boiled in my chest when the economics teacher, a Mr. Marshall, asked me to put the book away.

I slammed my knees against the inside panels of my desk, and my neck swelled like a cobra's.

"Damn!" I snarled loudly. "Shit!" Marshall pretended not to hear. This was not like me. I was only on page twenty-five of a Ken Kesey novel but already it was like being torn out of my natural skin and returned to an acid bath. Reality was too painfully slow, too physically uncomfortable. I needed escape. The novels were medicine, psychic analgesics calming my disturbed neural motors; my soul felt satisfied to recumber in the rhythm of well-written prose. Reality had no language, gesticulated at me like an imbecilic mute. Irritated, I grew snappish, my voice gained a mean edge. It took some time to return to a natural sense of wonder, which I *was* capable of. But even then it was a false kind of peace produced by an overtaxed mind imaging an ongoing, orderly, novelistic narrative onto the randomness and disorder of actual life, imposing meaning where there was none, and, if necessary, rendering reality to conform to the sense of unfolding, spontaneous plot development.

In a sense I was writing my life in the air, had already done away with the page.

I discovered the invisible, celestial, unseen publisher of human experience whose booklist was subscribed to only by mad people and angels; a book club joined by animals and children and dying people in the last burning hour of life.

By three o'clock on the afternoon of my second day at DeWitt Clinton High School, I had already proven myself a mentally disconnected flake to more than half of the teachers in my scheduled classes. I was in such a state of disembodiment with starts made on five different novels that I kind of floated onto the football field for tryouts in a state of literary hallucination. The smell of the locker room, however, quickly restored me to planet earth.

The varsity had lockers, which they stood before, naked in jockstraps, their muscles rippling with the casual stresses of suiting up, while I and the other candidates for jayvee stood by a bench along a wall that was to serve as our dressing station, slowly peeling off our clothes so as not to betray our lack of muscle conditioning to the narrow, cold scrutiny of varsity heroes.

A squat, fat guy with the pig-snout face of a tuskless boar and dressed in a jayvee uniform came scraping in on cleats and snarled at us: "Hurry up, sez the coaches. It's gettin' late," and scraped out. I took a real dislike. On the way he slapped five with a few of the varsity guys who seemed to know him, calling his name: "Shert-zer! My man!" and so on.

Shert-zer, I thought. Fucking Shert-zer. Yeah. We'll see about that. We'll just fucking see.

The varsity trotted out like gods in their pro-style bubble-shaped helmets and red-and-white uniforms. We were segregated from them like contaminated homunculi. They practiced on the big soccer field while we assembled on a patch of sparse grass and dirt off near the fence, in our hodge-podge, bedraggled, motley sweats.

Assistant coaches Steve Shiffman and Harvey Danis busied themselves with weeding us out. The thought occurred to me: A kind of "selection" is about to take place. Like that on the platforms of Auschwitz, Treblinka, Sobibor. Those who will live and those who will die. Those who will succeed and those who will fail. To fail struck me as awful a fate as to die. Coach Shiffman had the power then of a Dr. Mengele or Auschwitz camp commandant Hoess. His coach's whistle a riding crop. His low-cut cleats high black boots.

I began to think of things to say and do. My whole existence now bent itself to the purpose of persuading him to permit me life among the chosen, the opportunity to play, continue, survive. I imagined those who failed as disappearing right in front of us on the field. As walking off in a state of dejection and literally, in mid-stride, evaporating before our eyes. Who would remember them among the anonymity of the gassed and burned? What would recall them back, unless they splashed their energies and determination across the front pages of the human soul again and again, became in deed the daily news of important people, again and again, in published words and heroic football feats.

Here it would have to begin for me, with a well-aimed shoulder block; here on this plot of dirt I would have to begin to carve my name into a monument of eternally advertised enduring presence with a capital P. Here represent my ghost kingdom whose dead faces watched me, commanding me to ruthlessness, success at any price, so that I could bring the message of their obliterated existences back into the fabric of public consciousness, from which it had been brutally erased, so that each time I slammed my head into your guts you should feel a taste of their former muscle and bone, each time I laid you flat with a forearm you should bite on the club of their annihilated potential, each time I helped you to your feet you should savor the warmth and courtesy of their exterminated life-forms.

Shertzer ordered us to form ranks. He then lead us in a warm-up. He was in surprisingly good shape for one so hefty. Had us squat-thrusting till we groaned and doing push-ups with his cleats planted painfully on our backs. I was reminded of a *kapo* leading naked camp inmates through life-sapping calisthenics outside barracks in the heat of summer or dead of winter: The grunting, groaning boys; Shertzer's harsh, sarcastic orders barked over our heads, and off to the side jayvee coach Steve Shiffman, blond and blue-eyed, dapper in his coach's outfit, a handsomely attired SS man amused by our suffering.

It was a cold gray day after a night of rain. With my nose in the mud and the taste of weeds in my mouth, I glanced over at Shiffman and hated him. His word would send any of us into oblivion. Now and then he took someone aside in the course of the calisthenics, spoke a few brief words, petted the stricken boy's shoulder, and sent him to the locker room. Which is to say, sent him to the gas. Twice, his cleats passed before my eyes, paused, moved on. I jumped to my feet, heart pounding, ran in place. Shertzer's voice sounded German in my ears. I appreciated his contempt for us, identified with his cruelty. Jumping jacks: "One, two, three, four, one, two . . ." Next, wind sprints. One poor spindly bastard just collapsed on his face half-way to his mark.

Oh, well. Off to the locker-room gas with you. Next!

So it went. My only hope was to take heart from the example of the far-off varsity, like risen gods of Hades, faces in shadow behind their cages; they had survived and triumphed. They had become, in effect, the supreme elite of the tormentors. My job was to reach them, become one of them, and then I too would survive.

Suddenly, head coach Prezioso was among us. His presence swept through us like a shudder. We imploded, humbled by the absolute authority he possessed. Perhaps to another he was a tough but friendly head coach trying to speed up the tryout process so that he could get on with the business of shaping his team. To me, it was like the arrival of an SS chieftain to the camp. A special selection would take place in his honor. The method decided upon was a game called Bull in the Ring.

We formed a ring, in the center of which stood a boy. Prezioso called upon one of the boys in the ring to combat the boy in the center. Whoever was left standing became the bull in the ring. To survive you had to beat at least three combatants. Losers trotted off to the locker room, gasping for breath, astonished, shocked, dizzy.

I alone defeated five opponents. The last was a six-foot four-inch sperm whale whom I met with a forearm slam to the nose that literally lifted him off his feet. He landed so hard that the earth shook. "All right, Kaufman," laughed Prezioso with that gravelly voice, "but remember: I don't care how many you beat here today—and you did goddamned good, Kaufman, goddamned wonderful—remember: Jews don't play football. It's unnatural. Too much going on up here." He tapped his forehead with a thick, stubby finger. "Goddamn it, they think too much."

The reward came at the end of the day. Sixteen of us survived from a possible two hundred candidates. Shertzer jogged over, barked: "Jayvee, follow me to get your equipment," and in a two-column, slow-trotting line we proudly huffed behind him, past the varsity who watched us with taunting smiles that contained traces of the approval I so badly craved.

I nearly cried with gratitude when they handed me the helmet. An old black leather padded thing from the days of Knute Rockne, and I was asked: "What number you want?"

"Seventy," I said, and was given a white-and-red jersey emblazoned with the number 70 and the word CLINTON stitched across the front and back. I was in. I had made it. The best high school football team in New York City. Had armfuls of fiberglass and leather gear to prove it.

Padded pants and shoulder pads, rib pads and forearm pads, a lot of protection; the first, in fact, I had ever known against violence, and so a kind of luxury to one used to naked blows. Marty Wasserman, the varsity line coach, came over, thrilled me by saying: "Those are nice cleats. You've got high good ones, perfect with those thin ankles of yours. You wanna break 'em in now so that by the time you get to varsity they're as soft as a woman's ass."

I nodded with mute gratitude. It was a hint that he had already made up his mind to play me on varsity someday.

"And by the way," he said. "What Prezioso said about Jews playing football is true. It's not really a game Jews go out for. Jews like basketball. You know, all day you see them out there by the handball courts playing full-court. Even the girls turn out for it. Basketball's a Jewish game. Football's for the goys. I know. I'm Jewish. But there's gotta be something wrong with a Jew who wants to play football. I ended up playing a season for the Green Bay Packers before an injury took me out for good. I hope there's something wrong with you. I hope the reason you're here is because you're sick in the head. It's the only good reason for a Jew to be here. And to give it back to the goyim for kicking our ass all the time."

"Don't worry," I nodded grimly, "I'm crazy all right."

I was glad not to have a duffel bag or a lock for the locker I was assigned. I could ride home with my gear proudly displayed and the jersey pulled over my school clothes. I was a walking advertisement of proud membership in the DeWitt "C" jayvee—and loved it. Going home on the bus, no girls seemed to be especially interested in this fact, but I saw envy in the eyes of a few boys.

When I got home, I burst through the door, barely able to contain my excitement. The equipment suddenly felt strange, unreal in my hands, the potent totemic power debunked, almost by a kind of self-centered, indifferent lethargy that saturated the atmosphere of our dark little flat.

My parents were lying abed, as usual, dressed in their underclothes, listening to Muzak and reading trashy porn/snuff magazines.

"I made it! Look, Mom! Pop! Look!" I held out the official uniform and football gear of the biggest all-boys high school in the world, an American athletic powerhouse school, almost as though to say: We're official now! Real Americans! Societally as approved as you can get! And I'm a recognized school athlete and potential candidate for the *Daily News* all-city team roster, and maybe even someday NCAA college ball, and even pro—look, Mom, Pop, we made it, the ghosts have made it, the living dead are really living now through me, so many charnel bones and ashes and particles of smoke can be so proud that one of us has come all the way from the kingdom of death to this great sweating vital cheek-blooming, power-expressing rodeo of human energy and is a Jew, the son of the disappeared people in Mom's valise of snapshots!

My father laughed uneasily, said: "What are ya getting so excited for? Calm down. OK, OK. So you made it. Good. That's good. Go put the equipment away somewhere so it shouldn't be in the way. . . ."

I looked at him, stunned. "In the way?"

"Yeah, you don't want people trippin' over it."

"Please, Abie," whined my mother, "I'm not so happy you made the *fakacta* team, to tell you the truth. I would have been happier if you didn't. I don't need more heartache, and I will worry now you should break your neck like in *National Enquirer*, with that boy in Idaho played for high school football. But you don't want to listen. Good. We'll see. I just pray to God you don't end up like him, in a wheelchair."

"But look at me, Dad, Mom. Look at me. Look how happy I am. We should celebrate. If you was normal parents you'd have a celebration. Look how happy I . . . look . . ."

My voice trailed off weakly. I went to my room, threw the equipment to the floor, and lay there, shaking my foot and biting my lip, deep in thought. I felt shocked, angry, betrayed, and disappointed. But I told myself that they were ignorant. They didn't understand what I had achieved. On the day when they attend my first varsity game, I told myself, and see the marching band and the cheerleaders from neighboring Walton High, our sister school, and with TV cameras from local stations covering the play and college scouts with handheld 8 mm cameras shooting from the stands, they'll understand, boy will they ever! Nonetheless, I felt dispirited, lonely in my joy, which was waning quickly, until all I was left with was a faint flow of pride in myself that by nightfall had become a cold, staring sense of regret that I had ever been born.

I led a double life, on the field and off: football player, writer. The two didn't seem to mesh. All busted up, bruised with hurt, Ace bandages holding together sprains, iodine-soaked gauze pads plastered over cuts and slashes, once a week I limped into Mr. Greenhouse's creative writing class, after days of skull-ringing contact. My eyes had the dark-scored, shell-shocked look of soldiers serving in Vietnam, the war that was going on at the time. People were calling it a worse war than Korea. Who gave a shit? With my bad asthma, I knew that I was exempt. I had doctors' files coming out my ass all the way back to kindergarten. Every year: asthma, asthma, asthma. Especially in fall and winter. I still had it bad. On some days it kept me out of school, seated in my underwear on the edge of my bed, gripping the sides of the mattress, head hung, wheezing, or taking a pull on the inhaler that my father put to my mouth with tender care. "Here, Abe," he said solicitously, "take some of this," and his big thumb pumped on the aluminum canister and temporary relief went down and spread through the branches and roots in my lungs like in the Primatene Mist ad in *Life* magazine. That figure in the ad was me in profile, faceless, disabled by lack of air. Then, when I felt able, I went to school and ran myself ragged in practice, sometimes doped on phenobarbital-laced Broncotabs—I had an unlimited supply, permission from Dr. Siegal to use them at will. They really fucked me up, put me on another planet. I experienced these dramatic rushes of serenity alternating with sudden manic outbursts of intense, irrational rage. I was an unreliable player—could go either way, benign or ferocious, alternating sometimes from play to play. Consistency of mood was unknown to me.

And yet, for all that, a sense of peace and safety came over me the moment I entered Greenhouse's room, and saw him leaning against his desk and Fred Henry's dream-struck, old man's skeptical smile and Joey Goldman's frizzy hair and stoned eyes behind John Lennon wire-rim spectacles, and others, like Neal Abramson with his greaser ducktail haircut and sad, sad tragic air of Jewish longing for redemption and hopeless street punk mindset.

One day, when Greenhouse saw me limp in, his hand shot to his beard. He stroked it, pulled it thoughtfully, and said cautiously: "Yo, my man! What's doing, dude? You look . . .—his eyes narrowed for inspection and assessment—"like you're coming back from the war. What's with the bandages?"

"Football," I said dismally.

He looked astounded. "Football? Here? At this school?"

I nodded. The others in class studied me with increased interest. I was already highly regarded for my stories and poems. But this really put me over the top in their estimation. Greenhouse went loco, really ran with it.

"This is wild! So wild! Kaufman, my man! Did you know there's a whole tradition of sports and writing? I mean, baby, that puts you squarely in there with Hemingway and Kerouac, my man! *Pow! Wow-w-w-w-w-w!* Too heavy, man! But dig: it's like such a *contradiction*. You know, the jock shtick with the poetry riff. I mean, they are so opposite."

"Not so much," I said. "They're both a kind of statement."

That observation really floored him. All this took place before I had a chance to reach my seat. It was great, really. I'd come in all consumed with my team troubles and problems at home, and he'd pump up my confidence and get me thinking about writing before my ass could hit the chair. By the time I sat down I had resumed my role of writer, was ready again to take up this ephemeral impulse that only we in the room appeared to know about, have contact with. We were appointed to commune with invisible forces, muses, inspirations, and understood fully that we were set apart from society, born to be misunderstood. Part of the dialogue was about biography, our spiritual biography. Life is God writing us in the third person, which we, from our hopelessly disadvantaged perspective, are capable of experiencing only in the first person. How can language ever hope to capture this?

"Tell me, Kaufman," said Greenhouse. "Does anyone on the team know that you write?"

I snorted: "No way! They'd call me a twist; you know, a fag."

Greenhouse nodded vigorously. "That's wild, baby, totally wild," and he'd seem to go off in his mind, leave us for some other realm, peering out the window at the autumn trees, thoughtfully stroking his beard.

"How ya doin', Fred? What's up Joey?" I'd greet those around me. "Write something new?"

Fred and Joey already had, but usually the others hadn't. Most had taken the class because they heard that it was an easy pass. They were right. You didn't even have to come: no attendance taken. I had never experienced such a class. It was all up to you, your love of the thing. It all depended on what you wanted. I was clear about that: I wanted to be published, and I wanted to be editor in chief of the *Magpie*, the school's literary magazine.

The post was up for grabs. Greenhouse was thinking about who to ask. I knew that it was between me, Henry, and Goldman. No one else seemed to give a shit. In the back sat a tall, willowy horse-faced boy with long blond hair and bulging blue LSD eyes. His name was Bo. Elsewhere sat a boy so frail-looking that the effort to speak seemed to bring him close to expiring. He just sat there. Neal Abramson spoke volumes but wrote little. Still-born brilliant novels poured from his mouth. But the moment he set pen to paper, the magic vanished. It came out stiff, wooden, pretentious, shallow. His sorrowful eyes and hangdog face were countered by the matchstick wedged in the corner of his mouth and the hoodlum air of scornful insincerity that contributed to the sense one had about him that he was really, underneath it all, an asshole capable of robbing you blind.

Suddenly, Greenhouse snapped back to reality. "OK," he said to no one in particular, "what say we let Kaufman be the *Magpie* editor and Henry and Goldman can be associate editors. How does that sound?" He studied our faces with a look of profound uncertainty. Henry and

Goldman exchanged sarcastic looks, as though they'd been expecting this, and shrugged. But I was caught completely off guard, and stared at Greenhouse, then at Henry and Goldman, and back at Greenhouse again.

"Are you . . . kidding?"

"No way, baby. Dig it. A football-playing literary editor. That's about as hip as you can get. What do you say?"

"I say . . . I say . . . Sure!" and issued a loud, braying laugh of low self-esteem, a coward surprised at his own audacity.

The post came with privileges. I had my own office in the bell tower. Had a key in my pocket that I could use as I pleased, yet I rarely went up there. It was too dauntingly authentic; being up there brought me close to feeling the reality of actually becoming a great writer and I couldn't stand it. I would sit there and my head began to spin so crazily with dreams that I had to leave, couldn't last a minute more, rushed out so fast I left my swivel chair spinning on its pivot. Once, I found boxes upon boxes of old *Magpies* and, pulling them out, rifled through year after year of discouragingly unknown editors and contributors, until I saw in one issue the name James Baldwin listed under EDITOR-IN-CHIEF and shouted "Oh, shit!" I had touched the secret personal life of a famous author; was suddenly linked to greatness: it had passed here before. Shipwrecked in the Bronx, alone, undiscovered, I had found a footprint in the sand. Quickly I thrust the old *Magpie* into my briefcase. It was a magic totem, a kind of charm, and I wanted its power to work for me. But then I thought that someday someone just like me might kneel to the boxes, searching as I had, desperately, for a sign of hope, and I must leave something for him to find. Perhaps someday he won't have to search that far back; will find the issue containing my name and gasp: "Holy shit! Alan Kaufman edited the *Magpie*," and to his amazement dis-cover that James Baldwin had as well. Together we'd provide incontro-vertible proof that anything is possible with persistence and talent.

I wholly believed this, and put the magazine back where I'd found it. I'd try to write, seated at the big old oak desk, pen poised over my open composition notebook, but no germ of a story or poem unfolded in my head; instead, my brain whirled, unhinged by fantasies of me, the famous novelist, dressed like Greenhouse in a sports jacket with patched elbows, a blonde in a red cocktail dress on my arm, recognized wherever I went: London, Rome, Paris, or San Francisco.

I stayed up writing into the night. I had these pure, emotional visions that were indescribable: of the surging relentless river of life; of the parade of hacked and charred and chewed and wrinkled faces, as well as the smooth-skinned and the twinkle-eyed, all proceeding together down a river in Lethe; of every moment as a galaxy of changes, of human life as essentially a play in which God has failed to tell the actors that it's only make-believe. I saw plots, themes, motifs exploding in my skull like brilliant fireworks that disappeared, consumed by their own dazzling lights. In such moments I understood that literally anything was subject matter for literature, that with language I could penetrate the secret life of Man, that I only needed the skills that I would learn from Greenhouse, and that with discipline and hard work the Nobel Prize was absolutely within reach. I had still not yet written a word. Couldn't. The seething both enthralled and defeated me. It inspired me one moment, robbed me of my confidence the next. I felt that I had tricked my way here. How could I know that the very thought was the trickster, not I?

How was it possible that the hand of destiny could reach into such a godforsaken place as the Bronx, touch the life of someone as inconsequential as myself?

Or, in a flash, I saw the absolute glory that was possible to attain and rushed out, unable to contain my joy.

BOARDING THE FREIGHT

THE LOAN

TO REACH SCHOOL I took the D train down to 59th Street and Columbus Circle, where I transferred lines in a station with the color and smell of a war-gutted city. The number 1 train to 137th Street and City College shrieked, its headlights boring through the black tunnel to the platform. I stepped aboard, my long black hair framing a hand-some nineteen-year-old face, lean, tan, ear sporting a gold crescent-shaped earring, body sinewy with sensual disillusionment, and face hungry with dreams of literary greatness. I left my mother's door a dis-couraged, oversized boy, but by Manhattan my latent, welt-laced potential had emerged. My brown rebel eyes were smoky with defi-ance, my features recalling a Persian prince's, my spirit a tumbling effu-sion of as-yet untranscribed language—but in my brain still the shell-shocking, perpetual din of my mother's voice: "Why, Abie, do you wear that gold earring like a girl in your ear?! Take it out! This is not what a Jewish boy does! This is for goyim! It is pagan! You are making an enemy of God! He will punish you!" I don't even respond. Stand there punching the elevator button as she berates me, my eyes heavy with rebellious indifference, charm, mystery, like Leonard Cohen, whose manner I affect; I've never actually seen him, only listened to one album and devoured his image from the LP's cover, but I think I can imagine what he's like. In costume, I let my clothes speak for me: the frayed flannel shirt buttoned wrong, the jeans with intentional rips, my Frye boots in which my sweating, blistered feet anguished as I stumbled down the hot streets of a New York Indian summer, and best of all, the red hobo bandanna tied around my wrist! This last item drove her to distraction when I wore it in the house. She plucked at it contemptuously at the dinette table during breakfast or dinner: "What is this?" she seethed. "This hobo stupidity. Why don't you dress for college like a normal person? A nice wine-colored cardigan, nice chinos, nice penny loafers. For campus wear." She knew the term "campus wear" turned my stomach, made me physically ill—her little way of getting back at me. Usually I had to leave the house at this point, to avoid a fight.

Boarding the train to City College—famed, I've been told by one professor, as the Harvard of the Proletariat—I didn't merely travel to school, but climbed aboard the train of destiny, to be among educated people who were sure to recognize the profound quality of my illimitable gifts. I smoked cigarettes constantly, Tareytons, for I intended to be taken seriously and Tareyton struck me as a serious, adult brand. The very name, Tareyton, evoked a poet laureate of England, or an English Lord: Lord Tareyton. I was a Jewish Byron, a Semitic Heathcliff intent on becoming an all-American goy boy.

The campus had for me the declining grandeur of an Oxford or Heidelberg. It was no longer the intellectual stronghold of blue-collar Jewish genius: open admissions had changed the complexion of the student body. Afros and dashikis were everywhere, and Latinos in swell, hand-tailored threads and stingy brim hats, and serious Asian students in button-down collar shirts. But mostly it was the explosion of long-hairs, myself included, who made it seem less a Harvard of the Proletariat than the Delancey Institute of the Mentally Doomed. The campus stank of pot. There were Italians. Polish. Irish. Many were Jews. We Jews were there in force but being Jewish was the last thing we wanted to talk about. Whatever we were, our respective ethnicities had been left behind in the stellar dust of drug-expanded consciousness. For myself, I was less interested in learning the Story of Ruth than in memorizing the lyrics to "Lovely Rita Meter Maid."

My course load was almost entirely devoted to literature and creative writing. Already my writing teacher, the poet Marvin Cohen, had declared me a budding Proust. After his class, which ran from 7:30 to 9:00 P.M., Cohen invited me back to his cubicle in one of the faculty annexes that dotted the overburdened campus, where he broke out a pair of baseball mitts and a hardball and we took turns pitching sizzling fastballs at each other. Cohen, lisping in a manner reminiscent of the comedic actor Red Skelton, gushed with praise for my spontaneous prose poems.

I also shined in Valery Krishna's class on world literature, where we studied Malraux, Nietzsche, Sophocles—I ripped through them all, churned out A+ papers, and remained after class with Krishna and a select few to wrestle with great ideas. "You have a natural gift for apprehending and explicating literature. It's remarkable!" she wrote at the top of my first paper.

The high priest of my pantheistic rapture, however, was Professor Edmond Volpe, who taught the class on American literature. Volpe, a tall, broad-shouldered man with a sensitive, intelligent face graced by a salt-and-pepper goatee, embodied literature with a capital L. The campus library's stacks groaned under big volumes of literary criticism bearing his name. His command of the field, from the classic texts, to the biographies of the important authors, to the historical period of American writing that ran roughly between the Civil War and the middle of the twentieth century was breathtaking. He spoke as if Herman Melville or Hart Crane were personal friends; raised the specter of

Emily Dickinson before our very eyes, invited her to sit and tell us why she wrote in solitude. The ghost of T. S. Eliot entered, took a seat in the back of the room, interjected a comment now and then. I absorbed all of this in a state of religious fervor—you could hear a pin drop in that room. We had been warned before registering that the failure rate in his class was phenomenally high, that it was a full-year commitment and that at best one should not hope for a grade higher than B, so that those who nevertheless registered were as determined a bunch as could be imagined; the freakiest, dorkiest bookophiles from the five boroughs, the crème de la crème of the college's literary and scholarly upstart aspirants.

Volpe smoked cigarettes in class and permitted us to do likewise. In an air thick with smoke, through phlegm-constricted throats, while coughing, with wheezing voices, we issued carefully chosen words in a manner hesitant with complex intellectual thought; we groaned stammering pronouncements on Hemingway and Pound, Cummings, Stein, and Dos Passos, less like a gathering of relative ignoramuses from the proletarian underbelly of the five boroughs than a passel of eminent scholars manning an MLA panel.

I felt I knew all about Hemingway, but Ezra Pound was a revelation. I thrilled at the image of the bearded young Ohio farm dandy disporting in velvet through fusty old London and, later, in Paris overturning first English and then American literature, fielding brilliant unknowns like Frost and Joyce, Hem and Eliot, to challenge the hegemony of the stagnant canon. There was something said in class about his having broadcast for the Fascists during the war, but I shut my ears, let it pass through my system like a radio wave; suppressed it, just as I had when I came across words like *kike* in Hemingway's story "Fifty Grand," or flinched at his jeering, contemptuous anti-Semitic portrait of the Jew Robert Cohen in *The Sun Also Rises*. "That's just how they talked then," I told myself. And so with Pound. I didn't need to know more about it. Just some fluky aberration of his, I felt certain. Nothing to do with me. When Volpe asked us to adopt an author on whom to write our midterm and final term papers, I boldly chose Pound, even as an anxious pang knotted my midriff, a hollow, aching shame of mysterious origin.

Volpe liked my choice but asked after class, cigarette in hand, why I had selected Pound. I thought before responding: "Because he wore a half-moon-shaped green velvet earring as he was conquering his field." This nice detail I'd picked up on my own from some essay, and now, turning my ear, I showed my own earring, to which Volpe chuckled approvingly and said, nodding: "Very good, very good."

The one class I loathed and anguished over, cursed myself for taking, and slid hopelessly behind in was American Yiddish literature, taught by one Chaim Mendel, a Yiddish scholar of some apparent note, seventy years old if a day, short but upright and white-haired like Ben Gurion, and always dressed in white shirts and baggy trousers held by suspenders. His mien and particularly the look in his eyes were discomfortingly youthful, so that you turned aside from them on too protracted contact, for they seemed to say that this flesh which houses the man, me, Chaim Mendel, is quite near the expiration of its earthly term but the heart which beats, if sluggish, tired, weak, is yet the very same as that young, idealistic Jew who came from Poland half a century before, this brain the same, my hopes the same. Be warned, said his eyes, you who mistake your youth as perennial, who treat your Jewishness as a curse, for one day you'll wake up filled with self-hatred, still Jewish but now thick-waisted and wearing pants that hike above your belly!

He looked, despite his vigorous manner, very ill. A dying man instructing us in the literature of a dead language. In this respect we had something in common. Only I felt our dead worlds to be in some sort of competition. His had been lucky enough to have a language, to have not so much died as evolved, from Hester Street to Fifth Avenue, I. J. Singer to Saul Bellow, *Die Welt* to *Partisan Review*. But there was no language for Auschwitz, only silence. No evolution, only profound transmutation, from flesh to smoke, pain to death, identity to obscurity. Thus spoke my secret pride in being the son of the ghost kingdom of my mother's obliterated universe. I not only did not see myself as a Jew,

I saw myself as a sort of inversion of Jewishness, its photo-negative: a fourth-dimension ethnic and religious warp inhabited by corpses.

Nonetheless, though the bespectacled and Yiddish-inflected Mendel bored me to tears, I attempted to sample the Singer brothers and company but just could not bring myself to enjoy what I regarded as these charmless lowbrow folktales, or imagine what any of this had to do with me. Instead, in class, I drifted into my obsession with Pound's Imagist movement, Wyndham Lewis's Vorticism, Eliot's *The Waste Land*, and Hemingway's "Hills Like White Elephants."

One day at home, my mother leafed through my Yiddish lit textbook. She seemed to be looking for something, had paused red-faced and sweat-beaded in the middle of her household chores to flip the pages. Since she spoke fluent Yiddish it seemed natural to ask: "Do you like Yiddish literature?"

"No," she snapped. "I'm only looking to see if there's something here about your famous great-uncle Abraham Cahan, the Yiddish writer." She resumed her search while I sat there stunned.

"Oh, here he is. Look, Abie, he looks a little like you."

I got up, stared at his picture and the text with astonishment. He had been the preeminent American Yiddish writer and editor at the peak of the Lower East Side's immigrant culture, publisher and guiding force of the world's most popular Yiddish newspaper, *The Jewish Daily Forward*, a figure so seminal that Mark Twain and William Dean Howells valued his friendship. She was right: despite the difference in age of forty years, the spectacles, the bushy mustache, he bore a slight resemblance to me.

She, who stood there looking down at it stupidly, had withheld from me for nineteen years something so vital that at the thought of it I barely gasped out: "What do you mean? . . ." A futile, even self-consciously melodramatic question, but I had nothing else to fall back on; she always reduced me to cheap melodrama. I knew and understood everything in a flash: how it would have fired my imagination, stoked my courage to know that literary lineage ran in my veins, how such an example could have led me out of cultural darkness onto a path of naturally evolving Jewish identity. I wanted to strangle her.

"Tell me . . ." I said.

She looked up, a sweat drop clotting her impertinent nose. Her blue eyes were masked in obvious deceit, yet she pretended not to know the question coming.

"What?" she said.

"You . . ." I said.

She waited.

"You dithering . . ."—a good word; I had just learned it in comparative lit; used by Dickens—" . . .dithering . . ."

Her eyes retreated, rolled in her head.

" . . . nincompoop!"

"George!" she called, and walked out. "Your son is starting with me!"

"Didn't I tell you to shut that big mouth of yours or else?" came his voice from the bedroom. He didn't bother to rise from his E-Z-Boy recliner though. He knew: Confront me and I'll argue with you till the sun goes down and stay at it till it rises once more.

"I can't believe you didn't tell me that I'm related to Abraham Cahan!" I howled.

"Related my eye," he hurled back. "He was my mother's first cousin. That's not related."

"That's related!" I yelled. "That's related! I thought that my only relations in this world were you and Uncle Arnold: in other words, illiterate criminals and dead Holocaust victims. You know how badly I want to be a literary man! Why didn't you tell me about this person?! It would have helped me so, so much!! How could you be that selfish! How could you care so little about me?"

"Listen to this imbecile," my mother called out to the other room. It was strange, the two of us arguing our case to a disembodied voice— he still hadn't left his chair. So it must have been in Biblical times between Hebrews anguishing points before God. "I suffer memory loss from all the medication I take. Who remembered? Besides, what does it matter. Your grandfather didn't like him anyway."

"That's right!" growled my father, now stepping into the room across the oilcloth in his house shoes, the rest of him leisuring in fresh white T-shirt and paisley boxing shorts. He pulled the cigar from the corner of his mouth and pronounced: "He was rotten, that Cahan was. When we was hungry, my fathah went to him for a job and the creep threw him out of his office! Why would I tell you anything about someone like that? A real lowlife! The hell with him! Mash, is there still some of that cheesecake left?"

"I saved you the last piece from this one," she said, tossing her head knowingly my way.

That was the end of it. More about Cahan they would not say.

It did not surprise me that Cahan had thrown my grandfather out of his office. Izzy was a notoriously violent drunk who lost his laundry business to the mob over astronomical gambling debts. The most famous story about him was that once upon a time the son of a Polish super beat up my father, so my grandfather limped over on his gimp leg and beat the super's wife nearly to death. And when the super came by he too was beaten half to death. "Your zeder had some fists," my father would say in awe, which I did not share.

And anyway, it was too late. My corruption was complete. Not only was I doomed by crazy family genes, I was ignorant of my Jewish heritage and now, more than ever, had no wish to learn. The hell with it all! My discovery of the Cahan connection only exacerbated my already painful sense of exclusion from Jewish life. Embittered more than ever, I plunged into my studies in literature with tremendous resolve to become at least as knowledgeable, if not more so, than my goyish professors. Sat up nights with stacks of books, literary criticism, biographies, anthologies, full-length works of fiction, poetry, nonfiction. Yeats, Pound, Eliot, Joyce, Hemingway, Hugh Kenner, Leslie Fiedler, Philip Rahv, Malcolm Cowley—like a mantra in a hallucinated, modernist paradise, they were my gods, the idols I worshipped, the names I incanted to stave off a chronic sense of despair. To them I brought the woeful devotion of an inspired young Talmudist. And though I gave myself no credit for all this hard work and had, deep down, no real hope that it could bear fruit for one such as me—regarded myself warily as an unreliable demonic kid with a powerful writing compulsion at best, which I believed in, yes, but not really—I persisted in my efforts. Persisted, though, with the same sense I'd had all my life, that anyone coming from my sort of circumstances stood no chance. Inside, I was still the fat, helpless little boy hiding red welts on my arms. It was the great wall-like fact against which, nonetheless, I persisted.

Spring term came. My old schoolyard crime partner George Auria, now a sophomore at Columbia University, had been living since fall in the dormitories. He was majoring in art history while playing football on a full scholarship. For him the schoolyard dream of college ball had come true. He was not using drugs or drinking but worked out hard and wore his hair buzz-cut. Still, I sensed beneath the surface something churning. He looked mostly miserable. He had, irony of ironies, hooked up with a Brooklyn Jewish girl attending school across the street at Barnard, Columbia's then sister school. Alexi had frizzy black hair, a big nose, overgrown eyebrows, and wore thick-lensed spectacles. Come to think of it she looked a little like his brother, Mike. I couldn't guess at his reasons for seeing her, unless it was some old guilt for his youthful escapades as a schoolyard tormentor of Jewish kids. Alexi exacted a succinct enough revenge whether or not she knew about his past. An emotionally high-strung girl with no sense of humor whatsoever, she wept angrily at George's coarse schoolyard wit, and had him so on edge about saying the right thing that dark rings appeared beneath his eyes. To counteract what she at once saw as his latent anti-Semitism, she forced him to visit the headquarters of the Lubavitcher Chasidim for lectures on Judaism. With his baldy crew cut, inflamed, boil-sized acne pimples, dark rings, and bodybuilder's physique, he looked like a zombie robot soldier for a Haitian voodoo general.

One night we went out to the West End Bar to pour pitchers of piss beer down our budding alcoholic gullets. George sat hunched over his glass, gaping vacuously at a beer puddle.

"College . . ." I began.

". . . sucks," he finished.

"You gotta get out a little," I said.

He nodded.

"You look ready to explode, George. I know you a long time. You're borderline psychotic."

"You think so?"

"No. I know so. I've never seen you so . . . down. What is it? Alexi?"

"I don't know," he said. "It could be." He nudged the edge of his napkin with a timid finger. I shook my head.

"You know Klein?" he said.

"Your friend who dropped out?"

George nodded.

"What about him?"

"He's working in a motel in Denver, Colorado. He said if I want I could come out there and put up in the motel free. Maybe I should take him up on it. Wanna go?"

"Where will I get the bread for a trip like that? I'm still living at home on allowance until my student loan comes through."

"We'll hitch," he said. "I'll spring for food and stuff. Klein said we could pig out in the motel's dining room after hours."

And oh my God, suddenly I saw it. The great cavernous domed darkness of my Bronxian claustrophobic prison cell blown to smithereens by a great red, white, and blue depth charge of Kerouac-Wolfe-Steinbeck cross-country thrall. Finally, to get some red Kansas dust on my Frye boots, some fabric-fading Arizona sun on my disgustingly unweathered flannel shirt! I started trembling in my seat like a Dostoyevsky character struck with a nineteenth-century novelistic "brain fever" yet struggling not to erupt, knowing how fickle someone as chronically depressed as George could be, spooked by the least hint of supernormal joy. No, rather than cartwheel with suspect enthusiasm, I appeared to weigh the matter, one doubtful finger tapping my pursed lips.

"Free room?" I said.

"Yeah."

"Denver."

"Denver."

"I never been," I said.

"Me neither."

"Ah, what the fuck. Sure. OK, let's go to Denver." I shrugged and expelled a long, sad, exasperated breath as though I had just made, for the sake of his clearly deteriorating mental health, an enormous personal concession.

We weren't leaving right off, though; would need to wait until March, when George could take a break from off-season football training. This was still many weeks away. Nonetheless, I thought of nothing else.

The coming trip spurred me to take drastic action for my independence. I applied for student loans. I wanted out of my home forever, though I didn't dare tell myself as much. Rather, I thought: I might need the bucks for something, so why not try? I pressed the student loan people to speed things up and received almost overnight a federally subsidized student loan for thousands of dollars. I could hardly believe the ease of the process. A form filled out, followed up by a few impatient phone calls, and two thousand smackers courtesy of Uncle Sam dropped into my lap.

I didn't understand what I was getting into, had no grasp of fiscal responsibility. To me, it was free money. I thought of it as the long-overdue checks I should have gotten for my Bar Mitzvah, or government compensation for surviving as my parents' son for as long as I did, or just free cash for being young, handsome, and gifted in the United States. The largest sum I had ever handled to date was fifty, sixty bucks. Thousands? That was a king's ransom. And my father actually cosigned the mysterious thing as a guarantor. He barely glanced at the release form. He was smart. His hand was guided as much, perhaps, by a desire to be rid of me as my request was by self-justified resentment.

I just said: "Pop, sign this, will ya?"

He said: "What's it for?"

I said: "Student loan. It's on my head, not yours. But since I'm only nineteen, I need your permission, OK? It's nothing. Go ahead. Sign."

And ever so cooperatively, he said: "Awright. Don't say I never did nuthin for ya. And once you get it, I presume you know what you can do as far as I'm concerned."

"I know, I know," I said with a grin, fighting to mask my shock. He, my own father, was telling me to leave! "You have nothing to worry about on that count, believe you me," I said with a false chuckle.

So he wanted me gone! I'm outta here. But inside I cried. Even when three weeks later arrived the letter approving the loan, I studied it ambivalently. Was I really ready for this world? My intention was still masked from myself, I couldn't bear the thought of actually leaving home. Was I obliged to? Did she want me to go too? Rather than discuss it with them, knowing there was no hope in that, I moved robotically—had been doing so for years—in a state of unconscious self-mutilation, reported as instructed to the headquarters of the Chase Manhattan Bank. The "suit" who interviewed me at the bank noted my torn jeans, ragged sneakers, wine-stained flannel shirt, and unfocused eyes, but once I had produced a student ID and he ran a two-phone-call check uptown with the City College registrar and loan office, to verify my current enrollment and application status, his only question was: "How would you like the loan paid out?"

Unnerved by my success, which I now saw as the pitiless hand of fate, I stuttered: "Uh, I don't know. What'd ya, cut me a check? I don't even have a bank account."

"You'll receive the money here and now. All I need to know is, do you want to open an account and or have it all in cash? It's your call."

"Cash," I said, in a dream.

He went off and returned ten minutes later with a check for the full amount made out to me—the very first check I had received in my entire life, and for more money than I'd ever known—and led me to the teller, whom he instructed to cash the check in full. Then he gave the tips of my fingers a quick handshake and walked off, the heel taps of his buff black shoes ringing out across the marble floor.

It came to me in hundreds and fifties. I made a thick wad and jammed it down into my jeans pocket, then emerged squinting into the warm, windy day; crossed the corporate plaza with its giant bronze turd sculpture and high flagpoles flapping with state and company flags, my hand resting on the cash bulge as if to monitor its actuality and with an eye on my own emotions, to see how independence felt.

And with a surprising sense of profound pleasure I felt myself expanding to embrace the enormous city. Walked up through the financial district, the crisscrossing crowds of lifted, purposeful faces, each different, unique, a great symphony of peerless originals yet somehow collateral. The bonanza in my pocket inspired a sense of belonging. At this moment I could command anything that anyone else could: rent a priceless piano, dine on the best haute cuisine, purchase an ivory-handled walking stick, bed a long-limbed girl. I could rent a suite in the swankiest hotel, summon a limo, see a show. The towering skyscrapers, sheer walls of sky-reflecting glass, leaned close above my spinning head, peered down with sunburst flashes that I hallucinated as signals of divine investiture in the guild of free souls. Then I knew all at once in a rush of joy that what I had been thinking all along, that what my father had hinted at, was really what I most desired in my soul: not so much to leave home as to move out in order to find myself.

Then I knew what to do. I brought out change from my other empty pocket, the nearly depleted left one that I had arrived with to the bank, examined the needed coin slowly, watched the slot of a public phone gulp it down, and listened with a pounding heart as the line rang once, twice. She picked up.

"Hell-lowww?"

"It's me."

"So?" she said crossly.

"I'm not coming home tonight."

"I don't care," she said. "I already know what you're going to do. You think I'm stupid? That I don't know what you and your drug addict friends do? Stay out, and I hope you find yourself nice and dropped dead in the city morgue."

"I'm not coming home tomorrow either. Or the next day. I'm moving out."

There was a pause on the other end of the line, heavy breathing.

"You called to aggravate me?"

So, it was him, not her, who wanted me gone. In that moment I both feared and loved her terribly for her devotion.

"You're not gonna believe this, Mom. I actually didn't call for that reason. I actually didn't think about how this would effect you at all. I called to tell you it's over. That I'm never coming back. . . ." Tears erupted from my eyes. No, I told myself, drying my cheeks on a sleeve, no, it's not OK for a man your age to cry in the street—no!

Still, I wept.

"Why are you crying, stupeed," she said. "You know, I already don't feel so hot. My heart. Dr. Feely's pills are not working that good. Why do you cry, A-bie?"

Her voice sounded rigid, remote. I wanted it so badly to break, like mine, to bust out with a sob, to weep, to say I love you, to decide maybe we've both been wrong, to suggest: let's think this through together as a family. But it grew wooden.

"Where are you going to move? You're broke." This said not from concern but with a kind of incredulous disdain.

"I applied for a student loan."

"For how much?"

"Two grand."

"Imbecile. You think they'd give you so much money?"

"They already gave it. It's in my pocket as we speak."

Checkmate.

Here was one time in which siccing my father on me just wouldn't work: he was in fact part of the conspiracy. Beating me with a hanger or slapping my face was impossible now. Controlling what I ate, wore, spent, desired, dreamed, believed, knew, was bound to fail. There was nothing she could do to influence me or the direction of my life or my view of the world or history. I had two thousand smackers in my pocket, was of legal age to live on my own, and I was leaving home, and back there in Apartment 4F on 1475 Wythe Place no one could drag me back.

I walked up through Manhattan from Trinity Place to the Lower East Side and over to Soho, Tribeca, Little Italy, Chinatown, and then from the West Village to the East Village and Alphabet City. Just to feel the freedom of a man in the greatest city on earth. I stopped in at bookstores to leaf through Willa Cather novels and e. e. cummings' poems; stood in the aisles of St. Mark's Bookstore deeply immersed in Allen Ginsberg's *Howl* and Jack Kerouac's *Desolation Angels*. The city is: shelved books at your beck and call, racks of clothes to try on; it is strolling legs, it is stepping feet, it is long strides, shuffles, limps, swinging gaits, and the camel dip of slouched or ramrod shoulders. But most of all, the city is faces all pretending not to see you, so that I felt like a watchful ghost among the living but loved it all anyway—the image-reflecting shop windows, leaf-drifty passage of October autumn time and the slow, darkening chill that rose in the moody light as afternoon wore on.

In one store I stopped off and bought completely new clothes, changed everything. New jeans, the kind I'd always wanted, Levi's with flared cuffs, and a black turtleneck with a new brown corduroy shirt, and a watch cap such as nineteenth-century barge sailors might have worn, or any river rat shore dweller up and down the Hudson hunched at his fire as the night boats whispered past. By late afternoon I had reached the Columbia University campus, my legs aching but feeling more content than I had ever felt. I called George, told him what I'd done. He gave me the number of his brother, Mike, who lived in a railroad flat on 111th Street with Abby Luttrell and Ed Cranswick.

"Mike's got a room to let," said George. "Ninety a month."

"I'll pay him up for a year," I said.

"You're on."

I called Mike, told him I wanted the room. Ran up there. It was a long corridor leading to a lurid kitchen that looked straight out of the poker-night scene in *A Streetcar Named Desire* with a checked tablecloth, red walls, and stained-glass chandelier.

My new room was big, with a paint-spattered wooden floor and a view looking down onto the tree-lined street. I counted out eleven hundred dollars, told him to keep the change, and he gave me the key. That night I slept on the bare floor, cradling a bottle of Gallo port, using the bottle cap for an ashtray that soon overflowed with Tareytons—but I didn't care, and I had a newly purchased copy of Kenneth Patchen's *Selected Poems* for company from which I read aloud to myself into the late hours, head pillowed on a shirt and otherwise uncovered. I shivered and tossed on the cold floor that night, but when I woke in the morning, I was aware that I had just spent the happiest night of my life.

I put together a habitation for myself, constructed out of found things mainly, or thrift shop purchases. Repainted the walls a weird avocado green to resemble the tawdry set of *A Rage to Live*, Kirk Douglas's portrayal of Van Gogh, and on the wall hung an unframed reproduction of a portrait by Vermeer. Despite my mother's threat to lock me out, when I snuck home one night at one o'clock in the morning I found the chain off and quickly threw into a duffel bag the few belongings I owned while Howie watched from his bed, perched on an elbow.

"How long do you think the money's gonna last you? A few months at most."

"Well, then, I guess I'm one messed up scarecrow, huh dude?" I said.

"Stu-pid A-za," he said.

Suddenly I was on him, knee in his chest and twisting around his throat a fistful of pajama top. "Don't you ever, ever talk to me like that again," I hissed calmly. His fists flailed out but I slapped away his feeble swings. He had never been much of a fighter, had always relied on me for protection, even as he put me down. Then, just as suddenly I sprang free, grabbed up my things, and left.

My mother was in the foyer, sleepy in a turquoise nightgown.

"Here's the imbecile. Go ahead, hit me too while you're at it. You're lucky your father's not home. Look at you. You smell of wine. Look at that ridiculous hat. You want to hit? Hit me! C'mon . . . here! I'll give you hit!"

She reached to strike me but I charged past, batting her hand away, which made her shriek out: "Look! He hits his mother! Animal! We disown you! You hear?! Never come back!! Now you have no home! Go! Go!"

But I was already gone.

And down those empty Bronx streets that held practically my whole life, streets that had raped my pride and banged my knees with glancing blows, the schoolyard shadows that had beaten down my heart and the glass-strewn ground that had shredded my elbows, those brick walls against which my head had struck frustrated glancing blows of self-murder, the alcoves and lobbies in which I had cringed in the throes of enemy beatings, those windows that had followed me up and down the friendless alleys like the thoughtless, glassine gaze of my mother numbed on pills, I left forever—and yes, I cried. Sure. Nineteen years old and scared. All the way to the D train, and sniffled behind my sleeve, face tucked into my shirt, all the way downtown.

But by 59th Street, where I switched for the uptown number 1, I felt a lot better, and when I got off on the Upper West Side at 110th and Broadway, a block from my home, the neighborhood was jumping with night's revelers gathered under the cheap neon signs of student bars and phantom shoppers mulling in the big crowded all-night groceries over fruit stands heaped with luminous produce, and I nodded at fellow young longhairs like myself as I passed them in the street, one of their fellowship of drifting and orphaned intellectual pariahs of art and thought, like some sailor returned with shouldered kit back from journeys of years. For, in a sense, I had been away all these years, been away from myself, away from my own life, captive among a tribe of unhealed pain and historical sorrows; but now I was at last free to live the life of America, one of the road dogs whose skin goes berry dark on the long sunny highways to eternity-hopping, paradisical nowheres, and soon I'd be out there on the road's shoulder with a thumb pointed west, a feverish center stripe wanderer, hat tugged low over shaded eyes and my spirit open to anything.

DENVER

UP IN MY room, last hours before leaving, seated in the dark, clutching a bottle of ruby-colored Gallo port, drunk smile on my face, gulping mouthfuls of red courage. Any minute now George will come and we're heading west. This is the trip I've waited my whole life to make. Goodbye fetor of burning synagogues. Goodbye horse-drawn clip-clopping black-and-white documentary footage of ghettos where deranged, starved, and orphaned *kinder* wander babbling in circles beyond one's television reach. Goodbye grainy home movies of liberating battle-hardened British commandos stunned before corpse heaps at Dachau. Goodbye desecrated torahs, shorn *payos*. Most of all, goodbye fat helpless wheezing Yiddish victim-boy, Abie Kaufman, alias me: doll-puppet of wartime European distress. We are agreed: history is horrible. I'm thinking that if I like it out West enough to stay, maybe I'll change my name, grow long sideburns, wear spurs. Who knows? Spread before me on the floor, anointed with splashed wine, a Shell Oil map of the free, wide-open, anything-goes, forty-acres-and-a-mule, mine-eyes-have-seen-the-glory, for-purple-mountains-majesty United States is yielding up the enigmas of its automobile-encoded circulatory system, and bringing close a cigarette lighter to study our route—80 all the way–I mutter aloud the names of sacred states we'll pass through, an incantation, my American freedom prayer, like levels of Mahayana consciousness: "New York, New Jersey, Pennsylvania, Ohio, Indiana, Illinois, Iowa, Nebraska, Colorado . . ." I am going, after nineteen years of familial incarceration, and who knows what I'll meet out there, what I'll see, and how the encountering will broaden my mind. In bed in the Bronx, sequestered in monkish seclusion, for years I leaned on my elbow over Wolfe, Kerouac, Steinbeck, Twain, Hemingway—a passenger in fantasy with Eugene Gant, Neal Cassady, Tom Joad, Nick Adams, and Huck Finn. Now my turn had come to claim the country for myself.

When George knocks, I'm ready, a bit drunk but warm inside with that sweet confident glow of having nothing more to do than hitchhiking in a state of mild intoxication.

George looks a little worried or miffed. Hard to tell.

"What's up, man?"

He shakes his head. "Nothing. You ready?"

"Yeah! I'm ready. You sure you're OK?"

"No," he says. "But let's go."

During the subway ride north on the old clanking number 1 elevated subway, down tracks erected rooftop-level above poor little neighborhoods and dark side streets, past rivers of cars, red taillights streaming corpuscular into the veins of night, past troops of cats' eyes under neon invading the alleys, past drops of blood glistening on lobby floors, George bitched about how Alexi was still messing up his head, had him meeting with the Lubavitcher Chasidim in this crazy expiation of his anti-Jewish sentiments, and for me it was hard not to laugh. Poor George, paying for old crimes of youth: stupid, mindless, vicious utterances against Jews--even among his own circumcised friends, most prominently me, and now went and fell for a most sensitive newly liberated Barnard Lilith—avenging Judeo-demoness spirit of all the Robert Cohens he had ever tormented. I encircled his prejudice-cleansed shoulder. "I forgive you, man," and he chuckled sourly. "You can't forgive. You need to be forgiven. You were worse than me."

Shocked, I come back quickly, voice shaking: "Why do you say that?"

"C'mon, Alan. You were the craziest. What about the Unholy Alliance? What about that time you had us play 'Back to Bergen Belsen' and made Ronald Stringer dig his own grave in that snowbank in the schoolyard and then you and Louie stabbed him with pieces of that broken stickball bat? What about that time Tommy Ritter came down with that German helmet from his father's closet and you put it on and went into Friedhoffer's Bakery, up to that old Jewish guy behind the counter and ordered strudel in that Colonel Klink voice?"

I listened with a frozen smile.

"I was . . . c'mon . . ." I stammered. "You know what it was like for me. Gimme a break."

George spread his hands with a leering grin. "I'm not saying you didn't go through it. I'm just saying we both did some sick shit. Yeah, I'm saying it was sick, it was wrong, but coming from you it was twice as sick and wrong. Why don't you own up . . . ?"

"We were kids."

"You did that helmet thing just two years ago."

We fell silent. The Washington Heights station, where we'd pick up the bridge to get onto 95 and take that to 80, lay just two stops away.

"Look, man," I said over the shrieking train. "OK, yeah, we were sickos. But George, this trip means a lot to me, man. And I'm going out there . . ." I waved my hand out toward some imaginary "West"—"I'm going out there clear, you dig? Clean. With a free heart. And I don't want to take sick memories with me. I've been through enough, done enough that I'm sorry for. But everybody deserves, you know, a fresh start. A new beginning. That's what this is for me, OK? No Hitler. No Jews. Just me and the wide-open spaces. So I'm asking you as a friend: No more, OK? Enough. Just leave it. Drop it . . . enough."

We stared at each other. I waited. He shrugged, looked away.

So there was this quality of sadness about the trip's inauguration and the old intractable oppression of New York's dense brick gloom settled in my nerves. I looked away, rode numb, faced away, him faced away and rocking and swaying with wheels and track turns of the furious train. And when we arrived we took the big stinky steel elevator upstairs to the main lobby of the bus terminal and walked out into the grimy crowded Washington Heights streets. We weaved through dense foot traffic—mainly locals shopping in the bargain basement stores with perpetual CLOSEOUT SALE signs that had hung in the windows for decades—and as soon as we could, we turned left off the main avenue and hoofed at a slow trot through side streets over to the George Washington Bridge.

The bridge: a great silver harp laid over the dark Hudson River against a warm but remote night sky. We crossed on foot, pausing to glance down over the side into the swirling suicidal currents, green-blue, icy-froth, and depthless, and the river so wide, the Palisades jutting its forearms in challenge for an arm wrestle with the New York shore. One cliff followed another and extended all the way up to the Tappan Zee Bridge, which looked thin, distant, barely visible, a ghost structure veiled in mists.

I remembered sitting upriver as a boy, with George and Louie and Mike and Earl and others, roasting hot dogs in a big trestle fire, and I now mentally waved to my own childhood—a yearning boy figure squatting on the shore, peering into the future in which I now stood, yet unable to see me. If we met now, would I like what I saw of myself? Was I the man I'd hoped at thirteen to become? I was trying to live out the boy's dream as best as I knew how. I just needed a little time to make it come true, I told myself.

On the Jersey side, in Fort Lee, I faced the immense vehicular river pouring out of the eastern city of my birth into the western night. The road wasn't beautiful. There weren't old Hudsons jammed with bop kids in T-shirts, or rickety old Dust Bowl jalopies piled with Beverly Hillbillies, or haggard *Grapes of Wrath* Joads in rumpled caps, or any of the highway fantasies I'd had. It was an eight-lane monotonous hemorrhage of steel and exhaust pipelined into ultimate darkness—-though in fact we were going back in time, not forward, losing time as we moved west. We watched the Mars-red sun sink below the horizon. A chill wind gusted up our jackets, which we zipped up to the nose to protect our throats, and we shrugged and hopped in a desperate roadside dance to stay warm.

Right off, the wind chill had us up on toes, pirouetting thumbs out, auditioning for the drivers, hoping, praying, but no one stopped, and after an hour of this it didn't look like we were ever going to leave Jersey. Then, suddenly, in that skittish, fateful way that a road will remind us that we are on it only by its whim and that alone—and whether or not we get further will depend purely on luck seasoned heavily with determination, chance, and superstition—a rig so huge, so powerful, so bent on being a rig made for transcontinental travel (and so why ever would it bother to stop from its barreling flight down an overcrowded road merely to pick up two *shlubs* like us?) pulled over majestically onto the shoulder of the road and rolled to a stop. Then it just stood there with its signal lights blinking. George and I gaped back with uncertain hope, and then George's face contorted in that funny awestruck look he'd get, and shouted, "Holy shit! A ride! Let's go!" and we were pounding gravel to that rig like an end sweep in the season's climax game. From the rig came a sharp bugling steam-whistle blast of acknowledgment—its horn, I guess, only it sounded more like the prehistoric mating honk of a Tyrannosaurus rex—and when we got up to the cabin, George grabbed the big door handle that took both hands to jerk wide, tugged, jumped in, and I followed. We were high up there like in an airplane pilot's cabin, behind a huge dashboard, and the driver was this skinny, wiry, rooster-looking grizzled guy in his forties, with a baseball cap emblazoned with the words NAVY SEAL in grease-smudged tall gold letters.

He shouted from an orthodontically challenged mouth of snaggled, slime-coated teeth linked by yawning strands of repugnant spittle: "Well, that took you damn long enough! What the hell were you thinking about?!" which we each needed time to think over and reply to, which seemed to only make him madder. He was angry as hell, shaking his head in virulent wonder, shouting, "What the fuck!!" and pushed down on his gears, throwing the rig into drive. He stomped and released his gas and hydraulic brakes as he walked the immense machine back onto the road, howling: "You look like a couple of first-timers. Well, if you gonna stick your thumb out and some road dog's dumb 'nuff to pull over, the least you gotta do is—you boys listening to this?—"

"Yes, sir!" we yelled back.

"Good! You put your thumb out, you take your ride—so take your ride, boys, take your ride, goddammit. I could tell you was new. You boys new at this?"

"First time!" I shouted.

"Well, OK then, you coulda said so. Truck stops, no driver's gonna wait forever while you figure out what made him do it, even though it was your own thumb that flagged him down in the first place. You reading me on that?"

"Yes, sir!"

"Good. Because most truckers will not stop to pick you up off the road like I did. You know how goddamned lucky you are to be sittin' up here with me? You gotta go get your lifts around the truck stops. You got that boys?"

"Yes, sir!"

"Good! How far you going?"

"Far as you'll take us," shouted George.

That upset him.

"I asked you how far you going?"

"Colorado," I shouted.

"Trucker asks you straight, you tell him straight, or else. Colorado?"

"Colorado!"

"Well, I'll take you as far as Bellefonte, Pennsylvania."

"Awright!" I hollered. "Yeah!"

He looked over, all red-eyed, sleepless, a little drunk maybe, and grinned at my exhilaration. "Well, yeah," he enthused back, flatly. "That's more like it. Take a look at these. Wanna see somethin' nice?" He tapped his finger at two playing cards suspended by a chain from his rearview mirror. They each bore the picture on back of a naked woman posed lasciviously against a velvet curtain.

"I know and have intimately fucked each one of them women. What do you think?"

George and I looked at each other, grinning. He caught that from the corner of his eye, he was sharp and quick, saw everything.

"You making fun of me?"

"No, sir!"

"Cuz you funnin' me I'll let you right off here and thank you very much for nuthin, if you prefer so?"

"No, sir, we're not making fun of you," George explained. "We're just happy."

"Huh! Well, then, all right! Happy is where it's at. You boys like women, don't you?"

"You bet!"

"Well here's a pair. Here's two pair. Check out them tits. Them tits have kept me awake for ten thousand miles of road. Have you ever seen, have you ever had, have you ever made love to tits like that? Even in your wildest wanks?"

Truthfully, I never had.

"Not me," I shouted with polite regret in my voice.

George didn't respond. I thought of Alexi's figure, couldn't understand his curious silence.

"Him neither," I shouted, nodding at George, and the rigger laughed though George looked unamused.

"Are them not the most beau-tee-fool tits this side of Missoula?"

"They're beautiful! Where are the girls now?"

"Well, Cheri, the redhead, she's in El Paso, and Billy, the brunette, she's up in Reno. Billy's a dancer. Topless!"

"Wow," I enthused. Then he balled the jack and we took off down that highway like some supersonic killer whale, weaving and surging and churning effortlessly, dusting whole schools of insignificant and minnow-sized Chevies, Volkswagens, Falcons, and Toyotas, and shot past lots of little no-count suburbs and towns, and the driver howled: "Lets get us some poon!" George looked at me with raised eyebrows as if to say "Huh?" and next thing we know we'd fallen in behind an attractive blonde in a red GTO, tailgating dangerously close, and if she slows even for an instant we'd roll clear over her, crushing her flat, and you could see her irritated then scared glances in the rearview as she tried without success to shake him, left, right, accelerating, all without success, and it felt terrible to be part of this, a kind of road rape or highway gang-bang on wheels, but unfazed the driver kept it up until, literally, she had dropped to the right over four lanes and got off at the first exit she could and he howled: "Hooooooooowweeeeee! That was fuu-unnn with a capital fuckin' capital a-right! Want some more pussy?"

And we both shouted back "No, sir!!" and he nodded grimly and shouted: "Open up that glove compartment!" which I did. The door fell open, and inside it was dark, stuffed with things, including a gun, and he said, "Pull that whiskey bottle out there!" which I did—a pint of Wild Turkey.

"Take a pull and pass that down!"

Which I did and passed it down the line, and all the way to Harrisburg he kept it passing back and forth, and when it ran out he had me crawl in back to where he slept and he had a shotgun back in there. I brought out a fifth of Johnny Walker that he kept going among us and he howled, "You boys smoke pot?"

"Yes, sir!"

"Well, I don't. I'm a whiskey man!" and this avowed as we hurtled on a bridge over the Susquehanna River.

"Pot's good for you," shouted George. "But whiskey'll kill you!"

"Truth's the 'xact opposite!" he screeched. "Whiskey's good for ya! Weed'll turn you into a vegetable. My son Josh smokes dope. He's a do-nuthin, brainless, non-workin', incapable of fucking, unproducing veg-etable!"

Night boiled the car shapes into pure red taillights swimming and weaving on the big windshield, and overhead, with thrilling frequency, big green-and-white billboards announced turnoffs for Nanticoke and Hazleton, Bloomsburg, Milton, the highway crazy, a big throat, endless and on either side nothing to be seen but one after another truck stops, diners, gas pumps, like interplanetary stations where the transports pulled in to fuel up, then charge out into the alien space road, and I couldn't imagine how the driver managed to stay awake gaping at this big electric-lit hallucination days on end, or had the energy to shout: "And so I told Josh, I said I tell you what, I tell you what!! I'll make you a bet, I'll bet you I can smoke all the pot you throw at me but your lit-tle puny skinny-assed punk shit of a body can't hold all the whiskey I'll give you to drink. And I'm buying the whole fucking thing, booze and weed! And he took me up on it. . . ."

"Did you get high?" George shouted, laughing.

The driver's indignant head rose in the shrill, neck-tensing pose of a fighting cock: "Hell, high no! That grass weed shit didn't touch me at all! Not at all! I smoked that bag of stuff and said gimme another and smoked that bag too and in the meantime that boy of mine was vomit-ing sick and green on his knees like the little pussy that he is and I said, 'Your body is a worm, shithead, scrawny motherfucking little no-account snail from all that weed you suck 'stead of picking up some weights and women like your daddy do and drinkin' whiskey and be a real man, goddammit! A real man! I—am—real!'" and fell over laughing on the wheel, the huge truck sliding left to the shoulder and him all psychotically shook with mirth but George and I too scared to say a word, and then he shot straight up grim-faced, urged the wheel to the right and, correcting his coarse again, balled the jack, sent us flying through interstellar nighttime America and left us off at Bellefonte, just as he'd sworn to; pulled into a truck stop, alongside another rig, and shouted at the trucker in the cab: "Hey, champ, you westbound?" and the driver nodded and our guy said, "Take these boys down a piece, will ya?" and he waved us to "C'mon," and we thanked our driver, gushing gratitude, and jumped in with our new host, who was a quiet man, did not say three words the whole way through the rest of Pennsylvania: we passed DuBois and Brookville, got almost to Grove City itself, bypassed the turnoff to Pittsburgh, but there were still big mournful steel mills in the night visible from the roadside, huge chimneys pouring smoke that reminded me of something I shuddered at and erased from memory—determined to not so much as even think thoughts about *that* out here, and he dropped us off at Sharon, just short of the Ohio border, and roared away down the road.

We slid on an embankment, found a patch of grass where we lay under the stars for a few minutes, to catch our breath and savor the thrill of being this far from home. George leaned up on his elbow, looked west. "Ohio's right over there," he said.

But I just lay there brimming up at the stars, overflowing with it all, my freedom, a floating sense of high yet everything so sharp and clear, each grass blade, the buzzing gnats, and yellow light needles poked from the flowerhead of a giant overhead Freon lamp. I was all of these and no one, nothing—didn't need to be. It was fine to just lie here, smell the fresh night breeze. First time in my entire life I felt that way, too, my nerves all unbunched, no agenda. No one to save, nothing to be, no persecutions to detect or escape. I could feel myself spinning, hidden from the road, wanted some great hand to lift me up, hurl me up at the sky, send me farther and farther to some nameless place where history did not exist, even my memory of it erased, even my memory of me.

"This is pretty great, isn't it," said George.

"God! Yeah. How long you figure to Denver?"

"Triple-A said thirty-two hours if you drive nonstop."

"Let's do it!" I said. "I can't wait to get there. Let's just hitch straight through."

We chugged back up the embankment, stuck out thumbs, surging with confidence, and in no time an old bubble-shaped blue Buick pulled up, driven by an unshaved, sick-looking guy in a dirty T-shirt who said he was going as far as Montpelier on the Indiana-Ohio border. We took the ride and so it went, without a snag, ride after ride, no breaks to eat, right through the night, one catching quick snatches of snooze in backs of cars while the other kept up the lively stream of meaningless gab that most drivers expect in return for a lift, just to stay awake, and by morning we stood on the outskirts of Danville, Illinois, and it was unbelievable that we had already made it through so many states; the people who picked us up were gas pedal lovers, who floored their engines flat out and loved to streak ahead like bullets of light.

This was beginner's luck, but we didn't know it, how could we? Road innocents, we were riding in a dream and the drivers were genies sent to take us to Paradise. Cities and towns rolled by, interspersed with long stretches of nothing: Warren, Niles, Cuyahoga Falls, Cleveland, Norwich, Clydem, Fremont, Bowling Green, and up to Perrysburg and west over to Maumee and Montpelier. And we shot right through Indiana, hunted by longing, tired, hungry, but too excited, too driven to stop or eat anything more than stale donuts and sticks of Slim Jim beef ripped off truck stop counter displays, and smoking, smoking, smoking, even George smoked now for that nicotine rush that kept you awake mile after mile through Lagrange, Elkhart, Mishawaka and Portage, gazing out of windows, enunciating the strange names to myself with a smile, and gazing back at my curious eyes were kids with noses pressed to station wagon windows, sedans driven by portly matrons, a Jag commandeered by what struck me as an Englishman with the palest complexion I'd ever seen—he looked dead—and we just stayed on 80 all the way, it was the greatest road imaginable, through Illinois now, passing Joliet of prison fame and me envisioning us as escaped fugitives hunched sullen in the Mustang of a Joliet schoolteacher who was babbling happily about the time he taught in New York City, while Kenny Rogers warbled on the radio and George snoring in back and my eyes washed over by the sheer vast yellow-tinted fluorescence of the endless road, numbing galaxies of sleeping homes coming awake in Morris, La Salle, Peru, Malina, and Rock Island, where a truck delivering a load of cheese dropped us across the state line in Iowa, on some side road, and we gaped blearily at a vista in oblivion. Cornfields as far as the eye could see. And here our luck seemed to run out. Somehow we had ended up miles from 80, on some obscure and nameless road, hearts pounding with uncertainty.

I tried not to look at how big Iowa seemed but kept my nose pointed at my shoes. I didn't want to see the hopeless 5 A.M. road either. It was still pitch black, so that a car ten miles off looked like a yellow bead. The bead rolled up and down the serpent curves of the road hidden in darkness. It was a lousy place to be but there we were. I tried not to look at George either.

We started playing a game to pass the time. At first he didn't want to but once I started he had to, because all those years in the schoolyard we had played it and the rule had always been that once one started, the other had to, so I said: "Two blondes."

He clucked irritably: "*Tsk, tsk.* Sick bastard."

"Two blondes," I persisted, stubbornly refusing to cut him slack.

"Heh, heh. All right: in a Volkswagen bus."

"Volkswagen bus," I agreed. "And smoking weed. Stoned out of their minds."

"They got a cabin," he laughs.

"Two rooms. I don't want to have to see your hairy ass make the beast with two backs."

"And one of the blondes is your mother," he scolded.

A breeze rose, with a waft of cow shit. We hadn't eaten since New York. "So, we go there, to the cabin," I said irritably, "and when we arrive we're just sitting around listening to radio music. A Joni Mitchell marathon . . ."

That really threw a wrench in his works. "You like that shit?"

"Hell, yeah. The *Blue* album is the best music to get laid by. It's the best music for fucking. Her voice wants you to fuck. Go ahead, dreamers, her voice says, fuck and drink wine."

"Ray," he said simply.

"Ray? Are you nuts? I love Ray but fucking no way is Ray it!"

"Ray is it," he said. He sang, "I got a woman, way over town, that's good to me, ohhh yeahhhh!"

"The Eagles," I said.

He thought a moment. "All right," he had to concede. No one can deny that the best music for two people to fuck by is the Eagles.

Then: "A car's coming!"

The bead was coasting down the second curve in the spine and three more to go. At times a roll in the serpent's back obscured our view of the bead's progress, so we would watch it coming the whole time, even when we couldn't see it, because at any moment it could pop into view. We were big footballers, had been traveling now a full day, and though we were no danger to anyone, still, to stop now for us, the way we looked, at this hour, all ragged, on this lonely deserted road, one would either have to be dangerous or else suicidal. So I felt a little afraid that the car would actually stop, feared the ride I prayed for. And kept praying.

It would be great to get out of here, but the closer it came it brought closer and closer the uncertainty of what it brought. That might be a carload of rednecks with pick handles, or it might be a sane scared guy who just ignored our frantic hand signals, drove on, which is certainly what I would do under the circumstances. Or it could be the blondes. Yeah, right.

As the car approached I saw it wasn't a Volkswagen but a sinister-looking black T-Bird. It stopped. I muttered, under my breath: "Shit!" Inside, lit by a green dashboard, hulked a huge Native American man with shoulder-length black hair who leaned over to the passenger-side door, popped free the door's security button, and swung it open.

"Get in," he said.

George gave me a "should we?" look and shrugged. So I leaned my head into the window to check him out better. He was big. He was scary-looking.

"How far you going?"

"Just before Des Moines," he said, deadpan.

"We better take it," said George.

It would have been very easy to disappear. No one who knew us had the slightest notion of where we were at this moment. I sat up front while George slumped in back. He had a lot of room back there, might have caught up on his snooze while I entertained in front, but he was too tense. Every so often I turned and found him staring in alarm.

The driver responded to my small talk with an occasional grunt. The queer dashboard light gave an eerie lit-from-beneath shadowy look to his face. He didn't speak. Eventually I clammed up. I figured he was taking us to his underground torture chamber.

Instead, after we had traveled for an hour in the brightening dawn, he said: "You boys hungry?" and we said "Yeah." So he took us to eat. Pulled into an all-night truck stop restaurant complex that rose out of the deserted stretch of road.

"On me," he said.

We ordered the hot turkey open sandwich platters heaped with mashed potatoes, string beans, a stack of bread, a deep-dish gravy boat, and wiped our mouths on big clean white cloth napkins and thanked him effusively but he didn't respond, just said: "I'll take ya down the road some more" and took us all the way to the gates of Des Moines and drove off. And that was where the sun came up on us to show us where we were, which was exactly smack dab in the middle of nowhere and it getting suddenly light very fast and the turkey dinner in my belly a big sweaty lump.

We stood patiently gaping at the empty road. Along came a Volkswagen putt-putting up the highway, and we stuck out our thumbs and as it slowed, two amazing blondes with faces craned to see, smiled prettily at us, and we waved and gestured pleadingly and George actually fell to his knees in prayer, all with big stupid grins on our faces, and

I raised my arms hallelujah-style to the sky, hopped up and down shouting, "Come back, come back!" and damn if the Bug didn't slow as if actually thinking it over, and next thing it had come to a full stop. Shouting "Ho-ly shit!" we grabbed up our dusty packs and ran for our lives to make that ride, fifty yards in under 5.0 seconds, some kind of new world roadside record, and the door fell open and the girl on the passenger side stepped out barefoot, grinning in this polka-dotted thing tied around the sweetest breasts, and a big show of flat tanned belly and her thighs gorgeous in cutoff denim shorts. We jumped in the back like a couple of golden retrievers and she slid in and we took off.

"How far you going?" we shouted through air thick with pot smoke.

"Not far," said one. They both looked pretty zonked. "Want a hit?"

"Sure!"

We passed it back and forth, each inhaling deeply to get a good lungful.

The driver's name was Mary, and Charlene, or Charley for short, was her best friend. They couldn't take us any farther than the other side of Des Moines, but on the way we could "scoop the loop" with them if we liked.

"What is it?" I asked eagerly.

"You'll see," Charley teased with a seductive look.

I tried to think of what anatomical female part was loop-shaped but couldn't imagine it. But I stood ready to scoop whatever she wanted me to, into the loop, out of the loop, I didn't care, I was game for it all.

"Have you seen Big Foot?" asked Mary, and Charley snorted.

"Big Foot? The Abominable Snowman?" I asked.

They both nodded, choked with amusement.

"Not me," I grinned. "How about you, George?"

"There is no such thing," said George.

The girls grew indignant at this.

"There sure as hell is! It's been chasing us since we got on this road. Don't you see that green sphere following the car? That follows Big Foot wherever he goes. It means he's around."

George and I swung around to look out the rearview window, saw nothing out there. And again they choked with laughter.

"And that weird, bad smell . . ." said Charley, rolling her window down. "You smell that? It's Big Foot's smell. . . ."

And in fact, as the fresh air rushed in it brought a foul smell I'd never experienced before. I began to feel a little paranoid, not only about Big Foot but also about the sanity of these two, and of myself.

It suddenly hit me where I was: Iowa! A huge uncontrollable goy-land thousands of miles removed from scenes of my mother's blows, warnings, threats, judgments, insults, shrieking now through my stoned brain. I dropped my grimacing face, clutched my head. "What's the matter with him," I heard the girls say.

I said: "Nothing's the matter. Want to see my earring?"

And they giggled in delight. "Let's see," said Charley and as I leaned my face close to hers, hair pushed back to expose the gold crescent. She took the lobe between thumb and forefinger, stroked it ever so gently, and said: "It's nice!"

Suddenly I shouted: "Drive quick! Before Big Foot gets us all!"

And Charley said: "So you think it's true?"

"Hell, yeah!" I crowed, and they both screamed in delight, and Mary floored the gas pedal all the way into Des Moines, where I learned that "scooping the loop" is taking a turn around the main square in down-town Des Moines.

Remarkably, crowds of young people were still up, noisily congregat-ing around parked cars in which some of them sat and talked with heads or feet hung out the window, and every so often Mary pulled over to chat while the curious—male or female and almost all of them blonde and blue-eyed—leaned in to look at her captives, and I pressed out my head and called "We're from New York," which made no impression on anyone whatsoever, and after a half hour or so of this George and I grew numb with boredom and sat slumped in back, heads sunk between shrugged shoulders, resentful looks on our faces. Mary saw, said to Charley, "Let's drop them off." She seemed sorry to see us go and said, "Too bad my daddy's friends are all using the free cabin or you'd for sure be welcome and we could have a fun party, just us four." I had a feeling though that the party would be little more then the four of us snoring unwrapped in dirty blankets on the unswept floor of some ramshackle wood hut, and said: "Oh, well!" and Charley smiled and shrugged and they left us off a little sourly on the other end of Des Moines. The whole thing shaved about two precious hours off our travel and we were no closer, really, then we had been before their arrival. The fantasy of stoned blondes in VW Bugs died forever in the Iowa dawn.

We were still a good piece from Denver, with half of Iowa and all of Nebraska to go before we even reached the Colorado border. We got quick-hop rides out of Des Moines, the Sunday traffic picking up at about 8 A.M. or so, and two guys like us were no big deal in a state where every high school produces NFL-sized freshmen with their eyes on pro ball. So we took it as slow and tired as we felt, just grateful to be moving: Adel, Atlantic, Avoca, Harlan, Missouri Valley—all slipped by through the rattling breeze-stroked sun-squinty windows of the dusty pickup trucks and old Dodges that took us down a piece. Our drivers mainly drove in silence, some in T-shirts, others in church suits, all with arms out the windows, big blond guys alone and with nothing to fear. There was not a lot to see: highways are not built for their scenic views. Fields went by, endless under the enormous, bland Iowa sky, and the towns, what I could see of them, lay on the plains like little development models of sterile and supermodern bedroom communities, with the usual diners, gas stations, and movie theaters.

We entered Nebraska through Omaha, which was a big city with lots of somber buildings fading in the terrific heat and men in tipped-back straw hats and rolled white sleeves congregating on the corners; got a ride all the way to Lincoln, a slightly smaller version of Omaha, where we jumped into the station wagon of a plump bald man with bright blue eyes fixed in rigid, righteous conviction, the nature of which I had a sickening feeling we were about to learn.

He was dressed in white shirtsleeves with a big gold cross hung around his neck, on his way to some religious convention in Kimball, just where 80 dropped into the southwestern-most corner of Nebraska before becoming 25—the road that would drop us in a straight free fall right into the very heart of Denver.

Feeling it that close gave me patience for anything, or so I thought. I hadn't reckoned on Reverend Bob Sills of the Pentecostal Church of Our Holy Creation of Omaha.

"My name's Bob Sills. You boys are not religious," he decided the moment we were settled in our seats.

"No, sir."

"It shows on ya," he announced, beaming as though this were not necessarily all to the bad. "You got the look of being tired, though, of carrying a big weight, of feeling all alone in this world. Do I read you right?"

George sank down in his seat, drifting into sleep. "Sounds just like Alan," he said before dozing off.

"Nice to meet you, Alan."

"Feeling's mutual."

"So I was, at your age, so I was, the very same: alone. No one understood. I searched high and low for love and could not find it. In the lap of my beloved family. In the arms of women of low repute and high standing. In intoxicants of all kinds. I smoked pot. Yes, that's right. You wouldn't think it, would ya? That was ten years ago. Did the wild party circuit. I sought in politics for love. In labor. In the arts. All such things, for I was intelligent, above average if you must know. In none of these things, however, did I find the consolation, the deep, deep feeling of connection that I so desperately craved. And for years I quite honestly felt abandoned in the blackest, darkest, existentialist sense of the word 'alone.' Alone without love of God or Man. Alone without the comforting solace of another commiserating human soul. I even tried the church. Went, sat in the pews, kneeled, and prayed. Talked to the priest. Took communion. Recited novenas and whatnot. Perused the Bible, old and new, with an open mind. The result of all this effort? Tears, my friend . . . tears."

It occurred to me that he was going to make some pitch at any moment, to recruit me to the ranks of some religion or other, and that I could save us both a world of trouble simply by letting the good reverend know that I was Jewish. But I imagined that doing so would spoil something I had experienced all through this voyage until now: freedom from that very thing. No one knew or asked about my religion, or seemed—contrary to everything I'd ever heard about the country beyond New York—to much care. I had reveled wordlessly, greedily in my unchallenged American-ness, a status reflected back to me in the unsuspicious eyes of the truck drivers, farm girls, clerks, teachers, Moms, gardeners, graphic artists, grease monkeys, and every other conceivable kind of person who had picked us up so far. So I said nothing, let Bob talk on about Jesus Christ, my candidacy for salvation, and all the way through York, Wood River, Shelton, Gibbon, Kearney, where he bought us lunch in an all-you-can-eat Howard Johnson's fish fry and showed us wallet photos of his wife, Fancy, and his two daughters, Karen and Darlah, who was a knockout, and then on through Elm Creek, Cozard, and Gothenberg, where we crossed the Platte River and I stared out at the most far-reaching desolation I had ever seen, a landscape of dust and sky, amazing—a kind of earth moonscape with just hints of life here and there in the form of skeletal abandoned tractors and ghostly barns and not a single living thing for hundreds of miles in any direction. All through this Reverend Sills continued unabated his headlong assault against the bulwark of my heathenism, now even straight-out offered to convert me, bathe me in the waters, even offered lodgings, a place to live, and dropped hints that Darlah, the beautiful daughter in the pictures, was sitting at home still waiting for Mister Right—one of course who had been properly sanctified in the waters of our Christ's salvation—and for a moment I even toyed with the notion. It was so different from anything I'd ever considered. Saw myself in the button-down collar shirt with rolled sleeves and loosened tie, sweating in the pews, face flushed, head flung back, singing "Onward

Christian Soldiers" with a hard-on as my blonde *shiksa* goddess fondles my hardened cock under the jacket folded in my lap. Several times I was on the verge of telling him my real story, since he seemed, despite his lunatic obsession, so sincerely, so likably concerned about saving me from Hell, the poor guy little realizing that my own mother had already been there and that I had been born, so to speak, with the burn wounds of that visit spread over one hundred percent of my spiritual flesh.

"Alan," he said somewhere between Ogallala and Big Springs, "I want you to know that I know, that I have known; what I mean to say is that since a while back, your Jew blood, I know . . . I know."

My Jew blood quickened and chicken-fat heart began to ache.

"What makes you think that?" I said, struggling for nonchalance.

He nodded with this knowing smile. "It's as plain as the nose on your face," he said. And blushed: "I mean, *my* face. At least out here, anyway. That's all right! That's all right! Look . . ." His right hand fell on my knee, stayed there, not sensual, just reassuringly friendly, as your hand might feel to a stray dog you're trying to befriend. But that hand did not acknowledge my humanity. Still, I left it there, listened. He patted my knee to make points. I felt like a woman getting mauled. Felt paralyzed to stop him.

"It's not your fault. Do you understand?" He laughed at the sheer irony of it all. "Why," he said, "you're already forgiven. Christ has already set that place for you in his kingdom. . . ."

I envisioned my spot sandwiched between those reserved for German shepherds and toy poodles.

"Christ in his loving mercy sees the Jew child born into the darkness of his parents' misbegotten ways and holds forth his hand to say: 'Come unto me, to be bathed in the waters of conversion and regeneration.'"

"You want me to convert?" I gulped. It really hit me now. And I felt weak. Shockingly powerless. As if, despite my size and tough Bronx demeanor, I might say yes, from sheer unbraked helpless fear.

"Yes, Alan! Yes! Come over to us! We are your *real* family!"

And so forth.

I don't know where the courage came from, but I said: "That's nuts."

And George woke, looked out the window—he had slept the whole way through Nebraska.

"Where are we?" he yawned, unaware of the frozen silence chilling the air between the reverend and me.

"Almost at Big Springs," I said woodenly.

He looked at his pocket map, still ignoring the reverend, whose livid face had turned purple.

"That's it. That's where we cross into Colorado," said George.

The good reverend absorbed this exchange; had invested hours into my prospect and wasn't about to let this catch off the line quite yet, for dreams die hard. He could probably still imagine himself parading me into the church, to the buzz of his excited congregation: "I've brought us a Jew from New York City who is coming back to Christ our Lord!" and the love-starved women fainting at the sight of my handsome otherness as his daughter in her Sunday best grows wet at the Jewish boy-toy he's brought home for her sanctified jollies.

But there was the sign for Big Springs, and I pushed his hand off and said impertinently: "Pull over here, Reverend. This is it!" with all the savage authority I had acquired from years of schoolyard life, and with positive dismay he looked at me, his expression hangdog, betrayed, unable to accept that I could reject the sheer power of his naked, unbuffered oratory, let alone refuse his near-adoption of me as a son-in-law, and I grinned back cruelly and said, 'Right there, Reverend. You see that . . . what's it . . ."

"That feed store with the pennants," shouted George, and the good reverend eased onto the gravel service road before Wayne's Feed Company of Big Springs and sat gripping the steering wheel with a cold, injured smile as George and I trundled out with our gear and leaned down to offer one last glimpse of our beautiful, unshaven, and Godless faces, and he drove off, leaving us unsaved at the crossroads of Nebraska and Colorado.

We had to hoof on foot three miles to pick up 30, which would take us to 76. A ride sped us along the South Platte River, past Brush and Fort Morgan, where we caught a long-haul lift squeezed in the back of a crowded van of hippies who blabbed nonstop on methamphetamine while George and I dozed on their bundled sleeping bags and flea-infested blankets. And then a ragged nasal voice from up front said: "This is it, man, you're here," and we struggled out. "Here" was Larimer Street in Denver, Colorado, right across the way from Arcade Buffet, which boasted the longest bar in the West. According to Mike Klein's instructions we were only a mile or so from the Sandman Motel, where he worked.

I had met Klein once, briefly, in his freshman year at Columbia; had dropped in on George's dorm room in Livingston Hall on campus and there was Klein, a short, dour-looking guy with spectacles who smoked cigars and prided himself on his grasp of immaterial trivia.

Klein knew, for instance, not only how many miles of sewerage ran under the pavements of New York but the number of manhole covers dotting its streets and could break down for you borough by borough the numbers of fire hydrants. His wardrobe was uniform, without variation between changes: khaki work shirt with double button-down pockets, black chinos, white socks, brown shoes, alligator belt. One could imagine him wearing the same outfit sixty years from now, ripping up no-win off-track-betting ticket stubs and throwing them to the floor, then going out to nurse a beer through a long afternoon of dirty sunlight filtering through grim bar windows. He was already old, washed up before he hit twenty. Klein smoked a lot of pot, too; was dealing out of his room when he dropped out of Columbia—and left town, some said, after getting in over his head on dope deals he couldn't finance. His departure, for one who loved New York with a passion bordering on mania, was suspiciously abrupt. Known only to George, he resurfaced in Denver.

When we tramped into the motel's lobby, there he was, chatting with the clerk behind the check-in desk, a fat young man with rosy cheeks and lively blue eyes who took in our appearance with alarm until

Klein said in that emotionally drab voice of his: "Hi George. Hi Moony." Then turned to the desk clerk: "It's the ones I told you about."

He couldn't have been more blasé. We shook hands all around and Klein said to the clerk: "So, Toby, just this one time let's put them in a dayroom and then, only after two P.M., after that, OK? And if there's no vacancy on those days, well . . ."

"Into the gutter with 'em," grinned Toby, who seemed a likable guy.

As Klein led us to the room under discussion, he mounted a low-key dolce-voiced blathering engulfment of trivia that we felt too exhausted to resist. It was a nice room with double bed, color TV, pitcher of ice water, Gideon Bible on the night table.

"George, Moony, this is the only day you can use this room, because unfortunately—it's so really lucky that you actually *found* me here at all, because I had no idea when in fact you'd be present, physically speaking, in Denver, and thought I'd hang around today just in case, because normally, in fact starting tonight, I am the night shift desk clerk, which begins at two A.M.—-OK? Er, that's two A.M., A.M. being morning, not afternoon. . . . Have we got that so far? Yes? Great! You'll both have to find ways—this doesn't apply today. Today, we rest from the long, exhausting haul. God! I can't even imagine it! A couple of real Kerouacs you are—find ways, as I said, to keep yourself amused until two A.M., and only then can I give you a free room if one's available, and if not, well, no, not into the gutter with you both, of course not, but, well, we'll find somewhere to put you two—maybe a floor back in the office? It's a possibility . . . we'll see. Also, free food, all you can eat on my shift, so pig out, really, the owner doesn't mind. Seriously. All the pie and ice cream you like . . ." And so forth, on and on. We stood swaying by the beds, and then, like on cue, collapsed into them in our dusty road clothes and passed out. I guess he got the hint.

Denver bristled with energetic urgency—it bustled with endless bars, pool halls, winos, babes, cars, dope, police, clubs. And we bustled along with all that. Ducking in and out of saloons, knocking back cheap beers for a quarter a glass, bobbing on the street to dirty-faced Denver bluesmen riffing on catgut string guitars under headshop awnings; getting into very intense dialogues with yippies, heads, hippies, freaks, diggers, politicos about Washington, the Panthers, the Chicago Seven, the War, none of which I really knew anything about but suddenly cared so intensely! Because I wanted to be a hippie, and hippiedom was in full bloom—up and down the Denver streets they barefoot-moseyed in flowery groups, longhair couples in paisley and denim with weed-stunned toddlers in their arms, bands of stoned run-amok teens, and we heard there was a crazed LSD scene booming nearby in Boulder that tempted us to actually try some Orange Sunshine, but at the very last second we drew back, returned the tabs; and thank God, too, for I might have ended up in the loony bin out there, for all the ennervation I felt! I was literally out of my mind with excitement. Living a hallucination of Rocky Mountain goyisha freedom, Jewish-less, religionless, spontaneous belonging. We visited a crash pad, Octopus's Garden, situated in an old rotting Victorian where downstairs a fat Mama Cass–type stirred a big witches' pot of meatless communal stew while upstairs couples—some clothed, some not—snoozed or coupled or toked or whatever on a sea of sheetless marriages spread over the floor wall to wall. We stood in the doorway, gaping in: a big black Richie Havens wannabe jumped to his feet and raced around the room, babbling incoherently. The place smelled of dope, piss, vaginal secretions, and sperm. Even George couldn't stomach it, turned away. But I stood there, gaping, fascinated; actually considered moving in, maybe become one of the Octopus's tentacles, open to anything. It was fun to test myself against new things. I began to understand: that's what freedom is. The right to experiment, see what fits, what doesn't. It's how one learns who one is and who one isn't. I found I had a natural predilection for this. And I loved it.

We had good luck with the motel too—there were always plenty of rooms available and we'd return drunk with a hot bag heaped with fresh-baked bagels bought from a nearby all-night bakery and pull out big tubs of ice cream from the freezers behind the food counter, fill bowls with mountains of the creamy stuff, and dip our hot bagels in and tear off steamy chunks between our eager teeth. The high altitude made us hungry, and the unchecked freedom made us Dionysian. We drank joy juice all the time. Maybe it was too much latitude, certainly more than we were used to. Maybe we were afraid of happiness. Whatever we were, we were relentless in the pursuit of pleasure.

In the Arcade Buffet, longest bar in the West, we stood up against the old mahogany serving counter, which looked as long as a freight train, knocking back boilermakers, cheap wines, beers, Bloody Marys, martinis, and carousing with the barflies. We wandered into dance halls, grabbed laughing cowgirls by the waist and hugged them close, and got our faces slapped. Ranch-hand types glared at us and we invited them to dance too. We were, in a word, nuts. One night we instigated conversation with a dour-looking, pretty girl in a wheelchair. Lisa told us that she lived in a hotel across the street and invited us to her room to meet her pet rat, Hermes. Half-blind, we went.

A neon-bathed flophouse. Run-down balconies dripping rust tears and odd-looking degenerates loitering in the lobby, including one guy with an eye patch who Lisa pointed out as one that trafficked in body parts or illegal babies, what's your pleasure? Shuddering, we climbed creaky steps in a dark stairwell while she rode the rickety elevator up to the third floor, where she waited for us at the door of a small, cream-colored room with the highest ceiling I'd ever seen. There were vast, thick cobwebs up there that looked half a century old, and I tried not to think about the size of spider that made them.

Hermes was this pathetic white rat with red beady eyes and a sickeningly pink rodent's tail, but Lisa made a great fuss over it, as though it were the most beautiful animal on earth, some rare lynx or something, and to her, I supposed, it was.

"Do you want to hold Hermes?" she said, but before I could decline, she dropped it in my lap, where it snagged its sharp nails into my trouser leg, which hurt like hell. When I tried to pick it up it dug deeper. When I failed to pull it off, and pleaded "Please," Lisa grinned, "Not like that," and lifting it by its neck fur, gently took it back, little hands and feet spread and a glazed, trusting look on its face.

"He keeps me company through the long hours alone," she said, and George looked at me and I shrugged.

"Don't you got no family?" I asked.

"No," she said. "I was an orphan raised in a home. Now I live on social security. This place is all I can afford. They take state vouchers, ya know. What about you. Have you got family?"

I swallowed hard. "In a manner of speaking. I wish I didn't."

She shook her head. "You should never say that. No matter how bad you think they are, they're your family. I'd give anything to have one."

We thanked her, left—me with my healthy legs and sick family yet still not feeling as grateful or lucky as she seemed to think I should. Maybe she was right but I just couldn't see it.

What I did share with her but hadn't her courage to express was a sense of waiting in loneliness, though for what I couldn't say—perhaps to learn who I was? I didn't feel I knew. Denver only made me seem more a stranger to myself then ever, lost in its noisy streets and beckoning bars. It was a heartless city in its way. Crowds pushing in a frantic rush to get into the clubs from which spilled music, and the women looking very fine but cold and most on the arms of guys who looked like they knew what they were about and hated out-of-towners, and sure, people spoke to you all right, but you had the sense that their smiles just weren't real. And yes, it hurt the way their eyes quick-checked us, hardened, and turned away. George and I felt like a couple of drifting hobos stopped into town for some impoverished R&R, which wasn't far from the truth.

Still, it was beautiful. Over it all loomed the big blue Rocky Mountains, a night sky streaked with red and gold, like a desirous woman's hair, last traces of the Western sun. But how long can a sunset sustain you?

One day, in an Arby's roast beef joint, George and I hooked up with two countergirls, Joan and Rita, who invited us to meet up after work for a big car trip to Central City in the mountains. We gave them our address at the motel, just to make us seem legit. They'd swing by to pick us up at three.

We hurried back to the Sandman even though it was only late morning, told Toby about our big date and begged him to let us use a vacant room to clean up our acts. Reluctantly, he admitted us to a room, where George drew a bath and soaked while puffing on a stogie and reading aloud from the Gideon Bible about Onan, history's first chronic wanker. I sat on the edge of the bed nearest the window and stared out into the hot afternoon, where the snow-veined mountains shimmered pale in the distance under a sky so hot it looked white.

I didn't dare admit to George or myself how disappointed overall I felt in our Western experience. I even preferred the grueling hitchhike to the actual arrival. Although generally things looked more pleasant out here than in New York, and although it was nice to be free and far from anyone I knew, it was still the same old rat race of money and loneliness everywhere, and I could see how easily I could disappear, vaporize, into all this; how anyone could. Get a job locally. Learn to drive. Share a flat. And begin to move on the mindless treadmill. Get smashed on weekends to anesthetize the pain of the week. Watch the year fly by, the years add up. When enough had accumulated to make me think I was wasting my life, I could marry, have kids, flee to the burbs. What is this life? What does this have to do with who I am? How will it be any different than in New York City? There, at least, ideas mattered, were fought over, hotly; at least it was so on campus. But off campus? Probably the same numbing grind to live, without knowing why or what for, except for the immediate gratification of nervous cravings. I imagined that any noble values that one learned in school would play out in real life as anguished farce.

Still, the prospect of company restored my spirits. I showered and shaved in the ringed bathtub that George vacated, then slipped into the fresh new shirt and jeans and loafers I'd brought all the way from Manhattan.

I was now ready for my sexual conquest of the American West.

The girls came round dressed to kill in these pretty short summer dresses and sandals, their fair lips painted like bright red cherries. I jumped in back with the one called Rita; George rode up front with the cantankerous Joanne, who leaned over and gave him a big wet kiss on the cheek that turned his ears and neck a burning purple.

"Look at him blush like a little boy," she said, turning in her seat to smile at Rita. "Isn't that sweet?"

Rita and I looked at each other and she kissed me too.

"How was that?" I said.

"Like a nibble on an ice cream cone," she said.

I could hardly believe our good fortune. I just leaned over, put my arm around her, pulled her tight, and Joanne threw the car into gear and we roared out of the parking lot with Toby waving in the office door and the ice blue Rockies awaiting our arrival, for it was to them we were headed. Central City was this old deserted mining town, Rita explained, and some developers had turned it into a fun-filled tourist trap. We climbed along roads that made me airsick—to my immediate left steep gorges, the way barely able to hold a small Fiat let alone some big clunker like Joanne's Buick. But she was a hot driver, steered with one hand, the other in George's lap while my childhood idol sat there tongue-tied, withdrawn, strangely morose. I slapped him on the back of his pimply neck.

"Hey, what's with you?"

He looked at me as though something very obvious was wrong but I was too dumb to see. I couldn't guess what was up and snuggled down with Rita.

"What's the matter with George," she asked.

"Ahhhh, who the hell knows? He's a moody bloke."

She nodded that she understood.

"So," I said, "did it embarrass you to kiss me like that?"

"Yes," she said.

"So, why'd you do it?"

She thought a moment. "Because Joanne did."

"Yes," I smiled at her truthfulness, "I'm like that with George. If he does something I'm following right behind. It's hard to have a mind of your own. I'm trying, though. Actually I've got one but it's a secret mind. No one knows about it but me."

"Oh," she said. "Why is it a secret?"

"So I can dream as big as I like. So no one will laugh, or tell me I can't do this or think that or be whatever."

"It sounds to me like your fantasy of something is stronger than the real thing."

"Probably it is," I laughed. "Probably it is."

"So what brought you to Denver?"

"That secret mind. You see, I grew up in this crummy little room in the Bronx with a view of the alley out my window and just enough sky for one pigeon to crawl through on its belly. And I dreamed of a big America with big sky and full of people and adventures, and I swore to see it all someday." I looked out the window at the wild, rugged mountains. "As big as that," I said.

"And how does it feel?"

I shook my head. "I don't know. Strange. Like I can't connect. Like my insides are a shut suitcase. A suitcase full of pictures, and I'm waiting for someone to pop open the snaps, take a picture out, and ask for an explanation."

"That's interesting," she said. "So, I'm asking: Who's in the pictures?"

I started to say "murdered Jews" but stopped myself. She searched my eyes, saw everything without understanding what it was. I looked away.

"I've come this far," I told her, "and I can't look in your eyes. Maybe I've come this far to learn that I can't. Maybe that's why I came."

"You're strange," she said. "But in a nice way," and she touched my hand lightly with the tips of her fingers, our hands enfolded as we rode to Central City in silence the rest of the way, looking out the window at the jagged blue peaks and plunging chasms. Ever higher we climbed, to the old ghost town. When we arrived it announced itself with a hollowed-out ramshackle saloon that had the color and texture of a mummified moth. There were hired actors dressed as silver miners strolling about, leading well-groomed pack mules with reddish, shimmery coats. A lot of obese tourists snapped photos. And that was all that was left of the West I had sought.

We got drunk off our asses in Central City—knocked back endless whiskies, beers, and the girls were putting away martinis. Then we bought a big gallon of cheap table wine and found a deserted spot behind a big faded wooden ghost town barn that hadn't been made into any kind of attraction and sat with backs to the wall, faces to the sunset, slogging back wine and making out. I tried to pull Rita away to where we could have more privacy, but she kept saying, "Uh-uh, not that, no," and crushing herself all the harder against me, moving up and down rhythmically against my leg, but when I'd try to go further her little hand stopped mine with steely determination and again: "Uh-uh, no!"

"Why not?"

"Because I can't."

"Can't what?"

"You know. Do it."

"Why?"

"I'm with someone."

"Who?"

"Just a guy. But I swore I wouldn't cheat."

"This is not cheating?"

She blushed. "No!"

"Well, what is it?"

"Just having a little innocent fun."

"Fun! I'm suffering, here, baby! You've got me going wild over here. I'm . . ."

I waved my hand over my testicles. "They're all swollen. They hurt." It was the old problem. The pain was intense.

"Maybe I could help," she said.

"Yeah," I said seriously. "Please. Help!"

"But you promise that's all."

I promised.

We came to our feet, and she led me limping to the side of the barn, where we "helped" each other in a way that allowed us each to remain "faithful."

When we returned George was pulling on his pants while Joanne brushed dust from the seat of her dress. They also looked both happily spent and fidelitous.

We rode back to Denver and they dropped us off at the motel, where we all hugged, said our goodbyes. I explained that we'd be leaving soon, maybe even tomorrow. They seemed relieved to hear that. No chance then of their boyfriends ever finding out how faithful they'd been.

When they were gone, I asked George: "Is that what you meant in the car by that funny look you gave me on the way up to Dollar City? You figured out they were with other guys?"

"That's right," he said.

"How'd you know?"

"There was this ankle bracelet . . . she must have taken it off at the last second when she picked us up. It was lying on the floor by the gas pedal. It said 'Bo Loves Joanne.'"

"Well, poor Bo the *shmo* will never know," I said wistfully.

"That's for sure," said George. "That's for sure."

We'd seen enough. Felt tired. Our money was low. Klein wouldn't be able to put us up much longer. It was time to head home. For myself, I had seen enough of America for now.

We decided to travel back by a different route. We'd catch Greyhound up to Cheyenne, Wyoming. Klein hardly remarked our impending departure. Treated it as no more then a Brooklyn subway trip back to Manhattan. Stood there behind the desk in his khakis, the cold stump of a stogie in his mouth, his rimless spectacles thrust forward on his nose as he tallied the day's books.

"Did you have a good time?" he asked without looking up.

"Great!"

We explained about leaving on the morrow.

"Fine," he said. "Don't forget to leave the key in the door. Don't worry about making the beds. The maid will be in there. Have a safe trip back." Still looking down at his books.

"Klein," I said, just before going.

He looked up. "What?"

"What exactly are you doing out here, anyway?"

He paused, then said: "Waiting for the wait to end."

And that was all. The next morning we hoofed down to the Greyhound station. By afternoon we were across the state line, aboard "The Dog," and barreling into Wyoming's Big Sky country.

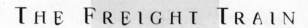

THE FREIGHT TRAIN

GEORGE WAS THE first to notice the freight train, parked in a gully visible only from the rearmost window of the Big Boy's restaurant in Cheyenne, Wyoming.

"Do you see that?" he said.

"Illinois Central," I said.

"On the eastbound track," he grinned.

"But school. If we get held up we'll never make it back in time."

He scratched a week's growth of beard.

"It *has* been a week," he said regretfully.

"That was pretty decent of Klein to put us up."

"Wasn't that a great motel?"

"The Sandman!" I chuckled.

We both paused to remember how we'd shown up just after he came on shift and already was at his ledger books. We'd walk all the way to the outskirts from the center of town and would enter the lobby almost limping and Klein would wave his hands over the numbered Peg-Board weighted with room keys. "Any of the suites," he'd say grandly, looking up from his math work in the ledger.

"Remember Lisa, the Rat Woman?" said George.

"Jesus H. Kay-ryst. Poor kid," I said, sadly shaking my head. "What was that pet rat called?"

"Hermes," said George. "Hermes." He shook his head.

"Besides, how long would it take? How do we know it's even going to Chicago?"

"We don't know. But I'd say Illinois Central hitched to a Union Pacific train on the eastbound track of the Cheyenne, Wyoming, station has a better than fair chance of ending up there."

"True."

He was always right about freight trains. His father was a retired switch operator for the Penn Central line. George knew which trains would come from north or south along the Hudson River. George could read the color codes tagged to the passing freights and say where they were going or coming from. We'd tell our parents we were going to a YMCA dance, then ride the subway north to Riverdale, where we marched upriver with a backpack of hot dogs, buns, cupcakes, orange juice. This was before liquor, at thirteen years old.

We'd build a cooking blaze so tall it tickled the overhead wires, the hot dogs glistening with melted fat, and once found a dead stray that we threw in and watched burn. When a freight came we ran alongside, then swung aboard and rode it miles in the night with the salt smell of the river air and the red-and-white lights of the Palisades. The densely forested embankment flowed by with cold, sweet, green-smelling shadows. George called out: "This one's from Canada!" or "This one's going west!" and it seemed like we were in Alaska, with wolves and Mounties, Indians and trappers and buffalo.

"But school," I said.

He chuckled. "It's that bad?"

"It's pretty bad. I'm an irresponsible student in just this one class. But I don't want to catch a fail. You're the diligent motherfucker with school. Who are you to question that?"

"Your mother is John B. Diligent."

"And your mother's anus is assiduous. But if I'm not back three days from now he's going to give me a fail. I haven't really been there all semester. He wants a paper too."

"What's the paper on?"

I looked at my sneakers. "I can't believe I got roped into this."

"So?"

"It's a Yiddish literature course. So to try to get a pass I told him my great uncle was the founder of the oldest Yiddish newspaper in America."

"Is that true?"

"Yeah. He was a big deal."

"I never knew that. So what's the paper?"

"The *Jewish Daily Forward*."

"I've seen it."

"I said I'd write this big thesis on the guy's life and work."

George shook his head. "What was the guy's name?"

"Abraham Cahan," I said. "On my father's side, the American side of the family."

"I didn't know," said George, biting into his hamburger.

"Or about me and Alexi. You don't know what we've been doing while you sleep."

"Sick animal," he said. He looked at the train. "So? Do we go?"

"The term paper," I said.

He nodded. "I wouldn't want to mess you up about that," he said gravely.

"I'll flunk," I said.

"Right."

My hamburger's melted cheese had gone hard. "What do you think this meat is? It tastes like butchered winos."

"But say it's really going to Chicago. From there it's a day's hitch back to New York. We'd be on the Upper West Side by Wednesday. That's a day early."

"Yeah, but what if it's a slow-crawling train?"

"No," said George authoritatively. "Crossing those big states, with so few main cities in between, they open up the throttle. We'd make good time. Think about it. What's the instructor's name?"

"Mendele. Chaim Mendele."

"Old guy?"

"White hair. Great face. He speaks mit accent like dis."

"I didn't know you're into that roots stuff."

"I'm not," I said. "I don't know what got into my head to take it. It's bored the hell out of me from the first class. I've showed up just enough to keep my hand in. Not even. Just barely."

George nodded, finished off his burger, and slowly wiped the grease from his fingers in the wrapping. He leaned back in his chair. "So?"

We slid easily down the loose dirt of the shallow gully, clutching at stubborn, leafless brush, the raised yellow cloud powdering the train, heat waves rising from the big rust-colored boxcars. The dust coating my nose made my breaths taste like dirt. We walked down the line, searching for an open car, the train seeming to stretch for miles. Sweat beads broke out on our faces. There were stacked automobiles mounted on trailer rigs, and open coal cars, their steel sides burning to the touch. A hawk hovering in the breezeless sky before a range of pale blue mountains was the only sign of life.

Then George broke into a hopeful trot, the instincts of his Penn Central upbringing aroused. Sure enough, there it was. Mountains and sky showed clear through its open dark interior. He jumped in, I followed, my torn jeans and flannel shirt, hands and sneakers plastered with greasy straw.

We did not say anything to the two men in hiding who peered out at us from a shadowy corner of the boxcar. Then the one with long hair said: "It's a good car you found. We'll be moving soon."

They were seated right in the thick muck that covered the corrugated steel floor, backs up against the wall. The Mexican-looking one held
out a bottle.

"No," George said.

"We got cards too, if you want a game. Helps pass the time."

"How long you been on?" said George.

"Me since Winnipeg," said Canada. "He got in at Billings. Anyhoo,
he's a wetback. Going to Chicago to look for work. That right? You
from Me-hi-ko?"

He nudged Mexico, who watched us with a deadpan expression that
did not conceal his distrust of us for refusing the drink.

Mexico nodded.

"We're going back to New York," I said. "Back to school."

Canada nodded. "College?"

"Yeah," I said.

"We been sitting here two hours about."

"Had many stops on the way?" George asked.

"This has been the longest. Next big stop is North Platte, Nebraska.
We'll be there about four hours. It's a humpyard there. They'll break up
the boxies for going east or south. This one to Chicago for sure. All this
back of the train is Illinois Central. Then Union Pacific. First boxies just
behind the engine is Sante Fe Railroad. Anyhoo, they'll uncouple us
down the middle, hook up another loco, switch us to clear track, and
point us east. Should be OK."

"Sounds like you've done this before," said George respectfully.

Canada nodded. "Few times. Always worked out."

Then we all knew everything we had to. George and I settled to
the floor to wait. My hands and pants legs were black, and broad
swaths of grease stained George's face, and mine too, I presumed. A
sharp jolt rattled the car. Then it lurched, shrieked. With a gratifying
peal of slammed steel the train began to roll. The men stood to their
feet. I got up, poked my head from the western side door, to see
where the tracks curved into miles of shimmering plains. At the very
end of the train the yellow engine pulled us into a slow arc as the

smoothed-out gully became flats of service roads, trailer parks, and heat-crackled billboards.

You could not sit. The floor rumbled through your spine. Fatigue drove you to the ground, pain brought you to your feet. We all stood around with downcast looks through the long wait of the crawling train. I looked at Canada and thought him a liar. No one could stand this all the way from Winnipeg. But when I found the good place to sit I liked Canada again. I liked Mexico too. And God bless George. Now the train was all right. It was the best ride of my whole life. You sat on the edge, legs hanging out the door. The reinforced frame absorbed the shock and you were just fine with your nose in the breeze. O beautiful for spacious skies, and I could love America all I pleased without a single condescending caddish smartass to show me wrong. Distant Wyoming hills held wild black rams picking their way up a burnt umber mountain's face, and there was ranch fencing stitched through abandoned stagecoach trails, dry creek beds, and old ghost towns. And I could love it red white and blue all I pleased, without my mother's mournful voice reminding of her suffering.

I was healthy and brand new, U.S.–born, passing through, the open range belonged to me the same as non-Jews. And I didn't want to think now of any difference between Jew or Gentile, though I was, not with eagles banking on the updraft from a windy bluff, beside a cold rushing creek scalloped with white froth. And I didn't want to remember about mass graves or the ovens, though I did, before a gorge carpeted with purple sage under an old suspension bridge. Habits die hard, I told myself. Jewish history was a habit I had to break.

As the cooling afternoon chilled the metal car, I rolled down my shirtsleeves and buttoned up. Great dead wind-seared barns and silos, gray with rot, rose from untilled land without a single tree or life sign, in a desolation that ran for heart-sickening hours, interrupted by the rusted red hulks of deserted threshing machines and tractors and of abandoned and once white water tankers bleeding orange rust and sometimes the ghostly shells of old ranches and farms.

"This is Nebraska," yelled Canada, and they all gathered beside me at the door, standing, to watch the vast erupting emptiness—an outer space of rural life. But then sharp and sudden and kissed by gold stood big corn rows, a Milky Way of shimmering stalks bursting with silk husks filled with good food. Our hearts lifted. On a dusty red clay road through the fields I saw two boys in faded blue jeans walking along, hands jammed in pockets, having a talk. Here's what I'd hoped some-day to see, when as a boy cramped in our onion-smelling slum I lay awake nights peering out an alley framed in fire escape iron, not even a sliver of sky for my own. Then, I too walked in imagination under the laughing crows with my best friend for life, my faded overalls sun-warmed on my corn-fed back, making plans for the conquest of the world, the two of us on our way to secret club headquarters in a ter-mite-gnawed, ghost-haunted house somewhere.

And the real boys and crops blinked by now, my eyes fixed on the horizon-converging rows of hypnotic memory in which a dreamlike Buick bumped down a service road that suddenly became a city.

"That be Lincoln," shouted Canada, and Lincoln unreal in granite, glass, and steel—then more fields, endless fields, ranks of brick resi-dential walk-ups, Roman–style banks, and gaunt municipal buildings and a few arrogant skyscrapers and all that petering out into car deal-erships and then factories and warehouses with muddy lanes and long brown puddles, the fields again forever and the blood-red sun turning the earth's shadow into bronze.

Now there rose up stationary trains and boxcars, row upon row, a field of trains, the great capital of trains, a blood-red Wailing Wall of all freights everywhere, and Canada shouted: "North Platte humpyard!" and sure enough the train slowed in a heart-stopping wail like grief that brought our hands to our ears as a mile and a half of metal anguished to a halt.

I withdrew my legs and came upright. Canada and Mexico had retreated into shadows again, their eye whites floating above their dim silhouettes.

"Gotta watch for yard bulls around here," said Canada in a dropped voice. "They might come to check along the train. Anyhoo, best talk low, huh?"

Mouth caked with dry spittle, I huddled with George and croaked: "Need water."

He nodded. "Go find a pump," he whispered, dry-mouthed too. "I'll stay with our packs. If you see something coming get back here and we'll break"—he pointed—". . . for those fields."

My sneakers thudded on hard dirt and I looked around at half a world, blocked from the rest by the train. Parked on sidings stood uncoupled cars for miles, but no one in sight. Nothing stirred along our train. We seemed to be the only ghost riders aboard.

Now I walked hurriedly toward what looked like a basin and spigot. It was water for sure, and I stuck my head under the warm wet trickle. I slaked my thirst, then filled the canteen to the top and screwed it tight. Then I stood, listening. Something I had heard. Far off—under the train—advancing: tires! Now a dust cloud! I ran shouting, "George! George!" and out of the train flew two backpacks, then George. I saw the running feet of Canada and Mexico under the train leave dusty puffs behind.

We crashed through the cornstalks blindly. Then we broke into a wide dirt road, stopped, bent double under the sickening exertions of our chests and bellies.

"I think we lost them," George gasped.

"Look again."

"Don't run. Just walk normal."

"I think we should run. We can hide in the field."

"He'll see us go there."

"So what? Let him. He'll never find us. It's almost night."

It was dark, a lava flow of light boiling through the sky, but over the fields and the road dusk had fallen, ashen, and we were all turning to shadows, even the pickup truck stenciled with Union Pacific on the doors, that drew up.

Canada and Mexico were cuffed in back. A blond and blue-eyed man, young as myself, with a wide, fresh, clear face got out. He wore a chocolate-brown uniform with a holstered revolver on his bullet-studded belt.

"Yard bull," said George.

"He looks OK," I said.

The bull called out to Canada in a voice without rancor. "Are them the two?" and pointed at us.

Canada nodded irritably, as though we were the cause of his misfortune.

The bull approached, then stopped in the middle of the road with his feet spread wide and left hand hovering near the gun. His left-handedness increased my nerve because in stickball I have always hit well against left-handed pitchers and duked well against lefty fighters.

"Morning, gentlemen," he said nicely, which cinched it for me. He was a pushover.

"Morning," I smiled, with lots of teeth.

"Hi," said George, more circumspectly.

"You gentlemen were aboard the incoming freight and have committed trespass of railroad property. I'm obliged to take you in."

"Take us in. Take us in where?"

"To the county jail in North Platte."

"Look," said George. "Why don't you just issue us a ticket and we'll call it a day."

"I'm not authorized," said the yard bull.

"Look," said George reasonably, hand rubbing his jaw, proceeding to negotiate. In the meanwhile I closely studied the yard bull's face. His blue eyes were set in a squint, and though his manner was gentle I detected a thin-lipped rock-hard obduracy in him.

I suddenly interrupted with: "Hey, mistah? We're walking out of here."

The blue slits shot a cold look my way. He said very gently: "I'm afraid that's not possible."

"C'mon, George," I said. "Let's go."

George looked from me to him, uncertain. "Well, why don't we just talk it out reasonably with the guy," said George.

"No!" I snapped, trembling. "We go now. Let's go. Start walking." I was fighting to keep the fear checked. I now saw where we were, clearly: in a Nebraska cornfield, a thousand miles from home, whereabouts unknown to others, trying to escape abduction by an armed stranger.

George looked at the yard bull, chuckled. "Well, I guess we're going."

"I wouldn't advise that."

"Don't explain to him. He's no cop. He's a security guard. We're off the property. That's good enough!"

We started to walk.

"Halt!"

"Don't look back," I told George.

"*Halt!*"

"Keep walking," I said.

" I said *halt* or I'll fire!"

We both stopped, turned, and saw it: blunt, black, and ugly, a snub-nose pointed straight at me.

The smile returned to my face, the show of teeth. My arms spread wide, I stepped forward, chest offered to the barrel. I said in a voice older then my years, maybe centuries old: "Shoot! Go ahead! What are you, nineteen, twenty, maybe? Same age as me. Look at this blue sky, brother. Look at this nice field. It's a nice day. What are you, gonna shoot us down for riding a freight? We're Americans, my man! That's what we do. You did too, probably, at some time. You're gonna shoot us for that? That?! I don't believe it. Go ahead, shoot! Shoot!!"

I waited.

He lowered the gun. "Know what?" he said, humiliated. "I'm gonna do worse. I'm gonna get the Sheriff to take you in! You'll wish I had shot you!" and spinning on his heels, he walked back to the truck, slammed the door, and drove off in a hurry with Canada and Mexico avoiding our eyes.

• • •

We sat down by the quiet field and looked each other in the eye.

"We're up a creek," said George.

I glanced over at the tall, dense, crashing rows of corn, the blue sky above. Insects crept in the dust, their backs and heads powdered with dust. The truck's treadmarks had gnawed deep into the ground and left scars.

"He's coming back with bad news for sure," I said.

"Yeah, I can feel it."

"I think maybe we should hide."

"Hide? Hide where?" George looked around. It was just before night, when things fade before your eyes, and the field was fading, but also his face was disappearing.

"Anywhere," I said. "We'll lay low. When it's dark enough and late enough we'll slip away."

"C'mon, man! Get real! These are country guys. They'll find us with no trouble. And if they don't they'll put out APB's and have their whole gang out fun-hunting us all through the county. Then, when they catch us, we'll really be in for it."

"You know, I'm surprised at you! You never struck me as the laying down type."

"Your mother's that type too," he said. "Lies down with anybody over sixteen."

"You know, I'm not kidding here! I'm pretty amazed. When the chips are down, here you fold. Here? In this godforsaken nowhere you lose your nerve! That's pretty sad, man, pretty sickening."

Abruptly, I stopped. What was I saying? This was George, one of the nicest, bravest men I knew. He was just being sensible. But something told me sensible made no sense in these kinds of situations. I had a hunch that to survive you must act.

I could tell he was hurt. He stood to his feet. A flock of crows exploded from the field and waved good night.

"I'm gonna start walking," he said. "And either down that road I'm gonna get home or they're gonna come get me. But I'm not gonna run like some fugitive out here in this crazy place. It's a mistake. You want to play chain-gang fugitive, good luck!"

He started walking. The crows were black bits of whirling ash against the night, the last sun a thin bleed of red light seeping from the wounded sky. It smelled so unfamiliar here, like a different earth, and the rising breeze brought an alarming waft of smoke. I had never felt so alone, and bowed my head. Sometimes the very soil in a place, the air it gave you, contained a threat of pain so subtle that it made dread seem normal. I felt small, attackable, a ragged coat you could tear apart with bare hands.

"George," I called softly, "I'm sorry."

He walked.

"George!"

I started after, not hurrying; knew where he was, his dim outline confined like mine to the bare road through the cornfield.

But then the headlights from a ways off appeared, and now George and I trotted to each other without hesitation, nakedly afraid.

"Maybe we should hide," I panted.

"I'm telling you no! That's a mistake!"

"Something tells me, George. I don't know. How're they gonna see?"

"They won't give up until we're caught and then there will be hell to pay."

"There's gonna be hell to pay now, I can tell you that!" I said.

We started walking, hearts pounding so loud I could have sworn I heard his above mine.

The crickets swelled to a maddening volume as the truck approached with a crunch of tires on the pebbly road. Headlight beams lanced the space between us, until we were flush in the eye of the white-hot middle and it felt like the big chrome grid might scorch our backs. Then it braked but we hurried on. A door slammed. Boots hit the ground with a hard thud.

"Hold up there!"

We stopped without turning, caught in the headlights.

Footsteps approached, a voice said, "Put your hands straight up in the air."

Neither of us moved.

The voice that was now full upon us said, surprised: "No?"

A powerful hand grabbed the back of my shirt and whirled me about. I stumbled, came to a full stop in a crouch. The deputy, dressed in khakis with a silver badge and a white Stetson, was armed with nothing more then a savage-looking nightstick that he used to point at the back of the truck. His face with the light just behind was a blank dark oval: "Get up there. Now!!"

I complied.

He pointed the club at George:

"You, the same!"

George trotted over. We stood there uncertain about what to do, hands raised, the yard bull aiming a flashlight directly at our faces despite the headlights' blinding force.

Then the deputy ordered: "Turn and face the truck, put your hands on the panel, spread those legs—I want you both up on fingers and toes. Fingers and toes! Let's go!"

We went on fingers and toes. It was torture. He rapped the nightstick against the truck's running board.

"Wider!" he shouted.

We spread as wide as our legs could. He shook us down, threw the items pulled from our pockets to the ground for the yard bull to collect. And watching all this earned me the first blow, the nightstick exploding against my inner thigh, and I fell to my knees in agony, moaning.

"Get up!" he growled.

I got to my feet.

"Fingers and toes!"

I got on my fingers and toes.

George bought it next. He groaned. Then I took it again.

He went at us back and forth. At the end we were curled on the dirty road.

"All right then," he said. "All right then."

He looked at the yard bull. "They're a little tamer now, would you say, Fred?"

Fred looked at us contritely and said: "Yeah, I think I can handle them now."

"Don't trouble yourself," he said, lunging forward to his knee, hand-cuffs held up in his right hand. He pushed me over on my face, jerked one arm behind, cuffed me, then the other, cuffed it, and I was rope-tied. He hauled me to my feet by the cuffs, which sent shooting anguish through my joints, and kicked me into the back of the truck. George got the same.

Then the deputy and the yard bull climbed into the cabin and start-ed up the engine.

George and I couldn't look at each other or bear to speak.

The truck drove slowly through the town, which was crowded with pedestrians: big blond men in clean white shirts, blue jeans, and straw Stetsons; the women wore floral-print summer dresses and sandals. The deputy waved and the yard bull honked his horn at acquaintances, who stopped to wave back and gape with cold smiles of mingled alarm and disdainful curiosity at the two game prizes manacled in the rear of the truck.

"Welcome to North Platte," smirked a girl with a ponytail who walked past at a stoplight.

I pursed my lips, blew her a kiss. She glared.

We passed a sign that read NORTH PLATTE: HOME OF BUFFALO BILL CODY.

"Yipee-ah-yoo," I said to George.

But my sarcasm was bluff. Actually my head felt lucid, a deadly calm, nothing about our circumstances seemed strange to me; had this gut feeling that somehow I had always known about this place, was meant to be here. Even the police station, a two-story building of yellow Masonic and green sun-tint windows with the words NORTH PLATTE POLICE STATION in raised stainless steel letters on the outside wall, looked familiar in a way I couldn't explain to myself.

Canada and Mexico were being arraigned in the narrow walkway before a long counter on the other side of which were several desks, a file cabinet, and the back-lit, bright red plastic of a loudly humming Coca-Cola vending machine. Behind one of the desks sat the sheriff. His cowboy boots were up on the desk and he was leaning back in his chair with a plastic Baggie containing several ounces of pot held up before his nose. He sniffed.

"Good shit," he said with great jocularity.

He looked us over with striking gray-blue eyes. He was in his early sixties and despite his mirth bore the remote detachment of a career veteran. He held up the bag. "You boys come in on the train with our Canadian friend. You part of the dope smuggling ring?"

"We never saw this man before in our entire life," I said angrily.

"That's right," said George.

"Well," he said, "I know you never seen him before. Could tell that by your accents. Deputy, give our guests arrest forms to fill out. Pretty please." He laughed so warmly that we found ourselves smiling along. "Well," he said, bouncing the bag of pot up and down in his hand. "It really is good shit. Too bad!" He put the pot in a desk draw and slammed it shut. "Put your belts and laces up here on the counter, please," he said.

We did as asked.

"Deputy, give these boys receipts for their personal belongings and let's have a look at what the other two suspects have writ on their admissions applications. I'm always curious to know who are these people so desperate to cross all the way from other countries and such, just to stay at our little old North Platte alma mater, whether we want them here or not."

I dutifully filled out the information requested of me. In a way the form was reassuring, with its letterhead bearing the seal of the State of Nebraska, showing the picture of a blacksmith hammering on an anvil out in the great wide open while behind him a freight train chugs through the pass, and over it all the words EQUALITY BEFORE THE LAW. It meant that regardless of the fact that no one on earth knew that we were here, held hostage to armed strangers with tin stars who hunted and manacled and even beat you in the performance of their duties, at least we were all under the same purview of state and federal government, which assured us of certain inalienable rights.

I filled out the form in copious detail; spent extra time outlining my academic background, emphasizing my collegial status, as though that entitled me to greater leniency. I was a nice young man, my remarks implied, who will have learned his lesson well enough if let off with a mild warning.

The form had a space for religion/race. I was confused. My first thought was to skip the question. But my eyes kept coming back to it. You should put down "Jew," ran my thought. All your life you have run from that fact and now it's time to declare yourself, and in the most difficult of circumstances.

But why provoke trouble, countered another line of thinking. You don't know how these people will react to such information. You don't imagine there could be a single Jew in all of North Platte, or in all of Nebraska for that matter. Be smart. Have nothing to prove. What can you prove by telling the truth? Go ahead, put a line through the space.

"Jew," I wrote.

When done, the forms were collected, as were the pencils we'd been given to write with and the ID cards we were asked to produce. I gave my college ID, the only real form of identification I owned. George gave his. The sheriff returned to his desk and studied the ID cards closely.

"You're Alan," he said.

"Yes, sir."

"And you're George."

"Yes."

He smiled at me.

He reached for the forms.

"Kaufman, Marvin, Alan," he read aloud. The he read on in silence, glanced up at me with that oily smile, then down again at the form. "So, you from what they call, you from 'Jew York,' is that right?" he said without looking at me, so merrily it made my heart sick.

A white-hot fear knotted my gut.

"Is that right?" he repeated.

"I'm Jewish from New York City," I replied, struggling to keep my voice steady.

"It says here you in college. What you studying?"

"I'd like to make the phone call I'm entitled to under law."

"Say, Deputy. You hear that? College kike from Jew York wants to make his legally guarantored phone call. What you says to that, Deputy?"

"I says the prisoner best stop making trouble. He's already in a world of it. He's a real troublemaker type, Sheriff. Those people generally are."

"I'm not trying to make any trouble. The law guarantees it."

The sheriff looked at me hard. "Not here it don't."

"He's the law here," said the deputy.

The yard bull said: "But just listen to what you're told to do and you'll be all right."

I looked at George, who hadn't said or showed anything by his expression.

"What are we gonna do, George," I said in a way that no one could help but hear. "They're violating our rights under Miranda."

"I think we'd better shut up," said George. The "we" meaning "you."

Stung, I nodded. The eighteen hundred miles between us and home, that vast continent about which I'd romantically fantasized, read hungrily, and written rhapsodizing reams, became a painful void that filled itself with the cruel black ocean of a pitiless fate. Yet I did not want to believe that I was cut off, utterly alone.

"You a college boy too," the sheriff said to George.

"That's right."

"What you studying?"

"Pre-med."

"You the smart one, I can tell. That's good advice you gave your friend."

"How long do you intend to keep us here?" I erupted. I couldn't help it. I was terrified.

The sheriff looked at me with disbelief. Then over at the deputy.

"He ain't too smart for a Jewboy, is he? I heard you folks were smart enough to take over the whole white world if us folks aren't careful. What happen to you? You a little retarded or something?"

The deputy burst out laughing and the sheriff looked around him in mock astonishment with his hand raised toward me, palm up, pointing: "Am I wrong? He's in my jail, in my town, committin' crimes in my county. And he's pullin' weight!"

"He's just nervous," the yard bull blurted out. "Why don't I take 'em up to their cell."

"Why, Fred," said the sheriff. "You makin' your play for the deputy's job? Hear that Deputy, you got competition here."

I detected some peevishness in his tone of voice.

"He just wants to play like a real cop 'stead of a low-wage hired gun for the damned Union Pacific," said the deputy.

"I don't even work for them," said the yard bull. "I'd be glad to be a company man. I'm just a freelance gun for hire."

"You oughta become a cop. Young man your age needs a right start. This is a good place."

"I just might take you up on that, Sheriff. So, OK if I show them to their cell?"

The deputy glanced sharply at the sheriff, who nodded his assent with reluctance, and the deputy leaned over the counter, fished around, and came up with an enormous keyring.

"Here you go. Put 'em in number three, with Charlie Ryder."

The yard bull said with a hard smile: "Is he up there? You're kidding. How long has he been out this time?"

"Just picked him up at his mother's house. Neighbor saw him and called it in. He'll be picked up by Marine Corps MPs and taken back to bread-and-water detention in a hellhole brig. I heard they rough up AWOLs pretty harshly the third time out. Wouldn't wanna be in his shoes."

The yard bull's hard smile softened a touch when he said to me: "Let's go. And don't give me any of your smartass talk."

"Go get 'em, Fred!" said the sheriff, feigning amusement, though I could tell he wasn't sure just now where Fred's real loyalties lay.

He led us up two flights of corrugated steel steps to a white corridor flanked on both sides by mostly empty cells. We were taken to number three, where the Marine sat on the floor, back resting on the wall, one knee bent, the other leg extended. An unlit cigarette dangled from his lips. Fred unlocked the cell, let us in, and said: "I'll come by to check on you sometime near morning when I'm off my shift. You'll be all right."

" I hope so. You heard how your sheriff spoke to me," I said. I could tell that he felt bad about it.

"And how about your deputy going wild with that nightstick?" said George.

The yard bull got flustered in a surge of conflicted loyalties. "Well," he sputtered, color rising in his face, "that's what you get for being a smartass." He turned to the Marine.

"Charlie Ryder."

The Marine looked at him. "Fred Wattel."

"You going back I hear."

The Marine picked a shred of tobacco from his teeth, flicked it away. "I never left," he said. "This here talking to you is an illusion of being home that I'm fantasy-projecting out of my brig cell back in Quantico."

The yard bull looked at him queerly and walked out. George and I stood staring at the Marine. He said: "You boys gonna watch some color TV?"

"Sure," I said. "Any distraction's welcome."

He pointed to the small barred window in the corridor that held a view of the night sky and a few roofs.

"There goes your color TV. Only one station though."

"Son of a bitch," George muttered.

"They can't do this," I said.

"They're doing it."

"I mean about the phone call. And they didn't read us our rights."

"I got a feeling no one knows about Miranda around here."

"Look at what they call a toilet."

George screwed up his face and shook his head.

"Look at this."

"The bed," said George.

"Isn't this, like, a human rights violation?"

"No," interrupted the Marine. "That's the next town over. This here is North Platte."

"You're the AWOL guy."

"That I am, that I am."

"You scared?"

"That I am, that I am."

"They put you in the brig for going AWOL?"

"Yes, they do."

"That deputy put his nightstick to us."

"You mean Cory? Cory the guy arrested you?" He spit.

"You know him?"

"Grew up with him, practically. He's a mean one. Never liked him."

"What about that sheriff?"

The Marine's eyes shifted around, avoided looking right at me as he carefully chose his words. "He's . . . he's into some . . . Put it this way. If you can, stay on his good side."

And it was like the roof caved in on any vestige of composure left to me. I felt pure molten panic surge through my guts. "What do you mean?" I said. "I'm gonna get justice here, ain't I? This is a legal jail. I have rights. I'm an American. It shouldn't matter what he thinks about me personally. Like me or not, I'm protected by law."

"Only law here is you cross him he'll nail you."

"He didn't seem to mind you," I said to George. "But he had it in for me."

"I don't know about that," said George. "Sounds like he was just, you know, pushing you."

"Pushing me!" I exploded. "You call all that anti-Semitic crap 'pushing'? I feel my life threatened here, man. I'm . . . I'm a . . ."

It was hard to say it. The Marine was watching and George was watching and it didn't feel like they would understand, but I felt a need to say it, air it, put it out among us. "Look, I'm a Jew. He's calling me Jew-this and whatnot."

They looked blankly at me, stranger and old friend alike, with a shared coldness.

Bitterly I walked to the mattressless cot where I was supposed to sleep and stretched out on the springs, head pillowed on my hands. There was no blanket but it was hot anyway. I closed my eyes, tried to rest. George and the Marine fell to talking about baseball.

She would sit on the edge of the bed looking through that ratty old valise full of photographs. The pictures were of friends and relations who had died in the war. She was left on the shore of the living to fend for herself, but sometimes I thought she wished she had died. No one understood her pain about what had happened.

For a time I had tried to understand but then I didn't want to anymore. I was tired of her tears of loss. It wasn't interesting to hear the same old stories of how this one was shot and that one burned in the ovens. I didn't care anymore about the fat aunt who drowned in the river trying to escape a German police dog, or about the eight-year-old cousin who hid for two years in a potato sack in a death camp. I didn't care about that. It was a war long done and this was a brand new world. A world of football and Howard Cosell, ABC's *Wide World of Sports*, hopping freights, Bob Dylan, and Lori in my American literature class. There was Vonnegut, Kerouac, Heller, Beckett, Steinbeck, Hemingway, Pound, Joyce, Yeats. The Irish knew how to write the best. How badly I wanted to be an Irishman. A Brit. A Wasp. For my heritage to include hunting and fishing, sewing up wounds with catgut, hay-baling, horse-breaking. Buffalo Bill. Not men in black caftans shorn of their earlocks by torturers who grinned like the sheriff had. The same SS grin, the same gleam in the eye, the same deadpan mirth of one with hands dipped in blood. There was not supposed to be such blood-drenched mirth in my new world. I was a hero bound to hop the great freight train of the new world with a free heart.

With a start I sat upright at the edge of the cot, fighting a sense of dread. Hours ago there had been a version of myself who walked with

élan on the balls of his feet and felt himself heir to the harmonica blues
of the adventuring night, child of Kerouac and Melville, a great travel-
er vagabonding through America, a cinematic dreamer bred on Peter
Fonda and Steve McQueen, filming with his eyes the mighty epic of his
life. But he was dead now, replaced by a scared Jew surrounded by foes.
I had a picture of the old me leaning from the freight train, hair blowing wild, grease-streaked wide-open face happier then it had ever been,
nineteen years old.

Now I was incarcerated by a hate older than me by millenniums and
I felt small against it, helpless, powerless to understand. Just wanted
out. To be home. Free.

The lights went out. The Marine said: "Lockdown. Time for bed."

George stretched out on the cot next to mine.

The Marine remained waiting on the cold cell floor, his back to the
wall. The lights remained on bright in the corridor, throwing long
striped shadows over his face and shirt. No one had brought us any supper; it had been a day and a half since the last meal in Cheyenne and
my stomach ached for food. I stretched out with my nose pointed at the
top of George's head, whispered his name.

"What's up?"

"Look, man. Try to understand." I felt so ashamed of my fear.

He didn't respond.

My voice came out low and harsh, strained to make itself felt. I spoke
fast: "I'm a Jew. They kill Jews, you understand? Remember those civil
rights workers? What's that guy's name? Goodman? Down in
Mississippi? They murdered him. Well, crap, this is Mississippi spelled
with an N. Don't play dumb, man. You know what I mean."

"Are you calling me stupid?" he said coldly.

"No!" I croaked. "No! I think I'm in trouble, George. Rednecks don't
like Jews. The goy . . ."

"The goyim, huh?" he said sourly. "Well, I'm a goy. That doesn't mean
I kill Jews."

I gave up, rolled on my back. Soon the deputy came and peered into
the cell. The Marine stood up and moved close to the bars to talk. They

spoke for minutes, and once looked back at me with deadpan eyes. I lay there frozen, afraid to move. I heard the word "kike"—or thought I did, their voices low—and fought back tears of hopeless dread.

Then he left and soon the sheriff appeared. When he went away I heard in the stairwell a loud cacophony of excited laughter. It must have been around midnight.

And then appeared a man who stood there for a time, looking into the cell while George and the Marine slept, the man staring furiously at me, not speaking, and I sensed his hatred all over me, in every inch of me, though he said nothing while I lay there pretending to sleep. He was considering something, it seemed to me, calculating, with my heart ripping out of my chest, its beats booming in my ears, a terrific pounding pulse tearing at my neck.

Something told me not to move, that to stir would provoke a terrible decision, or was this just a child's way of thinking? I didn't know but followed my intuition blindly. You are dead so you cannot move, I told myself. This afternoon you died so you cannot even blink or breathe. Just lie here still on this slab dead; soon he'll go away. Besides, you're dead. The dead are under no obligation to respond to a stare so full of hatred.

But oh, I wanted so badly to answer his stare. With my fists in his face, my knees in his abdomen, ill will for ill will, violence for violence. For him to be in the cell with me would have been such a relief, to be face to face without bars; anything but this humiliating state of complete exposure without even the dignity of a zoo, which at least presumes the danger posed by the animal, the honor of being a threat, whereas this felt merely obscene, as in some racial peep show, the Jew on display, a spoil of war, a trophy to perhaps be tinkered with—only the latest in history's longest unbroken manhunt.

He left. Finally the yard bull came, still in his chocolate-brown uniform. I swung off the bed to my feet, approached the bars with a terrified stare. We looked at each other warily. I was trembling.

"Are we going to have breakfast in the morning?" I carefully studied his face for signs that there would be a morning.

"I couldn't say," he answered evasively.

We stood there, not speaking. Then I blurted out: "Find me a priest!" And I listened to the words as from a remote distance, and felt so ashamed, almost wondered who had spoken them.

The words were left to hang in the still air, impossible, even ludicrous in their request.

"You don't need a priest. You need the rabbi," he said matter-of-factly, without innuendo. And added uncertainly: "I thought you're Jewish."

"Yeah, I am. But I want to convert," I said. "Please. I'm not kidding. I need to. I can't take it anymore." And by this I meant: Certainly you, my tormentors, will understand. These bars are just a detail. I've been in this cell for nineteen years. I want to come out. I give up. Let me be one of you. I'm ready.

And this man actually assumed toward me a posture of unsolicited reverence.

"Well, that's just very fine, that's just very fine," he said, and repeated himself—the same phrase—over and again several times with astonishment. And then he left and I retreated to a corner in the shadowed recesses of the cell, near the toilet, where I huddled, self-respect utterly broken, waiting for morning to come and not knowing anymore in my fear-hallucinations and shame whether or not there were other visitors, though there appeared visitations, incorporeal, obscure, some in uniform, others not; maybe they were Marine MPs who came to take away the AWOL, or maybe they were SS men whose faces I'd viewed from birth in my mother's eyes, in a film that had always played there, that I didn't want to see but that she was helpless to stop: men with eyes steeled against their own humanity and deadened into attitudes of inflexible scorn. They played like shadows slow-motion on the bar-striped walls of my fear-jailed mind. My hands tried to crush them out like rodents. Like rodents red-eyed, sneering, gray, filthy, venomous. Then clown faces floated shrieking through the air, green, jeering. I wondered how to kill myself; didn't want to live but had no way to end my life. So I tried to end it with sleep, black deep sleep, if only for an hour, and lay shuddering by dawn's blue light until fatigue and fear, hunger and shame, had worn me out and closed my eyes and I could not open them again.

George's shoe kicked me awake and walked off.

I came to my feet but had to brace my hand against the wall to steady myself.

George and the yard bull stopped talking long enough to look at me. "How'ze it goin'?" said George.

I nodded noncommittally. "It's going."

"Would you like some breakfast? I know you were worried about that," said the yard bull.

I studied him. "No," I said.

He nodded.

There was an embarrassed silence between the three of us.

"Why don't you eat it anyway," said George, always the practical one. "They're letting us out today. After the fine, there won't be much left for food."

"What fine?"

"The twenty-dollar fine you each gonna pay to get out of jail," said the yard bull.

Now the deputy came in bearing a tray that held cinnamon rolls and coffee.

He looked straight at me as if nothing had happened. "How'd you sleep, New York?"

I shuddered when he pronounced the name of my city: the way he said "New"—the N was obviously a disguised J.

I looked away with disgust for both of us, received the tray and ate it. Every last drop.

We went up before a justice of the peace who ordered us fined and took our money.

The yard bull drove us in his pickup to a fenced-in lot near the highway's entrance ramp. The fence bore a red-and-white sign: CAUTION. When we jumped out we stood there and he leaned his face from the window, sunglasses filled with the Caution sign and a fenced-in hot blue sky. He didn't say anything. I looked away. Then he said: "It was my job to arrest you and it was my job to get you out, too. I did that."

"You did," I said. "You did."

"I didn't know it would be like that," he said.

"Neither did I," I said.

He nodded. I turned away. George told him to take care. He drove off. Not too long after, a truck stopped that took us to Moline, Illinois, and from there we had favorable luck all the way to Harrisburg, Pennsylvania, where a high school music teacher in a red Datsun and who hailed from Queens, New York, picked us up and drove us across the George Washington Bridge.

George and I parted ways without any fanfare at all. Hardly a word passed between us. We just hugged coldly and he turned and walked off, stopped and waved, and kept walking—going, he had said, to visit his cousin Nino in Yonkers.

After the fierce light of the Western sun it was a shock to be clattering home cooped up in a coffin-shaped subway car, underground with pasty-faced, miserable-looking subterraneans. But God bless these moles, in some ways the most tolerant people on earth. I was burned by the sun and lean from the road and my eyes, hair, and lips bore the ravages of dust and wind. I might have looked the free soul but inside felt dirty, contaminated, harboring a grotesque secret that I didn't feel anyone else would understand.

When I got home, after a shower and a night's sleep, rather than attend school I lay in bed with a bottle of scotch, nursing it under my arm and chain-smoking Marlboros. Over and over I replayed the night in the jail, my gradual breakdown to where I was willing to do anything to save myself. I felt like a terrible coward who had behaved badly and should crawl into a hole and die there. I had lived up to Hemingway's contempt for Robert Cohen, to Eliot's disdain and Pound's vicious spite. I drank for three days running, and on the third day picked myself out of a string of bushes in Riverside Park. I didn't know how I had gotten there. Beside me flowed the placid gray Hudson River. An empty bottle of vodka lay on the ground. I brushed the dirt from my clothes, gaped at my dirty, shaking hands. "This is ridiculous," I said aloud. And shouted at the river: "Ridiculous! Ridiculous!! *Ridiculous!!*" and began to sob softly.

I still had the spring term of freshman year to complete. Haunted by flashbacks of my terror in the cell, I continued in my studies. I passed Professor Volpe's class in American literature, on some level no surprise. And yet my second paper on Pound—basically a three-page rant against Pound's anti-Semitism—so profoundly disappointed him that he called me at my home to pick it up personally from his apartment, as he wanted a word. I went over.

He lived on Claremont Avenue, down the street from the Columbia campus in a big wedding cake of a building, on the ninth floor, with bay windows overlooking the Hudson. He was casually dressed in a sports jacket and smoked a filterless cigarette. Placing his fist to his mouth to smother a hacking cough, he handed over the paper, which bore no grade, just a big red question mark.

"It's not what you're capable of," he said. "Look. You can disagree with Pound. You can condemn his anti-Semitism, which you rant about as though only you've just recently discovered it. I'm not telling you what you should believe, only saying that any view you posit must be intelligently presented, as I know you're capable of doing. This paper however is not intelligent. So I'm not going to grade it. It's unworthy of you and unworthy of a grade. That's all I wanted to say. Thank you for stopping by. Did you take the bus? I hope it wasn't much trouble."

"None. I live close."

"Oh, really? Well, that's very good." He turned, smiling, to show me the door.

Quivering, I said: "Professor Volpe, just one minute here, if you don't mind."

Surprised by my impertinence, he stopped and looked at me.

"Well?"

"You know, I had nothing but the greatest regard for you, sir. I practically worshipped you. So I don't disagree on some level with what you're saying, and yet I have to wonder if you can . . . Can you really understand, not being Jewish, what it feels like to encounter anti-Jewish hate rhetoric in the work of a poet of the first rank, whose reputation in the field of letters is just short of God?! I mean, you, someone like you, so 'intelligent,' admire him terribly, as I see it. And I wonder how you can admire someone— In fact it breaks my heart that you admire someone who participated in the murder of six million men, women, and children . . ."

"Well, that's not exactly what he did," said Volpe, unfazed. "He was broadcasting speeches over Axis radio, this is true, however . . ."

"However nothing! That is *exactly* what he did!" I snapped. "There is no 'however' here! In fact, that word is the problem: 'However.' How easily you accomodate the Unspeakable with just one word. Yeah, sure, he was responsible for actively supporting a system that burned Jewish children alive, 'however,' look at his brilliant translations of Chinese poetry! It's true that he publicly accused the Jews of economic world domination schemes in a manner complicitous with the aims of the most murderous torture-death regimes in the history of humankind, producers of Auschwitz and Dachau and human lampshades, and that hunted my own mother like an animal in the war, 'however,' look at the wonderful editing job he did on Eliot's *Waste Land*! Look at the fine poets he discovered! Eliot, who was himself a Jew-hater of the first rank! And Wyndham Lewis, who despised Jews. And Hemingway, who thought we were all just weak little kikes! Well, Professor Volpe . . ."—I tore up my paper in front of him—"here's one kike who says: Fuck that kind of poetry. Fuck your literature! Fuck you academic soul-sell-outs. And most of all: Fuck Ezra Dog Pound!" And shaking uncontrollably, I walked out.

I never attended his class again. The A+ just turned up on my record unsought.

In my Yiddish literature course I earned a B for turning in an A+ paper on my newly discovered famous Jewish relation, the Yiddish author and editor Abraham Cahan. In doing the paper I learned that the building that once had housed his newspaper, *The Jewish Daily Forward*, still existed on the Lower East Side of Manhattan. One weekday morning I rode a subway downtown to see it. I climbed up the stairs at Essex Street station. Candy wrappers, blackened chewing gum, and cigarette butts littered the sooty steps. The air smelled of urine. It was early still. Rusty old dull metal gates masked most of the closed storefronts and buildings. Junkies and drunks stumbled past. They lay on the sidewalk, asleep. One slumped with chin to his chest, swollen eyes shut, snoring. The corner street signs were in Spanish, Yiddish, and Chinese. The buildings wept black tears of ruin and rage, their windows bereft of habitude. Some of them were so old they seemed blind, and so terribly brittle that their fire escapes were liable to crumble at the touch.

A traditional Jewish woman in a wig and babushka hobbled up the street, exiled in time, like something stepped from a sepia-toned turn-of-the-century photograph. Several bearded religious Jews dressed in black caftans stood on the corner talking. I nodded but none responded, regarded my passage with an air of imperious contempt.

Feeling their cold eyes on my back, I stopped and looked up at the disintegrating skyline of warped antennas, splintered water towers, and ornate stone scrolls and gargoyles. I recognized from the photographs I'd seen the conical peak of the *Forward* building. At each of its four corners was said to be the face of my famous uncle, but the faces were not there, torn away.

I walked hurriedly up the front steps. Nailed to the impressive doors was a sign that declared this to be the home of the First Chinese Congregationalist Church of the Lower East Side. I gasped with outrage, tried the doors. They gave. Inside I found some stairs and climbed to the second floor, seeking some trace of the old Yiddish newspaper's operations, and more so, of my great uncle, Abraham Cahan.

In a large, pale, cream-colored room, cheaply painted, I found old lime-colored office partitions with beaded glass behind which, conceivably, the editors and reporters had once sat tapping out their stories. I passed through the room sniffing for the ghosts of the bustling newsroom. Nothing. I approached two large sliding doors that I threw open. They gave onto a huge, completely empty chamber that contained a single piece of furniture: a scarred old desk. I pulled open one of the drawers. My heart leaped: it was lined with parchment-yellow sheets of the Yiddish newspaper, so old they might have dated from the turn of the century. There were indentations on the room's scuffed wooden floor, which I kneeled to, ran my fingers in the grooves. Here must have stood the massive presses, for there were also the unmistakable greenish-black blotches of spilled printer's ink. This was the actual place where the paper had been published.

The great machines rose in my vision, and laboring among them the phantom press operators, printers, and journeymen wearing visors and ink-stained rubber aprons and moving briskly amid the clattering roar as the printed sheets spit out into high stacks of Yiddish print.

Here were headlines and columns and advice to the lovelorn that were baled and tied still wet and rushed out on the shoulders of newsboys straight into the early morning streets of immigrants, and shipped all the way to the Pacific Coast and around the world to Warsaw, Cracow, Moscow, Berlin, Paris, Prague.

I saw those stains and dents as encouraging proof of my uncle's victory over tremendous odds, from Russian pogroms to American nativist prejudice; his battle to educate himself, his successful entry into the arena of literature, and his attempt to uplift his fellow immigrants by helping to indoctrinate them into the ways of this strange new world, while also modernizing and extending the rich heritage of Yiddish culture. By the end of his career he had become one of this country's notable men of letters, friend to Mark Twain and William Dean Howells.

For the moment it was all there for me to see in that deserted building, in the heart of a neighborhood whose apex had long ago passed, now crumbling back into an aimless nullity.

The hope, the vision I sought in an explanation of the past was to be found only in myself. I was that future toward which so much striving—echoed ghostly in that room—had aimed. I, its embodiment, was the new generation for which my mother had survived, anguished, and sacrificed. I, the dream that had outlived the best efforts of Hitler and his ilk.

In this reverie I moved toward another door, found my way blocked by a wall of wet, hanging laundry: T-shirts, shorts, socks, towels, sheets. I began to unpeel my way forward through these layers when suddenly, turning aside a T-shirt, I surprised a Chinese man in his skivvies, who jumped back, gaped at me, and began to shout in Chinese, pointing at the stairwell. Bewildered, I looked around.

I stood in the man's living quarters: bed, hot plate with a boiling pot, kitchen table, dresser. Contrite, I tried to voice apology, but he was having none of it, his admonitions grown louder, his fingers stabbing angrily at the door stenciled EXIT. Nodding in confusion and shock, I left.

The stairs led straight to the street. Expelled, I stood on the dirty sidewalk, surprised to be there; looked up at the hand-lettered sign of a Chinese church that my great uncle's Yiddish newspaper had become. I felt dislocated in time, culturally unexplained, torn. What was it all about, this business of being Jewish? Still I had no answer, only fragments, signs, indications, runes: snapshots of my mother's dead relations, the hatred of a rural sheriff and his cronies, the crumbling remnant of a Yiddish newspaper lining an old drawer.

My Jewishness was a hate-love affair! A confusion! A guilty dream! It was the sexy secret pleasure of the Yiddish tongue that I did not even understand yet always loved to listen to; the rich, comforting taste of love-spiked foods that fed your soul but ruined your health; a history that I fled from yet learned more about each day; the leg-aching stand and sit of the synagogue pew; the Hebrew prayers that I barely grasped, like the Kaddish, that could be so numbing and yet also filled my eyes with tears.

To be a Jew was to belong to crazy, outworn places like the Lower East Side, where my first Jewish-American immigrant ancestors walked, fresh off the boat from Ellis Island; where the foundation was laid that later, for better or worse, would absorb my mother's emigration from the flames of Europe, and house and feed and husband her, in a manner that was certainly not perfect but much better than anything she had ever known before. In this place that had birthed and educated and cared for me too, where I now stood at the point of our first entry to these shores, I also faced a choice: I now saw, as every Jew must, that I had to continue to confront my Jewishness with all my confusion and doubt, and struggle until I had an answer, or else learn to live with endless questions. Perhaps this last choice is the true essence of what it means to be a Jew. Most of all I must never be ashamed of who I am but, for better or worse, accept this tragic mantle given to me by the accident of birth and see where the road leads, and follow without fail.

It led to home.

One night I returned, quite late. My father had already gone to his night shift job. My brother was asleep. I could see on the floor outside her room a glowing apron of light. She was up. I crept softly over, peeked in.

She sat on the bed, her waist still wrapped in an apron, rummaging in the valise. I stepped into the doorway.

"Mom?"

She looked up, her face wan, her blue eyes shrinking from me with distrust. Quickly she averted her eyes, turning as if to someone else, some unseen party with whom she had been talking before I interrupted.

"I didn't hear you come in. So, you come home? *Shoyne.* Why don't you go to sleep?"

"Can I look with you?"

She shrugged. "Sit down."

I sat respectfully at the edge of the bed. She had a few pictures arrayed on the bedspread like a fortune-teller's cards. I pointed to a yellowing passport photograph, a bust shot of her father, Isaac, looking haggard, the collar of his ratty sweater peeking from an overcoat many sizes too large. He was a stern-looking man but with weak eyes, and the blond brush mustache above his lip lent his face a comic appearance, like Charlie Chaplain.

"He had tuberculosis in that picture. He took it right after the war.

Look how bad he looked." Her eyes filled with tears. She handed me the snapshot and I pretended to study, watching her from the corner of my eye. She cried like a child.

It was gloomy in the bedroom, dark with a darkness that the little night lamp did not so much lessen as resist, like a thumb stuck in a dike. The valise contained a world to which I would never belong but which I felt a powerful longing to belong to. It contained secrets I would never completely know, for she often evaded as much as answered my questions about who this was, and how did he end up, and when did this one die? Most of the pictures were of dead people, either murdered in the war or else wasted by war-related illnesses when the hostilities had ended and they were free to roam through Europe, homeless, penniless, ignored, and dying of progressive malnutrition, of diseases catalyzed by the nightmarish conditions of concentration camps, of prolonged hiding in attics and chicken coops, bunkers and caves. They were my legacy, a family of phantoms to which I belonged, come from a continent of eerie cities and ominous mountain woods that had been their slaughtering grounds, their graves, and this time I could imagine that she had been where I knew she had been, endured in childhood what I knew she had endured as I knew what I had endured. I could trace the trajectory that had delivered her alive from a European charnel house, from butchery behind barbed wire to the schoolyards and candy stores of the Bronx. I could connect these things: Hitler, trains, camps, crematoria, whips, black-uniformed SS with the plastic-covered living room, the television set that broadcast *The Honeymooners* and *Leave It to Beaver* and *The Beverly Hillbillies* and Ray Smith's dry sportscasting of Green Bay Packer games and Lyndon Johnson's drawling speeches about the Great Society. I could see my own life and world as in history. The Bronx was part of it. America was part of it. All my yesterdays were part of it, and all of my tomorrows. I had been born out of history, and she, one of its survivors, was my mother.

I pulled another photograph, put it back. I reached for her hand. She pulled it away: "What are you doing?"

"Mom," I said, rising. I circled the bed and stood before her. "I have to go to sleep. Will you let me kiss you good night?" And before she could answer, afraid of her answer, I leaned down, placed my arms around her stiffening shoulders, and kissed the top of her head. Her hair tasted brittle. Her hands reached up, pushed me away, and her cringing head ducked in to her neck like a turtle's, to hide from my lips. She freed herself.

"Good night," I said.

I walked out.

"I love you," she called after me.

AMONG POETS
AND THIEVES

The Fishponds

I GUESS THE dour-faced, middle-aged woman with short-cropped hair and dressed in a shapeless work uniform who greeted my arrival with a dry "Welcome" had seen thousands like me before. Her name was Nurit, she said. She spoke good English. She led me to the office of the kibbutz secretariat and handed me a form to fill out, to take down my vital statistics. I put down my name as "Alan Kaufman," my home as "nowhere," my occupation as "author," and my next of kin as "Jacque Jucht." Jucht is my mother's French maiden name. Jacque Jucht was my mother's black sheep brother who supposedly fought in the French Resistance, saved family members from the Nazis, and shortly after V-day vanished without a trace. Rumor said that he cracked up a sportscar in the Italian Alps and died. But there was always new gossip about him, related to my mother by surviving members of the family who lived scattered throughout Europe and South America and who called her in New York to report that Jacque had been spotted in a bank in Geneva or driving a truck up the Amazon highway or managing a brothel in Amsterdam. I don't know why he came to mind just then in the office. I hadn't thought of him in a while. But suddenly his name appeared on my lips. My mother used to tell me bedside stories about him. How he defied his parents to become a professional boxer. And shortly afterward he went to Spain, where he helped smuggle out the French volunteers hunted by Franco. "He was a great hero," she told me, tucking my blankets tight before she quit the room. At the door she said: "But he quarreled with the family. He was very mean. And they disowned him. But I still love him." And she added: "In my way."

"Where can we find this man in an emergency?" asked Nurit.

"In France," I said.

"But, you have an address?"

"Paris," I said.

She stared at me for a moment, then laid down the clipboard and said wearily, "Come with me." We went to a supply room where I was outfitted with two changes of work uniform, personal linen, heavy work boots, a kibbutz cap, and a ration book of coupons for the commissary.

"You can buy there all the personal things you want," she explained. "Toothpaste, soap, candy . . ."

"Liquor?"

Her eyes fell. "Yes," she said with open distaste, "liquor."

As she led me to my quarters, she explained about my job. "You will work in the dining hall."

My heart sank. "Uh, can't I work in the orange groves? You have orange groves, don't you?"

"Yes," she said, "in time. But all the newcomers must start in the dining hall. This is your room. You'll share it with three others."

We climbed the veranda of a ranch-style, one-story residential compound; stood at the entrance to a bare, gloomy little room just big enough for the four cots crowded into it, one along each wall. Mine was near the door. There were suitcases shoved under three of the cots, and towels hung from nails on the wall. The beds were made, and at the foot of each, a clean uniform was neatly folded atop a footlocker.

"You make your bed every morning. The washroom is over there." She looked in the direction of a lime-colored door with an opaque window. "Be careful how you use toilet paper," she warned. "We seem always to be in short supply lately. You'll begin work tomorrow. Have a look around if you like. Dinner is at six in the dining hall."

"Is it free?" I asked hopefully.

"Yes, it's free." I took her extended hand. It was stubby, gnarled, and callused with blackened spatula-shaped fingernails. "Good luck," she said dryly, and descended the stairs.

The character and quality of my roommates' luggage, peeking out from beneath their cots, told me about them. The one who owned the cheap American rucksack knotted with a bandanna and bearing decals from Marrakech was probably a long-haired freak, potentially a friend. The bed with the Lufthansa flight bag worried me though. He's just toured through northern Europe, I thought, felt sure it had to be so; couldn't imagine what an actual German would be doing in Israel—wasn't even sure they let them into the country. And I figured that the expensive-looking three-piece leather luggage set of English manufacture and bearing Her Majesty's imprint on the manufacturer's label belonged to a Brit, which was fine by me. I had no truck with John Bull.

I didn't bother to unpack my dirty laundry; undressed, shoved my clothes into the suitcase, and kicked it under the bed. Wrapping a towel around my waist, I went for a shower. Under the nozzle I took a blast of stinging needles, let the warm hydrotherapeutic water jab at my neck for a while until the corded muscles loosened. Then I rubbed myself briskly with a towel, and when I stepped out onto the veranda I felt wonderful.

The occasion called for beer and a cigarette. But for the first time since landing in the country, I could look around me without a drink in my hand or without squinting through a smoke cloud. My eyes flinched in the sun, as they would in exiting from a movie matinee, took moments to adjust to what really lay before me: two blonde and barefoot women dressed in bikinis, passing in the shade of a low, sweeping willow, looking my way with broad white smiles of sunburned mirth.

"Hello!" I called, and waved. They giggled but didn't break stride and passed from view. I looked up into the sky, had never seen such a sky before, of the clearest, palest shade of blue, the sun seeming to cut right through it without resistance, and suddenly I could feel the blistering heat, a ferocious furnace against my skin. I touched my hair. It was already dried out, parched, my skull glowing like a hot skillet. Throwing the towel over my head, I went indoors.

I'd always been handy with my fists, not adverse to violence, which made me temperamental since I knew, if reason failed, there were knuckly manners of persuasion. So I first considered when I woke up on my cot, in my half-sleeping state, to take a reasonable tack with the owner of the stamping boots at my back. On the boundary of dream I rehearsed my argument: Listen, I know you've got your good reasons for waltzing in your hobnails, but I'm sleeping, man, don't you see that? Where's your system of internal reality checks, that little voice inside your skull that catches your elbow when you act like an asshole and says: Stop, it's not friendly. For nothing outraged me more then the senseless flouting of basic etiquette. Because deep down I didn't believe in the other man's innocence. He's just trampling on your balls, pure and simple, my head told me. An instant later I shot up and landed, rocking, on the balls of my feet, fists clenched, jaw thrust out, feeling mean and able to pummel some noggin should it come to that.

"You see me sleeping there?!" I snarled. I led his eyes to my cot.

He was built like a swimmer. My approach surprised him. A shirt in his hands just lifted from a pile on his cot came unfolded. His cold blue eyes squinted at me through spectacles with a kind of haughty amazement, as mine did, for I realized that he was German! Then his shiny, stubborn, upturned nose sniffed and his red lips thinned around two rows of evenly spaced teeth into a kind of sickly smile.

"You are planning to hit me?"

"I looked at my clenched fists with embarrassment, put them in my pockets.

"Well, no . . ." I said in a voice ten decibels too low to be heard well. "But don't you see me sleeping there?" I looked sadly at the cot, as if I were still lying on it, pitiably innocent, as though to say: Why would you want to wake a nice fella like that from his dreams?

The teeth went away, his lips filled out, and his manner grew mulishly confident. He began to fold the shirt against his chest, the collar pinned under his lantern jaw. "It's a little room, and if one must walk one must walk. How should I go?" He held a sleeve at arm's length, folded it across his chest. Took up the other, folded it. "The boots, they are very noisy. They give us these work boots to work. I just come from work. They are very noisy. But it takes very long to put them on, with their laces. I cannot take them off every time I come. You agree?"

I slumped down on the bed, stared at him in wonder. Here I was in Israel, being reprimanded by a German!

"I don't know," I said, "maybe. You're German, right?"

"Yes," he said proudly. "My name is Joachim. What is your name? You are American?"

"Alan. From New York City."

"Ah! New York!" He dropped the shirt and took up another from the pile. His lower lip frowned as he folded. "The capital of the world now, yes? I always want to go to New York but not for the money. It is expensive. Did you live with your parents?"

"No. Alone."

He grunted. "Alone. That is a luxury. I live with my father. I have no money for an apartment. But I took this trip."

"What are you doing in Israel?" I asked curtly, trying to sustain the resentment I felt obliged to feel despite the fact that I found myself, paradoxically, liking him.

"What?" he asked rhetorically. "I am an archaeologist. I came to Israel to see the digs. There are no digs in this valley. But I am in no hurry. It's a nice kibbutz. So I stay on a few months more, yes? Why not! I have no appointments!!" He looked up at me with glee, the shirt still pinned beneath his chin, and repeated: "No appointments!!" and shook with amusement.

Just then the door flew open and in tromped my other two room-mates, who without a word staggered to their beds and flopped down. The owner of the American rucksack did have long hair, but the incurious way he looked at me, then shut his eyes, betrayed a spoiled suburban mentality that earned my immediate dislike. The other sought to avoid my eyes, would not even look my way. He was a peculiar sort with a furtive smile, seemed to have something to hide, wore a black eye patch, khaki drill shorts, high kneesocks, and brown shoes. I soon discovered what he was hiding. I went down on my knees to fish my boots out from under the bed, where I discovered some twenty odd balls of crumpled toilet paper. I retrieved one and examined it. The roll of toilet paper perched on eye patch's footlocker exactly matched my specimen in color and kind. What the hell was this? And then I remembered Nurit's words about missing toilet paper. I stood to my feet and thrust the toilet paper under eye patch's nose. "Excuse me," I said, towering over his cot. He opened his good eye, a soft brown oval twinkling with deceit.

"Yes?" he said mockingly in a South African accent.

"Well, I notice that my bed has been used to squirrel away these peculiar looking nuts." I turned the crumpled tissue ball for his examination. His good eye twitched in nervous recognition, his cheeks colored. I held the evidence up against his roll of toilet tissue. "Looks like a match. I'll leave it up to you to collect your little treasure from under my bed and find someplace else to hide it. I don't think under my bed's the best place for it. Someone might get it into his head to look there and make off with the whole kit and caboodle."

"I don't know what you're talking about," he said coldly.

"Ah! Now that's a big mistake. You can see that, can't you?" My fists clenched.

He jumped to his feet. We were physically about evenly matched, which made me feel a lot better about what I had to do. My stomach knotted and adrenaline coursed through my veins.

"Well," he said, "here you are. Have a go if you like."

I don't think he quite expected me to accept his friendly invite. But I learned my manners young, had a proper Bronx schoolyard upbringing to live up to. So I drilled one straight into his one good eye and the next thing I knew, hands from behind were dragging me to the floor and there was a terrible commotion.

They sat on their beds with hangdog looks, like bad little boys, while Assaf stood before them with his arms crossed, grinning. He was the supervisor of the overseas volunteer workers: fair, chunky, Israeli, with a raspberry-colored skin cancer on his face; the result, I later learned, of too much sun exposure during the '73 war and its aftermath, the War of Attrition, during which Assaf lost a brother and served almost constantly. He winked at me. Then he turned to the others and said: "I don't know who is the right or the wrong, but no one fights on kibbutz. Never. If others hear they would be shocked. But I promise not to speak. If you promise not to fight. Or else, if they hear, they will tell me to throw you from here. But this you do not want. I like good workers. Everyone should be happy, OK?"

Of course, my hippie American colleague opened his big yap at once, spoke with a middle-class suburban drawl: "That's *so* unfair! This new person comes in here and assaulted my roommate. Look at Arthur's eye, for God's sake! And he's a visually challenged person too!! This violent nut should be arrested! In America this would be a crime!" Arthur looked up pathetically and squinted at Assaf through his puffy eye, his mouth set in a sorrowful frown. Poor bastard looked pretty awful.

Assaf nodded soberly. "If you want to call police, that is your business. But you should know that we don't like police on kibbutz. We take care of our own problems. And when everybody knows, they will throw you off, all of you. It's your decision. I cannot make this decision."

"Well, just throw this guy out! He punched Arthur! He's guilty."

"I don't know what happened," said Assaf. "You all have been fighting. You all look guilty to me."

It was true. They looked like a bunch of silly guilty bastards, with their faces cut up and noses bruised and caked with blood. I didn't come out too badly though, considering. My knuckles stung a bit; that's all, really. And the ripped kibbutz shirt. I was sorry about that. It was kibbutz property and now it wouldn't serve to mop a floor with.

"I want to speak to you outside," Assaf said, and I followed him out. Just before he crossed the threshold, he stopped and said: "OK?"

The Three Stooges nodded grimly. He broke into a smile. It was all an act. "Yoffi!" he said.

As soon as we descended the steps his manner changed. He became shy. Admiring almost. "Come," he said respectfully. We started at a brisk clip down the path.

"What does 'yoffi' mean?" I asked.

"Beautiful," he said.

"Where are we going?"

"To eat. It's six o'clock."

"But we're not heading for the dining room. Aren't we eating there?"

He made a face. "Come," he said, again with that trace of shy admiration. "We eat some real food."

So I followed along and we came to a row of white houses with red roofs and neat little lawns. From the screened-in veranda of one of the houses a delicious smell carried to us on profusions of smoke. I could make out the shapes of people seated and standing and heard the murmur of voices conversing in Hebrew, punctuated by explosions of laughter. We turned into a path which took us behind the house, to the backyard, where a group of men, dressed in T-shirts and shorts, were having a barbecue. The kitchen window faced the backyard and I saw several young women inside busying themselves.

When the men saw me they stopped talking. Assaf broke into a grin and said something in Hebrew. The men laughed and those sitting came to their feet. All extended hands to me.

"Yitzak. Nice to meet you," smiled a tall, thin, sunburned man with short kinky hair and a handlebar mustache. "Hello, how do you do? My name is Haim," said a strikingly handsome, broad-shouldered man with a Latin accent. "Yossi," said a third, with a grip like a vise. He was built like a brick wall and his shoulders, arms, chest, and legs were covered with a light brown fur, except his head, which was partially bald. The fourth man, big, heavyset, with red hair and beard and crazed blue eyes, nodded without offering his hand. "Buki," he muttered, and lifted his hand in a disconsolate wave. Then we all sat down on lawn chairs, except Buki and Yitzak, and a cooler was opened and beers passed around. There were small steaks and fish fillets grilling on the range. Assaf caught me staring at the food and chuckled: "Hungry, huh?" I nodded. He laughed and slapped my back. "Fighting makes you hungry," he said, and winked at the others.

"Tell me," said Yitzak, leaning forward with his hands folded on his knees, "what makes you do this?"

I explained about the toilet paper and they listened without amusement.

"That fucking maniac South African," Yitzak said in English, turning to the others.

They nodded.

"And what about the German? What did he do?"

"He was German. That's enough," I said.

They laughed till tears came to their eyes and they were holding their sides with pained expressions. Several times Assaf slapped me on the back and almost fell to the floor. A woman poked her head from the kitchen and looked at me suspiciously, then at the others with cold disgust, and said something dourly in Hebrew. Then she said to me: "You shouldn't think this way. Many of the younger Germans like that one come here to make a sacrifice—what is the word? To repent, for the past. It bothers them." Indeed, I felt a bit ashamed, since I had taken a liking to Joachim.

Buki, who laughed harder then anyone, waved at her to go away. She spit a reply and withdrew. The next moment, the door flew open. A parade of ladies bearing huge bowls of food appeared. They were all dressed in halters and shorts, had terrific figures and won my complete attention. But when I noticed Haim and Yitzak scrutinizing me, I quickly averted my eyes. I wasn't even introduced. Plates were passed around and food from the grill slapped on. This was followed by big ladles of various kinds of salad. Lastly, warm pita bread was tossed into my lap. Then the women each took modest portions and seated themselves on the arms of the mens' chairs. Buki's woman received a slap on the butt for blocking his view of me, and with a scowl she lowered herself to the floor and sat there cross-legged, staring at me. In fact, all the women were staring at me as though I were some chimera fallen from the sky. I suppose I was, in a sense. They began to ask me questions in uncommonly good English, while the men hunched over their food and ate abstractedly.

Where was I from? Why had I come to Israel? Didn't I have a good life in America? What did I do for a living? Was I divorced, single, separated, have a girlfriend, children? Was I ever going back? If so, when? If not, why not? Etc., etc.

The food was cooling on my plate and I was too starved to go on talking. I smiled apologetically at the last question, lowered my face without answering, and plunged in. It was delicious! I ate ravenously while the women watched with satisfaction. When I had scraped up the last of the potato salad with my fork, one of them rose, took the plate from my lap, and piled it high with more food. This too I dispatched in no time. The women were impressed. The men looked at me with approval.

Then they began to talk to each other as though I didn't exist. Finally, Yitzak nodded several times to Assaf who spoke passionately and, turning to me with a grave air, asked: "Alan, where did they put you to work?"

"In the kitchen."

Buki rolled his eyes at heaven and the women sighed. "Don't you want to work in the kitchen?" one of the women asked. She was adorable. I smiled. "I might," I said, and she giggled. "No!" Yitzak said somberly. "You come work with us."

"Where?"

"In the fishponds," he said, and the other men waited to see my reaction, as though I had just received the highest honor bestowable upon a human being.

"Fantastic!" I said.

They looked at each other with concern.

"What is fantastic?" said Assaf testily.

"That you asked me to work with you."

"What does it mean, 'fantastic'?"

"Ahhhh . . . it means . . ." I thought. "It means *yoffi.*"

"*Kol HaKavod!*" laughed Assaf. "All honor to you."

The others slept but I was up, seated on the edge of my cot, shuddering with cold as I laced up my boots at three o'clock in the morning. Last time I got up this early was a New Year's Eve when I and John O'Connor brushed off the sawdust of the Kilarny Rose Bar on Trinity Place in Lower Manhattan, stumbled out into the early morning streets, trembling with hangovers, and went for a climb to the top of the Manhattan Bridge. I hurried down the path to the parking lot. There were lights on in some of the houses but no one in sight. Up ahead, the dim shapes of the fishpond crew stood around two green and white jeeps. There was a Great Dane the size of the Baskerville's hound, dancing on its hind legs, paws resting on a jeep fender. At my approach he jumped down and emitted a low, guttural growl. I strode right up to the beast, prepared to see the sky blocked out by the spring of its attack, and growled back: "You've got teeth but I've got *this!*" I poked my fist under its muzzle. The big sloppy old pup nuzzled my fist with a lathering jaw and whined. The men laughed. "Awwwwww," I cooed. "You poor little puppy fellah! You're just like me. Everybody thinks you're mean just because you're big!"

"Alan is fighting again!" roared Yossi. "He is going to beat up Igor!" He slapped my back in greeting and pumped my hand. His arm collared my neck like a pillory yoke and he led me into the crew's huddle. They nodded in greeting.

"So, are you ready to work?" said Haim.

I breathed warmth into my fists. "Sure, but you should have warned me to bring a rubber wet suit!"

The men looked at each other, puzzled.

"What is this?" asked Yitzak, twirling his handlebar mustache.

Yossi shrugged, turned to Buki, who raised his brow as if to say "Beats me."

"No, no, no," I laughed. "Wet suits are for scuba diving. It's a joke!"

Yossi swallowed hard. He said stiffly: "Let's go," embarrassed to have missed the point.

We piled into the jeeps. The motors roared to life and our headlights swept the parking lot as we pulled out in military caravan formation, Igor trotting alongside. The armed, shivering sentry at the kibbutz gates lifted his gloved hand in a dismal wave as we rolled past. Instead of turning left or right onto the main road we simply drove straight across it and jumped, jeep after jeep, onto an unpaved muddy track through what looked like a misty swamp. Then, suddenly, we broke into a clearing.

Here were the ponds for as far as the eye could see: big, rippling ovals of incandescent water, each containing an image of the rising sun and encircled by low-flying blue-white herons which struck the waves with outstretched wings and flew off, silver fish wriggling in their bills. It took my breath away. The jeeps bumped in high bulrushes under skies billowing with the kind of lavender clouds that float like smoke puffs above desert buttes. We pulled up to a shed, jumped out, and stamped inside. It was as cold as a refrigerator in there. Like the others, I struggled into enormous rubber overalls and a pullover and sheathed my frozen hands in rubber gloves. I tugged tridents from the walls and helped Haim to drag out a heavy net. Outside, Yitzak waited, shirtless, stripped down to shorts and sneakers and perched on the red bucket seat of a John Deer tractor hooked to a flatbed truck. We dumped all the equipment on and sat around the edges. The tractor pulled out like a tugboat on choppy seas. Down to the ponds we rumbled, holding on for life against crazy vibrations.

We crept up on the fish commando-style. Before we set off Yossi had asked me: "Do you know the story of Sixty on Six?" Nope, I didn't. In the '67 war a squad of Israeli commandos surprised a Syrian military encampment sixty meters away by creeping up on them on bellies and elbows for six hours. "This is how we surprise the fish, or they hear us and swim away. OK?"

We didn't take six hours. Fish aren't that smart. We crept on tiptoe down to the bank, and then me, Yossi, and Haim fell to our knees and crawled through the high grass dragging a heavy rope behind us. Yitzak and Buki waited with the other end of the rope clutched in their fists. When we had circled the head of the pond, Yossi put his finger to his lips and pointed. There was a small boat. We inched up to it, tied the rope to the bow, and stood up. Inside the boat was a piled net. We scrambled in. "OK!" Yossi shouted to Yitzak and Buki. They jumped to their feet and began to pull us across the water.

We paid out net until we reached shore, then hopped out, feet sinking in the soggy banks and clipped our end of the net to a waiting tractor. "Go on," Yossi shouted at Haim, "get the refrigerated truck!" In the meantime Yitzak detached the flatbed from the second tractor, jockeyed around the fishpond to the opposite bank and hooked up his end of the net. "Alan!" Yossi roared, "get up on the tractor and drive!"

"That's a big mistake, Yossi. I can't even roller-skate."

"So? You learn!"

"He has that much faith in his fellow man? OK," I thought, "I'm game." I sure as hell was, too. Climbed into that bucket seat, absorbed a sixty-second lesson, then kicked the motor over. When Yossi said "Gun the engine," I pressed on that gas, the diesel engine roared, the tractor sputtered, and—coughing like a big motorized lawn mower lurched into motion—I was rolling through the high grass with the sun climbing higher.

Yossi rode on the sideboard while I drove, coaching, grabbing the steering wheel to adjust my route, but basically I had the hang of it. "Go slowly, Alan, slowly. You see how Yitzak goes? You go like him." As we dragged the net between our tractors, Yitzak and I, the pond's surface erupted in lesions as tens of thousands of fish swam to escape.

At the head of the pond our haul writhed in a grotesque heap, perishing for lack of air. Since these fish were destined for transfer to another pond, the trick was to get them out before they died. Each species expired at its own pace—carp and amnon and burrie were fragile delicacies, but the very first to go were the silver fish: big, sleek, shiny things with scales like stainless steel and a habit of shooting from the depths like little surface-to-air missiles, which is beautiful to watch from the shore, but just try and stand as I did, thigh-deep in a dying mass of them and shoveling fish into a little trolley that ran on a track commencing at my knees and rumbling up the muddy banks to dry land, where it dumped its contents into the storage tank of a refrigerated truck idling on the shore. If I'd known it would be like this I'd have worn a bullet-proof athletic cup. "Damn!" I howled, as blunt, silver-colored heads rammed my scrotum. My newfound "buddies," most especially Yossi, hooted and hawed on the banks. It was some kind of fishpond initiation. "Hey, Alan, give those fish a break, huh? No farts, hey!" Well, I didn't think it so goddamned funny at the time, but I didn't throw in the towel either; I stayed until I had scooped out something like three tons of fish and my arms just wouldn't work anymore. Then I just slumped to my chest in fish and gave out, and they came in and hauled me to shore and tussled my hair and tossed into my lap a big sandwich of hard salami wedged between two great hunks of fresh-baked bread and thrust an uncapped bottle of ice-cold black beer into my hands and squatted around me while I ate, talking in Hebrew, and when I had finished they helped me to my feet and back to the pond we went, to finish the job, and with their help it was easy.

But by no means was the day done; it was just beginning in fact, because once the fish were gone it was time to drain the pond of water and jump back in with a net and drag the mud bottom for the dying survivors who flapped in the muck, thousands of them. Forming a chain with the net between us, we marched in muck to one end of the pond, dumped our fish on the shore, and then slogged back the other way and dumped our haul; back and forth we went under the hot sky, and I fell to my knees, gasping, and Yossi: "Feeling your cigarettes, huh, Alan baby?" And when it was over it was sundown, the air had turned cool, and we were seated on the banks of another pond under an immolating sky, stripped naked and smeared with mud like fantastical heathens, and even lighting up a cigarette was a monumental effort, and Igor paddled through the water, his head barely above the reflected, fiery surface while crying herons, returned from moon voyages, descended to the flames.

CALL UP

IN THE WAIST of the bus sat a party of black-garbed Chasidim, including one pale, ascetic boy of sixteen or so who looked deathly ill. Behind me two border policemen were laughing riotously. Sprinkled among the passengers were several attractive young ladies. The driver was a gray-headed, ruddy old lion with a spectacular handlebar mustache. From time to time his surly blue eyes met mine in the rearview mirror and frowned suspiciously.

Beside me a dozing field artillery sergeant was rolling his head against the back of the seat. Several times he recruited my shoulder for a pillow and I pushed him away. He appeared to be under the influence of a powerful sedative.

I was traveling from Jerusalem to Ramla. From Ramla I was to catch a second bus to the base. My orders were to report to my reserve unit at 07:30 punctually. It was the second week of the war in Lebanon but I was on my way to my own private war in the Gaza Strip.

Also aboard were three elderly couples, traveling as a group, who appeared to be heading for a vacation. They sat with arms linked and kept up a lively storm of chatter from which members of their party occasionally broke to perform a kind of public relations service for the rest of us. Turning in their seats, they smiled broadly at both sides of the aisle and blinked merrily as if to say: Hi! We're old and there's a war going on, so pardon us for our good time. Listen, it's not the first war and it won't be the last.

The seats directly in front of me were occupied by a movie-handsome couple in their early twenties who seemed to be very much in love. I gathered by the young man's short-cropped hair and rankless field fatigues that he was in the regular army. His confident bearing and the monotonous authority of his voice indicated an officer, probably second lieutenant rank. They were both intently studying a bill from the Jerusalem Plaza Hotel. Probably he had received a twenty-four-hour leave and rushed down from the front to spend the night with her in a posh hotel. The hotel bill came to quite a lot for a young man's pocket and he appeared very proud of himself having spent it. She was resting with her nose and lips pressed to his shoulder and her long-lashed eyes blinking lazily at the impressive hotel bill. Every so often she murmured "Mmmmmmmmm," in reply to the young lieutenant's speculations about the various items on the bill. The young man was all acumen and worldliness: "Five percent room service! For what? A bucket of ice cubes and a towel." She said, "Mmmmmmmmm, but it was a nice hotel, wasn't it?" "Sure," he bristled, all leathery and indigestible. "Still, next time we'll take a shot at the Hilton." He paused to consider this. Then added: "I hear good things about the Hilton." "Mmmmmmmmm," and she nuzzled closer against his rhinoceros hide and stroked his marble hands. The cords in his neck bunched and he looked down at her with a hard-boiled smile. The glory that filled him very nearly blew off the top of his head. She then cuddled even closer,

God knows where she found the room, and said: "But it was a nice hotel, wasn't it?" and kissed him.

Four loud blips cackled through the ceiling's speakers and everyone froze to listen to news of the war: a voice droned statically about intermittent shelling in some areas, waves of bombings in others, here a tank assault and there combined offensives from land, air, and sea; then a revised casualty list was read. I leaned a cigarette into the cupped match of the soldier beside me who, on hearing the news, had awakened with a cigarette heading for his lips before his sleepy eyes could regain their focus. The old couples had unlinked arms to fumble in their handbags and shirt pockets for cigarettes. The Chasidim were leaning their faces over cupped matches in the aisle. The movie-handsome lieutenant and his girlfriend cracked open a new pack of menthol cigarettes and took lights from his lighter, which was wrapped in black electrical tape against sun reflection, a cherished target of snipers. We sat in the pea-soup fog of our own rapid exhalations until the broadcast ended. Then, one by one, windows were flung open and a hot breeze circulated through the bus, chasing away the cigarette smoke. The bus rocked from side to side like a boat. The august pine country of Jerusalem's surrounding hills had fallen away and now we were traveling through dusty plains along a cracked and bumpy two-lane road flanked by low, withered-looking orange groves and dust-caked rows of parched grapes on wrinkled vines.

We passed through villages of adobe-colored, villa-style ranch houses with cock-shaped weather vanes and squat corrugated huts pustulating with fat white chickens and tuck-tailed pariah dogs digging in the dirt and garbage, and the villages winked by between long stretches of sparsely grassed meadows and ploughed brown fields, with a funnel-shaped mounted combine pouring chaff out of its mouth like a vomiting grasshopper, and women stood in their doorways with their heads bound in kerchiefs and their hands folded on the pillows of their pregnancies, and old men hobbled past with nodding, skull-capped heads and *tsit tsit* fringes flapping about their beltless waists, and young, hard-muscled men in denim shorts and muscle shirts stepped into tenders loaded down with turnips, and then there were more fields stretching away in a flat plain to three cloud-grazing smokestacks trailing three plumes of black smoke—not Jewish ashes—from their spouts.

The bus rocked back and forth in the sickening cradle of the road, the soldier beside me staring gruffly at the clapping lid of an ashtray. The young lieutenant's lady friend was slumped in his lap, napping soundly, while he stared out the window with a rigid look of defiance, daring anyone or anything to disrupt their happiness and just see what happens! I waited to see what would happen and it was sad to see. You can't read a stranger's mind, but in time of war you can tell when a soldier is thinking about the war. A fear of going back to it went over his face like a soiled hand and painted his eyes and cheeks with smudges of anxiety and passed on, leaving its dirt behind on him.

I think he didn't want her to see what the hand had done to his face. That was a mistake: she woke, looked up into his eyes, saw it there, struggled to sit upright, her hand going to his face, but he pushed it away. His shoulder shrank up against the cold glass window filled with the world that he had defied to touch him and it had touched him in that strange way that war touches people and makes them prefer cold glass to a warm hand.

And then, up ahead, the face of the sickly looking Chasidic boy turned a life-renunciating white and he leaned his head down between the shiny knees of his black trousers and vomited an udder's worth of bile over his shoes and surfaced through his sickness to gasp air and then resubmerged to puke out more. His sickness spattered dress hems, pants cuffs, shoes; the border policemen in the rear stood up to see what had happened and began to guffaw, holding their sides in as though they too were sick, and an elderly Chasid with a bird's-nest beard opened his newspaper and began to hand around the war headlines, world and local news, gossip columns, opinion pages, funnies, and was down to sports when, clinging to his seat for his life, he groaned to stand. Thinking his balance regained, he let go, and with hands flailing wildly, his coat sleeves hiked to his white-sleeved elbows, he careened down the aisle toward the sickly boy and slipped to his knees in a pool of vomit.

Frantically, I sought for the bus driver's eyes in the rearview mirror, but they frowned suspiciously and returned to the road. Hands from everywhere assisted the elderly Chasid to his feet, and like a stroke victim relearning how to walk, clinging for support to the backs of seats with his vomit-stained hands, he shuffled gingerly to his seat.

The dismayed passengers nearest to the sick boy wiped their legs with newspaper while the boy hunched quietly between his knees, a thin thread of drool dangling from his open mouth; he appeared to be patiently waiting for the next convulsion. His face did not seem to be suffering at all, invested with the shocked composure of a drowning man who has regained sufficient self-control to paddle mechanically to safety.

The bus suddenly swerved hard to the left and, with a winding-down of the engine and the snorting of brakes, came to a full stop in the central bus station of Ramla.

Passengers crowded the aisle, pulling down their luggage and shopping bags. The boy remained throughout our exit hunched over his limpidly drooping lip, his dull eyes staring fixedly ahead at the reassuring puddle of his own illness.

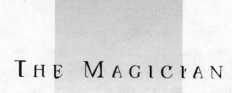

THE MAGICIAN

IN A LAUNDRY in the West Bank hamlet of Q., five Arab women huddle in a corner, shielding a nattily dressed boy. He is about fifteen years old.

The commander calls him forward, asks a question in fluent Arabic. The boy shakes his head emphatically.

I ask Amdu, our Bedouin tracker, to translate.

"He asks if they are concealing a Palestinian flag."

A woman steps forward, circles the boy's shoulder, and places herself between the commander and her son. As she speaks, the boy's face grows sullen with the burden of his pride. He must display defiance: he is male and the women are watching. But fear makes him deferent, too. When the commander repeats his question the boy looks up with agitated sincerity. Again the commander asks his question. Tearfully the boy gushes his denial. And now all the women are howling.

Then the commander says something that causes the boy and the women to freeze.

"He says he knows for sure where there is a Palestinian flag," Amdu translates.

Soldiers and civilians alike, our eyes fix uneasily on his back as he strides among the white laundry sacks with the omniscient air of a performing magician. Suddenly he stops, reaches into a sack, and wearing a strange, sarcastic smile plucks out a red shirt, a black sock, a green hand towel, holds them up and announces: "I have found a Palestinian flag. Take the boy!"

We stand stupefied, uncertain what to do.

"Take him where?" asks Amdu.

"We'll pull him in for questioning."

His mother's face strains with the effort to understand our Hebrew. "Come," I say to the boy, gently touching his arm. And now she bursts into tears. I seek his eyes; they look away. "Come," says Amdu, and taking his elbows we escort him out to the armored car, hands held before his face to block out the searchlight.

"What's this?" says Rami. He is reclining in his seat, smoking.

I help the boy up.

"We're pulling him in."

Rami scrutinizes the boy. "A Hamas man, huh?" He pretends to lift a rifle. His left eye squints. "You make boom-boom at the Israeli? You kill Israeli?"

"Give him a cigarette," says Amdu. "He didn't do anything."

Rami fishes out a cigarette. "How old is he?"

"Fifteen," I estimate.

He leans forward, offers the cigarette, stares with interest as the boy refuses. Then he pockets his lighter, slumps in his seat, and props his boots on the dashboard.

"Who can tell if he is a terrorist? He wears a tie and jacket? So? Arafat wears ties. For all you know, this one kills settlers."

The commander has emerged from the house. Ignoring the boy's frantically babbling mother, he motions to me and Amdu to mount up, climbs into the passenger seat, and orders us to blindfold and handcuff our "prisoner."

On the way to the garrison I squeeze his arm reassuringly; he misunderstands my intention, stiffens at my touch. I am filled with shame. I wonder what it must be like at his age (and given his clearly bookish disposition) to be blind and trussed among soldiers in an armored car, bound for interrogation. With every passing mile you are further from the fussing, smothering love of your mother, sisters, and aunts, and in your bedroom an open book on the table awaits you, betrayed by your inexplicable absence, your place in it marked with a plastic ruler.

Arrived in the garrison's parking lot, I watch in embarrassed silence as the commander leads him on. Just before the door of the interrogation room, he stumbles and the commander jerks him sharply upright.

RAID

OUR CONVOY HAS formed a circle on the main street in the Gazan hamlet of Z. There have been incidents of firebombing. We don't expect to find suspects tonight: usually they're gone before we arrive, and all other males as well. Still, you never know. At the door of a house, the commander retreats, grips his machine gun, and bursts open the door with a savage kick. He shines his flashlight on a woman's face.

She turns and hurries away. We advance into a courtyard, poking our guns at shadow-obscured doorways. The commander cautiously crosses the threshold of a dim wing of the house, his flashlight chasing a woman's shuttling slippers. Our ears stay pricked for a hand grenade's arming, the soft sliding-off of an automatic weapon's safety. We prod open a door at random, burst in.

The room is lit by a dim lamp. On the floor, a primitive pallet heaped with rags supports an old woman swaddled in blankets.

The commander walks out, wrinkling his nose, shaking his head angrily. "Look how these people live!" His eye falls on another door. "Let's go there." He pounds on the door. It opens and an Arab steps out. He is about twenty-five years old, a small, dignified moustache perched on his upper lip. Trouserless, he wears a black waistcoat over a long white shirt and is barefoot. I note that his toes curl in contact with the cold floor. Behind him stands his young wife.

"There is nothing here but women and children," he says in good Hebrew.

"Look," says the commander. "You people are firebombing our cars. Last week a woman and her three children burned to death. Who's doing it?"

The man's eyes go blank.

"Maybe there are firebombs in there? I smell gasoline." He points his chin at the apartment.

"No," says the man reasonably. "Of course, because of the troubles it is difficult to buy gasoline, so I keep a little in reserve. But not for bombs. I sell blankets. My children are in there, asleep."

"Who lives in the apartment above you?"

The man cranes his head toward the stairwell, at the next floor, where a group of women in housecoats are listening, hands white-knuckling the bannister.

"Only those women," he says.

"Where are the men?"

"They are in detention, sir."

The commander pauses to consider. "We'll have a look," he says.

And indeed, the apartment smells heavily of gasoline. The commander pulls the man aside and slaps his face. "Where are you hiding it?" The man howls and holds his cheek. I go to check a room. Finger on trigger, kick open the door, push away from the doorframe to the left, back to the wall, ready. Something moves. I shout, trained muzzle ready to kill. On the floor, in a neat little row, five children lying on straw mats. All of them are awake, their motionless eyes fixed on the ceiling. The voice of the commander grows loud and the man's voice is by turn tearful and querulous. Slaps sound through the house. Others from the unit have entered the flat, are searching everywhere. And I can't help but think that in my goggles, helmet, battle vest, armed, I loom over the children as once an armed German loomed giant over my mother's bed before they dragged her off. *I know it's not the same*, I tell myself, but can't help thinking it. I recognize the voices of Uri and Yoav. A table overturns. Things crash to the floor. *I know it's not the same.* Glass shatters. More glass. And Yoav shouts: "Here. The Molotovs are here!" *It's not the same.* But the children have not moved. They are afraid to look at me. I have stood in the room for some minutes now and not once have their eyes blinked.

THE TIME I DREW ANGELS

I ONCE DREW angels . . . during one of my marriages . . . no, actually after that marriage was over, when it was all in ruins. After I had run off with Rose (my wife's best friend, and my best friend's wife) and ruined that too, as the war dragged into its third year. All us men were in the army. I was close to a nervous breakdown. My betrayed wife called, invited me to her place; when I last saw her she had caught me in bed with Rose and broke a radio over my head. Police were called. She fled. I had since heard that she was threatening murder, had friends in the Israeli underworld—for a time feared that she would have me hit, but I went to her home anyway. Why not? I didn't care about myself anymore.

She had moved into a dingy tenement neighborhood, a bleak, slum-like project building, but she was putting her life back together and looked better than she had when I was shuttling back and forth between Rose's bed and the Gaza Strip and would spot her from a distance on a street, wearing dark sunglasses and dragging home fishnet shopping bags filled with bottles of cheap brandy. There were bottles out on the table now when I came in. She cooked a lousy dinner, eggs and hummus, some such crap. And the booze was out. With her, dinner was just an excuse to drink, that's all, and we drank now, as always. We were the ideal drinking mates. I had not even minded very much— such good mates we were—when she betrayed me with that cab driver one night; fucked him right in the backseat while I sat upstairs in the house, pouring myself tumblers of Rishon-Le-Zion. I even brought them down two helpings—but found them busy clasping white in a confusion of black lace and tense thrusting buttocks, so I took the glasses back upstairs and gulped them both down.

She unscrewed the cap now and poured me a glass. I was in bad shape. "You look terrible," she said.

"I'm full of remorse," I said. "I'm sick with what I've done to you."

She poured. She was silent. We sat and drank.

(OK, I'll own up. I *was* having a nervous breakdown then. Period. Was even having paranoid delusions in my army unit: imagined that my fellow soldiers, the best friends possible on earth, the bravest, kindest guys really, that they wanted to kill me with a bullet to the base of the brain—crazy stuff like that.)

"It's bad," I told her. "I'm having delusions."

She nodded. "Why don't you draw?" she suggested, "draw how you feel. My shrink strongly recommends it."

"OK," I said.

She rose, returned with watercolors, set out paper.

I began to draw, and sipped from time to time from my glass.

She swigged from the bottle straight. It was gold-colored in the room and felt safe. The pain between us actually formed a kind of embryonic womb, enfolding and protecting us. We each had already hurt the other too savagely to fear pain anymore. So, I drew. I drew people with wings on their backs. I drew an angel. He had on a news vendor's cap and a poor man's sports jacket. He stared toughly from the frame of the portrait. He looked gentle but tough as nails. He was full of the heartbreak of his love betrayals, full of the mercy that he felt for others. And it was beautiful, it was located in a kind of nighttime Brooklyn with a starry Van Gogh sky, and the angel seemed to say that never again on this earth for as long as the angel lives will the good or the gentle people of the earth be murdered or shamed or betrayed.

She liked my angels very much, she said. It was the first and only time that I have ever drawn angels. It was the last time that I was ever to see her too, because soon after, at the height of the khamsin winds, she got royally smashed, went down on all fours, and really tried to sever her wrists' veins on shattered wine bottles.

I never heard from her again.

THE THINGS CARL LITTLE CROW AND I DID TOGETHER TO STAY SOBER IN SAN FRANCISCO

I WAS paranoid, prideful, and newly arrived in San Francisco off a Greyhound bus with sixty-seven dollars in my pocket.

Carl Little Crow was half African-American, half Native American, a former back-alley drunk from Chicago with eighteen years of sobriety to his name. He was half my size and had a face like an alert animal. He wore an embroidered West African shaman's cap, a cowskin vest, baggy corduroys, and scuffed black shoes, and he carried a befeathered Native American tom-tom drum that he beat as he walked down Haight Street.

The things we did

1. Healing ceremonies atop Buena Vista Park in Haight-Ashbury. Carl claimed that a satanic sacrificial cult was operating in the area, abduct-

ing and murdering people, and that as spiritual human beings we must "cleanse" the area with our souls. For this ceremony, Carl's mentor, Roland, drove in from Arizona in a rusted brown station wagon. Also in attendance was Mike, sober ten years, known thereabouts as the Captain of Haight Street.

With only two months booze-free, I was the novice and appointed to carry the healing plant. The healing plant: a ratty-looking lobby shrub with withered leaves that Carl had salvaged from the trash outside a Tenderloin hotel. Carl took the plant home and fed it plant food, sunshine, Native American chants, water, and whispers of love until it was able to lift its head again. It still looked like a shitty plant from a flop hotel but vibrantly alive. And as I carried it, huffing, Carl led the way, chanting in a trance, beating the drum, walking in a slow procession up the slope to the top of the hill.

Deadheads and crack dealers watched us with interest. According to Carl, the devil worshippers were spying on us but chances were excellent that we wouldn't see them. It was strange, I thought; I'd shown up in San Francisco paranoid and delusional, clinging to my sobriety by bloody fingernails, gibbering about being pursued across the continent by devil worshippers, and here was Carl declaring that yes, they do exist, are a definite danger, and now once and for all we will rid the world of them. I felt both terrified and reassured.

Bringing up the rear was the Captain: tall, bone-lean, with a mean-looking handlebar mustache and a combative black beret set at a jaunty angle on his old gray skull. He had cold blue eyes and a big keyring jangling from his belt. He scanned the turf with sweeping looks, warning off anyone with the wrong idea. There's lots of such people around and they know Mike. While he may not beat you one-on-one the first time around, Mike will make it his religion to get even, even if it takes twenty years, and will not cease until you are effaced from the earth. His other hobbies are amateur photography, of which he is a very fine practitioner, and archiving local historical information and artifacts. For instance, he can show you, hidden near a drainage ditch covered over with dead leaves, a row of little white tombstones embedded like teeth into the cement that belong to a party of gold-mining 49ers killed in a drunken brawl "'round these parts nigh a hunnert and fifty years ago," as Mike would say. Only the accent was an affectation; he was really a marvelously bright and well-educated man whom alcohol had laid low, like the rest of us.

Behind him, at a remove of ten paces, walked Roland, and I was surprised at how average-looking he seemed. Like any road dog you might come across in the Arizona desert. That hermit smile and blue eyes bleached kind by extreme loneliness. He wore just a plain old black T-shirt, stone-scrubbed blue jeans, and embossed leather cowboy boots. He was more a dude than a hierarchically royal medicine man of the Black Foot tribe. But I figured what the hell do I know about it anyway.

My job was to carry and I did. My arms grew heavy. I wanted to drop the damned plant. But I held on as we inched our way up, led by Carl's mournful voice and the boom-boom-boom of the tom-tom, and soon we were at the top, where we proceeded briskly to a ravine and slid down the slope to a wide shelf, which Carl declared to be our healing ground.

It was a godforsaken place of dead trees with amputated branches. We sat in a circle and Carl Little Crow said something in Native American tongue, and Roland nodded and smiled. Then they all looked at me. "What's your spirit animal?" Carl asked. Surprised, I shrugged. "I dunno," I said. Carl's eyes burned into mine. "Name it!" I couldn't think of any. We don't have animals in the Bronx. What should I say: cockroach? Rat? This is how I knew that I was really in California now. Someone named Carl Little Crow asking me to name my spirit animal. "I dunno," I said again. Once more he burned into me with his eyes and said: "Name it! Name it now!" Suddenly the word "hawk" popped into my brain, so I blurted out, "Hawk!" and Carl hissed: "Look up!" and I looked up, and O my God, O my ever-loving fucking God, right there, over us, circling, two of them, enormous, right here in Haight-Ashbury. What are hawks doing here anyhow? And right at this moment no less?! Now I felt the presence of what he called the Great Spirit, what others call God, or whatever they call it. I felt it. And it freaked the living day-lights out of me. In a good way.

2. Walking down Haight Street together, Carl beating his drum, me holding onto his shirt, afraid to let go, that if I did I'd go drink. He led me up to trees and stood there talking to them, waving his hands with this ecstatic look on his animal-like face, and nodding his head vigor-ously with a look of delight, as though answering questions. "What're they saying, Carl?" I'd ask. "They're saying: 'Don't drink!'" he'd reply.

3. Take astral projection trips around the world. Actually, Carl took them while I sat there and watched. Usually we did this in the Café International on Haight and Fillmore. We sat at one of the scratched-up wooden tables embedded with hand-painted tiles, surrounded by electric paintings by young unknown geniuses, World Beat music play-ing, and Carl would close his eyes and begin to sway from side to side. It would seem as though the colors in the room were running together with acidlike intensity. You know how a GIF looks on your computer if the server crashes, like a kind of graphic ghost? Carl turned into that. If you'd clicked on him, nothing would have happened. He was else-where, transported by a spiritual metasearch engine into the hard drive of the Amazon jungle, or appearing on the interactive screen of the Himalayan Mountains. He was rapping with the Dalai Lama. He was reading poetry to the king of Sweden. Once he opened his eyes and I saw two white ghost buffaloes galloping in his eyeballs. When he did this it scared me but I preferred to stay by him rather than take my chances with my own mind, which was detoxing with d.t.'s and hallu-cinations that were trying to kill me. Each cell of my brain, my body, Carl had explained, had been perforated after years of drinking by a lit-tle hole that once I'd filled with alcohol but that now was empty, yearn-ing, yawning, craving, desperate to be filled, an almost sexual need, and that I must fill it with something else now. I must fill it with my soul. I must fill it with the Great Spirit of the Universe. I must learn to know

my spirit. That we were like two calling to each other across a great gulf. And that soon we would be reunited. So I sat and watched Carl Little Crow cavort with Dakota sandpainters and Ludwig van Beethoven. Ludwig, Carl informed me, was an abused child, like me.

4. Eat barbecue chicken wings. Carl had a shameless love of barbecue chicken wings. It surprised and disappointed me. I thought someone so spiritual would want to eat, say, a bowl of brown rice and drink a cup of green tea. Instead he'd take me over to Chicken Charlie's on Divisadero and order up big buckets of greasy, orange barbecue chicken wings and get all messed with juices and greases and bone smatterings on his grinning mouth, ecstatically cooing, "Yesssss! Oh, yesssssss!" I'd take a nibble off one and smile happily despite myself. It just didn't fit the picture, him tearing at those chicken wings and slurping up a thirty-two-ounce Cherry Coke. He had a bit of a belly, too. But worse still, he had this ugly weal of a scar worming down the center of his chest where'd he'd had open-heart surgery, during which he'd died twice and been revived.

During the time he was dead he had floated above the table, smiling down at everyone, and then left for a few seconds to take an astral projection trip to New York City, where he danced, he said, with a señorita in Spanish Harlem. That too shocked me. I mean, that's all one can think to do at the moment of one's death? Dance with a woman? "Not just any woman," said Carl Little Crow, "a Puerto Rican woman." He jumped up and down in his seat laughing like a happy kid with the grease all over him and I said very gravely: "That shit's real bad for your heart, Carl, and seems like you already had one heart attack . . ."

Carl grew still and I fought back tears but lost and sobbed out: "And what if you die, man! What am I gonna do? How am I gonna stay sober!?" Carl's eyes grew moist and he said: "By helping another," he said. "Remember! It's always by helping another that we are healed ourselves."

And I am crying even now, seven and a half years later, to remember those words.

5. Eat a whole half-gallon of peach melba ice cream. Another of Carl's
peculiar weaknesses. He'd have me at night seated on the floor of my
tiny room near the Hayes Street projects in the Mo', as we called the
Fillmore District, with the guns of battling crack gangs going pop-pop-
pop outside our windows, and squealing tires and screaming voices, and
a bundle of burning sage smoking in a bowl as we sat and breathed in
and out, in and out, watching our breath, calming our bodies. Then we
chanted a mantra: "God grant us the serenity to accept the things we
cannot change, courage to change the things we can, and the wisdom
to know the difference," and then he'd have me up on my feet dancing
a slow spirit dance around the room, waving my hands, moving the
energy fields around, as he put it. And when we were done, we then
adjourned to the communal kitchen that I shared with a bunch of pot-
heads and grunge maniacs, and took out a huge half-gallon of peach
melba ice cream and two spoons!

The sugar wacked Carl out for sure. His eyes would get all red and
he'd feel giddy and sway and stagger as he walked, and for a moment I
could see eighteen years ago to the back-alley drunk he must have
been, a little lethal menace. And it amazed me that he could have gone
so long without a drink and I'd feel hope. Then he'd leave and I'd sometimes find a ten-spot on the bed, maybe his last, since he was always
short of money and mostly unconcerned about it. I stretched out on the
bed with my boots on, head pillowed on my hands, listening to the
gunfire and the shouts and watching the fog roll over the last vestige of
the San Francisco moon. I was flat broke, my welfare general assistance
due to expire, and all that I had been, a father, a soldier, a lover, a boss,
a highly touted this, and a well-regarded that, all lay behind me now. I
remembered the park bench where I had laid down to die in Tompkins
Square on Avenue A in Alphabet City and from which I rose to live—
damned if I understand to this day how or why—when every blood vessel in my flesh demanded booze and booze and more booze and when
this disease I have, this disease of alcoholism, believed that it would
continue to drink even after I had died. I found help in the rooms of

recovery and, against the advice of the recovered drunks I met, boarded a bus with sixty-seven dollars in my pocket and a California sun rising in my addled, sleep-deprived, detoxing brain.

And this is what it means to be happy: to want nothing and to sit listening to the calm beating of your own heart as big wheels carry you off into a mystery lined with fast-food concession stands.

6. We got a man to detox. We happened upon him sitting on the steps of a Haight-Ashbury Victorian recovery home that had once been the residence of Janis Joplin, and just a few doors down from where novelist Kathy Acker once lived. (We'd see Kathy in her leather jacket hand-painted with skulls and roses and she, being a real dear woman under that tough exterior, always had a kind word.) He was dressed for business in a tie. He wore spectacles, his hair was thinning, and his hands were trembling violently. An overflowing suitcase lay open on the sidewalk and he was staring at its contents and moaning, "Uhhhhhhhhhh, God, uuuuuhhhhhhhhh, oh, God." And Carl said, "What is it, my brother?" and he said, "You God?" and Carl Little Crow breathed out meditatively and said, "No. I am a drunk like you." And the man looked at him angrily, then at me, and snapped, "I'm no drunk!" and burst into tears. "I *am* a drunk! Oh, I am a *terrible* drunk!" he whined. "What happened?" I asked softly.

"My friend lent me his apartment for three days so I got permission to leave the recovery house on a pass and went there and dropped all his acid and drank all his brandy and smashed up the house and I ran back here and they saw that I'd gone out and they threw me into the street! Now I have no place to go! My friend's back by now. He's probably looking to kill me. What'll I do? What'll I do?"

"Go to detox," said Carl. The man looked at him, astonished.

"Detox? I can't go to detox!! I'm middle-class!" How well I understood that pretense. But booze strips us down to our essentials.

"It's your only option," said Carl. And the man nodded his head and sobbed and I went up the street to the phone booth to call the Mobile Assistance Patrol van to take him in. For hours we sat with the man, waiting. And I told him the story of my last run. There I was, I said, living in Park Slope, Brooklyn. Had a sixty-thousand-dollar-a-year job. Married to an English actress and had a one-year-old daughter, a little blonde and blue-eyed angel named Isadora who would say, "Da'ddy, Da'ddy," over and over to herself as though I were ambrosia to her little soul.

Had a garden out back where I'd sit at night in a lawn chair under a tree of heaven counting stars. Had sworn off the liquor for good, figuring that nothing, nothing, must ever spoil my chance for a beautiful life with this little girl, nothing on this earth! Belonged to a gym, too. Got into peak physical condition. Was up for a raise at work; bringing in a lot of new accounts and money. Inside I felt miserable but I thought: "What the hell, I've always been miserable, it's just the way it is for me."

One day on my way home from work, passing through the twilight streets of my little neighborhood, I passed a local tavern, a real nice place for a respectable clientele, and I thought: "Why not? Why the hell not? Don't I deserve it? Look at how beautiful my life is. It'll be the proverbial cherry on the pudding." A bartender dressed in a red Eisenhower jacket was toweling a tumbler dry by candlelight. "Good evening, sir," he said as I settled onto a plush red-leather bar stool and rested my elbows on the polished mahogany counter. "Evening." I smiled with a terse nod. "And what will you be having this evening?" I lifted a finger into the air: "Chivas Regal," I said, and as he turned I lifted a second finger: "Make it a double." When he brought it I held it up to the candlelight and swished it around in the brandy snifter, its golden elegance proclaiming the vigor and achievement of my adulthood. I slammed it down with a gasp and said: "Gimme another," and that came and no candlelit reflection now, just down the hatch, and another and another, the bulkhead filling fast. I don't remember anything after the sixth. I experienced a black roaring pain in my head and my eyes winced open to the vague chilly paleness of a Manhattan dawn sky. I was still dressed in my London Fog raincoat, still clutching my attaché. And I was lying in bushes in the projects on 23rd Street in Chelsea, covered with vomit, urine, and blood. I staggered to my feet to stumble off to work.

And now I tore through my little daughter's life with cyclonic feroc-ity; took to sleeping at the office on an inflatable Boy Scout mattress and spent the nights in Billy's Topless on Sixth Avenue and 24th Street, one of whose dancing girls was found decapitated and dismembered, her body parts boiled for soup and served up to the homeless in Tompkins Square Park. It was front page in all the papers. They found the killer, too, a local nutcase version of Charles Manson. I remember the girl, a sweet Swedish dancer. I had stuffed a few bills myself into her G-string. It was that kind of place, and those sorts of people. I'd go home only to stuff some of my cashed paycheck into a measuring cup in the cupboard and then leave again to ride the subway back into Manhattan to Billy's. Once, late at night, I came home to leave some money. My wife didn't even bother to rise from bed. I put the money into the measuring cup and was heading for the door when I heard behind me the patter of little feet and turning saw Isadora, all of a year and a half, rush up and clasp my leg with her tiny arms and press her cheek to my shin and cling there, as if to say: "Please, Daddy, don't go." Never in my life had I ever loved anyone or anything as much as I loved her. I lifted her up, pressed her to me, kissed her cheeks with tears in my eyes, cradled her in my arms, and returned her to her place beside her mother, who lay there in the dark staring wordlessly at the ceiling. Then I turned and left. I went back to Billy's.

When I need to drink, nothing, no one, can stand in my way, I told the drunk on the stairs as we waited for the MAP van. It's not a thing that normies fathom. Nor should they have to. I am living proof that life is not fair, because if life were fair I'd be dead, slaughtered by the way I drank. Yet here I was, sober, and here was my friend and mentor Carl Little Crow with eighteen years. If we can do it, I told our middle-class friend, then so can you. And I knew that he believed me, as only one drunk can believe another who has been down the same road and lived to tell the tale.

7. From across the street a man with glowing eyes leered at me. Farther on a pair of tattooed and toothless motorcycle freaks eyeballed me,

plotting my murder, as I hurried down Haight Street. Like the man with glowing eyes, they had been following me for days and were all part of the same conspiracy. So too was a tall black man with a shaved head and wire-rim spectacles who received a signal from them and registered my presence as I passed his Mercedes-Benz. I knew that he thought I was an FDA agent sent to spy on his cocaine-smuggling operation. His eyes promised me a slow, painful death. By the time I reached the corner of Church and Market, I was faint with fear. I looked around for shelter, spotted a shop called Aztec Taqueria, and made for it. But as I crossed the threshold of the steamy little shop, I realized that this was the headquarters of an Aztec sacrificial cult who knew that *I* knew what they were: I had tricked myself into the lion's lair. Now I was really doomed. I couldn't leave, though. Paralyzed with terror, I stood at the counter. "What'll you have?" asked the counter help, a Mexican with tired eyes. My eyes shifted nervously to the open door of an office near the kitchen. Someone in there was staring at me. There was a video screen monitoring traffic. So that's how they did it! I watched to see if someone would emerge to close the store's front door, trapping me. But the counterman's voice was adamant: "What's it gonna be, man?" "Burrito," I stuttered. "Refried or whole beans?" I didn't know what to answer to this obvious test. The wrong response would unleash hidden minions in white uniforms rushing out from every corner to throw me onto the counter and hold me down for the high priest with the butcher knife. "For here or to go?" the counterman asked as he wrapped the burrito. He was looking at me strangely. Another test. "Here," I said. It was obviously the right answer. Only I had a plan. With shaking hands I received the burrito and paid him. A cauldron of white-hot panic boiled in my solar plexus as I made my way on wobbly legs to a table and sat down. I stared at the burrito without appetite, sure that a hundred eyes watched to see what I'd do. I must have looked white as a sheet. I just sat there. Had run out of steam. Felt ready to give up, stand, shout: "OK, then, murder me! Murder me!" It is what people who have completely snapped do in public with violent abruptness. Stand up on a bus or on a line, begin to shout about their crossover into the fifth dimension of insanity. Their way of saying that they hereby renounce their residency on Planet Normie. My plan was to sit thus until they tired of their surveillance, looked away.

I waited, enveloped in sickening fear. Then I jumped up suddenly, burrito in hand, and ran out the door. I hurried down the street, sure they were on my heels, and halfway down the block my legs wobbled and lost all feeling and I sprawled over the sidewalk. I lay there, thirty-seven years old, paralyzed with terror, unable to walk, rise, or speak, certain of imminent execution, not wanting to die, and so alone, so very alone. "Carl," I whispered, "where are you Carl Little Crow? Help me. Help me." And I saw Carl Little Crow's face before my eyes. He said, Pray for help to whatever you call your Great Spirit—ask for protection. And so I did. I called upon the name of God in Hebrew, Elohim, remembered from my Bar Mitzvah, without a clue about what it named or meant. I called out that name in sorrow, anguish, and defeat. And my legs regained sensation. And I stood up. And I began to walk normally. I did not feel the need to hurry. I still felt threatened by death, but walked in the valley of its shadow without fear. This was on Church Street in San Francisco, where later I bought a Jewish prayer shawl for a buck off a junkie selling stolen goods.

8. Carl Little Crow, where are you? Often I think of those times we spent together. It's been over seven years and, can you believe it, I have gone that long without a drink and I have become a poet. It happened because you said to me one day as we walked down Haight Street: "What do you want to do with this great gift that you have been given?"

"You mean sobriety?" I said.

"Yes. How will you use this miracle for the benefit of others?"

I didn't know. I said: "Maybe I should get a good job and set myself up, you know, more comfortably."

And you stopped and looked hard at me. "What were you doing when you went on your last run?"

"Earning sixty grand," I said.

"And was this true to your real nature?"

"Nah," I said. "It wasn't. I knew it. I hated it. And I hated myself."

"And haven't you learned here, 'To thine own self be true?!' Is this not the motto of our recovery? *To thine own self be true!*"

"Yah," I replied.

"So what is it you would do with the gift that is true to your being? Because sobriety is the Great Spirit's gift to you, but what you do with it is your gift to the Great Spirit."

And I said: "Well . . . I've always had this fantasy to be a poet, ya know?"

And you jumped in the air, literally, finger pointing at my eyes, and howled: "Ho! Then that is what you must do! And never waver until the last breath of your life! And remember, the hawk is your spirit, in your work! Call upon him when you most need help!"

And I have done as you advised. Since then I have performed my work before audiences around the world. I live in a beautiful apartment with a woman named Diane, who is a kindergarten teacher. Last year, forgiven by her mother, I flew out to see Isadora, my daughter, so as not to be a phantom in her life: We got along like a house on fire.

Where are you, Carl? Last I heard you were crossing the Southwest on foot. I want you to know how I am. My life is so beautiful now that sometimes I sit in a chair in my study just listening to the sound of my heart. There's a garden outside my window where birds sing. Doves and hummingbirds and sparrows and blue jays and robins. And there's a garden inside of me. There is a pond in which a great blue carp rests at ease in the shadows, unmoving for days.

I miss you, Carl Little Crow. I want to show you this place that I have found within, because it is you who first led me to it and helped me to plant the first seed. I see you laughing with glee, slapping your sides, rolling on the ground. I see you whacking at a coffee can with an oar, trying to get it open because we couldn't find a can opener. I remember you as though you were in this room with me now, strolling like a warrior down Haight Street, the proudest man I have ever known. I remember how your head bobbed like a mongoose and your eyes fixed on me with unflinching compassion when I told you that my mother had been in the Holocaust and had beaten me as a child. You said: "She was wounded and passed her wound to you. But that wound is the flower from which all will grow, if only you don't drink, and instead turn your thoughts to love and service for others." I am crying now as I write this, Carl Little Crow, unashamed of my feelings, another gift you gave to me. How your face, like a bust carved out of rock by a Mayan, would suddenly bear bright ribbons of tears caused by another's expression of pain.

Do you remember the trees you introduced me to in Golden Gate Park? There was the short black tree with white and yellow blossoms that you asked me to hug, and I did, in front of a group of Japanese tourists. There was the immense redwood that you slapped on the trunk with a shout "Ho! My brother!" and danced around while I stood by, bewildered by your energy and ignorant of your purpose. There was the eucalyptus whose leaves you snapped open under my nose to inhale and later brewed me tea from and told me of its healing properties. I remember how the little black birds that crowd the sidewalk outside the McDonald's on Haight Street would swarm over the sidewalk and sometimes land on your shoulder. Everyone around was too oblivious, consumed with their hamburgers, maybe consumed by them, to notice this extraordinary thing. "Yessssss, little brother," you sighed to the birds. "Ohhhhhhh, how are you, my friends? How is the food-gathering?" And you'd listen. I swear it seemed like they chirped back.

ON THE AUTOBAHN

LAST YEAR, AS news reports warned of a new fascism globally on the rise, I received three invitations to perform my poems in Germany. They came like sinister nods from fate.

Each time before leaving I anguished: How would I tell my mother, one of four thousand Jewish children arrested by Germans in Paris, July 16, 1942, for deportation to the gas.

I am her "memorial candle," her personal affirmation of Jewish victory over Nazi annihilation, and the one in the family whom she had chosen to carry the message of the six million into the future.

I couldn't bear to tell her, anticipating her fear: Since the original Nazis had failed to kill her, perhaps neo-Nazi skinheads rampaging in a reunified Germany might yet succeed in killing me.

Out for my first grand auto tour of Berlin in March, I expressed this very concern to Thomas, my host, the director of a prestigious literary institute. He is a German who has made the pilgrimage of conscience to Auschwitz. The confidence with which he pooh-poohed the neo-Nazi threat as so much media hype set me at ease. Moments later, however, he had to swerve to avoid hitting a police van loaded with riot troops, its siren shrieking toward an angry mob of skinheads.

In Munich, Frankfurt, Hamburg, and Berlin, audiences and media turned out to hear my poetry in a way that I have yet to experience in the United States. Germans love American poets. On television, before an audience of sixty million viewers, I performed "Who Are We?" my poem about the need that I feel as the son of a survivor to bear a message of social justice. But off mike, when I spoke further of the Holocaust, eyes turned hard. Conversation abruptly changed. Germans give the definite impression that they are sick and tired of hearing about "all that," their attitude toward the worst crime in human history like that of people living near the site of a popular tourist attraction: a kind of blasé weariness.

So, on performance tour I led two lives: by night hanging out with the literary avant-garde and by day visiting different sites of Nazi destruction. I saw deserted cemeteries with defiled, toppled stones and gutted synagogues still undergoing reconstruction fifty years after Kristallnacht, the Night of Broken Glass.

And yet, for the most part, I got along just fine with Germans of my generation. Some cared. Werner, who took me to see the museum of the former Gestapo headquarters, burst into tears when he discovered in the sign-in guest book the words "Hitler was right," left by the last visitor. I was less surprised.

But the hearty seniors whom one sees everywhere, with their snow-white hair and smug blue eyes, sparked rage in me, which I struggled to conceal. "What did you do in the war?" I wondered. And there was that doddering old man in Frankfurt who knew at once that I was an American Jew and seemed to come all alive on the quaint street, screaming in good English: "Jew filth! American kike!" and so on, then lapsed back into a senile fog. As he wasn't long for this world, I let Death respond for me.

In East Berlin my well-meaning hosts led me into districts riddled with bullet holes. Here, smiling long-haired young squatters worked at regentrifying ruins into architect's offices and underground discotheques. My guts wrenched as my hosts nonchalantly announced: "This was a Jewish quarter before the war." Sure enough, I saw on a brick wall a faded advertisement for Goldstein's furs, and farther on another, for Cohen's Bookstore. Gritting my teeth, I wondered: Where is Goldstein? Where is Cohen?

As I walked the *judenrein* streets of the new Germany like a ghost of Europe's vanished Jews, as I watched those smiling, long-haired youths with crowbars, tearing up the flagstones of old Jewish streets to plant gardens and build playgrounds, I thought: Maybe Hitler has won his war against us after all.

Months later I returned to Germany with a group of Spoken Word poets from America's cultural melting pot, including Paul Beatty, Patricia Smith, Luis Rodriguez, Neeli Cherkovski, and Dominique Lowell. In an increasingly xenophobic Germany, we did a crazy thing—for me a dream come true. Rather than reach our gigs by rail, we hired a Peugeot bus. The route we mapped ran straight through the heart of skinhead country. I don't know what possessed us—some spirit of Kerouac maybe, or Ken Kesey, with a touch of the Freedom Riders tossed in for good measure.

We were on the autobahn, doing 100 all the way. Patricia wrote poetry while Paul snoozed, Dominique deejayed, Neeli kibitzed, Luis drove, and I navigated.

We began to notice a proliferation of Confederate flags in shops and restaurants, adorning everything from key chains to automobile fenders. They serve as a far-right symbol in lieu of the outlawed swastika. Cars packed with skinheads drove past with Dixie flags prominently displayed. What an irony, I thought: that Jews and blacks riding together should once again recoil from that racist flag, only this time not in Mississippi but in reunified Germany. When we piled out at rest stops, we earned ourselves some bone-chilling stares.

During our tour, the Kohl government revoked its liberal asylum laws in an effort to end acts of skinhead terror through appeasement. The next day, Paul and I stood at a roadside newsstand studying a headline. We didn't need Berlitz language skills to deduce that neo-Nazi skins had murdered five Turkish women and children in Solingen, birthplace of Adolf Eichmann.

"We have no cause for rage," shrugged a young writer during the question-and-answer period following one of our Berlin performances, "we have none of your interesting American problems." He was explaining why Germans can't write the kind of in-your-face style poems that we perform. "Tell you what," I suggested, "write a poem about the agony of a Turkish woman as she burns alive with her children dying all around her." He stared blankly at me. "Or for that matter," I added, "try to imagine and perform the suffering of six million murdered Jews." The next day, Paul Beatty was verbally threatened for the color of his skin by a car full of skinheads, not a block away from the place of the performance.

Just recently, in the dead of winter, I returned to Germany for a third time as a guest of Berlin's Jewish community. I joined many prominent performing artists, writers, and thinkers, including Allen Ginsberg, Michael Lerner, and Kathy Acker, for a festival that paid tribute to the vitality of California Jewish life.

The event was held in a cultural center that had been founded on the site of a synagogue destroyed in the days of the Nazi terror. Above a blue-lit stage framed by fake California date palms hung an enormous Star of David. The effect was of a garish wedding reception. An odd, incongruous assortment of Jews crossed the stage, some with tattooed shoulders and reading cybersex prose, others chanting Buddhist-style Beatnik blues. Imported klezmer bands played sets, and a radical feminist Jewish juggler juggled. The audience, consisting of as many young Germans as Jews, showed their love with effusive applause. Before taking the stage to do my bit, I thought: As a show, we sometimes make no sense, but the important thing about the Jewish people is that we are here, alive, vital, together, expressing ourselves on the ruins of our near-destruction, and that is everything.

This time before leaving on the trip, I called my mother.

"Festival?" she said crossly. "What is there for Jews to be festive about in Germany?" But after repeated warnings to be careful and making me promise not to stray too far from the hotel, she confessed that she was far less worried about my going than I feared. "You're a survivor," she said. "You take after me."

EPILOGUE:
Dachau

NEAR THE EXIT door of the indoor exhibit, groups of students sat smoking cigarettes and eating lunch. A small contingency of Jews wearing yarmulkes stood around under umbrellas debating whether or not to go out in the pouring rain. I tramped past them, indifferent to the weather. What does it matter, I thought. What does it matter here?

But at Dachau concentration camp it mattered. Imagine the punishment of standing naked in the freezing roll-call square. Gravel crunched underfoot. Puddles exploded. I moved in a gray desolation punctuated by the white torsos of long low buildings with caged windows and black roofs. Huddled in my flimsy coat, I stopped to snap pictures with my camera like an infantryman from a liberation army squeezing off quick rounds as I advanced, but overall I received no impression of what I photographed. I hurried along, following arrows and signs marked: TO THE BARRACKS, TO THE CREMATORIUM, TO THE OPEN GRAVES.

Suddenly, a young woman bundled in a kerchief and a heavy coat stepped from the doorway of the barracks and fell into line just ahead. She marched into the powerful wind, huddled against the cold. I could not see her face. She tramped through puddles just like a woman I had seen in a picture in the exhibit, one leading her three children by the hand to the gas. She walked as if she were ordered to go, and furthermore must lead young children there. And we were going to the gas, to look, but she was unaware that I was behind her. I wanted to call out: Hey, I'm here, behind you! It's me. Alan from America. My mother is Marie, a Holocaust survivor! She made it. Look! I was born! I'm alive! I wanted to call out: So. We have finally come here. And before coming here, did you, like me, have the feeling, this strange feeling, that we were destined for here in the end? But instead, we walked on in silence, hunched over. The weather, I guess, made one walk that way, thrust into the loneliest parts of oneself. Bent over. It was so cold. Her back turned to me seemed as though it were turned *on* me. I almost felt rejected. It suddenly occurred to me that maybe it wasn't only the weather that made her, me, anyone, walk that way. Maybe *Dachau* made us walk that way, and feel as I did. Maybe a concentration camp is just that kind of place.

I went to the mass grave. It was a mound covered by smooth stones and surrounded by wreaths. Men, women, children, and babies were all here. I didn't know what to say, or do, or think. So I took out my prayer book; I said Kaddish, the prayer for the dead. What more could I do but to mourn in an appropriate fashion?

It has been said that silence is the only response. Prayer completed, I fell silent. I had come many thousands of miles and from over many years to this place, this monument in the rain. I had never known what to say about the Holocaust, and did not know what I should say now. Or feel. I felt silent. I felt *silence*. This is what has been given to my generation to do. To arrive at this site in Dachau, Germany, and to stand before it, incapable. This is the highest plateau of truth that my generation can attain. Imagination is unnecessary here. Arms can be laid down here. Art is only art here.

But it is not entirely human to only be silent. So, I said aloud, "I bring you greetings from my girlfriend, Diane, and from poets in San Francisco whom you do not know, but who would greet you, I am sure, if they could." Then I reached into my pocket because I like to carry stones in my pockets. I found a stone that I had brought from San Francisco for no purpose other than to rub it with my thumb as I walk. I took out this stone, laid it on the mass grave, removed a stone from the grave, and put it in my pocket. I like to think that in effecting this exchange perhaps I had given to the dead the gift of a bit of beautiful Mount Tamalpais on a crisp blue day, or a taste of Pacific sea air at Cliff House, or the cool feel of sand between my toes at Baker Beach.

But, of course, I hadn't.

WHO ARE WE?

Into the past
I go like a stranger
to discover why at night
I lay alone as a child
waiting for the front door
to slam, my father gone
to night shift work,
and my mother, Marie, to enter,
unable to sleep, and tell me
tales of childhood
war, pursued by those
who, as she spoke,

seemed to enter the room,
Gestapo men in leather coats
who ordered me to pack
and descend to a waiting truck,
for I am still going to Auschwitz
though a grown man in 1999
I am still boarding the freight,
crushed against numbed, frightened
Jews and Gypsies and Russian
soldiers and homosexuals
crossing frontiers to be gassed

I am her, in my heart,
though I am six feet two
and two hundred and ten pounds
and have played college football
and served as a soldier
and have scars from fights
with knives and jagged
bottles smashed on bars

I am still her, little girl,
hiding in chicken coops
and forests, asleep on dynamite
among partisans
I am still her, brushing teeth
with ashes
from the ruins of nations
gutted in war

I am still her brown eyes
and black hair of persecution
foraging scraps of thistle soup,

a star-shaped patch
sewn to my shirt

I am still my mother
every day in the streets
of New York or San Francisco,
the chimney skies glow and swirl
with soot like night above
a crematorium, or the Bronx
incinerator chute where I
threw out trash in a brick
darkness shooting sparks

I am still her in the streets
of Berkeley, walking among
sparechangers, dyed-hair punkers,
gays in stud leather, blacks,
Mexicans and Asians

I am still her rounded up
among poets and thieves
and politically incorrect
social deviants
on sun-drenched sidewalks
in the Mission and the Haight,
Greenwich Village, the Lower
East Side, or anywhere the weird
congregate in tolerance

And every day in this age
of intolerance,
in a mental ghetto
affirmed by the homeless,

I pass the dying
with the loud ring of my boots,
ashamed to think that perhaps
my heels are the last thing
they heard
Every day I am a
survivor of AIDS and poverty

Every day I sit in cafés
watching tattoos turn to numbers
and I grow angry
I want America back
I want America to be
the home I never had

And you, who are you
if you hear my voice?
Who are you, stranger,
if you read these words?

Who are we
who stand threatened
in these times of darkness?
Who are we, condemned to die,
who do not know ourselves
at all?